## Mercedes and Auto Racing in the Belle Epoque, 1895–1915

ALSO BY ROBERT DICK

*Auto Racing Comes of Age: A Transatlantic View of the Cars, Drivers and Speedways, 1900–1925* (McFarland, 2013)

# Mercedes and Auto Racing in the Belle Epoque, 1895–1915

Robert Dick

McFarland & Company, Inc., Publishers
*Jefferson, North Carolina, and London*

*The present work is a reprint of the illustrated case bound edition of* Mercedes and Auto Racing in the Belle Epoque, 1895–1915, *first published in 2005 by McFarland.*

LIBRARY OF CONGRESS CATALOGUING-IN-PUBLICATION DATA

Dick, Robert, 1953–
Mercedes and auto racing in the belle epoque, 1895–1915 / Robert Dick.
p.    cm.
Includes bibliographical references and index.

**ISBN 978-0-7864-7732-6**
softcover : acid free paper ∞

1. Mercedes automobiles—History—20th century.
2. Automobiles, Racing—History—20th century.
3. Antique and classic automobiles.   I. Title.
TL215.M18D53    2014       629.228'09--dc22         2004016405

BRITISH LIBRARY CATALOGUING DATA ARE AVAILABLE

© 2005 Robert Dick. All rights reserved

*No part of this book may be reproduced or transmitted in any form or by any means, electronic or mechanical, including photocopying or recording, or by any information storage and retrieval system, without permission in writing from the publisher.*

Cover photograph: Salzer (at the wheel) and Stegmaier
in the 17-litre Mercedes, September 1909

Manufactured in the United States of America

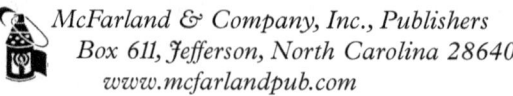

McFarland & Company, Inc., Publishers
Box 611, Jefferson, North Carolina 28640
*www.mcfarlandpub.com*

# *Acknowledgments*

I owe a great debt to the Daimler-Chrysler Archives (Stuttgart/Untertürkheim), especially to Martin Roland and Gerhard Heidbrink. Almost all of the images in this book are from that collection, including the Cresswell drawings from Pomeroy, *The Grand Prix Car*. I am also indebted to the archives of Renault (Paris), Fiat (Turin), Opel (Rüsselsheim), and Peugeot (Sochaux), which supplied most of the remainder of the images.

My particular thanks are reserved for Karl Ludvigsen, who did more than anyone could reasonably expect. Without Karl, this book would never have been published.

# Contents

*Acknowledgments* . . . . . . . . . . . . . . . . . . . . . . . . . . . . . . . v
*Preface* . . . . . . . . . . . . . . . . . . . . . . . . . . . . . . . . . . . . . . . 1
*Introduction* . . . . . . . . . . . . . . . . . . . . . . . . . . . . . . . . . . . 3

1. Scenery . . . . . . . . . . . . . . . . . . . . . . . . . . . . . . . . . . 5
2. Meeting Point: Eiffel Tower . . . . . . . . . . . . . . . . . . 9
3. *Système Panhard* . . . . . . . . . . . . . . . . . . . . . . . . . . 17
4. *Riviérà* . . . . . . . . . . . . . . . . . . . . . . . . . . . . . . . . . . 28
5. Mercédès . . . . . . . . . . . . . . . . . . . . . . . . . . . . . . . . 40
6. *Roi du Volant* . . . . . . . . . . . . . . . . . . . . . . . . . . . . 47
7. Simplex . . . . . . . . . . . . . . . . . . . . . . . . . . . . . . . . . 56
8. One-Tonners . . . . . . . . . . . . . . . . . . . . . . . . . . . . . 64
9. Sixty . . . . . . . . . . . . . . . . . . . . . . . . . . . . . . . . . . . 77
10. Towards Madrid . . . . . . . . . . . . . . . . . . . . . . . . . . 87
11. La Coupe Bennett . . . . . . . . . . . . . . . . . . . . . . . . 101
12. Hot Favorite . . . . . . . . . . . . . . . . . . . . . . . . . . . . 115
13. Muscle Car . . . . . . . . . . . . . . . . . . . . . . . . . . . . . 130
14. Grand Prix . . . . . . . . . . . . . . . . . . . . . . . . . . . . . 147
15. Italian Supremacy . . . . . . . . . . . . . . . . . . . . . . . . 163
16. Apotheosis . . . . . . . . . . . . . . . . . . . . . . . . . . . . . 179
17. Depression . . . . . . . . . . . . . . . . . . . . . . . . . . . . . 195
18. Blitzen Benz . . . . . . . . . . . . . . . . . . . . . . . . . . . . 202
19. Voiturettes . . . . . . . . . . . . . . . . . . . . . . . . . . . . . 215
20. Savannah . . . . . . . . . . . . . . . . . . . . . . . . . . . . . . 234
21. Grey Ghost . . . . . . . . . . . . . . . . . . . . . . . . . . . . . 243
22. Modern Times . . . . . . . . . . . . . . . . . . . . . . . . . . 251
23. Rivals in Blue . . . . . . . . . . . . . . . . . . . . . . . . . . . 270
24. Test Run . . . . . . . . . . . . . . . . . . . . . . . . . . . . . . . 283

25. Tactics ................................................. 294
26. Oval Tracks ............................................. 311
27. Wartime ................................................ 320

*Appendix A: Forgotten Cars—and Forgotten Heroes* ............. 329
*Appendix B: Technical Data* ................................. 337
*Appendix C: Race Results* ................................... 352
*Bibliography* ............................................... 357
*Index* ...................................................... 359

# Preface

This book narrates the early history of automobile racing from the beginnings in 1895 until the break due to the first World War in 1915, describes the technical progress of the cars and celebrates the drivers and engineers who have too often been underappreciated, misunderstood, or simply forgotten. Automobile racing had its origins in France, in Paris, in the center of the Belle Époque—the "beautiful era"—those glorious years between the end of the Franco-Prussian War in 1871 and the beginning of the Great War, when Europe was at peace, those who had money spent it freely, and the infant automobile came of age. French marques and the Automobile Club de France were dominating the scene, the language was French, and all the important races started from Paris. It was in 1901 that a foreign trouble-maker emerged, the Mercedes, or *Mercédès* as the French sportsmen called it. Named for the daughter of the man behind it, "Monsieur Mercédès" as he would come to be known, this German machine was to play a leading role, its career and evolution becoming an image of the whole period.

In those early days before the first World War, automobile racing gave invaluable assistance in improving the breed of the ordinary motor car. The era of the pioneers was one of the richest, one of the most exciting and inventive. Nevertheless it is regarded as prehistoric. Were these once-much-praised racing cars as crude and as primitive as they are often described today? They were not. Even at their worst, the early machines were technically competent. The men who built and drove them, with patience, tenacity and skill, were not illiterate, clumsy or unfit. They developed a new craft, laid the foundation of a new industry, conceived the modern high performance engine, and gave magic to a series of races which drew hundreds of thousands of spectators and thrilled entire nations.

Many particular questions and legends have been in need of clarification and reevaluation: the marketing of the original Daimler engines in France; the position and influence of "Monsieur Mercédès" Emil Jellinek and his favorite engineer Wilhelm Maybach; the French boycott and the great crisis of 1909; the origins of the voiturette movement; the Mercedes and the Benz successes in America; the role of Ernest Henry in the development of the revolutionary Peugeot. So the history of Mercedes and the other racers of the Belle Époque is worth telling in some detail.

It is beyond the scope of this book to include the history of the countless hill-climbs and sprint races which enjoyed great popularity but did not affect early automobile racing history. The descriptions of the cars, the race reports and the biographical data are based on contemporary factory records and contemporary journals made accessible by the Daimler-Chrysler, Opel, Renault and Fiat archives, the Bibliothèque Nationale, Paris, and the technical universities of Stuttgart, Berlin and Hannover. Secondary souces have been avoided as far as possible. The old French magazines *La France Automobile*, *L'Automobile—Revue des Locomotions Nouvelles*, *Omnia*, and the American *Motor Age* had little in common with their present day counterparts. Mass production and formula circuses were unknown in the early days so that these magazines had to meet the needs of only the enthusiasts and sportsmen: forthright, hard-hitting, well-balanced and highly entertaining publications, a gold mine of information about the races, the drivers and the cars. *L'Automobile* especially was outstanding. Its content was handled by Gaston Sencier, an experienced engineer and newspaper man who seldom fell for press-agent stories and who gave his journal a sort of clinical accuracy which none of the others shared.

All the illustrations, except for a couple of cutaway drawings sketched during the forties and fifties, come from the early days; most of them are images kept in the Daimler-Chrysler collection. The majority are credited to "M. Branger—photographe—5, rue Cambon—Paris," and were taken using 13-cm × 18-cm glass plates. Maurice-Louis Branger was born in 1874 in Fontainebleau. Later he renamed his shop "agence de reportage photographique," and was an established war correspondent.

As the historian Doug Nye remarked: "It's incredible to hold one of these panes of glass up to the light, to study the image upon it from the 1902 Paris–Vienna or 1903 Gordon Bennett or 1914 GP de l'ACF and to realise that this item you are holding was actually THERE ... it was actually in the camera being operated by that guy crouching in the roadside ditch that day. It vibrated to the rumble and blast of those great cars hurtling by ... Aah yes, nostalgia, The Real Thing..."

# Introduction

In 1894 the automobile was still content to chug from Paris to Rouen and to give proof of its reliability. One year later it ran to Bordeaux and back, as speedily as possible, and in 1896 all the way to Marseille. The French market promised a sensational turnover. But the agencies of the leading make, of the *marque doyenne* Panhard, were assigned long ago. Didn't Panhard use Daimler engines, built under license in Paris? Thus the businessman Jellinek took the train to Cannstatt, to order a Daimler, for the purpose of resale at the Riviera, of course with a fat profit. But the two-cylinder rattled in the wrong place, namely under the seat and not under a hood at the front. The sportsmen insisted on front engine à la Panhard. Cannstatt quickly changed its arrangements and built the Phoenix, a German Panhard which was such a hit that Emil Jellinek soon bought two-thirds of the Daimler production. Therewith his influence was sufficient to persuade Cannstatt to design a completely new car, the Mercedes, a Daimler which complied with the special wishes of the sportsmen. In the spring of 1901, the brand-new Mercedes promptly swept the meeting of Nice. The shocked reaction was: "Nous sommes entrés dans l'ère Mercédès!" The downright dominance of the *marque doyenne* was crumbling away. A pack of newcomers began to set the pace with exemplary engineering, on endless straights and triangle courses, in the Bennett Cup and the Grand Prix, on the beach of Daytona and the brickyard of Indianapolis. The "beautiful era" of the pioneers combined performance with style and charisma. It passed through ups and downs. It outlived the withdrawal of the old marques and the grave crisis of 1909. It thrilled to the birth of the modern racer. The Great War put an end to it.

# 1

## *Scenery*

They came together in 1867, at the Exposition in Paris, the self-propelled carriage and the gas-burning engine. No rendez-vous, merely coincidence, and no question of wedding. Full of expectations, the Nikolaus August Otto & Cie., founded three years before in Cologne, exhibited its low-speed gas engine, nothing more than an improved copy of the two-cycle machinery patented in 1857 by Eugenio Barsanti and Felice Matteuci. It was good for a scandal when the similarity struck the Parisian journal *Le Gaz*, and for a gold medal, for the favorable consumption of 1329 liters of coal gas (also known as methane or $CH_4$) per horsepower and hour simply put the 3166 liters of the competing machinery from Lenoir in the shade. On good days the tinkerer Otto drew up to one hundred explosions per minute from his two-cycle entity. Then and only then the 600-kg colossus delivered half a horsepower: unusable for the propulsion of a self-propelled vehicle, and no alternative to the ubiquitous steam engine. Hence it was steam which provided motive power in all motorized exhibits. Heavy and cumbersome machines bounced off the rails into the open country, tractors from England and France, forgotten makes like Aveling & Porter, Clayton, Garret, Ransoms & Simms, Albaret, Larmangeat or Lotz. Comfort and driving fun? The solitary motor coach from Guidez & Collin, a smoking and stinking railway carriage fallen off the tracks, furnished at best a touch of it. Of sports or racing cars there was not a trace anywhere.

What was all the rage? The cranked bicycle of Pierre Michaux, the "vélocipède," on which well-trained sportsmen whizzed over the recently extended boulevards. Had Baron Georges Haussmann, since 1852 the préfet of Paris, anticipated the course of things? By 1867, when the World Exhibition made its guest appearance at the Seine for the second time, he had gloriously transformed the city in the linear geometric spirit of René Descartes. Eugénie, the proud and beautiful empress of the third Napoleon, was behind it; now her Paris was outclassing the competitors London and Vienna. In the center of course were the Trocadéro and Champ de Mars, where the Exposition concentrated, but also the new greenery of the Avenue des Champs-Élysées, bordered by kiosks, music pavilions and elegant villas, the preferred playground of all gentlemen and dandies. For a promenade in a self-propelling carriage, for an automobile drive in the company of a lady, neither the environment nor the audience were lacking, it was the motorization which was missing. Thus, for the time being, the dandies still sat on their vélocipèdes, pedaling hard to attract the attention of Tout Paris' demoiselles. It was no surprise that the capital of the beautiful Eugénie soon turned into the metropolis of the cyclist; that in 1869 more than three hundred vélos per day left the factories of Michaux, of Tribout, Meyer & Cie., of Truffault or Rousseau; that Richard Lesclide, the former secretary of Victor Hugo, published a vélo gazette; that the sportsmen ran against each other towards Rouen.

Who would be the one to manufacture a self-propelled vehicle, if possible with a lightweight high-performance engine? Rail-fixed trainmen obviously not. Unconventional thinkers from the guild of the locksmiths and carriage builders came into question, an unfaithful watchmaker, an ambitious foreman of a sewing machine or armament factory. And in fact it was a ... bell-founder who attended to the affair. His name was Amédée Bollée, and during the 1870 war, in his home town Le Mans, he had filled up his cash box by casting cannons. The money enabled him to construct a "voiture à grande vitesse," a fast steam car, that trundled along the unfirm paths of the département de la Sarthe from May 1873 onwards. Momentary full steam quickened the "Obéissante," as the 29-year old Bollée christened his "docile" five-tonner, up to a speed of 40 kilometers per hour. But after two years of everyday use, on weekdays for the transport of goods, on Sundays for the promenade within the family circle, after two years of patient development and elimination of all defects, the Obéissante was conspicuous by a hitherto unknown feature: reliability. Bollée dared a demonstration in Paris. In October 1875, the Obéissante took itself to the center of the nascent Belle Époque. A triumph. Over the Avenue du Bois, the subsequent Avenue Foch, the speedy steamer crested the hill of the Arc de Triomphe and demonstrated its agility under the applause of the Beau Monde, Paris' "Beautiful People." Then, by way of the Boulevards Extérieurs, the Parc Monceau and the Place de Clichy, it clattered towards the Canal Saint-Martin and disappeared in its shed. Not only did the *Figaro* report the event, but even the honor of a caricature was conferred upon the Obéissante: Cham let Madame Prud-homme reply to her husband: "Do you want that I am 'docile' like a machine?" Bollée received numerous inquiries, but no order. Thus, in 1876, he turned towards mass transport and built a tram in cooperation with the Parisian foundry Dalifol, before, in 1878, the "Mancelle" came into being.

Engine in front, drive through shaft and chains on the rear wheels: The Mancelle, the girl from Le Mans, granted the classic automobile its universal layout. No less inventive was the front wheel suspension by means of two transverse leaf springs which Bollée fitted to all 31 steamers which were to leave his workshop. It was no surprise that, in 1899, Amédée Junior, or Amédée *fils*, took over his father's idea for a racing car: what was surprising, however, was that the Sizaire brothers and Louis Naudin became famous in 1906 with a similar design... Of course Bollée displayed his modern Mancelle at the 1878 Exposition Universelle, where he offered it at a ridiculous 12,000 francs, while the archaic steam hutch of Randolph was priced at a horrendous 45,000. All the same Bollée got in touch with only one buyer, the Alsacian industrialist Gustave Koechlin. The car department of the bell-foundry Bollée did not take off running. Neither was the "Nouvelle" of use to change the situation, nor the speedy "Rapide," introduced in 1883 and running at 60 km/h, nor the liaison with a dubious entrepreneur named Léon Le Cordier. Amédée Bollée did not fail because of defective engineering, but because he was unable to sell his well-developed steamers in reasonable, cost-effective quantities. Disappointed, almost disillusioned and bitter, he returned to the family tradition. Bollée was an authentic, nowadays almost-forgotten, pioneer, father of all car builders, who not only helped to make the steam carriage popular and hence smoothed decisively the way for the gasoline automobile, but who gave a definite direction to the French scene: It would be Paris that looked for a definitive overall concept and made it marketable.

The gas engine? Far-sighted Paris did not drop it at all. The scandal-tainted two-cycle machinery from Otto & Cie was produced under license. It was the world's best engine. But how could it drive an automobile as long as it had to be hooked to a gas pipe? The solution could only come from Cologne. Immediately after the Exposition of 1867, the situation in the Rhineland was not really rosy, but still the shop visibly got going, so that at the beginning of 1872 Otto and his managing friend Eugen Langen changed the name of their company to "Gasmotorenfabrik Deutz," or Gas Engine Factory Deutz. The new name sounded more respectable, inserted industrial flair. Furthermore a technical director of top class was missing since the autodidact Otto was hopelessly swamped with the organization of the constantly increasing production. Langen engaged the Swabian Gottlieb Daimler, born in 1834, gunsmith, engineer of the Stuttgart polytechnic college, director of machine factories at Reutlingen and Karlsruhe. By the end of 1872, Wilhelm Maybach, who was 12 years younger and had met Daimler at Reutlingen, followed as deputy. The Swabians worked diligently in the Rhineland, upgrading the fabrication of the gas engines, still stationary two-cycle units, though improved regarding power output and fuel consumption. The staff rocketed from 66 to 231, the production from 20 to 50 per month. The gas-burning machine became slowly but surely a competitor of the steam engine and when, in 1876, Otto developed the four-cycle principle, Deutz had started on the right path. Neither Daimler nor Maybach ever preened themselves on the invention of the four-cycle concept. And Otto? Was he really the genial inventor or had he copied again? In 1862 a Frenchman, answering to the elegant name of Alphonse-Eugène Beau de Rochas, had published a description of the four-cycle method, only a manuscript, no practical realization. "Otto's neuer Motor," Otto's new engine, realized the dream, was promptly granted the patent with the famous number 532 which secured a worldwide four-cycle monopoly to the Gas Engine Factory Deutz, for ten years—until the pamphlet of Beau de Rochas reappeared.

In the meantime, Paris had a combination of weighty carriage à la Bollée with dainty filigree vélo in mind, an assembly of light tube frame and diminutive steam engine. Or more precisely, Albert de Dion had this in mind, a man from whom nobody in fact expected it. Count de Dion was born in 1856 in Nantes, succeeding to the title of marquis in 1901, after the death of his father. He was a wild libertine tightrope walker, as much at home in the Café des Ambassadeurs, the Alcazar, La Scala or the Folies-Bergère as in the posh salons of Parisian society, even if some ladies present there blushed at his sight. The count did not enjoy the best reputation! The boulevard press wrote about him, about affairs, duels, gambling debts. Even worse, especially in the eyes of his family, was Albert's fascination with everything which resembled a machine. Hadn't he built a small steam engine in his free time? Philanderer, musketeer, à la rigueur gambler, but inventor…

In the autumn of 1881, it ended in disaster. The count met Georges Bouton. Born in 1847 in Paris, Bouton carried on a small workshop in the Rue de la Chapelle, with his brother-in-law Charles-Armand Trépardoux. The name of their company was Trépardoux & Cie. and they supplied small steam engines and boilers to renowned toy retailers like Ducretet & Bourbouze or Giroux. The small but fine shop of Giroux was located at the Boulevard des Italiens, next to the Café Riche and the Café Anglais, just where Tout Paris used to gather and dine sumptuously without being concerned about an invoice of 25 francs. The Glacier Tortoni was also in direct proximity, in whose upper hall ice pyramids with waffles, cakes, tarts, Bordeaux, Madeira or Malaga could be savored in festive illumination. Of course Albert was in and out here after his standard promenade on the Champs-Élysées. So it was no wonder that one day, after a tête-à-tête, Bouton's small machine caught his eye and that he hurried to the Rue de la Chapelle: "Build a small steam car for me!"

"There aren't any boilers light enough" Bouton replied.

"Then build one, and work for me at a salary of ten francs a day each."

This was three more than the business received so far. Bouton began to work on the spot. In 1884 the enterprising trio found definitive premises in the Rue du Pavillon of the western suburb Puteaux, called the new firm "De Dion, Bouton et Trépardoux" and displayed the first steam-engined quadricycle. By the beginning of 1887, it was followed by a faultless single-seat tricycle.

This appeared at just the right time, since Paul Faussier, director of the journal *Le Vélocipède*, was organizing a race to be held on 18 April 1887, especially for the steaming three-wheel runabouts. The route led from the Porte de Neuilly to the Grille du Bois de Boulogne and back. Race? Bouton was the sole starter. When he crossed the finish, he had averaged 30 km/h: a great sport had been born. Faussier did not feel daunted by the lack of competitors. In 1888 and 1891 he planned further contests between the Pont de Neuilly and Versailles. It was too early for keen participation since the engineering was still so inexact and obscure; on the other hand the vehicles inspired the enthusiasm of a marveling and applauding vélo scene. In his lithograph "Retour du Bois, le Dimanche," the Swiss illustrator Théophile Steinlen set out the colorful bicycle scene.

As a De Dion tricycle ran against the clock at Vincennes around the Lac Daumesnil, the police suddenly stopped the fast journey: A lady had been frightened. Despite the grandiose fuss the foxy de Dion was left empty-handed as he wanted to sell his small cars. But he achieved something marvelous. The environment of the vélo scene, and not least the numerous publications which described technology and sport, provided massive publicity. Everything was in readiness for the reception of the first gasoline carriages.

# 2

# *Meeting Point: Eiffel Tower*

Lightweight, gasoline-burning, high-speed engines made up the Daimler range, from 1882 onwards, for stationary purposes, for driving saws and fire pumps, for smaller locomotives and trolleys, for boats, and from time to time for a self-propelled carriage. In that year the stubborn Swabian Daimler had dropped out, at 48, in the middle of the midlife crisis, after ten years in the position of a technical director at the Gas Engine Factory Deutz, after ten years of friction with the four-cycle pioneers Otto, Langen and Schumm. Gottlieb Daimler moved to his native Swabia, as usual with his adjutant Wilhelm Maybach on his coat-tails. Since their common time at Reutlingen, Daimler and Maybach had the reputation of being inseparable. At Deutz however, the situation was different: "Neither Langen, neither Otto, nor Schumm approached me to hold me back at Deutz after Daimler's paying off… Schumm set Bela Wolf on my chair so that I did not see any other solution but to follow Daimler's invitation."

The friendly councilor Keppler procured a villa in Taubenheim Street at Cannstatt. The masonry was rotten, but the park large and the greenhouse perfect for a workshop extension: the secret hotbed of the high-speed gasoline engine. Maybach moved nearby, to Ludwigsburg Street, and rummaged in patents. Hadn't he learned it at Deutz from Otto? The cards had just to be properly shuffled to find the aces. And there was a first experience from Deutz times: "Some day, I simply held a gasoline-impregnated piece of cotton waste in front of the air intake of a running gas engine, closed the gas valve, and the gasoline engine was completed!" With a "vaporising apparatus," the gas engine could cut the cord of a fixed fuel supply.

Did Amédée Bollée know that, in August 1883, the bell-foundry and fire-pump factory of Heinrich Kurtz manufactured a first engine to be supplied to the shop on Taubenheim Street? Certainly not. The affair was top secret. Daimler was not allowed to stalk within the Deutz district for five years. And the famous patent number 532 was still valid, to say nothing of the protected detail solutions that Maybach was working up. And could not everything blow up? Paul Daimler, the stubborn Swabian's eldest son, remembered: "The old man tried in vain to convince mankind that air was necessary for an explosion. The greenhouse played an essential role since we could work there without being seen from the street. The gases were usually led into a cavity in order to absorb the exhaust noise. But once we choose a straightline exhaust pipe which immediately produced more power due to the suction effect." In 1885 the small single-cylinder engine with the bore/stroke dimensions of 58 mm × 100 mm developed half a horsepower, at 600 rpm, four times the gas engine standard. The door to success? A small-bore platinum tube, closed at its outer end, screwed into the cylinder head and maintained at red-heat by a Bunsen burner: The famous hot-tube ignition which was patented on the spot.

The high-crankshaft-speed wonder weighed just 50 kilograms and was promptly mounted in a self-propelled vehicle, in the "Reitwagen," the Riding Car, a wooden-framed two-wheeler: "Gottlieb Daimler built the bicycle deliberately because in those days the minor roads were trenched by deep grooves. Later cars used to skid while the Riding Car passed through without any difficulty." One year later the high-speed single rattled in the stretched dimensions of 72 mm × 126 mm, output now an entire horsepower, enough to drive a classical horse carriage, a four-seat américain. The motorized hippomobile speeded up to more than 15 km/h, threatening all passersby, dogs and horses between Cannstatt, Untertürkheim and Esslingen until the authorities strictly forbade "further driving trials with the auto-carriage." Gottlieb Daimler realized that in the Germany of 1886 there was no artifice that could sell a gasoline carriage, neither from Cannstatt nor from Mannheim, where Karl, or Carl, Benz, at the beginning of the year, had presented his "Patentmotorwagen," his Patent-Motor-Car and was left empty-handed just the same, despite sales brochures, despite the Work Machine Exhibition in Munich, despite the favorable price of two thousand goldmarks. But it was not for nothing that the stubborn Daimler wore the title of a technical director. He knew how you

**Gottlieb Daimler and his son Paul in the américain.**

should sell yourself and your inventions. From the outset the Riding Car and the américain were little more than spectacular demonstration objects to sell the high-speed engine as power for saws, pumps and boats. His efforts were not without success, since the greenhouse workshop in Taubenheim Street soon burst at the seams; in 1887 Daimler moved to the former nickel plating works of Zeitler & Missel on the Seelberg at Cannstatt.

Then he approached cosmopolitan Paris, his friend Édouard Sarazin who managed a consulting office in the middle of the vélo scene's shopping center, at no. 62, Avenue de la Grande Armée. Sarazin had in mind the leasing of gas engines as well as the exploitation of French and foreign patents: "Location de Force motrice par le Gaz, Exploitation d'Inventions françaises et étrangères." Since the seventies, Sarazin had looked after the Parisian interests of the Gas Engine Factory Deutz, after license manufacturing, after infractions of the four-cycle patent, culminating in the creation of an official agency, of the Compagnie française des Moteurs à Gaz. After a visit to Cannstatt, after demonstration of the Riding Car and the américain, Sarazin began instantly to think in vélo dimensions, of a gasoline-engined quadricycle, Benz and De Dion fashion. Daimler held off, but that did not prevent Sarazin from placing an order for the manufacture of three high-speed engines in Paris, with Panhard, Avenue d'Ivry. This was just the right moment since Ivry was suffering a heavy setback, and Sarazin knew it only too well. Since 1876 Panhard had built aplenty two- and four-cycle engines under license, in the middle of the eighties certainly four hundred units per year, which were cancelled overnight when the Rhinelanders, with Sarazin's help, established their Compagnie française. Wasn't the high-speed engine from Cannstatt a perfect compensation? Daimler on the other hand could not imagine better French partners. Did not Panhard belong to the established large concerns of the Paris area, with the corresponding periphery, with the most modern tools and machines, with qualified workmen, with proven distribution channels? And then there was the steel, some of the best in the fin de siècle world! Paul Daimler on this: "The old man appreciated the alliance with Panhard. The French had gained their experience with bandsaws. They cooked their steel in their own mines, best compounds up to vanadium steel. In fact only England and Sweden supplied high-grade steels. But the French had raised their production at least on the same level, while in Germany not a quarter as good material was available."

After all Panhard looked back on forty years of tradition. It was in 1845 that Jules Périn, a spirited carpenter of the eastern faubourg Saint Antoine, had obtained a patent for the blade guide of bandsaws. The innovation spirit paid off, perhaps slowly but surely, since it took 20 years until Périn employed 75 men and moved into a more spacious workshop in the Rue de Charonne. Shortly after, in 1867, in the same year when Otto exhibited his first two-cycle machine at the Exposition, the shop was suddenly known as Périn, Panhard & Cie.: With fresh qualification from the École Centrale des Arts et Métiers the young René Panhard had joined in. The shop continued to prosper, not only because of the fine wood and metal saws but first of all because of the cannon for the 1870 war. It was not that the enterprise outgrew the carpenter Périn, but with increasing age he took things easier and left the helm to the younger generation.

René Panhard, born in 1841 as son of a well-known Parisian carriage maker, looked for reinforcement. He had Émile Levassor in mind, his schoolfriend, just two years younger. Panhard offered him a 10 percent share. And of course Levassor accepted and looked after expansion and equipment of a freshly acquired estate south of the Seine, a large deserted locksmithery in the Route d'Ivry, the subsequent Avenue d'Ivry. And how did the small Sarazin office get in touch with the giant Panhard? On one hand Sarazin was the agent of the world's largest gas engine factory and hence afforded an open door, on the other hand he was acquainted with Levassor since the mid–1860s when they were both at Cockerill in Liège, the Belgian license partner of Deutz.

Thus all the brains behind a new industry were in touch. Moreover, two deaths affected the course of things. Périn died in 1886; Périn, Panhard & Cie. was renamed Panhard & Levassor. Sarazin died in December 1887; his wife Louise inherited a big parcel of shares from the Compagnie française des Moteurs à Gaz. Certainly not without good reason the widow Sarazin worried about a drop in value in case of competition from the high-speed engine from Cannstatt. Hence she offered Daimler her services only as an interim measure, "till discovery of a new representative." Now it was the stubborn Swabian's turn and he intervened on the spot, on 4 January 1888, in most elegant French: "Concerning our business, I am not in a hurry to look for another representative in Paris. I liked to hear that you are up to date on everything and that you want to be helpful to me, what I herewith accept cordially. I see also that you appreciate my engine, exactly as Monsieur Sarazin did. It stands to reason that you are anxious to avoid that the fruits of your dear husband's work will fall in other's hands. In these matters I hope to act entirely in your interest so that you too have an advantage therefrom. I cannot yet say in what way."

Gottlieb Daimler knew exactly what and where he wanted, and struck the right note at the first dash, since shortly afterwards Madame Sarazin took the train to Cannstatt, not alone but in company of her nine-year-old son Henri, as was right and proper. In October she came again, this time with no one else but Émile Levassor at her side. Now Daimler had the deal practically in the bag. Levassor prepared the grand entrance on the occasion of the imminent Exposition Universelle, the first World Exhibition with Eiffel Tower. On 22 December 1888 he wrote: "We have received the first three drawings of the two-horsepower twin-cylinder. Please dispatch the

Louise Sarazin, née Cayrol, from May 1890 Madame Levassor.

other drawings as soon as possible so that we can speed up the manufacture of the engine. The sample engines can in any case be shipped to us without being worried about the validity of your patents. Madame Sarazin enquired Monsieur Armangaud, who confirmed it."

Panhard & Levassor, the best possible license partner, had not only taken the bait but even applied pressure whereby the parts between Cannstatt and Paris were strictly allotted. Daimler supplied the design and the prototype. Panhard & Levassor developed further up to the serial production and shared sales and distribution with the widow Sarazin who moreover watched over the well-being of the patents. Herein she did a good job, especially when the frontier-crossing shipment of the sample engines evolved into a matter of delicacy. According to French patent law, the import of an engine meant direct competition for the licensee and hence invalidity of the patent. The Parisian clerk Armangaud was unable to resist charm and expertise at the same time. He acquiesced in this particular case if Panhard charged the customs clearance to Sarazin's account: Reason enough for Daimler to transfer the exclusive license and exploitation rights of the French patents to his representative in February 1889. As a counter-move Louise Sarazin remitted 12 percent of her turnover to Cannstatt. The promised benefits? "Madame Sarazin will use the patents as she thinks it best," was written in the contract, which meant nothing else than production in Ivry and 20 percent commission. A good deal for all parties, whose culmination followed one year later, in May 1890, when the single Levassor exchanged wedding rings with the widow Sarazin.

Émile Levassor, from 1873 partner of René Panhard.

It was Émile Mayade who looked after detail development and manufacturing at Ivry. He soon mastered the two-horsepower twin. Mayade, born in 1853, came from Clermont-Ferrand in the Auvergne, was the great practicality oriented chef d'atelier, the workshop chief, the *éminence grise* behind Levassor. With his wife Jeanne he lived above his workshop, at no. 14, Avenue d'Ivry. Mayade fussed unceasingly over the new engine: Two of the familiar singles arranged with the narrow included angle of 16° between them, a V-2 which guaranteed low weight and compact structure. The initial dimensions of 60 mm × 100 mm delivered 1.5 hp at 600 rpm and a compression ratio of 2.5/1. Until the nineties a complete range was available, with bore/stroke from 62 mm × 106 mm, 67 mm × 108 mm, 72 mm × 126 mm, 72 mm × 140 mm up to 75 mm × 146 mm and an output of 4 hp. The head layout followed best gas engine fashion: For the purpose of easy access in case of a failure, the valves were banished to a laterally located pocket and placed one above the other. The "automatic" intake valves were not mechanically operated and merely sucked in their mixture, opening all alone during the induction stroke with the help of the atmospheric pressure, and closing with the help of a light spring. The exhaust valves were operated by a rod worked by an eccentric double cam-groove in the face of the flywheel. In a flash the mechanism was converted and the V-2 backed off. Flexibility was not worth mentioning; the whole thing was virtually a constant-speed affair. The V-2 ran its six hundred revolutions per minute or it did not run at all, since a simple surface carburetor was still used to vaporize the benzine and a red-hot platinum tube to fire the mixture. A really minimal regulation was possible by tuning the bunsen burner and the centrifugal governor which interrupted the exhaust valve mechanism at the critical crankshaft speed. A drip-feed oiler lubricated the cylinder walls, and nothing else. From there residual oil flowed downwards and disappeared in the crankshaft bearings, a constant-loss system. A larger water tank served as cooler. Primitive? In all areas the V-2 was far above the standard of its time.

Daimler V-2, the primal engine of a new industry.

In April 1889, the Eiffel Tower was solemnly inaugurated with a 21-gun salute on the first platform. Paris met the rest of the world at the Exposition. Musketeer de Dion and his partner Bouton exhibited no fewer than four of their steaming tri- and quadricycles. Benz agent Émile Roger relied on a well-established Patent-Motor-Car. Les Fils de Peugeot Frères, the sons of the Peugeot brothers, displayed a crude, unsprung three-wheeler from steam artist Léon Serpollet, whose peculiarity consisted in a flash boiler, a heated tube bundle which vaporized injected water instantly. And Daimler's V-2 rattled at every turn. At the Pavillon du Pétrole, near the Pont d'Iéna, it fed 30 light bulbs via dynamo. *Le Tout Paris* was delighted! In a mini-tram it helped the *Beau Monde* to reach the train connection to the Rue du Caire, the center of the Colonial Exhibition. On the Seine it drove the *Violette* and the *Passe-Partout* and on 18 June it was finally granted its inevitable patent. The first order was not long in coming:

## 2. Meeting Point: Eiffel Tower

**Wilhelm Maybach at the tiller of the Steel-Wheel-Car; by his side Paul Daimler.**

Francisco Bonet purchased a V-2 for his weaving mill in Barcelona, and two singles in addition. At one point Armand Peugeot stood in front of it, one of the Peugeot brothers' sons, a Panhard customer of long standing. He asked for output and weight. Almost two horsepower from 100 kilograms, infeasible with steam, in any case enough for the brisk propulsion of a light tubular frame. This was exactly what the enterprising Peugeot had in mind and he was easily able to afford it since in the South of the Vosges, around Montbéliard, he employed two thousand men in the production of coffee mills and other household appliances, of all sorts of tools, and since 1885 of bicycles. Had not Maybach, since the first Sarazin visits, worked on a gas-engined quadricycle? The drawings were ready at the beginning of January.

Armand Peugeot required elegance, no clumsy copy of a Patent-Motor-Car from Benz or a quadricycle from De Dion, no wood-spoke wheels, no Cannstatt interpretation of a motorized carriage. Peugeot thought of attractive and fashionable styling with reasonable performance, of a double vélo, as delicate as possible.

Since Benz came also into consideration, Daimler reacted right away. The future NSU, the knitting machine factory Neckarsulm, quickly supplied a frame. Maybach mounted a V-2 including four-speed gearbox. The double-vélo named Steel-Wheel-Car arrived in Paris via train on 29 October. Peugeot nodded contentedly. His engineer Louis Rigoulot was the first who drove between the Eiffel Tower and Grenelle along the Seine bank. Shortly after, Peugeot in person stepped in the Steel-Wheel-Car, then Émile Levassor, René Panhard and finally Louise Sarazin with her children. Really, "a lady could be taken along, without risking dress and life!" Peugeot decided on the spot to build a French version. And Benz? In view of the existing business connections between Panhard and Peugeot, Émile Roger had only a few chances, if at all.

On 1 November 1889, a satisfied Gottlieb Daimler wrote to Louise Sarazin: "I have now decided to cede the exploitation of my French and Belgian patents for gas and gasoline engines to you and to sell them to you for the amount of ... francs, payable at success, but then at latest after the three following years. The fees are now to be borne by you. All subsequent mutual improvements and alterations are to the benefit of both parties. The products have to bear my name and you do not make me any competition in other countries. I hope that this is in conformity with your wishes." Daimler killed two very big birds with one stone. On one hand he made sure that Panhard and consequently Peugeot would use the engines made in France not under their own name but as "Moteurs Système Daimler." On the other hand he had definitively sold his patents now, and deliberately before the creation of the Daimler-Motoren-Gesellschaft, the Daimler Motor Co. Was Louise Sarazin conscious of the proforma action? As sure as fate! Already at that time one good turn deserved another. Had not Daimler promised certain advantages and kept his word? As in the case of his friend Sarazin the stubborn Swabian did not accept that the fruits of his own work would be of benefit to others. He alone would reap the fruits of his French patents, and nobody else!

# 3

# Système Panhard

While in Paris the Exposition attracted all the attention, at Cannstatt the creation of a Daimler Motor Co. was hanging in the air. Schoolmate Max Duttenhofer from the United Powder Factories Köln-Rottweil, who had often consulted Daimler at Deutz "because of his eminently suitable factory equipment," wanted to enter, not alone but with Wilhelm Lorenz from the German Metal Cartridge Factory Karlsruhe. On the German side of the Rhine the situation was not really pleasant. Sales of the high-speed engine even lagged behind the expectations. Hence that sly fox Daimler saw no objection, quite the reverse. In March 1890, the Daimler Motoren Gesellschaft, in short DMG, came into existence, "with the purpose of the exploitation and utilization of the petrol and gas engine inventions made by engineer G. Daimler." It was a 600,000-mark stock company, divided into six hundred shares, of which Daimler signed two hundred, brought in by real values, the Seelberg factory and the patent rights. Doing this the DMG took over "the contracts already closed by Mr. Daimler for the exploitation of his inventions." The clever armament sharks Duttenhofer and Lorenz completely overlooked the fact that they would not get anything out of France. Knowing for sure what he did, a cool Daimler had left open the exact selling price in his letter of 1 November 1889. Instead of regularly disbursing a part of her turnover, in future Madame Sarazin would pay a fictitious fixed amount by installments, and to Mr. Daimler privately. Years later Duttenhofer drew the balance: "The connection to France did not bring any direct benefit to our company, but was insofar of value that in Paris the Panhard & Levassor Company very actively worried about the production of Daimler engines and strongly promoted the development of the automobile vehicles. For Mr. Daimler this connection was very advantageous on the financial side."

In contrast to the just-established DMG, which planned to produce everything except for self-propelled vehicles, not only Peugeot but also Levassor saw their chance exactly there. As planned, Peugeot and his engineer Rigoulot followed the direction of the vélo fashion, bent into shape the Steel-Wheel-Car, placed the V-2 directly ahead of the rear axle, aiming at the wealthy sportsman and the dandy, as their customers. Levassor and Mayade had a machine of a different character in mind, a sturdy front-engined carriage for the cosmopolitan bourgeois, laid out according to the soon-inevitable *"système Panhard"*: V-2 lengthwise in front, rear-wheel drive via leather-faced cone, separated three-speed gearbox and chains. Hadn't the bell-founder Bollée used a similar layout for his Mancelle? On 31 July 1891 the front-engined carriage demonstrated its long-distance ability when Levassor and wife Louise, starting at five in the morning, chugged to the popular Channel resort of Étretat averaging 10 km/h over a distance of 225 km. The first Panhard catalogue

At the end of July 1890, Louis Rigoulot delivered the modified Steel-Wheel-Car of Peugeot make to the Avenue d'Ivry, with a request to sort out the V-2 number 14. At the tiller Émile Levassor. In the spring of 1891, Ivry sold the original Peugeot to Stockholm, to Zacco, Bruhn & Co.

appeared right away: "Voitures & Bateaux mus par Moteurs à Pétrole Système Daimler." Then it was Peugeot's turn. In September, Louis Rigoulot and his colleague Auguste Doriot joined the great bicycle race between Paris and Brest: 15 km/h over 2050 km, one day behind the pneumatic-tire-equipped vélo of the winner Charles Terront.

In autumn of 1891, Panhard sold his first batch of six cars, price per unit 3500 francs-or; the Abbé Durier was allowed a church rebate of 500 francs. Until then, Panhard had sold more than fifty moteurs système Daimler for stationary purposes. That the license fees did not flow into the DMG cash soon attracted the attention of Messrs. Duttenhofer and Lorenz. Of course they wanted to push Daimler into the cold, and appointed an incompetent engineer from Lorenz' following named Max Schoedter over his and Maybach's head. Schroedter's revised Steel-Wheel-Car emerged as a grotesque flop. In autumn of 1892, they contacted Armand Peugeot, wanted to sell the quadricycle outside of France as a Daimler. But only with the consent of Émile Levassor and his wife Louise! To this end they tried to bait Gottlieb Daimler, offered him the technical direction and the take-over of the majority of stock. To deceive his French friends, that was too much—the stubborn Swabian dug his heels in.

## 3. Systéme Panhard

In spring of 1893, he abandoned the DMG, relocated his work to the Hotel Hermann, of course in the company of his entourage, with accounting clerk Linck, adjutant Maybach and engineer Moewes. The hotel gang supplied rough drafts to Panhard and was strongly missed at the Seelberg where the high-speed-engine production crashed from 123 down to 70 units. Duttenhofer and Lorenz, more and more in a temper, asked the house bank to block the accounts. No fear! The old Swabian always alighted on his feet and continued collecting license fees, by the end of 1894 nearly 60,000 marks, about one hundred years' wages for one of his workmen! Paul Daimler related:

> The Hotel Hermann was an old, distinguished health resort with extensive Russian clientele. By the end of the eighties it stood empty, was divided into apartments, hence the nickname "rat-castle." Within the large park behind, there was a two-storied hall with circumferential gallery. This was the experimental workshop in which around 15 workmen were employed and between 30 and 40 cars have been built. Above, there were the offices where Maybach, Linck and Moewes acted. The cars could be driven directly from the hall to the outside into the park whose paths were rather savaged, good for first trials. The Phoenix engine was developed in the Hotel Hermann, the Panhard construction too.

But it was the float-type feed spray carburetor which came first. At last it took the place of the "milk bottle," the voluminous surface carburetor, and granted the V-2 a minimum of flexibility. Just the thing to promenade from Paris to Rouen, at the end of July 1894, in the much-heralded Concours of Pierre Giffard's popular

July 1894—Concours Paris-Rouen. Émile Mayade at the tiller of a Panhard *wagonette*.

*Petit Journal*. Winner was "the horseless car" which reached the finish "without danger for the passengers, easily controlled by the travelers, and not too expensive to run on the road." Every dream, illusion and form of motive power was represented. Among the propulsion delivering devices there were lever systems, clockwork, hydraulic, compressed air, electro-pneumatic and semi-electric engines, among the power sources compressed water and the weight of the passengers! Only the *perpetuum mobile* was missing. Twenty-five-year-old Paul Daimler was a passenger in one of the four works Panhard, while his father stayed at Rouen: "The first price goes with the same score to Messieurs Panhard & Levassor from Ivry and les Fils de Peugeot Frères from Valentigney, who both use the gasoline engine which was invented by Monsieur Daimler from Wurttemberg." The placing did not reflect anything else but the production: Panhard as well as Peugeot each had sold 93 vehicles, all equipped with a Moteur Système Daimler. Only Benz was able to match them, with 127 units "the world's largest automobile factory."

The Phoenix or Phénix celebrated its debut one year later, in June 1895, between Paris and Bordeaux, in the first true race in the history of the great sport. And how it celebrated! Levassor, mechanic d'Hostingue and their Phénix-motorized Panhard gave the competitors no chance, covered the 1192 km in 48 hours and 47 minutes, miles ahead of a Peugeot trio. Of course the Phoenix had been devised by Maybach, but it could hardly be called Daimler, since right away the DMG would have taken it under its wings. Thus it was called Phoenix, patented

July 1894—Concours Paris-Rouen. Alfred Vacheron, co-owner of the Phade foundry at Monthermé, had converted his Panhard, replacing the usual tiller by a volant, a steering wheel. Hence he was allowed to share fourth prize with Le Brun, for "important improvements to the mechanical car."

under the title "Wilhelm Maybach in Cannstatt." Duttenhofer and Lorenz should find the stubborn Swabian a hard nut to crack; with his new engine he would rise like a Phoenix from the ashes! The new engine was composed of two cylinders in line, initially in the dimensions of 66 mm × 104 mm, 67 mm × 108 mm or 75 mm × 120 mm, later of 81 mm × 120 mm and 91 mm × 130 mm. It still had automatic intake valves and hot-tube ignition, but differed from the V-2 by its exhaust operation via camshaft.

Ivry built the first French engine in March 1894 in the dimensions of 75 mm × 120 mm. Émile Mayade agonized until September and even by stretching the bore to 81 mm he was not able to elicit more than a disappointing 3.3 hp out of the Phénix. Mayade's brainstorm arrived during the winter:

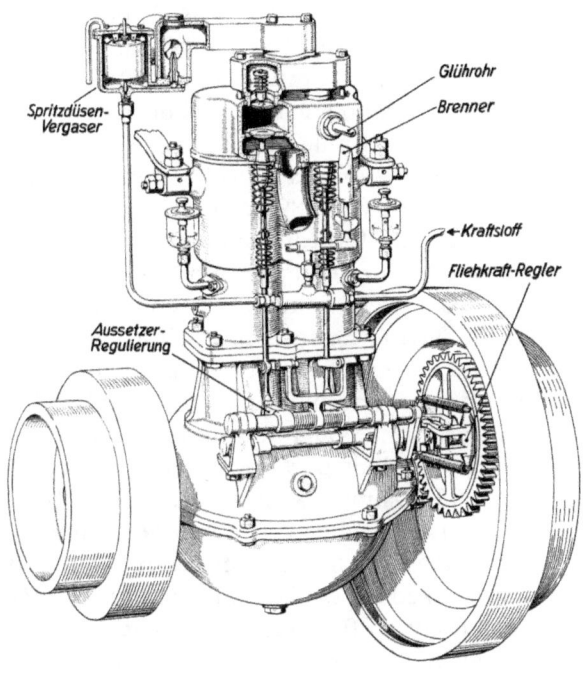

The Phoenix or Phénix engine.

new crankshaft, throws not offset at 180° anymore but concurrent, including a balance weight in the shaft center to struggle against vibrations. The result? Four hp at 800 rpm and 83 kg, the same output as the most powerful V-2, but saving 25 kg. No surprise that Levassor confiscated the Phénix for himself. At the finish near the Porte Maillot, he just said: "Tell Maybach to encapsulate the camshaft! And we need a four-cylinder!" Concerning the performance of the "Éclair," the modified Peugeot of the brothers Édouard and André Michelin, which hung behind because of innumerable tire punctures, he commented: "Why don't you fill your tires with cotton, cork or hay!"

In France nothing could now prevent the boom of the new industry. Based on the organizing committee of the Bordeaux race, the ACF emerged within the end of the year, the soon almighty Automobile Club de France, which ruled as "Société d'Encouragement" the direction not only of the races but of the entire scene. Albert de Dion and Étienne de Zuylen were at the club's head, a duo made for each other who had met during the journey to Rouen. De Zuylen (or, more exactly, van Zuylen), born in 1860, was the perfect club president, a pure sportsman, thus wealthy by definition, a disinterested promoter of the automobile. Disinterested? Wasn't he married to Hélène de Rothschild? And wasn't the Rothschild clique investing everywhere in the new industry? Many pioneers of the first hour joined in, first of all Émile Levassor, Armand Peugeot and Léon Serpollet, *Figaro* columnist Paul Meyan, *Vélo* director Paul Rousseau, Louis and Gaston de Chasseloup-Laubat, *Tout Paris* socialites Georges de Leuchtenberg, Pierre d'Arenberg, Henri de La Valette and Jean de Castellane, and two immigrant Americans just about to become prominent, William Kissam Vanderbilt Jr. and James Gordon Bennett. Panhard, Peugeot, the system Daimler engine and the well-developed Benz supplied a foundation on which all novices more or less relied, Émile Delahaye, Alexandre Darracq, Émile and Louis Mors as well as Amédée and Léon Bollée. The upcoming road races provided perfect advertising, a fact noticed even by Duttenhofer: "In the year 1895 Mister Emil Levassor made the first longer endurance run from Paris to Bordeaux and back. From then on a big upswing can be realised, and the races requested more and more speed."

If the DMG wanted to keep pace within the new scene, Maybach's work and patents had to be secured at all events. Moreover, not only was Levassor after a Phoenix license, he kept asking for his friend Daimler's definitive consent. Frederick Simms and his Daimler Motor Syndicate promised £17,500 for the British rights: reason enough for Duttenhofer to negotiate with the hotel gang and reason enough for the stubborn Swabian to reconsider his financial attitude. In December 1895, Daimler wrote to Levassor: "Since the English syndicate has paid the £17,500 my new contract with Duttenhofer and Lorenz is valid." Henceforth the license fees flew in the DMG cash. A clever move on the part of Duttenhofer, who had attacked the weakest link in the chain: Maybach was appointed technical director and given 30 shares. How could he refuse? And Daimler had to follow, he not only alighted on his feet but presided over the supervisory board, collecting 200,000 marks for the Maybach patents and in future 5 percent of the net profit.

In June 1896, Paris was celebrating. The Automobile Club de France, which held its first meetings in Albert de Dion's city apartment at no. 27, Quai d'Orsay, moved into a villa in the Bois de Boulogne, inviting four hundred guests among the *Tout Paris* for the inauguration banquet: "Boson de Périgord, Prince of Sagan, just accepted as club member, came in company of Princess Metternich." At Cannstatt the festivities were not quite so exclusive. The DMG drank to the thousandth engine, the beginning of production of the Belt Car, and of course to the peace treaty between Duttenhofer and Daimler. Belt Car? The "Riemenwagen" was the DMG's first serial vehicle, an unsprung rear-engine carriage, using a ludicrous flat belt arrangement as drive train, and a center-pivoted axle as steering. Were the achievements of the *système Panhard* unknown in Swabia? How could Maybach bring about such an archaic joke? On one hand Maybach was first and foremost an engine man; on the other hand in Germany the neighbors from Mannheim set the tone with the equally primitive Benz, and were able to sell nearly two hundred units per year. The customers regarded the belt drive as an advantage, making possible smooth starts and even power transmission, in contrast to a cone clutch and sliding-pinion gearbox which raised every speed change to a crashing and bucking adventure, jolting chauffeur and passengers out of their seats. Up to 25 km/h the Belt Car with its shaky steering was perfectly suited for field paths. Anyway the Riemenwagen did not speed up further since Cannstatt mounted only the small Phoenixes, either in the dimensions of 66 mm × 104 mm or 75 mm × 120 mm, either with three or with four horsepower. Before the production start at the Seelberg, the first Belt Cars were still assembled in the park of the "rat-castle," until the end of 1896 a total of twenty-four units, with bodies à la Benz: four seat vis-à-vis, two or four seat victoria, coupé or landaulet. The real sportsmen did not accept

## 3. Systéme Panhard

It was in the "Riemenwagen," in the Belt Car, that the Prince of Wales enjoyed the benefits of the gasoline engine for the first time.

the stone-age Daimler, but the unhurried socialites did and it was aboard a Belt Car that the Prince of Wales enjoyed the gasoline engine for the first time, while previously he had favored Léon Serpollet's whispering steamers.

The *marque doyenne*, the founder make Panhard & Levassor, dominated in the great French road races. Although in France more and more dangerous competitors were springing up like mushrooms, the German-French liaison of the systèmes Daimler and Panhard was able to stand up for three years, due to the close collaboration between Maybach and Mayade. A moteur système Maybach never did manifest itself, nor did a voiture système Mayade, since in the age of the fin de siècle the gray eminences had to remain gray. A consequence of the events that some patents had been granted on Maybach's name, and a consequence of the events too, that, in October 1896, the great practitioner and artisan Mayade won the race to Marseille. Towards the Mediterranean, the latest gasoline tricycles from De Dion & Bouton were hard to catch. With the help of spark plug ignition their quarter-liter single (67 mm × 70 mm) easily sped to 1500 rpm, delivering 1.75 hp. As a result of frictions with Daimler and Levassor concerning the external marketing of his quadricycle, Peugeot had abandoned the license engine. He centered his own twin (84 mm × 126 mm), designed of course by Rigoulot according to the best Phoenix or Phénix fashion. And the Bollée brothers joined in, the sons of Amédée *père*: on one hand Amédée *fils* with a big twin (95 mm × 160 mm) lying athwart at the front, on the other hand Léon with his name-protected "Voiturette."

A relief driver was out of the question for Émile Levassor. Completely exhausted, his Panhard turned over near Avignon when a dog ran in the way. Mayade had to save Ivry's honor. On the leg ending at Marseille, by the aid of a tailwind, the famous mistral, he forced his four-cylinder up to an average of 32.4 km/h. Now the small De Dions were under pressure, and promptly began to splutter on the way back to Paris because of spark plug problems. After 1720 km and a running time of 67 hours and 43 minutes, Mayade won in front of his teammate Merkel, while Paul Viet, Georges Bouton's second brother-in-law, was just able to hold third position with his light De Dion runabout. A four-cylinder in the Panhard? At the moment nothing else than two Phénix twins (81 mm × 120 mm) crudely coupled together on a common crankcase, whereby the output quite simply doubled to eight horsepower at an unchanged 800 rpm. After all 2.5 hp more than in Merkel's enlarged twin (91 mm × 130 mm). The deep mystery of whether power enhancement was to be achieved by using several cylinders or by simply increasing the single or twin cylinder's swept volume henceforth found its solution in the high-capacity four-cylinder. The limit of growth? A reasonable relation between output and weight since repressing rules were non-existent and still out of consideration: The sportsmen and the ACF were jolly glad that the machines ran at all.

Panhard now collected great profits, due to the peerless front-engine system

October 1896—Ivry. First four-cylinder: Mayade's Panhard averaged 32.4 km/h through the lower Rhône valley, and won the race from Paris to Marseille and back, in 67 hours 42 minutes 58 seconds.

which obviously ensured the success in the sport. Or did it? Three British sportsmen firmly believed it. Their names were Charles McRobie Turrell, Harry J. Lawson and H. O. Duncan, and without hesitation they paid 30,000 francs cash for the Bordeaux winner, and 75,000 into the bargain for the three front-placed Marseille racers. Just two years before, a wagonette with canopy was offered for 5650, a phaeton for 5300, and a mylord with pavilion for 6000. No isolated case! A Phénix, which had been ordered long before, left the shop of Ivry at the catalogue price of 12,000 francs. On the very same day it moved on for 22,500 and finally finished up for 45,000 in the hands of Alfred Harmsworth, the eccentric owner of the *Daily Mail*. Cannstatt seized the chance, reacted instantly and adopted the front engine. Production of the Phoenix started in 1897, a Swabian high-leg Panhard, which was named after its engine and which differed from its French counterpart by the bulky, typically German body. This was not done for the engineer's but only for the clientele's sake. The front engine and the corresponding hood turned the self-propelled carriage into an automobile with its own character. The sportsmen quickly accepted the new appearance so that overnight everything else looked old-fashioned, from the Belt Car to the Benz, to the Peugeot. And at Cannstatt nobody complained about the stinking Phoenixes clattering just in front of the nose: Initially only two-cylinders, from 1899 four, up to a 5-liter (102 mm × 150 mm), delivering 16 hp.

Levassor never recovered from the accident in the Rhône valley. On 14 April 1897, he succumbed to an embolism. In view of the new season Mayade improved only details, mounted for the first time a *radiateur en serpentin*, a tube coil radiator, which cut the huge watertank down to a mere 40 liters. Nothing else? Following the winter event from Marseille to Monte Carlo, further in the North the first difficulties arose with the approval of the long road races: Many rural communities were hostile to the automobile disturbance. The ACF was only able to arrange short-distance races to Dieppe and Trouville.

In 1898 the sportsmen were allowed to cross national boundaries for the first time, to venture out of France, thanks to Étienne de Zuylen's connections to Amsterdam. Of course Paris could not stand back, and the hitherto intractable bureaucracy accredited overnight the already classic run to Bordeaux! After Levassor's death Mayade officially chaired the Panhard engineering. By the beginning of the nineties, he had moved from no. 14 to no. 19 of the Avenue d'Ivry, living above the head office. As *directeur technique* he was at last allowed to give his fancy full scope and hence developed into the first engine-dynamics expert in history. Ivry sparkled. The newest four-cylinder (94 mm × 132 mm) was no longer simply made up of two coupled twins: The crank throws of the outer cylinders were offset at 180° to the inner ones, providing a speed jump of 25 percent up to 1000 rpm. The 3.6-liter engine produced 14 hp, nearly four horsepower per liter. A *volant*, a steering wheel, replaced the archaic tiller and the wheelbase was increased from the previous year's 200 to 230 cm. Michelin supplied tires, 900 mm × 65 mm at the front and 1100 mm × 90 mm (overall diameter/width in mm) at the rear, all this in view of better control of the Panhard which could speed at up to 60 km/h. The Michelin brothers were not the only specialized suppliers. Panhard driver Léonce Girardot recommended a small shop at no. 71, Rue du Moulin-Vert in the south of Paris, where Jules Grouvelle and Henri Arquembourg built their *refroidisseurs d'eau*, their water coolers. The finned tube radiator promptly migrated forward in the position of higher pressure. Thereafter, during the 1898

**July 1898—Ivry. Paris–Amsterdam winner Fernand Charron at the wheel of his Panhard.**

season, the Panhard could not be held up. The full-bearded Chevalier René de Knyff won the race to Bordeaux, while the former vélo star Fernand Charron averaged 44 km/h in the year's main event to Amsterdam.

On 18 September 1898, Mayade was killed in an accident while traveling through the Charrente Maritime when his Panhard collided with a horse and cart in the steep descent of Chevanceaux and turned over. The Avenue d'Ivry lost the thread and the *marque doyenne* its sole leading position, inter alia, because the creative exchange with Cannstatt was almost completely cancelled. Arthur Krebs, born in 1850, family from Germany, from Boppard in the Rhine Valley, infantry officer, balloonist and fire brigade captain, took over Mayade's heritage. In the first year of his activity he stretched the four-cylinder Phénix to 96 mm × 138 mm and 16 hp. In 1899 this was enough for the last two great Phénix victories, with Charron in the race to Bordeaux and de Knyff in the Tour de France for automobiles. Right at the end of 1899 the new four-cylinder Mors was suddenly in the limelight, after winning the races to Saint-Malo, Trouville and Ostend and a new record of 67 km/h between Bordeaux and Biarritz. The door to success? The established Société d'Électricité of Émile Mors, headquartered in the Rue du Théâtre of the Parisian district Grenelle, had engaged a pragmatist named Henri Brasier. Charles-Henri Brasier was born in 1864—in Ivry!—and he simply copied the best, improving it with his own ingredients up to perfection: four-cylinder front-engine mounted in a chain-drive frame, Phénix and Panhard fashion, upgraded by a low-tension ignition from his own shop. In the eyes of the customers it was hardly of importance that Ivry had handed over the lead in the great sport. The order books kept on overflowing. For a Phénix in the *système Panhard* the sportsmen had inevitably to wait at least one year. A Mors, even longer! A rear-engined Peugeot, a belt driven Bollée, a comfortable Benz, a nervous tricycle from De Dion? The real sportsmen wanted the unbeatable *système Panhard*, and nothing else. Then there was the way to Cannstatt. But Cannstatt was not allowed to sell to France...

# 4

# *Riviérà*

By the end of the nineties, the sportsmen still pronounced it Riviérà, and not Rivièra like the summer crowd a few decades later. It was fashionable to spend the winter months in Cannes, Nice, Monte Carlo and Menton, in the Cimiez, in the Riviera Palace and the Hôtel de Paris. The Excelsior Regina was inaugurated by Queen Victoria, "inauguré par Sa Majesté la Reine d'Angleterre." And the wide parks provided the proper distance to the *Beau Monde*. A playground comme il faut for the sportsmen! Who else but Albert de Dion, Étienne de Zuylen, the Marquis Louis and the Comte Gaston de Chasseloup-Laubat could urge the ACF to organize a race between Marseille and Monte Carlo? On 29 January 1897, 37 cars and motorcycles started from the Place Castellane, 16 of them on tires. On the straights Gaston de Chasseloup-Laubat and his two-and-a-half-ton steamer from De Dion outpaced all gasoline vehicles. Albert Lemaître in his Peugeot and Étienne Giraud in his Panhard struggled for second place. At Hyères the steamer replenished fuel, at Sainte Maxime water. The De Dion covered the narrow 17-km climb from Nice to La Turbie in just 38 minutes. The victory was sure since the dangerous descent to Monaco was not clocked because of snowfall. The steamer averaged 30 km/h, crossed the line more than half an hour ahead of Lemaître's Peugeot and a Panhard trio under Prévost, de Knyff and Giraud. During the following banquet in the Rotonde of the Hôtel de Paris, a bright-eyed Albert de Dion raised his glass: "We build the locomotives, Michelin the rails!" Overnight the automobile became presentable. Now even King Carnival stepped in the motorcar, promenading through the streets of Nice, decorated with flowers.

At the beginning of March 1898, the elegant winter society was eagerly waiting for the blue and white Jeantaud of the previous year's winner, a posh electromobile, that Count Gaston, befitting his rank, drove with white gloves. A new record in the climb between Cuzes and Fréjus was certain. But the Count did not even appear at the start in Marseille: During a test drive on the Champs-Élysées the engine had burned through! But the popular Madame Laumaillé came along, on her tricycle, a De Dion. Her husband provided entry fees and gasoline costs by getting on the train to Monte Carlo day after day, and gambling until 20 francs were in the bag. Soon the Laumaillés were even able to afford a refined villa… The brisk lady did not keep up with the leaders. *Les Rois du Volant* in their latest Panhards arranged the race among themselves. Fernand Charron was the first to cross the finish in Nice, then Gilles Hourgières, *nom de course* of the well-known Parisian socialite and future Mors director Georges Huillier, and René de Knyff. The elegant Charron was *Tout Paris*' first gentleman to go out without a top hat. Born in 1866 in Angers, he won his first bicycle race at 15, riding a grand-bi, received two francs 50 centimes, and a live chicken. In 1888 he began to work for Adolphe Clément, managing the Parisian shop. With bicycle champion de Civry, he founded the Vélodrome de la Seine, before taking over the French Humber agency. In 1895, with his friends Léonce Girardot and Émile Voigt, he launched CGV, Charron, Girardot et Voigt, one of the finest addresses in the Avenue de la Grande Armée, selling Panhard, Peugeot and De Dion. Hence it was no surprise that, after his Riviera success, he found on the spot an enthusiast who forked out 50,000 francs for his stylish racer, while de Knyff still collected 30,000. This made the winter tourist Jellinek think.

Emil Jellinek came from Vienna where he pursued all kinds of businesses and where, one year ago, he had sold a handful of Daimlers. It was not that somehow he was committed to Cannstatt, but mechanic Wilhelm Werner was working in Vienna, and that was the end of it. Currently the self-propelled collection was made up of a Belt-Car and a two-cylinder Phoenix, a Benz, a Voiturette from Bollée, an additional grasshopper from Ménard, and finally a Mors which he drove in the hillclimb to La Turbie in 1898. With the exception of the Phoenix all these vehicles were difficult or impossible to sell. Jellinek and his French business partner Léon Desjoyeaux knew that real money could only be made with a four-cylinder in the *système Panhard*. But the genuine distribution was already assigned everywhere. Thus on to Cannstatt! Of course Duttenhofer and his marketing manager Gustav Vischer accepted with pleasure the order placed for six brand-new Phoenixes, although Jellinek and Desjoyeaux forced the prices down to the minimum and required an absolute free hand for the resale. In addition, Cannstatt approved a second mechanic

Winter paradise for sportsmen: the Riviérà, the villas of the Mont Boron and the port of Nice.

Jellinek in Vienna, with Daimler Belt Car and chauffeur Hermann Braun.

and chauffeur for the purpose of on-site service, customer support and demonstration. Hermann Braun, born in 1878 in Cannstatt, moved from the Seelberg to Vienna, "entered Jellinek's employment." But the proposition of a French agency was a cause for concern. The Sarazin contract and the exploitation of the Maybach patents by Panhard prevented every direct sale across the Rhine. On this point the stubborn Swabian was not to be trifled with. Moreover the DMG would have shot itself in the foot: If only one component bearing the name Daimler would be shipped to France without Panhard consent, then, according to local legislation, all patents and hence license fees were invalid forthwith. Duttenhofer knew it only too well. Wasn't global marketing the real objective of a new branch established in Berlin? In fact, with a semi-official agency in non–French Monte Carlo, the DMG would not be breaking new ground. And six Phoenixes equaled 96,000 marks, in volume more than one-fifth of the 1897 engine production. And with the Riviera included, Jellinek and Desjoyeaux promised to purchase at least two dozen cars. Duttenhofer and Vischer pondered. What should they think of this Mister Jellinek?

Although born on 6 April 1853 in Leipzig, where his erudite father, a rabbi and the "most important preacher of his time," was giving philosophic Talmudic lectures between 1845 and 1856, Emil Jellinek was Austrian and grew up in Vienna. A peripatetic luck-seeker, he had no interest in scientific studies. In 1872 his father sent him to North Africa's Tangiers, as office boy and secretary to his friend Schmidl, the local Austrian consul. While riding through Tétouan he fell from his

## 4. Rivièrà

Spring 1898—Nice. Emil Jellinek at the tiller of his Mors, climbing up to La Turbie. The 8-hp 90° V-4 (80 mm × 110 mm) was hidden at the rear, under the seat, primary transmission by means of leather belts.

horse, just in front of the window of a handsome young lady named Rachel. Fortuity? The injury to his leg was severe, her fond care had prompt effect, and in 1874 Mademoiselle Rachel Goggman turned into Madame Jellinek. And Emil finished up in Oran, in the tobacco business of his parents-in-law. The first gold mine opened up at the beginning of the eighties: insurance in Algiers. After moving to his native Austria, where Jellinek took over the Viennese agency of the French life insurance company Aigle, the time of scrimping was over for good. The family spent the summer months a few kilometers to the south, in fashionable Baden, Wiener Strasse no. 37, in the house of his friend, wine dealer Hanni "whose daughter would marry Prince Auersperg." The business boomed so that Jellinek, in 1891, bought the adjacent plot no. 41 where he built the Villa Mercedes. Mercedes was the Jellineks' little daughter, born in 1889 in Vienna, whose name sounded like fireworks over the shores of the Mediterranean: Mercedes Adriana Manuela Ramona. The two sons born in Africa had been christened conventionally, Adolphe and Fernand! Was Rachel, in gorgeous Vienna, missing her Mediterranean birthplace Oran? She died of cancer in 1893, and in future Jellinek named everything which was beloved and dear to him "Mercedes." During winter, Jellinek used to headquarter in Nice, renting no. 57, Promenade des Anglais. This Mister Jellinek was no motorcar expert but certainly a good businessman and on this point he was on the same wavelength as councilor Duttenhofer. Cannstatt gave the go-ahead for the Riviera, of course semi-officially. The Phoenixes were delivered to Baden.

The clientele in front of the Viennese doorstep was far from being neglected. On 3 February 1899, Jellinek wrote to Rudolf Stary, the personal chauffeur of Princess Windisch-grätz:

Mercedes Jellinek. In 1909, at 20, she married in Nice Baron Carl von Schlosser, "in a glittering wedding." In 1923 Baron Rudolf Weigl, a sculptor from Vienna, followed as her second husband. Mercedes died in 1929.

> Although you did not take the trouble of replying to my letters, I wish to inform you that the Panhard cars are completely outdone by Daimler. In Baden you will see the latest twelve-horsepower four-cylinder, which climbs the Semmering at incredible speed. I have sold my Baden car to a factory owner at Lyon, since in the Estérel, between Nice and Fréjus, or Freischütz as you say, it beat all Panhards, even last year's fourth placed. However, here the car ran differently than at Baden where the oil nozzle was too large by half. After it had been downsized, the car ran wonderfully. Mister Spitz can tell you everything about it. At the moment I have a ten-horsepower car with electro-magnetic ignition. We drive from Nice to La Turbie in 37 minutes and 12 seconds and, using a 16 tooth sprocket, we hope to achieve between 30 and 32 minutes. Between Nice and Monte Carlo, everything is going in third and fourth gear, never in first and second. The president of the French automobile club, Baron Zuylen de Nyvelt, asks me to leave the car to him. You see, dear Stary, you were wrong. The Daimlers can, if they want, achieve great things.

It was difficult to convince the good Stary, who remained faithful to a *marque doyenne* which was just holding its position as never before and had run over the opposition in the great races towards Bordeaux and Amsterdam. Jellinek kept at it, replied on 13 February:

> With your opinions you remain incorrigible. Girardot achieved 50 km/h on a flat stretch. Yesterday, on the road to Cannes, I covered the kilometer in 58 seconds and the day before I drove from here to La Turbie in 34 minutes and 21 seconds. As a consequence I sold the 10 hp for 26,000 francs, to be delivered on 15 April, in fact to a gentleman who has a four-cylinder Panhard. Such prices have not been

Villa Mercedes at Baden, near Vienna.

obtained here so far. Alas my 12 hp will arrive only in April. In August I'll receive a 15 hp. Whether I'll enter the 10 hp in the races, I don't know since I fear that my 26,000 francs are gone if it is involved in an accident. I know the Léon Bollée cars, they are not bad. But unfortunately they have a belt drive and a hot tube ignition while our electro-magnetic ignition is wonderful and safe. Your will see the 12 hp during the Summer and find out how it speeds up to the Semmering.

By the end of March 1899, the Riviera focused on the speed week, the *semaine automobile*. For the first time the enterprising Jacques Gondoin, the president of the automobile club of Nice, held a complete meeting: The long-distance race between Nice and Castellane, then the touring car race from Nice to Magagnosc, the one-mile sprint on the Promenade des Anglais, the hillclimb up to La Turbie and finally an exposition and concours d'élégance at Monte Carlo. Albert Lemaître, the popular Peugeot star from Épernay in the Champagne, was unbeatable in the latest version of the rear-engine two-cylinder (140 mm × 190 mm). To Castellane and back he averaged nearly 42 km/h, achieved 1 minute $35^{3}/_{5}$ seconds over the standing mile, and climbed to La Turbie in 24 min 23 sec. And Emil Jellinek? For the run to Magagnosc he entered a 4.9-liter Phoenix (102 mm × 150 mm), for the driver "Mercédès." And after 85 km and 2 h 27 min 30 sec, it was Mercédès who won, averaging 34.5 km/h. Whom did Mercédès leave behind? Two additional 4.9-liters under "Dr. Pascal" and Arthur de Rothschild, the favorite customers of the Jellinek squad. Of course it was Jellinek who stood behind Mercédès. Behind Dr. Pascal was hidden the physician Henri de Rothschild, founder of the Paris Mathilde Hospital and of the Théâtre Pigalle, dedicated collector of skulls and nephew of banker Arthur. But most of the work at the wheel of the Rothschild Daimlers was done by Hermann Braun and Wilhelm Werner, at least when no distinguished on-lookers were in sight. Obviously pseudonyms were *de bon ton*. "Axt" stood for the publisher André Hachette, "Escargot" for Étienne de Zuylen, "Snail" for his wife Hélène, "Walrus" for Émile Mors. In the sprints, the Daimlers had no chance, their best time being 2 min 23⅖ sec, 48 seconds slower than Lemaître's Peugeot. Nevertheless a triple victory, even if the race was just a noble coffee-party and brimful order books, so that it was not difficult for Jellinek and Desjoyeaux to keep their word and to order two dozen Phoenixes. Of course they had the latest "ignition apparatus from Bosch" since Jellinek did not want to hear any more about incandescent platinum tubes: "Every hot tube ignition will inevitably set a car on fire." Ignition apparatus? A magneto supplied non-reinforced tension to an ignition pin, which protruded into the combustion chamber, and to a wipe contact operated by an interrupter cam at the right moment, generating a spark: the famous low tension make-and-break ignition.

For the next Semaine de Nice, Jellinek requested more power and less weight. Maybach and his assistant Josef Brauner applied the standard solution, enlarged

March 1899—Meeting of Nice. The Rothschild family before the start of the touring-car race to Magagnosc: on the left no. 102 with Wilhelm Werner and Henri de Rothschild, alias Dr. Pascal; on the right no. 103 with Hermann Braun and Arthur de Rothschild.

Winter 1899–1900—Cannstatt. Production director Hermann Balz testing the longer of the two 5.5-liter Phoenix racers, the duc "Mercédès I," wheelbase 217 cm.

the engine displacement and shortened the wheelbase. With 106 mm × 156 mm and 5.5 liters their pepped up Phoenix was on a level with the 110 mm × 138 mm and 5.25 liters of the latest Panhard but could not match the 119 mm × 165 mm and 7.35 liters of the Mors, the reference of the 1900 season. The power output fell between the 24 and 30 hp of the two French cars: 26 hp at 950 rpm. The weight of the engine was 320 kg, transmission via huge leather cone, separated four-speed gearbox and chains. As for the frame cut, Maybach and Brauner carried off the prize. While Ivry extended the wheelbase to 250 cm for better handling, Cannstatt offered either 190 or 217 cm! Nevertheless the massive Phoenix weighed 1400 kg, 350 kg more than the powerful Mors. The much-read Paul Meyan, no longer on *Le Figaro*'s payroll but meanwhile chief editor of *La France Automobile*, the ACF's more-or-less-official organ, justified the excess of weight: "The Daimlers are no racing cars. They are built so that in ten years they are still in the same condition as today, what in my opinion is no small compliment." The tire dimension was guided by the length of the contest, for sprints 870 mm × 90 mm front and 920 mm × 120 mm rear, for longer road races 910 mm × 90 mm front and 1020 mm × 120 mm rear.

In the Autumn of 1899, Duttenhofer dumped the small Phoenixes, built by the MMB, Motorfahrzeug und Motorenfabrik Berlin, the motorcar and motor factory at Berlin-Marienfelde, as anonymous products without Daimler emblem. Jellinek declined and Vischer commented: "Of course it is not in the interest of Mister Jellinek that the prices are suddenly beaten down so enormously since he has not yet sold a larger number of cars and he will be aggrieved all the more since the MMB is asking a delivery time of only three months in which case a considerably higher price can be obtained not only in Paris but in general. As well we think it is impossible that in Berlin within three months such a car can be completely tested and delivered. The further remarks that no Daimler patent has been hurt are almost a mystery to us and we are at a loss for words." The old Daimler was tired. His heart disease got worse. A cure did not help. While testing a new Phoenix he collapsed and fell from the car. On 6 March 1900 he died, just 66 years old. Of course Louise Sarazin came from Paris. And of course Duttenhofer stayed in Berlin: "Please ask Lorenz to place in my name a crown at the grave." Although Daimler's death did not change anything in the patent situation, Cannstatt was now able to move more freely and Jellinek received more backup. On 22 March, Cannstatt noted: "This afternoon director Maybach departed to Nice where the races will take place during next week. Then it depends mainly on the result whether or not the deal with the 30-hp racer will come about." Thirty hp? Jellinek had ordered a brand-new engine, a "moteur Mercédès." Only with a new engine bearing a new name could the Riviera, Paris and France be opened, since Panhard applied pressure, preventing—via ACF, patent and customs offices—any official import or race participation of a Phoenix.

La semaine de Nice was inaugurated on Sunday 25 March 1900 by a *corso fleuri*. "A very distinguished society gathered in the grandstand, the King and the Queen of Saxony, the Prince and the Duke of Oldenburg, as well as many in automobilistic circles well known personalities." The highlight of the winter season followed on Monday, the race from Nice to Marseille, distance without neutralizations 197 km. The Jellinek camp entered two short-chassis Phoenixes, both with 26 hp and 1400 kg: Hermann Braun alias Mercédès I drove the duc Mercédès I on the longer 217-cm frame, starting number 6; foreman Wilhelm Bauer alias Mercédès II the ultra-short 190-cm spider Mercédès II, no. 8. Both Phoenix racers were forced to start under the name Mercédès since the AC de Nice accepted the entries only under this condition. And then only because Desjoyeaux was a club member! Two purely private 5.5-liters were accepted as Daimlers, the no. 10 under Prince Lubecki and the no. 15 under race doctor Pascal who right from the start drove at the back of the field. Wilhelm Werner was hibernating in Vienna, looking after the cars of Baron Alfred Springer.

The contenders were the 16-hp Panhard (96 mm × 138 mm), especially the cars of Charron and de Knyff, and the brand-new 30-hp Mors (119 mm × 165 mm) of Levegh, anagram of Alfred Velghe, the uncle of the Mercedes driver who crashed so tragically in the 1955 Le Mans race. Braun finished up in the ditch, just 15 km after the start. Charron was delayed by a spluttering engine. Levegh lost half an hour by reason of a puncture. De Knyff won in 3 h 22 min, Bauer finished tenth, nine minutes back. Maybach cabled: "After 66 km, the most difficult section, Bauer led by four minutes. Then three tires burst successively. Arrived in Marseille 45 minutes back. Braun had accident, Braun healthy, car out of order." The drive back was not clocked because of poor weather. As in the previous year the touring car race ended successfully. After 192 km between Nice and Draguignan, Englishman E. T. Stead's 4.9-liter crossed the finish in front of Paul Chauchard's Panhard. It was the climb to the summit village of La Turbie which came to a bad end. Bauer was at the wheel of the short spider, Braun as riding mechanic by his side, when in the first corner careless spectators crossed the road. Bauer attempted to swerve and ran into a wall of solid rock: "Foreman Bauer crashed. Will hardly survive the night." Bauer died next day of his injuries, leaving Braun with multiple fractures. Jellinek cancelled a start in the subsequent mile sprint.

Paul Meyan commented in his *France Automobile*:

> Again and again it is claimed that the accidents with the two Daimlers are due to their construction, that they are too powerful, too heavy, too high, hard to control at speed. I cannot share this point. I have seen the cars, taken a close look and found striking details. I even was passenger in one of the cars, towards La Turbie, and I have to admit that I was extremely surprised how this heavy mass of 1400 kg took a gradient of 10 and more percent at a speed of 42 km/h. Before the race, Bauer had practised the hill forty times. He knew it better than anyone else. But at 70 km/h he had to avoid a group of all-too curious spectators, lost his way through the corner and slid into the rocks. Could Bauer who was not a pure racing driver stave off the disaster with a lighter car? Perhaps. I am not saying this to condemn the Cannstatt cars. With their good comfort they are perfectly suited for touring journeys. Due to the magneto ignition their engine is exceedingly flexible, can be run if necessary on two, three or four cylinders. The question remains about the foreign competition. The Daimlers are German and as such we have to reject them. In the environment of Nice there are already a lot of them. But as far as I know, with three exceptions, they are all in the hands of foreigners, in the hands of Baron Springer, Prince Lubecki, Xantho, Jellinek and Stead. They come to the coast during the Winter and bring their cars along. Give everyone the possibility to buy in France without delivery time! How can we forbid the import of the Cannstatt cars as long as we are ourselves building with American tools?

Phoenix production: the Seelberg factory at Cannstatt.

Duttenhofer wrote: "Now it was easier for Jellinek to convince the DMG that the unsuitable design of the Daimler racer caused the sudden death of the Cannstatt foreman, that the frames of the Daimler cars had to be built even lower, wider and longer. And if the direction of the DMG would agree to build new cars exactly after his specifications then he would take a whole series against fixed payment." In May 1900 Paul Meyan paid a visit to the Seelberg factory, and met many friends. Peugeot star Albert Lemaître was there, the Brazilian balloonist and aeronaut Alberto Santos-Dumont, Desrousseaux and Farconnet from Marseille, and Bertier from Le Mans, who was picking up his 28-hp. And of course Arthur de Rothschild who had a close look at his 20-hp. Meyan wrote: "Do you know on what Cannstatt is working? On a brand-new engine which has been devised by Wilhelm Maybach, the inventor of the Phoenix. This engine has been named Moteur Mercédès. Emil Jellinek alias Mercédès and Léon Desjoyeaux have bought it from Maybach. It will be constructed in the Daimler factory."

Jellinek provided full employment. In 1900, 344 men worked in the Seelberg factory, nearly three times as many as in the founding year 1890. They assembled 210 engines and 96 cars, occasionally still a Riemenwagen but mainly the two- and four-cylinder Phoenix. The turnover just exceeded two million marks of which a quarter million were labor costs, half a million "used materials" and a further four hundred thousand "general expenses." By July 1900, Jellinek had taken 34 wickedly expensive four-cylinder Phoenixes, paying no less than 638,000 marks for them,

November 1900—Hillclimb of Chanteloup near Paris. Henri de Rothschild and his brand-new 5.5-liter Phoenix achieved fastest time of the day, covering 1820 meters with a gradient of 11 percent in 3 min 45⅕ sec: victory against a rather weak opposition.

April 1902—Meeting of Nice. The 5.5-liter Phoenix of William Zborowski climbed in 25 min 21.6 sec to La Turbie, fast enough to win the four-seater class. The Phoenix was ordered on 13 April 1899 and delivered on 15 January 1900 via the Motor Carriage Supply Co., London.

one-third of the annual turnover! No wonder that he could assert his wishes and that Cannstatt rolled out the red carpet even for his secretary Ferdinand Spiegel. Desjoyeaux localized his operation to France, keeping an eye on Paris. It was Desjoyeaux who transformed the Phoenix into a *voiture chic*, despite its German origin, despite the over-solid and heavy body, despite its massive appearance, with a flair of goldmark and Bagdad-Bahn, of Riviera and Grand Hotel, of breakfast at Maxim's and four bottles of champagne in the spider. In December the moteur Mercédès appeared in *La France Automobile*. Then, in the last issue of the year, the Mercédès shone in full splendor on the front page. On the front page of the ACF's semi-official organ! *Le Tout Paris* was marveling.

# 5

## *Mercédès*

If the stubborn Swabian Daimler ever met the top salesman Jellinek, then certainly it was only pro forma. Anyway Daimler would have continued to behave with integrity and loyalty towards his Parisian friends and would instantly have blocked the contract of 2 April 1900: "Mister Emil Jellinek founds in Monaco a company with enough available capital for the sale of Daimler automobiles and engines." Only after Gottlieb Daimler's death could Cannstatt approach the French market so directly and circumvent the agreements with Panhard via the detour through Monaco. Every initiative of the Daimler heirs to collect license fees for the new moteur Mercédès was immediately nipped in the bud with the threat "that the proceeding of Mister Daimler in the French affair did not comply with the contracts and that the situation of the Daimler family against the DMG would be a very bad one in the case of legal action." But the head office felt uneasy. On 19 May 1900 it was noted:

> Today Paul Daimler brings us the copy of a letter written by Gottlieb Daimler to Madame Levassor dated 1 November 1889, concerning the cession of the French patents. According to Karl Linck, apart from this letter, there is no other special contract between Gottlieb Daimler and Madame Levassor or another French company. In this letter there is only the clause that on the part of Madame Levassor no competition is allowed outside of France while the reverse that Gottlieb Daimler respective we are not allowed to compete in France is not contained. Karl Linck justifies it with the French patent law which excludes a sale from our side to France since in this case the French patents would be invalid. This would not be within the meaning of the contract after Madame Levassor had bought the patents.

And, something which Daimler's secretary Karl Linck kept quiet discreetly, no French money would have flowed to Cannstatt anymore. At all events Cannstatt summed up "that a sale from Germany to France is not allowed because of this letter from 1 November 1889." A pity that the heirs did not sue.

And Louise Sarazin? On 17 September 1900, it was announced "that negotiations with Madame Levassor will take place during next week": In future, Cannstatt was allowed to sell the Mercedes in France and Ivry the Panhard in Germany. On 19 March 1901 "the office of the international automobile exposition planned in Berlin informed the DMG that Panhard & Levassor too had applied for space." Herewith the situation was clarified: "As we don't adhere anymore to the contract that Gottlieb Daimler made with Panhard & Levassor concerning the sales to France, it will not be possible to protest if this company opens an agency in Germany. In any case, as a result of this action, we would have a free hand in France and hence in our opinion we cannot do anything against the agency."

On 17 April 1900, two weeks after creation of the Jellinek company in Monaco, the substantial order from Nice came in. Vischer and Maybach forwarded the message to Lorenz: "Councillor Duttenhofer transfers meeting to Friday afternoon and Saturday morning. Your presence would be very desired. Jellinek places order for 36 cars. Value 550,000 marks." The reply was not long in coming: "Will arrive next Friday. Congratulations." Hereby 36 cars constituted only a part of the whole order. "A new engine design should be developed and named 'Daimler-Mercedes.' The orders of Mister Jellinek have to be preferred to all others. Only the orders of the German War Department have the parity with the orders of the Jellinek company." This meant nothing else than the exclusive distribution rights for the Mercedes, at a fixed selling price on the DMG's part. Originally Cannstatt planned five

Emil Jellinek, photographed by his friend Henri de Rothschild.

different types: 10, 12, 16, 23 and 30 hp for 12, 14, 15, 17 and 19 thousand marks. In return, Jellinek had to take "at least ten units of each size," thus a total of 50 cars per year, valid until the end of 1902. The actual profit was in the resale, for which at least 17, 19, 20, 23 and 25 thousand marks were valid—an average profit of 30 percent, "subdivided in equal parts, regardless by which party the sale is realised," or in Jellinek jargon "resale to compte-à-demi." In addition Jellinek was now bound to Cannstatt, obligated "to buy and sell cars or engines of more than 8 hp from other manufacturers only with the DMG's consent." In any case, with the Mercedes, the Jellinek company was able to thrive and prosper. Fifty cars equalled 300,000 marks, nearly one hundred years' salary of chief engineer Josef Brauner, the *éminence grise* behind Wilhelm Maybach!

By the beginning of July 1900, "Paul Daimler stopped working on his small car for the time being, in order to assist Maybach in finishing the construction of the new cars." From whom was derived the design of the new Mercedes: from Maybach, from the young Daimler, from Brauner? Despite the accord with Louise Sarazin, the Mercedes had to differ considerably from the Phoenix, the engine as well as the general appearance. Otherwise Panhard was still in a position to close the door. Jellinek, with the aid of his friend Arthur de Rothschild, provided the preliminary financing of the heavy orders. From French market connoisseur Desjoyeaux came the target: lower, wider and longer, and of course lighter, stronger

Cannstatt management: from left to right, Max Duttenhofer, chairman of the board of directors; Paul Daimler, who headed his own engineering office; Gustav Vischer, the marketing director; Friedrich Nallinger and Adolf Daimler, who headed the production with Hermann Balz. Maybach was absent, possibly on purpose, since his relationship with the Daimler brothers was not the best.

and faster. Maybach packed the difficult requirements of the sportsmen into a technically feasible framework. The team around Brauner put the lot decently down on paper. The young Daimler helped out, at times and grudgingly, before he disappeared over winter: "Unfortunately Paul Daimler is unhealthy at the moment and is staying at home since the beginning of January. At the recommendation of his doctor he will have to take a cure and for this purpose will depart to Baden-Baden within the next days."

Josef Brauner was born on 24 December 1863 in Lettowitz, Moravia, and went to school at Brünn and Dresden, thus far away from Cannstatt. It was at Dresden that in 1887 he began to design steam engines, at first for C. E. Rost & Co., then for Moritz Hille, and finally for Buss, Sombart & Co. at Magdeburg. On 1 July 1895, he moved to Karlsruhe, working under Wilhelm Lorenz. When a few months later, on 1 December, the Lorenz office was relocated to Cannstatt, Brauner had found his destiny. Under Maybach he devised gasoline engines for Schuckert, the engine of the Belt Car and the Phoenix. Particularly with regard to the Mercedes, his contract was renewed in April 1900 for another five years, and one month later he was promoted to department head, annual salary 3900 marks. His staff consisted of Eugen Link for the engine and the carburetor, Karl Schnaitmann and Wilhelm Kraft for the axles and the frame, Otto Pfänder and Hofmann for the gearbox, and finally Paul Denner for the wheels. Ernst Raustein, the eventual brother-in-law of 1914 works driver Max Sailer, remembered: "I entered on 1 July 1900. At this date the engineering work on the first Mercedes was in full progress. I worked under Eugen Link on the ignition. Robert Bosch himself was repeatedly in the office. Maybach's and Daimler's offices were strictly separated. I never saw Paul Daimler in our office. I can only remember one contact, when Wilhelm Maybach, at a later date, tried to use the scroll clutch developed by Paul Daimler for his own construction." Hermann Balz was responsible for the final assembly.

Overall, "lower" meant primarily a lower engine, without power loss; hence the dimensions of 116 mm × 140 mm in comparison to the 106 mm × 156 mm of the big Phoenix, displacement now 6 instead of 5.5 liters. But the head of the Phoenix, too, was rather cumbersome. Couldn't the hanging valves be turned upside down? And what should be thought of the "Centaure," the latest Panhard from the board of Arthur Krebs, of its magnetically operated intake valves which made it amazingly flexible? In some way the Mercedes intake had to be positively operated. Maybach, Brauner and Link chose the simplest synthesis, the T-head. In the moteur Mercédès, the intake and the exhaust valves were located in pockets on both sides of the combustion chamber, operated via two side camshafts at crankcase level. The end of the automatic intake era! The search for the best valve timing dragged on while appropriate valve diameters were quickly found, 53 mm for the intake and 51 mm for the exhaust, as well as a suitable name in hard-core German: "hammer-head." The two cylinder pairs were made of cast iron, with integral heads, fin de siècle fashion, whereas the crankcase was made of magnalium, the latest alloy of Berlin metal mixer Ludwig Mach, one part magnesium, nine parts aluminum, density 3.6. The Mercedes surpassed the planned 30 hp at first go, delivering 35 hp at 1000 rpm and a compression of 4:1, and weighed 238 kg, more than 80 kg less than the most powerful Phoenix. The combination of hammer-head with throttle valve carburetor and low tension ignition resulted in a usable speed range extending from 300 to 1300 rpm. And the hitherto unknown flexibility was typical not only for the 6-liter but also in its two scions, for the 2.9-liter 12/16-hp (91 mm × 110 mm) and the diminutive 1.75-liter 8/11-hp (75 mm × 110 mm). Thus Cannstatt did not offer five but only three different types, since the orders of Jellinek continued to focus on the 6-liter.

The transmission to the separately mounted four-speed gearbox and the cooling were provided by two rather expensive components, the scroll clutch of Paul Daimler, a spiral spring gripping the driven shaft, and the famous honeycomb radiator which was patented on 20 September 1900. In comparison to the

Mercedes engine: 116 mm × 140 mm, 6 liters, 35 hp at 1000 rpm. For the first time the intake valves were mechanically operated.

Phoenix and the current Panhard and Mors, the moteur Mercédès was mounted more centrally and lower in an all-steel channel frame, wheelbase 233 cm, 262 or 302 cm, track 140 cm, tires 910 mm × 90 mm front and 920 mm × 120 mm rear. Of course the smaller engines were available in shorter and lighter chassis, the 1.75-liter with 200, 210 or 232 cm, the 2.9-liter with 220 or 232 cm. Jellinek and Desjoyeaux left it up to the clientele to choose the body, common practice at that time. But in addition the sportsman could choose the axle and frame manufacturers, either Krupp in Essen or Arbel in Douai, either Mannesmann or Lemoine. The best wheels were available in Paris, Avenue Malakoff, from Jacques Rothschild & Fils, made of finest acacia or hickory wood. The wheel hubs were supplied via Lorenz by the German Armament and Munitions Factory, Karlsruhe, the ball bearings by the DWF of Ludwig Loewe, the unmatched "furnisher of complete factory equipments." Was the new car called Mercedes or Mercédès? In Cannstatt it was Mercedes from the outset, in France always Mercédès, and in Jellinek circles as it was convenient. Concerning engineering and packaging Jellinek and Desjoyeaux were satisfied, but not concerning reliability and the delivery situation.

It was on 22 November 1900 that the Mercedes was tested for the first time. Hermann Balz drove to Ludwigsburg, 13 kilometers in 20 minutes: "The frame twisted because of the dreadful roads." Three weeks later, Hermann Braun came from Vienna to test the prototype on the road to Heilbronn, had "to stop only four times to check if nothing was overheated." By the end of December, the 35 hp "sample car" was shipped to Nice via rail. By the end of January 1901, mechanic Huttenlocher was just able to correct the major defects, without wasting time on minor details. He changed the camshafts, turned all the engine and gearbox bearings, applied a layer of white metal, mounted a new radiator, a float chamber made of brass, a flywheel with "wrought-iron rings," replaced the front axle and the exhaust flanges. And Paul Daimler's scroll clutch did not work! "Since the first car has been completed, four different clutches have been necessary. The last one has been delivered three days ago. Four work-days per piece have to be calculated." And Hermann Balz had to wait until February to start the production at Cannstatt, "until two o'clock at night." Then Maybach himself took the train to Nice taking care of the remaining defects: "Universal joint of the steering worn. Spiral springs of the electric ignition bad material. Noise of the engine still blamed, remedy by inserting non-resonant material into the ringing gears. Second countershaft brake has to work better and automatically cut off the engine. Clutch has to be improved. Short countershaft vibrates, has to be better carried. Teeth of the sprocket too have to be hardened." Conclusion: "The assembly of the cars should be more precise."

But at Nice, on the Promenade des Anglais, the prototype caused a sensation. The ladies scrambled for a tour. The Mercedes was "delectable, inventive, charming and fresh." It was because of the lines, the new styling, the elegant honeycomb radiator, the low-profile hood, the raked steering column, the repartition of the masses. The Mercedes was the first motorcar which *looked* like an automobile. Didn't it instantly bring to mind great sport and fastest time in La Turbie? And then the engine, the new moteur Mercédès! How could the sportsmen calm down anymore? When the throttle was opened the engine speed rose, instantly. And when the throttle was closed the speed fell just as quickly, so far that the engine slowed the car down. Wasn't it mysterious? That in top gear everything was possible from 20 up

The 35-hp Mercedes sample car, the prototype, which appeared on the front page of *La France Automobile*, on 29 December 1900.

to 100 km/h resulted in a completely new experience for the driver. For all that the Mercedes was a classical grand tourer, a sports car in the sense of Paul Meyan, which was able to terrify every Panhard and Mors once the rear seat was removed. Henceforth driving a Mercedes was *de bon ton*. The sportsmen waited patiently for delivery of the 35-hp and accepted its initial shortcomings.

The first two cars were dispatched in racing trim to former Peugeot star Albert Lemaître and Claude Loraine Barrow, a well-known Panhard driver from Biarritz. Henri de Rothschild asked for "an unpainted engine, only cleaned thus not primed, filed off and oiled, levers nickel plated," profited from the usual rebate, paid just 20,000 marks, and placed in return a car with Prince Soltikoff. W.-K. Thorn, an American millionaire living in Pau and a satisfied Phoenix owner, personally took delivery at Cannstatt, paying 27,000 marks. William Turner Dannat, one of *Tout Paris*' most popular salon painters, sent his mechanic, paid by cheque. The Romanian distillery owner Xantho transferred 28,800 francs for "a common chassis for racing car with new spring construction, frame only primed, everything brass plated," and took delivery from Jellinek at Nice. So did Lubecki and Essling: "Prince Essling's mechanic receives 1000 francs and for all spare parts he buys 10 percent commission." Lemaître's friend Henry Simon requested delivery by mechanic Huttenlocher to the Villa Zénoide in the elegant Boulevard de Cimiez at Nice, and paid 27,500 francs for a white phaeton with red stripes, "seat in the rear wider, so that three passengers have enough space if necessary." C. L. "Charley" Lehmann, Jellinek's star salesman and subsequent agent in Paris, landed a big fish in the form of William Kissam Vanderbilt Jr., the American millionaire sportsman, who "will take delivery himself on 7 April and pay 20,000 marks." New York stockbroker Foxhall Parker Keene and Count Potozky, whose negotiations were handled by Jellinek's secretary Ferdinand Spiegel, had to wait until May. Phoenix owner Dr. Richard von Stern from Vienna obviously inspired no confidence as he had to pay before delivery, despite his previous year's victory in the race from Salzburg to Vienna. Gustavo Motschmann from Bilbao got the most luxurious coachwork, an elegant wooden tonneau, all in white, at the impressive price of 33,000 marks. And of course Willy Tischbein, in Hannover director of the Continental-Caoutchouc & Guttapercha-Compagnie, had placed his order with no tires, "delivery between 12 and 15 April." Cannstatt's definitive pricing to Jellinek was seventeen thousand marks for the bare 35-hp chassis. Mark and franc were more or less on the same level and Cannstatt's day rate for one mechanic was five marks.

The demand for the smaller 2.9-liter 16-hp did not come up to expectations. In addition to the demonstration cars for Jellinek, Charley, Léon Desjoyaux and his brother Noël, only four cars found buyers, among them Foxhall Keene and a Dr. Trousseau from Paris. Even worse was the demand for the 1.75-liter 11-hp, despite Cannstatt's offer of a "complete coachwork resembling the Panhard & Levassor": just three beside the demonstration cars found buyers. Xantho paid 11,000 marks for delivery on 15 June. Jellinek suggested cancelling the transmission brake, and reducing the price to 6000 marks. Promptly Willie Vanderbilt ordered a two-seater. Anyway Jellinek did not want to waste his time with small cars and a price war. He preferred to focus on his newest project, "electric cars," and placed an order for a dozen chassis "without transmission and without magneto, but with cooling device, steering, rear brake and tires." Jellinek had found something new on the doorstep, the "Jacob Lohner & Co. in Vienna, court car and automobile factory for electric and gasoline-electric cars according to the the Lohner-Porsche system." The moteur Mercédès drove, via a dynamo, two inner-pole engines in the front wheels. Once again it was the front page of *La France Automobile* which was used for the official presentation, at the beginning of November 1901, in melodious French: "Voiture *mixte* pétroléo-électrique Lohner-Porsche." Jellinek avoided any allusion to Daimler or Mercedes. A number of the regular customers were delighted by the smooth locomotion. Lubecki, Dannat, the Rothschild family and Simon ordered immediately, despite the additional price of 7000 marks.

When, in December 1901, the automobile became presentable, when a gorgeously decorated Salon moved for the first time to the noble Grand Palais, just off the Champs-Élysées, neither Jellinek nor Duttenhofer dared an official exhibition of the Mercedes. The Avenue d'Ivry was too close, the patent affair still too sensitive. It was not without good reason that the Mercedes *mixte*, the gas-electric hybrid, was named Lohner-Porsche in *La France Automobile*. On the other hand the Salon could not be missed. Under no circumstances! Thus the Mercedes was displayed by indirect means, via Jellinek's friend Victor Mathieu, via his Palais de l'Automobile, one of the finest Parisian showrooms at no. 218, Boulevard Pereire. It was there that Dannat had ordered his 35-hp. In the Grand Palais, Mathieu displayed his complete range: "Voitures légères Panhard & Levassor, voitures légères Mors, voiturettes Renault, voiturettes De Dion-Bouton." Only the best! And into the thick of it he pushed a 35-hp, a posh tonneau, "painted in red, plated in yellow, subtle stripes in black and gold," and a 8/11-hp, likewise a tonneau, "painted and upholstered in automobile-red." Now the Mercedes was definitively established, since it had long since posted its first successes in the great sport.

# 6

# Roi du Volant

For the real debut of the Mercedes, only the meeting of Nice was suitable enough, of course. Jellinek was consumed with impatience: "This year's race of Nice will probably be the greatest sporting event of this genre. Every factory takes part in the subscription of the awards. I ask you to give me the authority to subscribe 1000 francs in your name. Monsieur Desjoyeaux and I subscribe the same sum. Nowhere else you are able to achieve a better publicity and in no case can you accept to be outdone by Nesselsdorf. Since your interest to sell the cars is the same as ours, I hope that you will not enter with a refusal."

The driver selection presented problems and remained unresolved for a long time. Nobody at Cannstatt or at Nice had doubts about Hermann Braun's and Wilhelm Werner's skills. Nevertheless they were not counted among the kings of the steering wheel, among the *rois du volant*. Just after the turn of the century mechanics were no "kings." A mechanic lacked not only the contacts with the clientele but also the status in the ranks of the gentlemen drivers. An established *roi du volant* always bought at special discount directly from the factory, sold imperatively before the race and doubled the original exorbitant price after the victory. Braun and Werner had never learned about it, in contrast to Fernand Charron, the great master in this discipline. Jellinek approached Charron's friend Léonce Girardot, the "eternal second," who even came in second position in the name CGV, the Agence Générale des Automobiles Charron, Girardot & Voigt, meanwhile the most renowned—and most expensive—Panhard agency of them all.

They met at CGV, at no. 45, Avenue de la Grande Armée. They talked about the great races and the Parisian Mercedes agency. The liaison to Panhard was close. CGV was aiming to build its own cars. Arthur de Rothschild intervened. But Girardot had to decline. Baron Arthur kept on to mediate: "I have just met Monsieur Lemaître. He soon will marry and come to Paris for good. He leaves the vineyards in the Champagne up to his brother. I suggested a possible agreement with you if your negotiations with others do not materialize. He looked forward to a possible cooperation." Peugeot was just withdrawing from the great sport. Albert Lemaître was uncommitted and Jellinek quickly put him under contract. Cannstatt immediately delivered a 35-hp racer free to the door, payable on resale, whereby 50 percent of the return went into Lemaître's pockets. In addition the DMG shared with Jellinek a contribution to the expenses of 10,000 francs, in view of the entry in the meeting of Nice and the Gordon Bennett Cup. The Bennett race was one of the main reasons for the engagement of gentlemen drivers, since, according to the regulations, the drivers were required to be club members. Under no circumstances would the DAC, the German automobile club under the chairmanship of the stiff

Duke of Ratibor, have admitted a mechanic into its ranks! But Jellinek made a second find. As backing for Lemaître, the Englishman Claude Loraine Barrow switched over into the Mercedes camp, first and foremost because of his good contacts to the scene in Biarritz and not because of his minor successes in a 12-hp Panhard.

It was Claude Loraine Barrow who was at the wheel when, on 17 February 1901, the 35-hp Mercedes appeared at the start of a great race for the first time. In Pau, on the outward road to Tarbes, the Mercedes faced the 330-km of the Circuit du Sud-Ouest. It did not look too promising. Two days before, Barrow had to cancel his participation in the touring car run: "Mister Barrow had defects in his car and we have no sure information whether or not he will be able to race tomorrow. The races in Pau are of the highest importance and it would be very fatal if Mister Barrow could not take part in them." The Mercedes was to start first in the Circuit du Sud-Ouest, only to slow down after a few hundred meters by reason of a faulty gearbox: "The wheels have seized up and because of insufficient locking of the reverse mechanism, the gears broke out and the differential axle was twisted." Just behind Barrow, it was the turn of the president of the Automobile Club Béarnais himself, W.-K. Thorn in his 28-hp Phoenix. After two kilometers a cart and

The Mercedes was a toy for the sportsman. Daily locomotion was still provided by the horse drawn carriage, even in Nice. Standing in the carriage is Henri Degrais, then Étienne de Zuylen (back to the camera), and on the right Emil Jellinek.

## 6. Roi du Volant

horse crossed his way. Thorn darted sideways, plowed through the ditch and finally came to stop against a tree. He escaped with a dislocated arm and torn-open eyebrow, his Daimler with three broken wheels and slightly twisted frame. Obviously the Daimlers were not the cars of the hour. The Panhards of Maurice Farman and Léonce Girardot, both 5-liter Centaures (110 mm × 138 mm), struggled for the lead. The road between Dax and Bayonne was snow-covered. Girardot went into a skid, pulled the front axle out of shape. Maurice Farman won in 4 h 28 min 20 sec, averaging 76 km/h, one hour ahead of his brother Henry in his Darracq, who took the light car division, the freshly initiated *voiture légère* class. Since 1898 the weight of the midgets named voiturettes was restricted to a maximum of four hundred kilograms. The method had proven successful. Thus why not an additional category for light cars, weighing in at no more than 650 kg? The big bores continued to enjoy a full year of complete freedom. It was in 1902 that they were restricted to 1000 kg.

La Semaine de Nice opened on Sunday 24 March 1901, as usual with an elegant *corso fleuri* through the city. Arthur de Rothschild had metamorphosed his longish Daimler into a luminous flower garden. Princess Essling and Mademoiselle Rose d'Elchingen shared a blue and yellow ... chariot! Countess Potozka drove her voiturette under a yellow parasol. Baroness de Zuylen promenaded "in a very nice

March 1901—Meeting of Nice. The hero of Nice: Wilhelm Werner at the wheel of Henri de Rothschild's Mercedes; on the left Hermann Braun.

car, decorated with white and yellow ribbons and daffodils." Who received the Prix d'Honneur? The couple Just Fernandez in an electromobile.

The road race followed on Monday, starting at six in the morning, from Nice, via Aix and Senas to Salon and back, a distance exactly 462.602 km. Three short-chassis Thirty-fives turned up at the start, officially as "Daimler with moteur Mercédès," the Jellinek squad with starting numbers three and four under Lemaître and Barrow, then Henri de Rothschild's private racer with number five and Dr. Pascal alias Wilhelm Werner at the wheel. The weights? Two at 1100 and just 1060 kg for the perfectly prepared car of Werner. In full contrast to their bulky parents of the Phoenix range, the Mercedes, or better the Daimler-Mercédès, now stood at the lower end of the scale. The Panhard trio of Chauchard, Pinson and the Englishman Stead left the scales at 1250 kg, the lonely Mors of the Belgian de Caters at 1280, the Rochet-Schneiders of Degrais, Schneider and Marge at 1440. In the case of the comfortable Audibert-Lavirottes of Audibert, Lavirotte and Ollion the pointer even hit out into the red area, 1600 kg! The 400-kg light voiturette clique did not come into consideration for the overall victory, but there was potential in one of the tricycles, maybe Béconnais on his Liberator, the diminutive Georges Osmont on his De Dion or Léon Demeester on his Gladiator. Paul Chauchard, the full-bearded vice-president of the automobile club of Nice, was the first to be dispatched on the journey. At the time control at Cannes, Chauchard was still in front, then Lemaître, Werner, Barrow and Baron Pierre de Caters with his 20-hp Mors. In Salon, Werner clocked in front of de Caters, then Demeester with his incredible Gladiator tricycle on whose rear axle was enthroned a 6-hp single from Aster. In Nice, the sportsmen were eager to see the finish. "At 4 h 40, Werner crossed the line, the mechanic of Baron de Rothschild. He went through the distance in 6 h 45' 48". His Mercedes ran on the latest Continental tires with narrow tread." Just nine minutes back of him came Demeester, sitting on a piece of tube instead of the lost saddle. "The statisticians quickly calculated the average, 57.9 km/h for Werner, 56.6 for Demeester." In the heavy class Werner finished 26 minutes ahead of Henri Degrais' Rochet-Schneider, 29 minutes ahead of de Caters' Mors. Barrow followed in fifth position, Lemaître in ninth. The mechanic Werner had taught the gentlemen drivers a fine lesson. And Hermann Braun? In cooperation with Werner he had trimmed the Rothschild racer to top form. Then he took the wheel of W.-K. Thorn's 35-hp six-seater in the touring-car event to Draguignan. Thorn and his friend Stephen Knapp stayed in the rear, in company of their ladies, enjoying the landscape while Braun secured victory in the big class.

The much-read and often-cited Paul Meyan wrote, "Nous sommes entrés dans l'ère Mercédès"—we have entered the Mercedes era. And Jellinek cabled "that his car won yesterday's race with our former mechanic Werner at the wheel. Victory due to him and his colleague Braun. Request one thousand marks renumeration for both and publication through advertisements." The entry into the Mercedes era went on. On Tuesday, the Promenade des Anglais was closed off between the Pont Magnan and the Quai du Midi for the Coupe Henri de Rothschild, for the mile with standing start and for the flying kilometer. The steamer of Léon Serpollet was unbeatable, achieving 1 min 11 sec and 35⅘ sec. Werner followed in the Rothschild Mercedes with 1 min 16⅘ sec and 41⅘ sec, averaging 86.2 km/h over the kilometer. Then Richard von Stern in Prince Lubecki's 35-hp with 1 min 21

**March 1901—Meeting of Nice. In the race between Nice and Senas, Paul Chauchard and his Panhard finished sixth, 48 minutes behind Werner. In the Coupe de Rothschild, Chauchard achieved 1 min $25\frac{3}{5}$ sec over the standing mile, $43\frac{4}{5}$ sec over the flying kilometer.**

sec and $41\frac{4}{5}$ sec. Henri de Rothschild himself had a try, achieved 1 min $25\frac{4}{5}$ sec and $44\frac{1}{5}$ sec. The meeting closed with the hillclimb to La Turbie. "The week ended exactly as it began. Werner won again, the hero of Nice! With 18' 6" he beat the old record of Levegh by 56 seconds." But it was Béconnais who set best time of the day in 17 min 21 sec, thanks to his speedy Liberator, a 165-kg light tricycle with 6-hp single from Soncin. A humble mechanic was not invited to the elegant banquets, did not meet the clientele in select atmosphere, but a simple mechanic could devote his time to a better preparation of the racer. Werner was perfectly acquainted with the peculiarities of his Mercedes, adjusted his driving, reinforced and improved just where it was necessary, trimmed away where too much material provided unnecessary comfort (and weight). Thus Werner ran his gentle colleagues Lemaître and Barrow over and became himself a *roi du volant*.

Paul Meyan wrote: "I have foreseen the consequences of the Mercedes victories for a long time and I have announced them several times. This series of victories constitutes an irrefutable demonstration for the endeavor of the Cannstatt factory. The result is a flood of orders [for Mercedes]. And these same orders are lost to us. The Riviera market should not be neglected during the season. It is an international market which has formed a preference for a marque already at the beginning of the year only because it has drawn the first prize in the races of the automobile club of Nice. It is a huge mistake to disregard these races and to concentrate on the Bennett Cup or the race towards Berlin. They knew it only too well, they were warned that the foreign competition would enter new models, stronger and completely suitable models. They countered with old warriors. Within two months we'll pay back, they think. Possibly, but it is a margin of two months for the competition. And now Germany has gained a foothold."

In 1899 Jellinek had remarried, Madeleine Henriette Dittholer who was born in 1873 in Oran. In the evenings, at the Promenade des Anglais, Jellinek and Madeleine used to have the house full of guests. Of course Léon Desjoyeaux was present, and the Rothschilds, the Potozkys and the Esslings, Prince Lubecki and the Xanthos, Prince Alexis Orloff and the Duke of Leuchtenberg, banker Robert Katzenstein from Frankfurt and the rich American Clarence Gray Dinsmore. Every day saw furious activity. The 1902 production was nearly sold out, behind every order was a special request, and Cannstatt did not deliver in due time. "As an early riser Jellinek took care of his post immediately after receipt. Urgent inquiries were forwarded via cable. At table the telegrams received were replied to on the spot and one chauffeur after the other, one servant after the other, was sent to the telegraph office, until finally everybody had to pick up the food from the lift by himself. A large pad of notepaper was always resting on the table, with telegram forms, and a family member had the production list ready to hand." At Cannstatt, "every engineer and master received for the first time the Jellinek medal, five hundred marks in gold."

Nevertheless Jellinek and Desjoyeaux were not entirely satisfied, since the Mercedes had just been able to carry off the palm against a pack of tired veterans, against an older Mors with automatic valves, against a handful of obsolete Centaures from Panhard and against cobbled-up boulevardiers from Rochet-Schneider and Audibert-Lavirotte. In the strict sense Nice had been nothing special, albeit the first victory of a foreign make on French soil. Now, Jellinek required an international success. Run on 14 June 1900, the first race for the Bennett Cup between Paris and Lyon had not attracted any interest by itself; a boring affair, it had been won by Charron. That was reason enough for the ACF to combine the second Bennett event with the race to Bordeaux, starting in the western suburb of Saint-Cloud, on 29 May 1901, pre-dawn at four in the morning. "In order that Messieurs Lemaître and Barrow are allowed to take part in the Gordon Bennett race, they have to be members of the German automobile club." Starting numbers two, five and eight were allotted to the German club, for Lemaître, Barrow and an unknown named Becher. In the meantime Jellinek and his chauffeur Braun tested the latest Panhard of Maurice Farman and quickly retained it as a sample: "The new Panhard engine has circa 150-mm bore and circa-150 mm stroke, that is to say equal bore and stroke. I am in a position to acquire such a car immediately, delivery after the Berlin race, in fact for the equivalent of two Thirty-five chassis and 20,000 francs cash. I am thinking of making the deal since this Panhard can be resold easily at all times and currently is worth 45,000 francs." Vischer was reluctant "because it is debatable whether the Panhard car can be resold so easily after the race."

Jellinek did not discuss the matter for long, bought the Panhard from his own account, for 50,000 francs, and his friend Henri de Rothschild paid the same amount for the racer of Léonce Girardot. The new Panhard engine, a revised Centaure from the pen of Arthur Krebs, displaced 7.4 liters with dimensions of 130 mm × 140 mm, and delivered 45 hp. Of course the Panhard was faster than the Mercedes, although it weighed 1250 kg, 150 more than the German car. But towards Bordeaux the road ran straight ahead so that pure power and top speed played the central role. To avoid disgrace, Jellinek withdrew the Bennett entries. Only the private Thirty-fives of W.-K. Thorn and Foxhall Keene were entered in the open race to Bordeaux, nos. 54 and 72. Willy Tischbein, who had just established a new record between Mannheim and Pforzheim, had a start in mind, but he too withdrew at the last minute. Finally Thorn was the sole Mercedes contender who appeared in front of starter Horace Huet, only to break down during the first leg towards Chartres. The French team was alone in the Bennett section, the Mors of Levegh and the Panhard duo of Charron and Girardot. Charron gave up at Vendôme, suffering valve trouble. Levegh went like mad until the gearbox disintegrated near Châtellerault. Girardot finished and won the Cup. In the open event, Henry Fournier, in the previous year riding mechanic for Charron in the Bennett-winning Panhard, drove his Mors to an uncontested victory in 6 h 10 min 44 sec, followed by a Panhard quartet under Maurice Farman, Voigt, Pinson and Hachette. A pity, for in the Bennett Cup a well-prepared Mercedes would have had at least some chance.

The car of salon painter Dannat was well prepared, rebored to 118 mm and now displacing 6.12 liters. Higher pistons with four rings raised the compression to 4.5:1. A new drip-feed lubricator from the specialist Dubrulle improved the oil flow to the crankshaft, enough for 1200 rpm, output 45 hp, transmission via adapted ratios and a 22-teeth sprocket. The Dannat Mercedes would do more than 100 km/h and the painter was delighted, but with his 48 years he did not feel fit enough for the distance, and asked for Wilhelm Werner, the new *roi du volant* as driver. The event of the year, the race from Paris to Berlin, was imminent. There were to be three stages: the first day from Champigny via Épernay, Reims, Sedan to Aachen or Aix-la-Chapelle, the second day via Jülich, Cologne, Münster, Bielefeld, Minden to Hannover; and finally via Braunschweig, Magdeburg, Brandenburg, Potsdam and Spandau to the trotting track Westend. Cannstatt demanded an appropriate showing; the cars were now Mercedes-Mercedes and not Daimler-Mercédès anymore. Henri de Rothschild assumed two entries, nos. 38 and 39, Jellinek three, the 40, 41 and 82. In addition the popular Paul Baras, the great voiturette star from Darracq, had entered a Mercedes privately, no. 84. Jellinek made his usual application. "Lemaître receives 5000 francs, Paul Baras and our former mechanic Werner both 3500. Expenses for tires 3000 francs." In fact Baras came to Cannstatt and picked up a Thirty-five. On the way back to Paris, near Château-Thierry, a front tire burst. The racer flew over a sandheap, finishing up in a pond. With broken collarbone and slightly twisted Mercedes, Baras hobbled home to Paris and did not turn up at the start. By the end of June, Jellinek was not able to scrape more than three racers together, the rebored Thirty-fives owned by the American trio Thorn, Dannat and Keene, nos. 38, 39 and 40. At the wheel were Henri Degrais, who had shown such a fine performance in the heavy Rochet-Schneider in the meeting at Nice and who in future would open up the Belgian market, Wilhelm Werner and Albert Lemaître.

As usual Hermann Braun was allowed to promenade, starting on 22 June in the touring car event to Berlin. In addition, there were two 28-hp Phoenixes, a duc with refinery owner Henri Deutsch de la Meurthe and a tonneau with the Parisian Eisemann agent Henri de la Valette; then came Robert Katzenstein in a Panhard, Baron de Dietrich and Emil Mathis in De Dietrichs, Eugen Benz in a Benz, Madame Gobron in a Gobron-Brillié, Louis Mors in his Mors, Baron and Baroness de Zuylen in Panhards. It was an easy game for Braun, who won. On 27 June the *Tout Paris* pilgrimaged to the unpopular East, through the Bois de Vincennes to the *fourche* de Champigny, long before the start at half past three in the morning. Since the race to Bordeaux, phenomenal speed would be taken for granted. Fournier and his Mors had averaged a fabulous 85 km/h, faster than the express train, like the famous ride on the cannon ball! Bordeaux was a turning point for the great sport, the beginning of the heroic age, the emergence of the first genuine racers. Fastest of all was the Mors, the masterpiece of Henri Brasier, a bulky, long-stroke (130 mm × 190 mm) ten liter which, despite the obsolete automatic intake, delivered 55 hp, enough for 120 km/h on the long straights. The Mors was heavy, 1450 kg dry, but this did not bother either Brasier himself or Hourgières, Fournier, Antony, Rolls or Keene, who even preferred the speedy Mors to his Mercedes. Levegh had withdrawn after the race towards Bordeaux, and died at the beginning of 1904. The proud Panhard, the 7.4-liter Centaure, was not quite able to keep pace, despite the participation of 28 racers, of Charron, Girardot and Voigt, de Knyff, Farman, of the upcoming stars Georges Heath and Charles Jarrott, and *Tout Paris'* prince du chic: Boson de Périgord, Prince de Sagan. There was also a sportswoman, Madame Camille Crespin du Gast, wife of the wealthy co-owner of the famous Grands Magasins Crespin-Dufayel, who competed in a smaller 20-hp Panhard.

On the leg to Reims, Albert Lemaître and his Thirty-five were able to keep pace with the front-runners, in 16th place, just in front of Degrais. The Mors of Gilles Hourgières was in the lead, by a comfortable margin. On the way to Sedan, Fournier gained, while Werner suddenly slipped within the first 25. Fournier was first in Luxembourg, in front of Hourgières and a complete Panhard pack—Girardot, Voigt, Charron and Hachette. On the leg to Aachen, Degrais struggled with the light 650-kg Panhard of Étienne Giraud. In Hannover, the Mors of Fournier and Antony were trailed by the Panhard trio de Knyff, Girardot and Farman, then Keene and Henri Brasier. On the last stage, Antony, pseudonym of Debraye, withdrew with gearbox failure. Just a few kilometers after the start in Hannover, Degrais left the road, at half past five in the morning, when heavy fog concealed the countryside: "I drove in the dust cloud of the car ahead, unable to see the road. I resorted to steering by the tree tops. But suddenly the trees disappeared. The road seemed to go straight on, but deviated sharply to the left and then to the right. In the same moment the Mercedes lay headfirst in the ditch." Degrais escaped without a scratch, but his mechanic Baron de Schwyter was in the hospital for four months. After 21 h 29 min 49 sec Werner arrived at the trotting track Westend as the fastest Mercedes driver, 14th in the heavy class, 18th overall, six hours behind Fournier in his white Mors, having averaged 70.5 km/h. Close behind were the Panhards of the eternal second Girardot and de Knyff, then the Mors of Brasier. Lemaître crossed the line in 17th, just two positions in front of Madame du Gast. The placings were almost embarrassing, particularly in the face of the achievement of Louis Renault's diminutive Renault, which not only took the voiturette class but eighth place overall!

## 6. Roi du Volant

As usual the racers from the Panhard camp changed hands quickly, for 50,000 francs. Charron passed on to Count de Maigret, Henry Farman to Stéphen Ribes, de Knyff to Alexis Orloff, Jarrott to Dunlop director Harvey du Cros, Georges Leys to Lord Carnavon, the sponsor of Egyptian explorer Howard Carter. The winning Mors had gone to the Englishman Laycock, for—80,000 francs! And the 25-minute motion picture that Léon Gaumont, then director of the Comptoir Photographique in the Rue Saint-Roch, made near the Belgian frontier? The husband of Madame du Gast bought it on the spot.

The 1901 season closed near the Channel resort of Deauville, in Newport, Rhode Island, and between Schottwien and the elevation of the Semmering, just in front of the Villa Mercedes at Baden. In August, at Deauville, Werner sprinted in 1 min 12$\frac{3}{5}$ sec and 41$\frac{1}{5}$ sec over the flying mile and the kilometer, while on a dirt track in Newport, Willie Vanderbilt beat the Mors of Foxhall Keene. On 24 September, Cannstatt received a dispatch from Jellinek: "Stern won the Semmering race in great style in 12 minutes 30$\frac{2}{5}$ seconds. Werner second in 13 minutes 40 seconds. Stern's throttle valve carburetor has to be installed on all cars." Jellinek put on more pressure than ever, requested the perfect Mercedes, while Cannstatt proposed a new designation: "The new engine which will be put into production and which, in comparison to the previous construction, will be considerably simplified, should not be named the Mercedes engine anymore. We have decided to bring this new type on the market under the name new Daimler engine." Of course Jellinek and Desjoyeaux did not agree! The considerably simplified Mercedes could only be called "Simplex."

# 7

# *Simplex*

The general layout and the characteristic features of the Mercedes remained unchanged in 1902, the already famous hammer-head, the low-tension ignition, the honeycomb radiator and the scroll clutch. Simplex was the designation of the 1902 model range, a refined and "simplified" Mercedes range. The simplification did not make sense to everybody and His Majesty the Kaiser replied to Maybach's explanations: "My dear Maybach, it is true that your cars are very beautiful, but they are not very simplex!" It was in May 1901, in anticipation of the race to Berlin, that Cannstatt began to include most of the improvements in the racer of William Dannat. In autumn of 1901, the 35-hp with the stretched 118 mm × 140 mm dimensions was renamed 35/38-hp, wheelbase 233, 262 or 302 cm, track 140, while the unsaleable 1.75- and 2.9-liter were replaced by the 20-hp 4.1-liter (100 mm × 130 mm) and the 28-hp 5.3-liter (110 mm × 140 mm). On 20 June 1901, Jellinek placed an order for 20 cars of each size, delivery between February and July 1902, price 14,000, 15,500 and an unchanged 17,000 marks for the top model. Half the order was assembled as *voiture pétroléo-électrique*. "Mister Jellinek is free to order, instead of complete cars, either the entire lot or a portion of it as chassis with engine, but without transmission. The transmission of engineer Herz will be mounted later, and the price for the chassis including the engine and the assembling of the electrical components is fixed at 12,000 marks per unit. The electrical equipment is supplied by Mister Jellinek at cost price." The business volume of Jellinek was increasing, but his claims were too. He was no longer content with 50 percent of the profit. "When selling these cars, either with sliding-gear transmission or with electrical drive, Mister Jellinek receives two-thirds of the extra proceeds and the DMG one third."

The simplifications affected nearly all components, with detail improvements concerning the camshaft drive, the flywheel, the ignition system, the exhaust pipe, the worm-and-wheel steering and the lubricator supplied by Louis Dubrulle. The throttle valve carburetor, operated from the steering wheel via hand lever, became standard equipment. As a result of Barrow's breakdown in the Circuit du Sud-Ouest, all gearbox and differential shafts ran in ball bearings now. The weight of the 20-hp chassis was fixed at 840 kg, the 28-hp at 850 kg, and the 35/38-hp, with regard to the new heavy car class, at 950 kg. Willy Tischbein's Continental supplied lightweight rims and tires, and Rothschild & Fils the wheels made of hickory wood.

> The engines have to be as noiseless as possible. The fan is driven by a chain running in a groove so that it cannot jump out. The ignition has to be completed so that the many springs are cancelled. All the cars receive a worm and wheel steering which has to be protected against dust as on the Mors cars. The spur-gears made

## 7. Simplex

January 1902—Nice. The new 6.5-liter Simplex being tested at the Col des Quatre Chemins, between Nice and La Turbie.

April 1902—Meeting of Nice: Boulevard Gambetta. Emil Jellinek at the wheel of a Mercedes *mixte*; by his side Claude Loraine Barrow. Standing near Jellinek, with goggles, Henri Degrais; standing near Barrow, Hermann Braun.

of fiber with brass inserts are broadened by ten millimeters at least and are tested before mounting. A cock has to be mounted to check the oil level in the sump. In addition to the 50-liter fuel tank in the back, a tank near the front seat is added, as large as possible. The water tank to cool the band brake of the gearbox shaft is mounted below the frame. The theoretical speed of the 28-hp car with 18 teeth and 1200 rotations per minute should be 25, 55, 80 and 100 km/h. Better springs have to be mounted so that two and four passengers enjoy the same comfort. The steering column has to be inclined and to go as much as possible into the engine compartment. For all cars, wheels have to be ordered from Rothschild & Fils, made in the lightest design, possibly of hickory wood. Rothschild honors the guarantee for their wheels to a large extent and has to confirm it directly, respective Emil Jellinek will send us this guarantee from Paris."

In the autumn of 1901, the ACF decided definitively on the future of the heavy car class. (The ACF was no longer in the Bois de Boulogne but in the pompous Hôtel Pastoret at the Place de la Concorde, where the club had moved at the beginning of 1899). From the 1902 season, the heavy class was subject to a maximum weight of 1000 kg or one ton, 50 kg more than Étienne Giraud's original 950 kg proposition. The omnipotent Commission Sportive headed by René de Knyff conceded an additional seven kilograms to racers using a magneto ignition since nobody wanted to require the removal of the magneto, while the accumulator of a battery ignition could be placed alongside the balance in the twinkling of an eye. Of course, from

April 1902—Meeting of Nice. A Mercedes *mixte* duo using internal pole engines within the front wheels. Near the left car, Jellinek, Barrow and, behind the radiator, Charley Lehmann.

1902, the one-tonners competed in the Bennett Cup, hence the often-used designation Gordon Bennett formula. The clever sportsmen quickly found ways and means of bypassing the bothersome rules. Despite the commission's specification "en ordre de marche," they heedlessly discarded all possible components, from the hood to the seats, from the reverse gear to the brake! The henceforth holy *pesage*, the weight control and scrutineering, took place without battery, water, fuel and oil. Borrowed jockeys as oil-pumping assistants had no chance, since driver and riding mechanic together were restricted to a minimum of 120 kg, later to 140 kg. The other corporal consistency was not subject to any additional clause: According to the regulations, ladies were allowed to start. In Cannstatt, the slightly enhanced maximum ditched the plans. Suddenly the 35/38-hp was underweight!

Josef Brauner quickly devised a new crankshaft and, at the beginning of 1902, the 35/38 was renamed 40-hp (118 mm × 150 mm). In promenade trim, the 6.5-liter produced 40 hp according to its designation, at 1050 rpm and the tame compression ratio of 4/1, in the sharper racing trim it put out 50 hp at 1200 rpm and 4.5/1. The short Simplex Forty had a wheelbase of 245 cm, track 145 cm, tires from Conti, 910 mm × 90 mm front, 920 mm × 120 mm or 1020 mm × 120 mm rear. In January 1902, the Forty prototype arrived at Nice, painted in the Jellinek colors, cherry red with black stripes. The second Simplex was delivered to Willie Vanderbilt, at the beginning of February. And at the end of the month, it was the turn of the official gentlemen drivers, Lemaître, Degrais and newcomer E. T. Stead, then Richard von Stern, Standard Oil heir Harry Harkness Flagler, Clarence Gray Dinsmore and Foxhall Keene.

In January 1902, Charley Lehmann—whom everyone generally called simply "Charley"—took over the official Paris agency, of course via Jellinek, and placed no less than 13 cars.

Even a king joined the ranks of Mercedes owners: Léopolde of Belgium. Within the *Tout Paris* he was known as "Cléopolde," by reason of his supposed liaison with ballet star Cléo de Mérode. In 1896 Mademoiselle de Mérode was elected "reine de beauté" by *L'Illustration*. In fact she was the most beautiful *danseuse étoile* of the Opéra and, in 1901, was just compromising herself by dancing on the music-hall stage at the Folies-Bergère. It was reported that Léopolde was well known to the lady named Cléo and that, in August 1901, in her apartment in the Avenue Louise, he met her and the stylist Fernand Charles. The trio talked about the coachwork of the king's latest Mercedes, whereupon Mademoiselle de Mérode proposed two amply

The 6.5-liter Simplex, 118 mm × 150 mm, output in race trim 50 hp at 1200 rpm.

upholstered leather armchairs as seats. The king liked the idea, especially when Charles added a tulip-shaped aluminum covering for the seats. Messieurs Rheims and Auscher from the panelworkers Jacques Rothschild & Fils were responsible for the hand-beaten execution, which combined art nouveau, comfort and lightweight construction. No surprise that the "tonneau de grand luxe" coachwork was soon called "Roi des Belges." The snag? There is no proof that Cléopatre Diane de Mérode and the king were lovers and moreover the Avenue Louise was not in Paris but in Brussels. The smaller 4- and 5-liter Simplexes were more difficult to sell. In Paris, Charley was able to find just two buyers. A third car was sold to Vienna, to Marquis Alexander Pallavicini, another one to Italy, to Luigi Bruno, and a fifth one to Schwerin, to the Grand Duke of Mecklenburg.

By the end of July 1902, Barrow paid a visit to Cannstatt, threw up his hands in horror, and complained to Jellinek:

> I came to see if my 20-hp made progress. You promised delivery by 15 August. Vischer now tells me that a delivery before 20 September is out of the question! I cannot agree and you know it! The season in Biarritz is all over when the car will be delivered and I shall miss any opportunity to sell a Mercedes. I placed the order for the 20-hp in March and cannot receive it before the end of September. Isn't it ridiculous? Probably you gave Charley's cars the priority. If this is the way you treat me then keep the car for yourself! And then the 28-hp, it is exactly the same. Now it is said that it will be delivered by the end of September. And next month it will be the end of October! Please write to me in Biarritz to explain all these delays.

Of course Jellinek gave his Parisian star agent Charley the priority, since it was he who was able to sell the largest numbers, and by far. He had seized Barrow's 20-hp and had placed it elsewhere. The Swabians rolled out the red carpet for Charley's client: "A Mister Johnston has purchased the 20-hp car and he comes to Cannstatt to take delivery on 15 August. This gentleman has to be treated in the most obliging manner and every requested alteration has to be achieved. Mister Johnston is the man who helped Mors to come up. Johnston is American, engineer, very rich and is living in Paris." Howard Johnston was a well-known Panhard and Mors driver, spending most of his time near Bordeaux, either at the Château Danzac or at the Château de Beaucaillou, his beloved vineyards. Barrow was forced to wait. But his second order, a 28-hp, arrived in time, a "tonneau with canopy, painted in white with red stripes, frame and wheels in red, wheels with white flames, upholstery white." Barrow was a changed man: "My wife says you should call the new Mercedes "Excelsior" because they like to climb up the hills and always aim higher. Thus Excelsior, don't forget it! My wife cannot imagine a better car and the name Excelsior appeals to me." The Brazilian balloonist Alberto Santos-Dumont wrote on 2 September 1902: "Why don't you come to Paris anymore? Are you anxious that I'll buy an engine from you? But you know that this can be done in written form and I'll do it. I'll soon get the Santos no. 9 built, with Mercedes engine whose even running will prevent any vacillation. It is an airship for ten passengers and will be moored at Monte Carlo. Now to the business. Under which terms can you offer this 200-kg engine? Please reply as soon as possible, you know I am always in a hurry."

Countess Zborowska, whose husband was to achieve such a fine performance in the race to Vienna, acted with more subtlety than Barrow. This was no surprise:

## 7. Simplex

June 1902—Paris–Vienna. William Zborowski at the wheel of his Simplex Forty. He ordered the racer as a 35/38-hp on 30 May 1901 and took delivery on 10 June 1902, just a few days before the start of the race towards Vienna.

Countess Margaret Laura ("Maggie" to her friends) came from one of the finest houses. She was a grand-daughter of William Backhouse Astor, daughter of John Carey, was related in her first marriage to Alphonse de Stuers and now to the notoriously famous big game hunter William Elliott Zborowski. On 15 July 1902, the Zborowska wrote to Jellinek in the finest French when, on the occasion of a flying visit to Cannstatt, she stayed at the Hotel Marquardt in Stuttgart:

> My cordial congratulations for the success of the Mercedes in the race from Paris to Vienna. I am pleased that it was my husband who was able to show the superiority of the Mercedes above all the French makes to you and to everyone. A real triumph for the German industry! My husband acquainted me with your anticipation and I thank you most sincerely that you promised delivery of my car by the end of the year. I have just seen the car of my friend Hinckley and I am so delighted that I'll do without my coupé coachwork. I would be very grateful if you could deliver my car exactly as Mr. Hinckley's. He granted permission. I would be proud to show the car to my English friends who so far bought solely French. I am convinced that my Mercedes will have the greatest success in London. Are you not able to deliver the car in October? I would like to drive it before the winter, before the bad season which comes so quickly on the other side of the Channel.

There was nothing for it, poor Countess Zborowska had to wait for her elegant 12/16-hp until June 1903. But it was delivered as an improved 18-hp.

Simplex constructors in Cannstatt: At the wheel Hermann Balz; by his side Wilhelm Maybach; in the rear Gustav Vischer and Adolf Daimler; standing behind the dashboard Josef Brauner.

In Baden, the Villa Didier was added to the original Villa Mercedes.

## 7. Simplex

For some time Duttenhofer had intended to increase production and to offer prompt delivery. Now he produced relief with a new factory in close-by Untertürkheim, the official merger with the Berlin branch, the takeover of the Austrian branch, the Bierenz, Fischer & Co., and Paul Daimler's simultaneous relocation there. Would Jellinek soon be able to supply from stock, just like Darracq and De Dion? After the name "Mercedes" was registered as a trademark and after, at the end of 1902, the DMG displayed for the first time openly in the Grand Palais, Jellinek's future seemed secured. Meanwhile Cannstatt granted him a supply contract for 25 cars per month, thus three hundred per year, and remitted 20 percent for every direct sale. Jellinek expanded his summer residence in Baden: The Villa Didier had been added to the Villa Mercedes, in honor of Madeleine's firstborn son. The next step was a unified facade, then eight bathrooms and an early form of air conditioning. Finally, there was no. 54, Promenade des Anglais, the famous Villa Mercedes in Nice, in fact the Villa Mercedes number two. But Hermann Braun had to wait until the spring of 1903 before he could use its backyard for the preparation of the racers.

# 8

# *One-Tonners*

In 1902 the traditional Riviera debut was missing the great splendor of the previous years. It was not that the powerful Simplex Forty was unable to match its competitors, it was that the road race between Nice and Abbazia had been cancelled; the ministry of the interior and the préfet had refused permission. The *corso fleuri* was still held, as well as the hillclimb and the sprints. On 7 April, the Simplex celebrated a triple victory. Despite heavy fog, Englishman E. T. Stead, whom Jellinek had engaged in view of the London scene, achieved an incredible 16 min 37⅘ sec in the twisty 17-km hillclimb to La Turbie, one and a half minutes faster than Werner in the previous year. Did the Simplex perform so much better than the original Mercedes? Obviously it was due to a combination of Stead's acuity and driving skills since Lemaître was content with 18 min 25⅕ sec and Werner with 18 min 30⅕ sec. On the concrete pavement of the Promenade des Anglais, the Simplex was just able to win the class. It was Georges Osmont on his 8-hp De Dion tricycle who set best times over the mile and the flying kilometer in 57⅘ sec and 33 sec, equaling an average of 109.09 km/h for the kilometer. Wicked tongues accused him of a rolling start, but it was tolerated since his speedy De Dion had no clutch! In any case Degrais and his 40-hp Simplex left from a standing start, the result being 1 min 9⅗ sec and 36⅘ sec, or 97.82 km/h. Werner was next in 1 min 9⅘ sec and 37⅘ sec, then Lemaître, Rutishauser in a steamer from Gardner-Serpollet, Stead and the Belgian Camille Jenatzy in his Jenatzy.

While the mile sprint, the Course du Mille, had been limited to the hillclimb participants, the Coupe Henri de Rothschild was open to everyone. Léon Serpollet and his "Oeuf de Pâques," his steaming Easter egg, covered the flying kilometer in 29.8 sec and was credited with 120.32 km/h, a new world record! Stead congratulated: "Twenty nine, Master Serpollet, twenty nine!" Degrais in the fastest Simplex averaged 99.44 km/h, Stead was fifth with 93.42, Werner sixth with 92.8 and Lemaître tenth with 90 km/h. As usual the order books were full and Jellinek got in touch with a driver trio of which much more was to be heard, with Baron de Caters, Camille Jenatzy and William Zborowski, who, at the wheel of his two-year-old 28-hp Phoenix, won the four-seater class of the Turbie climb. That *La France Automobile* frequently dedicated whole pages to the novices from Cannstatt was no coincidence. For each publication Desjoyeaux paid one thousand francs! A privilege, since by no means would the elitist *Monsieur le rédacteur en chef* wrote about rattletraps. In any case Paul Meyan praised "the remarkably fine lines and the flexibility of the engine, the noiseless run, like an electric car!"

At the beginning of May, Willie Vanderbilt took the wheel of his perfectly prepared Simplex and drove to the southwest of Paris, where the ACF had just homolo-

June 1902—Paris–Vienna. At the finish in Vienna the order was inverted: no. 147, the light 650-kg Renault of Marcel Renault was the overall winner, 13 minutes ahead of the 1000-kg Panhard of Henry Farman. (Renault)

April 1902—Meeting of Nice. E. T. Stead at the wheel of his Simplex Forty. Stead was certainly one of the fastest drivers of his time, up to La Turbie nearly two minutes faster than the *roi du volant* Werner. In the background the 20-hp Darracq of Marcellin.

gated the flat, tree-lined straightway between the villages of Dourdan and Saint-Arnoult. On the timed section between the kilometer stones 37 and 38, Vanderbilt and the Simplex averaged 111.11 km/h, a new record for gasoline cars. Jellinek immediately remitted the promised bonus and Stead commented: "10,000 francs to Vanderbilt for one kilometer was very good pay. I would certainly rather do that than La Turbie." On 15 May, Vanderbilt and the Simplex went eastwards, to Champigny, to the start of the Circuit du Nord à l'alcool: The ministry of the interior had exceptionally granted a permit under the condition that the ACF prescribe alcohol as fuel. Vanderbilt broke down on the first stage towards Arras. It was raining. Despite countless skids on the slippery *pavé du nord*, Maurice Farman drove his brand-new Panhard to victory in 11 h 58 min 51 sec, beating teammate Charles Jarrott and the light Darracq of Marcellin by more than an hour. The alcohol race made few converts, but the sugar-beet fuel continued to be under discussion.

The race of the year was to be from Paris to Vienna, starting on Thursday, 26 June 1902. The race would cover 1120 km, in four stages, from the inevitable fork or *fourche* de Champigny via Troyes, Chaumont and Langres to Belfort, then at a touring pace through Switzerland, via Basel and Zürich to Bregenz, then at full speed again, over the 1800-meter Arlberg pass, via Innsbruck to Salzburg, finally via Linz to the Prater in Vienna. The Bennett Cup, combined with the main event, ended at Innsbruck. The Jellinek squad originally aimed at entering a team of six cars, six Forties with Lemaître, Barrow and Stead, with Werner, Braun and von Stern. But all the designated racers had already been sold. Four buyers wanted to take the wheel themselves, and the two others were on the way somewhere else. Braun even had to abstain from a start in the touring-car event, in which the two 28-hp Simplexes of Henri Deutsch and Baron Bratsen de Rehderoord kept the flag of Cannstatt flying. Barrow quickly accepted the wheel of a light De Dietrich, and Stead started in a Georges Richard.

Not a single official Simplex turned up at the start of the race to Vienna, to the hometown of Monsieur Mercédès! Had Jellinek backed down overnight and, in the face of the fresh armada from Ivry and Grenelle, disposed of the six racers as quickly as possible? Or was the reason the exorbitant prices that the clientele was prepared to pay at the beginning of the year? One of the designated Forties finished up in the hands of Doctor Suchanek for 35,000 francs, not as a racer but as a comfortable tonneau, painted and upholstered in red. It was a classified deal, since the Doctor requested "to keep secret his name." Finally four private Forties were entered, no. 26 with Zborowski, no. 27 with Baron Maurice de Forest, no. 208 with race doctor Henri de Rothschild and no. 218 with Bellamy. Maurice-Arnold de Forest, later Count von Bendern, was born in 1879, the natural son of the German industrialist, banker, financier and Oriental railway pioneer Moritz von Hirsch, a good friend of Robert Katzenstein's father. When he was in Paris, de Forest spent his time in the western suburb of Saint-Cloud, in the Château de Beauregard, where the third Napoleon had enjoyed his liaison with Miss Haryett Howard.

The scales of the ACF showed 978, 980, 994 and 990 kg, and in the case of the Forties this was a completely "en ordre de marche," in ready-to-race condition. The Commission Sportive had to check two hundred racers squeezed below the weight limits by means of all possible and impossible trickeries, so-called *voiturettes, voitures légères* and *grosses voitures* made up of 20-, 40- or 70-hp engines

June 1902—Paris–Vienna. Favorites: Henry Fournier and the 9-liter Mors.

set in chassis composed of accumulation of perforations, weighing in at 400, 650 and 1000 kg, and starting with 150 kg excess. Smaller (and hence lighter) engines were out of the question, least of all in the camp of the one-tonners. Suddenly the *marque doyenne* Panhard & Levassor turned up with cylinders of flour-bag size, with the bore/stroke dimensions of 160 mm × 170 mm, with a displacement of 13.6 liters and 70 hp: the famous Seventy. The frame was rather long: wheelbase 275 cm, track 125 cm. It dwarfed the Simplex! And where had Arthur Krebs saved the weight? Under the hood, by replacing the cast-iron pairs with four steel singles, a rather expensive solution: raw material costs were 2800 francs, workmanship an additional 2500. The heads, still made of cast iron, and the water jackets, made of 1-mm sheet copper, were welded into position. The crankshaft ran in five main bearings, instead of three. In addition Krebs omitted one speed in the gearbox, and eliminated the sub-frame, hitherto used to isolate the engine from any strain imposed by chassis twisting. The Seventy was a great success, a perfect one-tonner. The latest Mors had difficulties in keeping up. Henri Brasier had left Grenelle, was just establishing his Richard-Brasier company, with light car specialist Georges Richard and the aid of Rothschild money. The new Mors was much above Simplex level, displacing 9.2 liters with the dimensions of 140 mm × 150 mm and giving 60 hp. The backstairs gossip that Grenelle had mounted T-head engines in the racers of Fournier and Gabriel was never confirmed. Still, Rolls, de Caters, Vanderbilt and Keene trusted in the automatic intake. Thanks to the winding stretch through the Alps the light 650-kg Renaults and Darracqs were by no means without a chance. The Basque Darracq,

June 1902—Billancourt/Paris. The team of Renault Frères before the race to Vienna: on the left the four midget racers of the 400-kg voiturette class with Oury, Cormier, Grus and Lamy; on the right the three 650-kg voitures légères with Louvet, Marcel and Louis Renault. (Renault)

June 1902—Paris–Vienna. The 7-hp De Dion tricycles of Osmont, Bardeau and Lazon during the scrutineering at the Place de la Concorde. They weighed 210, 220 and 218 kg, started in the 250-kg motorcycle class, and used alcohol as fuel; hence the suffix AL behind the starting number. Georges Osmont won his class, reaching Vienna after 24 h 42 min 16 sec.

born in 1855 in Bordeaux, began his career by manufacturing the Gladiator bicycles and the motorcycle devised by Félix Millet. In 1896 he founded the "société Alexandre Darracq, Suresne," assembling the Aster-engined "Perfecta" tri- and quadricycles, under Léon Bollée license. The first pure Darracq appeared in 1901, designed by Paul Ribeyrolles. Finally worth mentioning was the participation of chief editor Paul Meyan in a De Dietrich, and of the young Marius Barbarou, who was just about to accept an offer from Benz, in a Clément.

The Bennett racers were to open the road, at half past two, well before dawn. Girardot in his CGV was first off, then Fournier in a Mors, Edge in a Napier, de Knyff in a Panhard and Herbert Austin in a Wolseley. The pack followed at two-minute intervals. For the first 80 km, Fournier averaged 113 km/h, but dropped out at Langres with a broken gearbox. The Panhard Seventy lived up to expectations. De Knyff won the leg to Belfort in 4 h 16 min 30 sec, followed by his teammates Henry Farman, Jarrott, Maurice Farman and the lighter 650-kg Darracq of Edmond. Zborowski lost 45 minutes, de Forest and Bellamy nearly two hours. Despite easy going through non-race Switzerland, the CGV and the Wolseley retired. When de Knyff left Bregenz to climb the Arlberg, the Bennett Cup was in the bag. Or was it? The differential did not stand up; with Innsbruck in sight, a pinion sheared off. Edge had only to finish to win the trophy for England. He reached Innsbruck in 11 h 2 min 52 sec. On the descent from the Arlberg, Eugen Max lost control of his Darracq. The

June 1902—Paris–Vienna. William Zborowski and his Simplex Forty at the start on the Plateau de Champigny.

brakes were red-hot. His mechanic jumped off. The Darracq went over the edge. Max finished up on a ledge. Nobody was injured! De Forest took the third leg of 369 km in 5 h 23 min. Bellamy withdrew. Henry Farman was in the lead with a total racing time of 10 h 34 min 1 sec. De Forest followed nearly one hour behind, then Marcel Renault in his 650-kg Renault, and Zborowski. In fact Farman had a comfortable margin. But the road between Salzburg and Linz was rough and bumpy: "The roads were crossed at frequent intervals by gullies of prodigious depth that were calculated to break the back of any motorcar, and probably its driver's as well." Farman could not use the power of the Seventy, needing to preserve the frame, while Marcel Renault staked everything on one card. Fifty kilometers from the finish he cut in front of the Panhard, winning the last leg in front of his voiturette comrades Grus and Cormier. Zborowski lost 46 minutes. De Forest was able to reach the trotting track at the Prater, but in tow of a horse cart, meaning disqualification. The 650-kg Renault of Marcel Renault took first place in 15 h 47 min 43 sec, the 1000-kg Panhard of Henry Farman was 13 minutes back, the Darracq of Edmond 23 minutes, the Simplex of Zborowski 26 minutes, after a 36 minute penalty.

The German *Radwelt* went to the barricades:

June 1902—Paris–Vienna. Marcel Renault at the Belfort stop. For the photo Louis Renault took the place of *mécanicien* Vauthier, who had to perch on the fuel tank. (Renault)

Didn't we forecast that the race officials would not allow the protest against Marcel Renault's victory? Count Zborowski has been downgraded to fourth place despite his better racing time. He, or more probably the German car, has to accept a penalty of 36 minutes because of a delay at the Swiss frontier, on a neutralized section, thus outside of the timed stages. Thereby Renault won in front of Panhard. De Forest who reached Vienna as fifth with his Mercedes was completely disqualified since he was pushed as he ran out of fuel in Switzerland, thus also within a neutralized leg. It puts an end to any discussion. Zborowski and his Mercedes remain the real winners. But we have to pose the question: Why is the victory of a German car not acknowledged? The Daimler Motor Co. has not fulfilled its duties as representative of the German industry. Panhard, Mors, Darracq and all the others started under best conditions, with specially built cars, with the best drivers. At every turn of the route there was an army of mechanics with a lot of spare parts. Daimler cancelled its entries. Why? This is out of the question in such a situation. Only two amateurs started in Mercedes. De Forest drove a Mercedes in a great race for the first time. Zborowski had so far taken part in a few smaller races. Neither the first nor the second can be compared to de Knyff, Fournier or Farman. Daimler just showed a lack of interest. The amateurs drove without any assistance and lost far too much time when refueling. Zborowski bought fuel in a pharmacy while everywhere full cans were waiting for the Frenchmen. If the factory, whose cars they drove, had granted just a part of the backup which was accorded to the Frenchmen, they would be first and third officially. The fame of the house of Daimler was dependant on a simple fuel can. The value of the French victory in the race to Berlin was demonstrated one year ago. What will be the value of the victory in the race to Vienna because the German cars have not been assisted?

June 1902—Bennett Cup: Paris–Innsbruck. Bennett Cup victors: the Napier of Selwyn Francis Edge and his cousin Cecil as mechanic.

**June 1902—Paris–Vienna. Henry Farman and his Panhard leaving Bregenz.**

Obviously the *Radwelt* correspondent forgot that the Commission Sportive imposed a 30-minute penalty on Marcel Renault too and that only the failures of the untested one-tonners from Panhard and Mors made possible the victory of the Renault and the front placing of the Zborowski Mercedes. To refuel in front of pharmacies was planned by the ACF from the outset and their exact location was part of the race documents.

At the end of July 1902, the racers gathered in the wooded region of the Ardennes. In small Belgium where permission for a town-to-town race over open roads was out of the question, the local club, upon the proposal of Baron Pierre de Crawhez, dared to take the step into a new dimension. On the "Circuit des Ardennes," the cars had to cover six laps of 85.4 km each, starting from Bastogne, going through Longlier, Habay-la-Neuve and Martelange back to Bastogne, without any control or neutralization: the first road race in a circuitous course of several laps. The prospect of racing round and round the same circuit by no means commended itself to all the drivers. Most of them disliked "monkey cages" and still preferred to roar over mountains and through valleys, to capture fresh landscapes. For the manufacturers and the spectators, it was a welcome innovation, the former saving practice costs and the latter seeing their favorite not once but six times. Charles Jarrott recalled: "It was only when I arrived at Bastogne the day before the race and realized from the nature of the roads and the number of the competitors that the race would offer a great amount of sport that I began to be interested." Zborowski, de Forest and Bellamy entered the familiar Simplex trio,

June 1902—Paris–Vienna. The 24-hp Darracq of Paul Baras in Vienna: 17 h 47 min 4 sec, third in the 650-kg class and sixth overall.

June 1902—Paris–Vienna. Marcel Renault turning his lap of honor on the Prater trotting track. For the first time in racing history, David had really beaten Goliath. (Renault)

nos. 51, 52 and 74. But Bellamy was caught practicing at racing speed, and was promptly forced to withdraw, while de Forest stayed at home. And Zborowski was not able to keep pace with the Panhards and Mors whose teething troubles were overcome now. The Ardennes circuit was fast, extremely fast. The Simplex Forty was not speedy enough to threaten the Panhard Seventy and the Mors Sixty. It was de Crawhez who took the lead in the ex–de Knyff Panhard, covering the course in 54 min 3 sec. Zborowski was just able to lap in 1 h 2 min 56 sec, losing more than six seconds per kilometer, putting him out of contention After de Crawhez collided with Coppée's Germain, Jarrott and his Seventy inherited first place and won in 5 h 53 min 39 sec, averaging 86.9 km/h. Nine minutes back of him came Fernand Gabriel in a Mors; 29 minutes back was Vanderbilt, also in a Mors. And Zborowski was thoroughly satisfied with his fourth place, his 6 h 46 min 40 sec and 75.6 km/h.

How fast the Panhard and the Mors were able to run straight ahead was demonstrated by the end of August, in the kilometer sprint at Deauville. The 9-liter Mors of Gabriel achieved 26$\frac{2}{5}$ sec, the 13-liter Panhard of Chauchard 26$\frac{3}{5}$ sec, the fastest 6.5-liter Simplex under de Forest 32 sec. The 136 km/h of the Mors and the 135 of the Panhard contrasted with the 112 of the Mercedes; de Forest was even slightly faster than Vanderbilt in May. Clarence Gray Dinsmore achieved 39 sec driving his four-seater. Or was it Wilhelm Werner who was at the wheel? Thirty-eight years later Werner lifted the veil of secrecy: "This race was driven by me since I was employed by Gray Dinsmore as racing driver. Because of his poor health, the owner

June 1902—Paris–Vienna. Zborowski's Simplex entering the Prater in fourth place, 26 minutes behind Marcel Renault.

## 8. One-Tonners

September 1902—Semmering. The victorious Simplex: at the wheel Wilhelm Werner, by his side his new employer Clarence Gray Dinsmore; behind him banker Robert Katzenstein. In the left hand back seat is Otto Hieronimus.

of the car was not able to drive himself." Baron Springer had fallen ill so that Werner drove for Dinsmore since the beginning of the year, for "the best known character in international automobilism." As American delegate of the Bennett committee, Dinsmore spent his time in Paris, either at his town house in the Avenue Marceau or at his villa just outside the town. The communication between Werner and Dinsmore was unique, since the former did not speak English and the latter did not speak German. The German *roi du volant* had just to glance at the quaint American, "then he realized immediately that he was driving too slowly. In fact it was never speedy enough, as long as it was safe for everyone." In autumn, Werner, his employer Dinsmore and Frankfurt banker Robert Katzenstein started off by road for Vienna. There, the four-seater was stripped in anticipation of the Semmering hillclimb, exactly ten kilometers with an average gradient of four percent, "in which the quality of the car and the skills of the driver came into their own." With a time of 10 min 37⅕ sec Werner won "the challenge trophy masterly crafted by Gustav Gurschner," nine seconds ahead of the Simplex driven by the previous year's winner Richard von Stern, ten seconds ahead of the Gardner-Serpollet steamer of the full-bearded Hubert Le Blon, then Ferdinand Porsche in his gasoline-electric Lohner-Porsche and a young Ettore Bugatti in a 24-hp De Dietrich.

Of course Jellinek, Desjoyeaux and Lehmann knew that the Simplex Forty would never be able to match a top-class one-tonner from Panhard or Mors. During the summer of 1902, Maybach and Brauner had devised something entirely new to better exploit the prescribed 1000 kilograms. A thoroughbred racer was on the drawing board, the first pristine Mercedes racer, the ancestor of the Silver Arrows. Meanwhile Jellinek searched for competent drivers. Barrow had definitively switched sides, having found a better position in the De Dietrich camp, but continued, on occasion, to take on a Mercedes for resale. Otto Hieronimus, a well-known motorcycle man living in Austria, was on the list. From the in-house squad there were of course Werner and Braun, while Degrais recommended his fellow countrymen de Caters and Jenatzy. On 20 August, the record holder of La Turbie, the extremely fast E. T. Stead, declined the offer:

> You are always lucky, and to find six good men to drive your cars next year for less than 30,000 francs is a chance which only you can secure. I am authorized to look out for some good drivers at "excelsior" prices and cannot find them. I offer you the good advice to make written contracts with your men or they may leave you at the last moment. As you have sold all your cars for next year, I think you are quite right not to incur the big expense of racing, just as I am certain you will not be annoyed with me for not driving Mercedes when I can make with another factory from 50,000 to 100,000 francs in the year. I suppose our very good relations will not be interfered with and that if business comes in for Mercedes I shall do it through you, in fact I have a letter from England inquiring about Mercedes and I shall see if I can do business for you. I understand you will be in Paris at the end of the month. I hope to have the pleasure of seeing you.

Moreover, Jellinek kept an eye on the great star Henry Fournier and his brother Achille, who, in association with E. Rabourdin, managed a fine Mors and Panhard agency named Paris-Automobile in the Rue d'Anjou. At the beginning of September, on the occasion of the elegant meeting of Longchamp in the Bois de Boulogne, Henry Fournier demonstrated a Mercedes *mixte* to the Shah. Hereupon, Rabourdin and Jellinek went to Vienna:

> During our stay at Baden, you told us that one of your racers is still vacant and that you could reserve it for the brother of Monsieur Fournier. Now we ask you to cede the volant of this car for the races of Nice to the famous American jockey Tod Sloan. This gentleman has already driven your cars and has additional experience with a Mors. He had a 40-hp Mercedes and at the moment he drives a 70-hp Panhard. He was never in an accident and we think that he is a good driver. Furthermore he is a customer of Paris-Automobile and, when he is allowed to drive a Mercedes in the races of Nice, he will order a car from us. Thus we ask you to reconsider the matter once more and to reply as quickly as possible. Monsieur Sloan's intention is to compete in all automobile races of 1903.

The lively jockey, who nearly disappeared behind the huge wheel of his monumental Panhard, never came into prominence with Mercedes nor another marque. Zborowski was quite interested in the wheel of a Mercedes. On 1 October 1902, he wrote: "I thank you very much for the friendly letter of 27 September. Yes, of course, I would like to drive one of the German cars, a Cannstatt chronometer. But I am living in England and I have already been asked to drive one of the English cars to defend the Gordon Bennett Cup. I cannot drive any German car in this race. As condition [of driving a Mercedes in the other 1902 races] I request that the German cars, thus your cars, will start in all races, except the Bennett Cup, on Falconnet, Perodeaud & Cie. tires and that the usual preparations are made for the drivers and the cars."

# 9

## *Sixty*

In the form of the Simplex, the Mercedes hit the mark, an automobile with inherent style, with a powerful and reliable engine, eclectic, agile and speedy. Small wonder that it set a fashion and that it continued to form the pivotpoint of the Cannstatt range, displacement three, four, five and seven liters, rated at 18, 24, 35 and 40 hp, dimensions 91 mm × 110 mm, 100 mm × 130 mm, 110 mm × 140 mm and slightly rebored 120 mm × 150 mm: "At the instigation of Charley, from now on the 12/16 hp should be specified as 18 hp, the 20 hp as 24 hp and the 28-hp cars as 35 hp." The small 2-liter, which was of high quality but much too expensive in relation to the engine output, was cancelled. Of course the revolutionary hammer-head sat atop all these engines. Typical for Maybach and his team, it had three advantages at the same time: it not only operated the intake and lowered the engine's height but made possible easy access in case of a broken valve stem. After unscrewing a simple butterfly nut the failure was cured from the top side in short order. Initially Maybach decided in favor of the hammer-head primarily because of the lower height and the easy maintenance, but it was only after two years of development, and only with the precise valve timing of the Simplex, that the Mercedes was able to outclass the mixture-sucking Panhards and Mors. Within the mysteriously squiggled pockets, an apparently turbulent and chaotic combustion worked perfectly. Due to low engine speed and low compression ratio, overheating of the exhaust pocket and subsequent self-ignition failed to appear even after longer full-throttle runs. The frames differed in wheelbase and track, in the section of the U-profiles, in the dimensioning of the wheels and other details. In effect every Mercedes was custom-made, not only in terms of the bodywork. There was no standard frame length. The small 3-liter was available with wheelbases of 220 and 232 cm, the 4-liter with 220, 232 and 243 cm, the 5-liter with 233, 262 and 302 cm, the 7-liter with 239, 275, 322 and 352 cm; track could be 135, 140 or 145 cm depending on the length. Usually Cannstatt fitted tires from Conti, although some French and English customers asked for Michelin and Dunlop. Sizes were 910 mm × 90 mm front, 920 mm × 120 mm rear, or occasionally the coach dimension of 1020 mm × 120 mm or the smaller and hence lighter 870 mm × 90 mm and 880 mm × 120 mm. That Cannstatt, because of the costs, often unscrupulously jumbled the components did not simplify matters. The last 2-liters and some 4-liters were mounted into 3-liter chassis, some 5-liters into 4-liter chassis.

The Simplex inspired copies all over the place. At the beginning of January 1903, Henri de Rothschild paid Cannstatt a visit with Adolphe Clément, Henri Degrais and Charley Lehmann. The full-bearded Clément knew all the tricks of the trade, having worked his way up with vélos and the French Dunlop license and invested in real estate in the Avenue d'Ivry, only to change it later for Panhard shares. The French asked permission to produce the 5-liter Simplex and the honeycomb radiator under license. Duttenhofer kicked up a fuss, writing to Jellinek: "I agree with you that a concession in this direction would bring us damage. But I do not ignore the fact that Baron de Rothschild is able to copy our engine and that we don't have good prospects when taking legal action. The same applies to the cooling apparatus." Jellinek was hesitant as he had in mind establishing a factory in France, with Maybach, who was reluctant. In fact, the wealthy Docteur de Rothschild had his "Pascal" built in Paris, a copy of the Simplex! The Baron was delighted to drive an exotic marque and sold a handful of Pascals to his friends, whereupon he donated the benefits to a charity fund. In the future Clément and Panhard produced their own T-heads and purchased their radiators from Grouvelle & Arquembourg. All parties were satisfied.

In addition to the Simplex range, Cannstatt planned a completely new engine which initially (and only internally) was called "Idiot," in the sense of antiquity: the unique, the inimitable one. Barrow and his wife preferred "Excelsior." But henceforth the sportsmen simply continued to drive Mercedes. In France, "Simplex" was never really adopted and in Germany it disappeared bit by bit. Since December 1901, Maybach, Brauner and Link were working on a lower-priced Mercedes. Above all, it was the complex T-head engine which hitherto was money-guzzling, since two camshafts were always expensive, whether low-mounted or not. Thus the team around Maybach went back to the original T-head alternative and applied the straightest way to update the obsolete, mixture-sucking Phoenix head. The existing low-mounted camshaft was made to drive not only the exhaust valves but in addition, via pushrods and rockers, the overhead intake. The 3-liter with the dimensions of 90 mm × 120 mm produced 18 hp at 1200 rpm. Cannstatt intended to force the price down to 9500 francs by using a crude shaft transmission, a standardized tonneau body and small tires of the dimension 810 mm × 90 mm. In May 1902, the management noted: "Car weight less than 650 kg, speed 50 to 60 km/h. Sample cars completed until beginning of December, to be displayed in Paris. Tank, housings, everything possible to be made of sheet steel. Jellinek prepared to take over distribution, 3 percent commission." The Salon presentation fell through. Cannstatt had to wait until February 1903 to see the prototype taking its first steps, whereby Maybach commented: "drive slowly!" The demand was slack. The sportsmen did not take note of the low-priced Mercedes.

But the new valve operation layout did save not only costs but also weight. Why not a similarly designed 9-liter for a powerful one-tonner, for a 50-hp? Jellinek was delighted right away. In May 1902, he placed an order for 20 cars, to be delivered between January and May 1903. "The last car has to be delivered on 15 May since in the face of the small number of prospective customers for such powerful cars a later delivery date is not possible anymore. The coolant pipes of these engines have to be shaped so that the hood will be as low as possible. The wheels have to be ordered from Rothschild & Fils, made of the best possible wood, with completely free hand in matters of manufacture. At all events the springs of these twenty cars have to be ordered from Lemoine, made of the best possible material." On 18 June 1902, Jellinek increased his order by additional forty cars. And the designation 50-hp was quickly changed, the 9-liter being called 50/60 hp, and, in July 1902, definitively 60-hp: the Sixty.

The four cylinders of the Sixty were formed in pairs from iron castings, Cannstatt fashion. The bore/stroke dimensions of 140 mm × 150 mm resulted in a displacement of nearly 9.25 liters. The camshaft, mounted on the lower left hand side, operated directly the exhaust valves which were situated in laterally located pockets, and, via pushrods and rockers, the intake which was placed in the center of the head: an intake over exhaust layout, in brief IoE, or F-head. While, at the left-hand side, the camshaft drove the water pump and the magneto, at the right-hand side, an interrupter-cam spindle operated the wipe contacts of the low-tension ignition via thin vertical rods. The 9-liter engine with a compression ratio of 4.5:1 weighed 310 kg and delivered 65 hp at 1100 rpm, more than 70 hp at 1200 rpm. At first glance it seemed surprising that the cancelled intake valve pocket did not affect the combustion process. Regarding specific output or mean effective pressure, the 9-liter was on the same level as its T-head forerunner. During the Belle Époque, at 1200 rpm and 4.5:1, the combustion process was quite slow by modern standards. "Because the races in France are likely to take place only with alcohol or carbureted alcohol as fuel, it is absolutely necessary that for the time being fourteen 60-hp cars be equipped for alcohol and gasoline operation." At the end of January 1903, Cannstatt sent an inquiry to Nice: "Please cable whether racing cars should be run either with pure denatured alcohol or the addition of 25 percent of benzene." Alcohol instead of gasoline meant an adapted carburetor jet and dual ignition "with Bosch magneto and spark plug apparatus." By March 1903, the French dropped their alcohol mania, and the Swabians the plug apparatus. In other respects, the equipment remained unchanged: the scroll clutch, the four-speed box and the final chain drive, the wheelbase of the pure racer 260 cm, the track 140 cm (for

Cutaway of the Mercedes Sixty. Valve timing: The intake opened 11° after TDC, closed 11° after BDC; the exhaust opened 45° before BDC, closed 6° after TDC (from Pomeroy, *The Grand Prix Car*).

Jellinek's *limousine de voyage* on the long 347.5-cm Mercedes Sixty chassis, for ten years his preferred touring car. Stepping in, the tall Dinsmore and banker Katzenstein.

the speedy touring tonneau the wheelbase was 275, and for a comfortable limousine 347.5 in combination with a track of 145 cm), with tires measuring 910 mm × 90 mm front and 920 mm × 120 mm rear. As for replacement of the intake valve in the event of a failure, in everyday use, the fast Sixty was seldom exploited up to the limit and was reliable, while a racer had to be frequently serviced anyway.

The Sixty continued the course of its forerunners as a classic grand tourer selling like hot cakes. And it pulled along the entire 1903 T-head range: 3-liter 18-hp (91 mm × 110 mm), 4-liter 24-hp (100 mm × 130 mm), 5-liter 35-hp (110 mm × 140 mm) and the slightly stretched 7-liter 40-hp (120 mm × 150 mm). In Cannstatt, Jellinek paid 11,000, 12,000, 15,500, and 17,000 marks for the T-heads and 18,000 marks for the Sixty. Then he added around 50 percent. He sold a complete batch of 24, 35 and 60 hps to Henry Fournier's Paris-Automobile "en gros" for 20,000, 22,000 und 28,000 francs. "En detail" it was more, at least 30,000 francs. Stead wrote from 22 Radipole Road, Fulham, London:

> Have you two 40-hp Mercedes for sale and at what price? I shall have to split the profit with a firm here if we make the sale. You might send me a telegram if you have these cars. You do not reply quick enough and have lost me the sale of a 60-hp on account of your delay. You promised me the option of certain cars when I was in Vienna, will you please write me at once what they are. The 60-hp I shall buy firm and pay you one-third down. I cannot get any news from Charly. Will you please reply to me very quick as I am travelling about so much. I leave London in a few days to make the race Circuit des Ardennes in Belgium (July 31). I then return to Beschill England to make the race August 4. I then return to Paris (August 15),

then back again to England to make the six days commencing September 1. Plenty of racing for me as you see and I have never asked anyone, they have all come to me. I did not wish to make the Belgian race and asked very high terms which they agreed to without hesitation.

A few days later from the Normandy Hotel in Paris: "I buy the 60-hp Mercedes as offered for 40,000 francs and I'll transfer a deposit of 15,000 francs via Baron Henri de Rothschild. But I hope that you will deliver the car before June 1903."

Claude Loraine Barrow had picked up Harry J. Lawson, the well-known British Panhard driver. At the beginning of January 1903 he wrote from the Villa Romana in Biarritz: "I think you should promise delivery of the 60-hp by 7 May. Didn't you promise delivery by the end of March? It's just for you that I accept the car in the first week of May." Almost all of the former Forty buyers ordered a Sixty now, since neither Panhard nor Mors was in a position to offer a comparable all-round vehicle. New customers included John B. Warden, Cup initiator James Gordon Bennett, Conte Carletto Raggio, who was just co-financing the establishment of Itala in Turin, and Willy Poege, "director of the Electricity Company, formerly Hermann Poege in Chemnitz." And, when a self-driving major overtook His Majesty's coach running at full trot, even Berlin changed policy: "At present the Kaiser wishes to acquire a car and he has already ordered a motor-lorry."

With its weight of 310 kg, the F-headed 9-liter produced 70 hp, as compared to the 247 kg and 50 hp of its T-headed 6.5-liter forerunner. The power-to-weight ratio of the new engine was 12 percent better. For pure racing purposes, considerably more than only a 9-liter could be packed within the 1000-kilogram limit. Suddenly Cannstatt began to dream in Panhard dimensions, of eighty horsepower and more, of fastest time to Bordeaux and absolute world record. The Jellinek squad stuck to the facts, while Duttenhofer wrote: "In Berlin I have just talked to Count Zborowski and he is of the opinion that a combination of racing and touring car involves a lot of difficulties. He favours pure racing cars, built especially for the race in which they take part. But in this case it can occur that the construction is too light so that the car will break down." Was Cannstatt not missing the necessary experience to play with the leaders in the great sport? And who would buy a handful of thoroughbred racers? Charley Lehmann quickly came up with four customers.

The racing engine "was commissioned" on 18 September 1902, an 80 hp which of course included all characteristic features of the Sixty, in particular the F-head and its valve operation through one camshaft mounted at the left hand side. The bore/stroke dimensions of 170 mm × 140 mm meant 12.7 liters, twice as much as in the Simplex Forty, but one liter less than in the Panhard Seventy, a consequence of the relatively short stroke, necessary to limit the height of the colossus. During first test runs the 12-liter delivered 85 hp at 1100 rpm, leading to the inevitable designation change from 80 to 80/90-hp. But soon the Eighty produced 95 hp at 1200 rpm and accordingly was called 90-hp! The combination of the smaller radiator, lighter four-speed gearbox, the wider 145-cm axles and the short 260-cm frame of the Sixty made for the ancestor of the Silver Arrows. The designation was never clarified. Depending on the office, the driver or the mechanic, the 1903 12-liter racer was the Eighty, the 80/90 hp or the Ninety! "The basic price for the four

Spring 1903—Cannstatt. The Mercedes Eighty, the ancestor of the Silver Arrows.

April 1903—Meeting of Nice. Hermann Braun at the wheel of his Mercedes Sixty, on the Promenade des Anglais. On the left Wilhelm Werner and Otto Hieronimus. In the background a Gobron-Brillié.

## 9. Sixty

80-hp cars is fixed at 20,000 marks. Three of them are sold to Charley for 90,000 francs. The profit resulting from the sale of these three and the further 80-hp cars is shared one half each."

Even with a night shift, there was not time enough to prepare an Eighty for an attempt at a new kilometer record on the Promenade des Anglais. On 16 March 1903, Duttenhofer wrote to Jellinek: "I am relieved to learn that you are resigned to the idea that the 90-hp car will not come to the race of Nice." The fashionable spring meeting of Nice had not been able to recover. A hesitant government had refused permission for the meeting of Pau as well as for the road race from Nice to Salon. Gastaud, Max, Terry and Albert, the newcomers to the Jellinek squad, were allowed to let off steam in a 600-km tour through the Alps. Hermann Braun supervised the preparation of the racers in the backyard of the Villa Mercedes at the Promenade des Anglais. Ten Sixties were waiting. Wilhelm Werner was there, and for the first time Otto Hieronimus, a 24-year-old engineer born in Cologne. "Final drives with 22, 24, 25 and 26 teeth" were mounted in view of the steep gradient up to La Turbie. Conti supplied wider tires, 910 mm × 100 mm front, 920 mm × 125 mm rear, but forgot to ship the tubes. Fortunately Michelin had proper tubes in stock. Hieronimus had gunned his Sixty in 14 min 26⅘ sec up to La Turbie, 19 seconds faster than Werner, two and a half minutes faster than Degrais, when starter Jacques Gondoin broke the race off. Just a stone's throw away from the corner

April 1903—Meeting of Nice. Three Sixties in the backyard of the Villa Mercedes. In the middle, Henri Degrais.

**April 1903—Meeting of Nice. The Sixty of Otto Hieronimus at the start of the hill-climb to La Turbie.**

where Bauer had been killed three years earlier, Zborowski took a bend with throttle wide open and crashed into a rock. He was thrown out of the brand-new Sixty and killed instantly, his friend and mechanic Hans Wilhelm van Pallandt seriously injured. Was Zborowski too determined to avenge what he considered an unjustified penalty at the Swiss frontier, his forfeiture of victory in Vienna?

Of course, on 5 April, the spirits on the Promenade des Anglais were depressed. In the combined standing mile and flying kilometer sprints, Braun achieved 1 min 3.72 sec, 32.8 sec and 112.5 km/h, Werner 1 min 4.3 sec, 32.99 sec and 109.1 km/h, beating Le Blon's Serpollet steamer and the Mors trio of Rigal, Augières and Gabriel. The gentlemen drivers Degrais and de Caters were holding off. In the subsequent Coupe Henri de Rothschild, Léon Serpollet and his steamer attacked the flying kilometer record. His older record was long out-dated. In November 1902, Augières, pseudonym of the famous Parisian jeweler Auger, had covered the kilometer in 29 seconds, 124.1 km/h, at Dourdan, at the wheel of his Mors. The concrete pavement of the Promenade des Anglais was slower. Serpollet failed in his attempt, was content with 29.19 sec and 123.3 km/h, his colleague Le Blon with 30.55 sec and 117.3 km/h, then Werner with 32.3 sec and 111.5 km/h. In a final sprint excluding the steamers Hieronimus averaged 113.3 km/h. "Just one hour later, after the wondrous mutation from stripped racer into comfortable four-seater, Baron de Caters promenaded in company of three elegant ladies over the Place Masséna!" This could only be done with

April 1903—Meeting of Nice. "Le Torpilleur," the steam-engined torpedo of Léon Serpollet, on the Promenade des Anglais.

The Villa Mercedes in Nice, no. 54, Promenade des Anglais.

a Mercedes. As usual Meyan analyzed "the southern market, the most important after Paris. It seems to be in the hands of three marques, of Mercedes, Rochet-Schneider and Renault. Others are present too, Panhard, Mors, De Dietrich and Serpollet. But the sun of the Riviera is primarily shining for the three former. Ah! The German competition! It continues to be in business, and more firmly than ever. We have permanently to bear in mind that with Maybach, the best engineer is standing on its side, and with Mercedes himself, the best salesman." The winter season closed with the opening of the Corniche. The scene looked towards Madrid.

# 10

# Towards Madrid

In fact the administration in Paris did not want to permit any road race at all. But the ACF kept at it. Albert de Dion wrote that "a great yearly test is indispensable for the automobile industry. The livelihood of twenty-five thousand workers depends on that test." Étienne de Zuylen and his friend Quinonès de Léon turned towards Madrid where an enthusiastic Alfonso XIII had just ascended the throne and promptly issued a decree approving the route from Biarritz to Madrid. Now Paris had to add its consent, and Cannstatt recorded on 11 December 1902: "The French automobile club has planned a great international race from Paris to Madrid and Mister Jellinek is convinced that it is necessary to take part. The expenses for this race will probably amount to 50,000 marks and Mister Jellinek will assume one half. For the time being Mister Jellinek has made a contract with one driver only, with Mister Degrais. He will receive a fixed salary, whether he will race or not, of 10,000 francs, payable quarterly in advance." On 25 February 1903, Willy Tischbein wrote from Nice: "I heard from Paris that Fournier will drive your Mercedes in the race Paris–Madrid. Of course, we are prepared to remunerate Fournier, when he wins the race, or is second, third or fourth. But we don't want to pay the enormous sums of the last year without any appreciable achievement. Please let me know if the car driven by Fournier is your property in which case he would anyway be forced to start on Continental, or if he has free hand concerning the tires."

On 7 April 1903, shortly after the races of Nice, Pierre de Caters signed a contract. The Baron came from Beichem near Antwerp, and undertook to drive the race to Madrid and the Bennett Cup in a Ninety. As remuneration he had the possibility either to keep the 12-liter racer or to pick out any other Mercedes, delivery within six months. For one of the first three places in Madrid or the victory in the Bennett Cup, Jellinek conceded an additional Mercedes of choice; for the fourth, fifth or sixth place in Madrid a discount of 33 percent, and for a kilometer or mile record 50 percent. The grading was clear: Third place in Madrid matched a victory in the Cup, and second place in the Cup counted nothing at all! In any case Cannstatt had to provide the service and to brush the worn-out racer up, free of charge for the Baron. Chain-smoker de Caters did not come alone but brought a speedy countryman. For the event across Spain he intended to lend his Sixty to Camille Jenatzy, the red-bearded driver who was the first to exceed the magical 100 km/h mark on 29 April 1899, in a high-tension duel against Gaston de Chasseloup-Laubat, on the chaussée at Achères north of Paris, at the wheel of an electro-vehicle called "Jamais-Contente," a never-satisfied cigar on four diminutive tires emanating from a Jules Verne novel. Meanwhile every child knew him as "éternel guignard," as eternal jinx who, with his ramshackle Bolide or Jenatzy, was standing still somewhere between Paris and Bordeaux, in trouble. Would the Mercedes withstand his outrages? In any case he was fast. Jellinek was aware of it and approved exactly the same conditions for the places one to six in Madrid.

As reinforcement for the three Belgian gentlemen drivers, Werner, Braun and (since his good performance in Nice) Hieronimus, were certain. Jellinek submitted ten entries, and the ACF allotted nos. 14, 27, 34, 36, 39, 86, 290, 291, 292 and 293. In addition, a batch of private entries came along, number 9 with Harry Harkness, the 99 with John B. Warden, the 114 with Foxhall Keene, the 123 for the Sixty owned by Gray Dinsmore, the 149 for William Dannat, finally the 155 for the older Forty of Eugen Max. Whether Maurice de Forest and Henry Fournier, with the 68 and 83, would start in Mors or Mercedes had still to be clarified. On 17 April, Conti director Tischbein was in high spirits once again and cabled to Jellinek: "I have heard rumor that Gabriel has left Mors and that he will drive a Mercedes in the race Paris–Madrid. If this is true, I ask you to arrange for Gabriel to start on Continental, because he will certainly drive one of your cars. Of course we are prepared to remunerate Gabriel accordingly."

Meanwhile Cannstatt was working on six Nineties. In the early morning of 18 April, Henri Degrais picked up the first one. On his way to Paris, he advised Jellinek per telegram: "Car is running brilliantly. Have left Stuttgart at six. Arrived in Nancy at two. Had breakfast in Lunéville." In the third week of April, Hermann Balz and Adolf Daimler released the next four racers. For several days Charley, Ferdinand

April 1903—Paris. On the left Jellinek with pale hat; in the center Desjoyeaux with bowler; and Fernand Gabriel at the wheel of the Mercedes Sixty.

Spiegel, Richard von Stern and Robert Katzenstein were allowed to test them without restraint. On 27 April, they summarised their experiences, "in order to eliminate the apparent defects immediately." In broad outline, everything was fine. Spiegel mentioned the leaking radiators which "can jeopardise the success of the race." Josef Brauner went to the radiator supplier, Wieland & Co. in Ulm, around 50 km south of Stuttgart, and supervised the manufacture of tightened tubings. Charley requested that the factory "pay special attention to the weight limit since the control would be very strict." But in particular it was the "rack-and-pinion regulation" which caused difficulties, the throttle control through shortening of the intake pushrods and accordingly reduced valve lift. The rack and the pinion wore down too quickly. Maybach suggested a pinpoint lubrication. Finally the complex device was simply removed in favor of "throttle control per old carburetor." "It is mentioned that the 80-hp engines are very hard to start, resulting in delays, mainly in the morning when preparing for the new stage." Maybach recommended "to lubricate with paraffin in the evening to avoid hardening of the oil." Von Stern proposed an additional small tank so that the engine could continue to run during short service stops, but it was impossible within the prescribed weight limit. Adolf Daimler wanted to convert the water tank used to cool the transmission brake, and "to give the mechanic a simple hand device for the sprinkling of the brake." The watering-can solution was "accepted and carried out immediately." Director Alfred von Kaulla expressed reservations "about a participation in the race." Charley set him straight, pointing out "the importance of the race for the whole business" and that the competitors too were polishing.

Then, on 3 May, it was again Tischbein's turn: "I cabled today: Approve 5000 francs for Gabriel. Particulars from Paris. Please try to conclude an agreement with Gabriel on our behalf too, by committing Gabriel to start until the end of 1904 only in Mercedes cars with Continental tires. We don't know how far we'll come with Werner in the race Paris–Madrid. Since in any case you have a lot of influence over Werner respective Dinsmore and since Dinsmore has bought the car on condition that he has to use it for the race, you can certainly put some slight pressure on Werner respective Dinsmore to fit Continental tires on this car. If Werner will then contact us, I can firmly promise you that Werner will not be on inferior terms with us. I don't know if Werner has a standing contract with our competition. But if he is free, of course we would be prepared to engage him for our tires during the rest of the remainder of the season." Jellinek, Cannstatt and Continental did not bid enough for the speedy Gabriel who was not prepared to switch sides for less than 20,000 francs. Two days later Gabriel wrote: "Yesterday I have met Monsieur Charley who could not give a definitive answer since a decision from Continental is still to come. To avoid a litigation, I had to go back to the house of Mors. But I have a new idea: At the moment I am on the books of Mors. With a corresponding allowance, I would be able to disengage in order to switch to Cannstatt. But this should happen before the 13th of this month since the drivers have to be definitively named until then. After all I know that Continental completely agrees with you and Charley will take all necessary steps to bring about a decision. You could divide the sum as follows: Continental 7000, Charley 7000 and you 6000 francs. Thus everything would be clarified and open." Jellinek applied for a higher contribution to the expenses than the hitherto-approved 25,000 marks. Gustav Vischer refused. Thus Gabriel drove the Mors no. 168.

In the meantime Degrais was crossing Spain. On 5 May, he reported:

> This night, I came back from Madrid, sadly by rail since the front axle broke in two on the pavement of Madrid, fortunately at only 3 km/h so that not even a tie rod was bent. But overall the road is good and tolerates high speeds. Indeed the pneumatics will suffer from the sharp stones unless everything is rolled before the 24th. Two legs are very dangerous: The Etchezarate and the Guadarrama where a gradient of 17 to 18 percent comes up in both directions. If it is raining the road will be extremely slippery. We have a stock of spare parts at different points and are working day and night on the perfect organisation and the certain success of the marque that only de Knyff seems to fear.

The other Nineties were staying at Cannstatt, ready for pick up. On 7 May, the young German bicycle star Paul Albert who, on the recommendation and with the assistance of Willy Tischbein, was to drive the Sixty no. 291, informed Jellinek:

> My car has been assembled a few days ago and runs perfectly. I am making daily practice runs which were satisfying so far. The maximum weight is not attained although I still have retained both brakes and no component has been cancelled. It is certainly interesting for you to hear some news concerning the racing cars. The Eighty is below the limit by a hair's breadth, and is below for certain after the utmost has been saved. In my humble opinion the engine itself is too heavy, while Mors for example is using steel cylinders in their thoroughbred racing cars whereby the weight is greatly reduced. Indeed these cars don't withstand much more than one race, but in this one they serve their purpose. You certainly know that the Eighty has just one foot brake, a lighter gearbox than the Sixty and a radiator saving eleven

May 1903—Paris—Madrid. *Pesage* in the Jardin des Tuileries: The Mercedes Sixty of Foxhall Keene.

## 10. Towards Madrid

May 1903—Paris–Madrid. *Pesage*, the weigh-in or scrutineering, in the Jardin des Tuileries: The Mercedes Ninety of Pierre de Caters.

kilograms. Testing was satisfying so far. Especially uphill the Eighty is much superior to the Sixty, about in the same degree as the Sixty to the Forty. In contrast, at the moment there is no clue for the maximum speed on the level since the local road condition makes a full exploitation of the power impossible. Yesterday Werner tried his Eighty for the first time, reportedly without complaint. Today the car of de Caters, who arrived yesterday in company of Jenatzy, should be finished, the car of Jenatzy presumably the day after tomorrow. Jenatzy has brought along an electrical clutch for his and de Caters' car, but wants to fit it at a future date only. Vanderbilt took delivery of his car two days ago and drove directly to Paris. Dr. von Stern is still here and is apparently very satisfied with his car. On next Monday he wants to drive with it to Vienna. Degrais has left 14 days ago with Rothschild's car. You have certainly obtained details concerning his test drive to Madrid. On 17 May all cars should be in Paris. I hope to be able to drive along at least a part of the route from there. I'll bring the car to Paris on the road. Drivers other than those mentioned are not here yet. Until 17 May, four, at most five, of the Eighties are likely to be ready.

On 15 May, Albert was killed during a practice spin after having misjudged a gully.

Jellinek was making his visit to Paris, stayed at a suite of the Hotel Élysée Palace. The French Conti agency, J. Loeser & Fils, confirmed free service on the way to Madrid. On Wednesday, 19 May, the *pesage* opened in the Jardin des Tuileries, just across the Concorde, on the doorstep of the ACF headquarters. Cannstatt had in fact assembled six Nineties. All of them lined up, painted in "*matte* white," in the morning the 14 and the 27 with Wilhelm Werner and Pierre de Caters, in the afternoon the 34, the 36 and the 39 with Degrais, Hieronimus and the inexperienced Köhler, the substitute for Gabriel. In the early morning of Thursday appeared the 86 with Jenatzy who was lucky to be at the wheel of a 12-liter. The Sixties followed later, the 99 and the 114 with Warden and Keene, finally the 290, 292 and 293 with Terry, Braun and Gastaud. Obviously Braun preferred to start from well back, so that the originally allocated 123 was cancelled. Max and his little Forty retained their 155. Albert's 291 was nullified. De Forest and Fournier took the wheel of their Mors, while Dannat preferred to paint and Harkness to sip cocktails. The proceedings lasted until Saturday, for the Commission Sportive had to scrutineer 224 racers: 88 one-tonners, 47 voitures légères, 36 voiturettes and 53 motorcycles. Even Cannstatt was in high spirits now: "Approve 10,000 francs advertising Paris–Madrid!"

The *matte*-white squad competed against an awesome armada—fifteen Panhards, fourteen Mors, twelve De Dietrichs and a pack of Gardner-Serpollets, CGVs, Gobron-Brilliés, Napiers and Wolseleys from the heavy class, as well as ten Renaults and eight Darracqs from the smaller classes. It took just one year to convince Grenelle to adopt the expensive steel cylinders, Panhard fashion. With 145 mm × 175 mm the new Mors displaced 11.5 liters and delivered 80 hp, more or less the same output as the 80/90-hp from Cannstatt. Further Mors features included a welded-on F-head, cone clutch, four-speed gearbox, frame stamped out of 4-mm sheet steel in U shape, wheelbase 265 cm, track 146, tires 910 mm × 90 mm front and 920 mm × 120 mm rear, 120-liter fuel tank. At least for the first, extremely fast, stage ending at Bordeaux, all Mors drivers preferred an automatic intake, so the pushrods and rockers were disabled for the time being. The valve timing was not completely *au point*. At Ivry, Arthur Krebs had not changed the previous year's 160 mm × 170 mm, but had given his big Panhard a second camshaft, and thus a T-head, output 85 hp. Technically, the notable feature of 1903 was the almost universal adoption of the mechanically operated intake valve,

May 1903—Paris–Madrid. *Pesage* in the Jardin des Tuileries: The Serpollet steamer of Hubert Le Blon.

## 10. Towards Madrid

**May 1903—Paris–Madrid.** *Pesage* in the Jardin des Tuileries: The Wolseley of Sidney Girling.

which could now be found all over the place, down to the voiture légère class in which Darracq as well as Renault showed up their highly ingenious "L-head," a pure product of the weight limit. In principle it was a simplified and distorted T-head, whose camshafts and valves had been compressed on one side of the engine, all the valves standing above a single camshaft, the intake and the exhaust in the same pocket: "A T-head arrangement involved the provision of a second camshaft which seemed almost intolerably clumsy. The L-head, which was by far the simplest way out of the difficulty, involved sacrificing the size of both sets of valves." Whether the idea originated from Suresnes, Billancourt, Darracq, Renault, Paul Ribeyrolles or the De Dion renegade Paul Viet remained open.

For the first time, the *matte* whites started in a road race as hot favorites, alongside the Panhards of René de Knyff, Henry and Maurice Farman, Georges Heath, Charles Stuart Rolls and Pierre de Crawhez; the Mors of Henry and Achille Fournier, Victor Rigal, Gabriel, Salleron, Augières, Maurice de Forest and Willie Vanderbilt; the Serpollet of Hubert Le Blon; and the De Dietrichs of Charles Jarrott, Claude Loraine Barrow, E. T. Stead, Henri Rougier and Madame Camille du Gast, Paris' "Valkyrie of the machine." Many constructors were driving themselves, including of course Charron, Girardot and Voigt in CGVs and Louis and Marcel Renault in Renaults, but also Émile and Charles Dombret in Motoblocs, Herbert Austin in a Wolseley and Marius Barbarou in a Benz. Much more was to be heard from a lot of newcomers, including Gustave Caillois, Arthur Duray, Vincenzo Lancia and Luigi Storero in F.I.A.T.s, and Victor Hémery and Louis

May 1903—Paris–Madrid. *Pesage* in the Jardin des Tuileries: The Mors of Maurice de Forest.

May 1903—Paris–Madrid. *Pesage* in the Jardin des Tuileries: They both came from Marseille, the Turcat-Méry and Henri Rougier. De Dietrich built the Turcat under license.

Wagner in Darracqs. Alfonso Sanz, the son of the twelfth Alfonso and the opera beauty Eleonora Sanz, started in the voiturette no. 228 by the name of Passy-Thellier. Jockey Tod Sloan intended to drive a Georges Richard towards Spain, Ettore Bugatti a revamped De Dietrich.

In three stages, via Bordeaux and Vitoria, the route led to Madrid. The race would start on Sunday, 24 May 1903, as usual before dawn, at half past three at Versailles, Route de Saint-Cyr. The course then ran over the finest, fastest and dustiest motor-racing road in France, through Rambouillet, Chartres, Châteaudun, Vendôme, Tours, Châtellerault, Poitiers, Ruffec, Angoulême and Libourne to Bordeaux, a distance of 552 km, with town neutralizations totalling two and one-half hours. *Le Tout Paris* was going berserk. On Saturday evening, tens of thousands thronged to the stations of Montparnasse and Saint-Lazare to reach Versailles on time. As the dawn neared the atmosphere was clear, crystal clear, without the slightest breath of wind. The lull before the storm was eerily underpinned by the magnesium flashlights of the photographers. Jarrott and his De Dietrich had drawn number one. Henry Fournier approached, whispered a last word in his ear. It was still too dark to start. A quarter to four, and the De Dietrich shot off on its journey, followed by de Knyff, then Louis Renault, then the rest, at two-minute intervals, and finally the motorcycles, in broad daylight. Hundreds of thousands, millions, were bordering the road everywhere on the endless straights where the big Panhards, Mors and Mercedes roared

May 1903—Paris–Madrid. The Mercedes Ninety of Jenatzy in the hairpin near Pétignac.

May 1903—Paris–Madrid. The Renault of Louis Renault. (Renault)

by, averaging 140 km/h. Over a timed stretch at La Bourdinière, between Chartres and Bonneval, the 650-kg Renault of Louis Renault was said to have averaged nearly 150 km/h. And Louis Renault was the first to reach Bordeaux, a quarter of an hour after midday. Jarrott followed half an hour later, just in front of the blockbuster, Gabriel, at the wheel of his Mors no. 168. He had left Versailles 82nd in the starting order and pushed right through the scores of cars, driving inevitably in a dust cloud nearly all the way. He covered the 552-km distance in 5 h 13 min 31 sec, averaging nearly 106 km/h, a stunning performance; "as an extraordinary piece of driving it stands unequalled and will always stand alone." Louis Renault's light Renault had lost 20 minutes, Salleron's Mors 33 minutes, Jarrott's De Dietrich 38 minutes.

And the *matte* whites? Jellinek cabled: "Warden very well classified in Bordeaux. Your 80-hp are the dung carts I predicted. Renault, Mors, even De Dietrich in front of us. Fine disgrace!" John B. Warden's Sixty reached Bordeaux in fourth place in the one-tonner class, fifth overall, 43 minutes behind Gabriel. "Warden drove the whole distance in third gear since he wanted to take no risks because of the dust." Nine Mercedes crossed the line at Bordeaux, Gastaud in seventh, Jenatzy in eleventh, Max twelfth, Braun seventeenth, de Caters twenty-first, Köhler twenty-second, Hieronimus thirty-second, finally Degrais in thirty-sixth place. The *roi du volant* Werner? When leaving Chartres, he was seventh and moving up. After the Tours control, he was hot on Louis Renault's trail, until the rear axle of

**May 1903—Paris–Madrid. The De Dietrich of Charles Jarrott at the Bordeaux control.**

his Ninety broke. Near Coignières, Terry's Sixty struck an apple tree, turned over and burned. The "eternal jinx" lived up to his reputation when he roared through a host of gnats. It was inevitable that one of the many insects would find its way into the carburetor, and by the time Jenatzy discovered it, nearly two hours had elapsed. Braun and Hieronimus struggled with their tires. Köhler had to replace a coolant pipe. De Caters plowed through a field and drove on without the foot brake. In Châteaudun, Degrais poured ten liters of water in the fuel tank. The *Motorwagen*, the favorite gazette of the self-driving Prussian officers, drew the balance: "Werner, Jenatzy, Warden, Max, Gastaud and de Caters drove dashingly, as well as Braun, all others slackly."

Mere trifles! "La course meurtrière," the murderous race, was the headline. The goddess of speed took a deadly toll in this event. A few kilometers beyond Couhé-Vérac, a village between Poitiers and Ruffec, Marcel Renault in his 650-kg Renault caught up with Théry's Decauville, tried to pass, got his wheel into the gutter, swung round twice and overturned, succumbing to his injuries a few hours later. Claude Loraine Barrow in his De Dietrich swerved to avoid a dog, crashed into a tree, and was catapulted into a pond. Mechanic Pierre Rosez, a Spaniard and old servant of Barrow's, was killed on the spot. Barrow died a few days later when pneumonia set in. Leslie Porter saw a rail crossing too late, tried to steer into a field, and hit the wall of a farmhouse. His Wolseley caught fire. Mechanic Willie Nixon was burned to death. Just beyond Angoulême, Tourand in a Brouhot skidded into the

May 1903—Paris–Madrid. Race of the century: At the wheel of his white Mors, Fernand Gabriel averaged 106 km/h between Paris and Bordeaux.

May 1903—Paris–Madrid. The Mercedes Ninety of Jenatzy on the downhill straight of Sainte-Maure.

June 1903—Circuit des Ardennes: Kilometer sprint at Huy. The Benz (160 mm × 140 mm, T-head) of Marius Barbarou covered the flying kilometer in 30⅕ seconds.

crowd, killing his mechanic, a soldier, a child and another spectator. Georges Richard collided with a horse and cart, suffering severe injuries. Near Saint-Pierre du Palais, E. T. Stead and Salleron brushed too close. Stead's De Dietrich ran into the ditch and turned upside down, pinning its driver underneath. Madame du Gast stopped to render first aid, refusing to leave until an ambulance arrived to take Stead to Libourne. Having lost three hours, the Valkyrie rejoined the race and finished in 45th place. The road was covered with innumerable wrecks. A total of 114 cars, just half of the actual 224 starters, reached Bordeaux. Paris stepped in and stopped the race, and Madrid followed suit. Cars were not even allowed to pass through the streets of Bordeaux under their own power and were towed to the station behind horses and carriages, returning to Paris by rail. This was the death-knell of the town-to-town races, the end of the heroic age. On 25 May, Gustav Vischer wrote: "The impression of the frightful race Paris–Madrid is still fresh in my mind! I hope that the news published in German bulletins concerning the ban of the race will not only be confirmed but that the ban will be final and put an end to these criminal activities once and for all." Meanwhile Paul Meyan commented on the likely finishing order in Madrid: "In view of the classification in Bordeaux, the subsequent sections and the condition of the cars, I believe that Mercedes could have won the heavy class, followed by De Dietrich, Panhard and Mors." Indeed, Meyan bet on the homogeneous Sixty, not on the powerful, perhaps too powerful, Ninety.

June 1903—Circuit des Ardennes. Émile Voigt, the "V" of Charron, Girardot & Voigt, drove his CGV to seventh place.

Just a few weeks later, on 22 June, the sportsmen returned to their "criminal activities," although no Mercedes was entered in the second Circuit des Ardennes. De Crawhez and de Caters drove their Sixties in a kilometer sprint at nearby Huy, and a short 1350-meter hillclimb. Barbarou in a Benz won the sprint in 30⅕ seconds, in front of Osmont's Darracq and Hanriot's Clément. Katzenstein commented: "Caters has been well and truly beaten by Benz. Allegedly, a cart forced him to throttle down. Fools like Keene and Caters who race on their own are very dubious advantages for a cause." In the main event, over six laps of 85.4 km, Pierre de Crawhez drove his Panhard to victory, in 5 h 52 min 7 sec, twenty minutes in front of Léonce Girardot and his CGV. The great French marques continued to dominate.

# 11

## *La Coupe Bennett*

A Napier was hardly able to match a Panhard, a Mors or a Mercedes, but nevertheless was able to win the 1902 Bennett Cup since French interest was still at a low ebb. As driver Selwyn Edge commented: "We have won the Gordon Bennett through others breaking down." That the Cup was not displayed in the Hôtel Pastoret at the Place de la Concorde but somewhere else on the other side of Channel bothered Paris little if any—until the breaking-off of the race to Madrid. Overnight *la Coupe Bennett* began to monopolize the headlines. James "Jamie" Gordon Bennett was born in 1841 in New York, the son of the founder and publisher of the *New York Herald*, a gentleman and dandy who was responsible for Henry Morton Stanley's 1869 search for explorer David Livingstone. JGB promoted ballooning and yacht racing, each one with a Bennett Cup. He practiced the sport of coaching, astonishing his neighbors by riding through their formal gardens with a coach and four, at midnight, naked. In 1877, on New Year's Day, JGB disgraced himself when attending an open house at the home of Miss Caroline May, who was noted for her charm and daring. Already well-served with punch, he proceeded to insult his hostess and to relieve himself into the grand piano. The next day, Miss May's brother stepped up to JGB's carriage as he arrived for lunch at the Union Club, and they grappled in the snow. After a duel in which nobody was injured, both men declared themselves satisfied. Bennett, however, removed himself from New York society and agreed to represent the *Herald* in Paris. At the turn of the century, JGB spent his time either at Versailles, in the former love-nest of the fourteenth Louis, or at no. 104 of the Champs-Élysées, or aboard his 100-meter yacht *Lysistrata*, in company of seventy guests and a crew of one hundred, the crew all clean shaven, British Navy fashion.

In 1899, Bennett presented the ACF with the "Coupe Internationale d'Automobile," a horseless carriage crafted in best Art Nouveau style by the famous Rue de la Paix silversmith André Aucoc. To the public the Cup quickly became known as "la Coupe Bennett," the Bennett Cup. Influenced by JGB's yacht club past, the Bennett Cup was to be contested by national automobile clubs recognized by the ACF, and represented by teams of one, two or three cars, in an annual race, run between 15 May and 15 August, over a distance of between 550 and 650 kilometers. Not more than three racers could be entered from each country. "The cars have to be driven by members of the competing clubs" and "the cars must be entirely constructed and all their parts manufactured in the country which such cars represent," with the exception of the Swedish iron of the magnetos and the Belgian close-woven fabric of the tires. Foreign manufacture of a car under license, potentially giving a marque more than three entries, was not prohibited specifically.

The drivers could be of any nationality. From the outset there were enough seeds of contention.

After the 1902 Napier victory, the organization of the next race fell to the British club. But where could the event be held? Since a speed limit of twelve miles per hour, not even 20 km/h, was strictly enforced throughout the United Kingdom, an Act of Parliament was required before the Bennett Cup could be staged on British roads. Club secretary Claude Johnson suggested Ireland. While a bill exempting cars from any speed limit on the day of the race received the royal assent on 27 March 1903, the Bennett committee selected a circuit close to Dublin, shaped somewhat like a figure eight, with the start and finish between Athy and Kilcullen. On 2 July 1903, competitors were required to cover alternately three laps of a shorter 40-mile or 64-km eastern loop through Castledermot and Carlow, and four laps of a longer 52-mile or 83-km western loop through Kildare, Monasterevin, Maryborough and Stradbally, for a total distance of 327 miles or 527 km. Like the 1901 event it was shorter than the originally submitted minimum of 550 km. The course was rather narrow, combining long, partially bumpy straights with angular corners and twistier sections. Despite the disgrace on the way towards Madrid, Cannstatt was preparing three Nineties, the 12-liters belonging to de Caters, Jenatzy and Dinsmore. But the selection of the drivers was still in the lap of the gods.

July 1903—Gordon Bennett Cup, Ireland. Camille Jenatzy and the Mercedes Sixty amid the Irish Midlands near the Moat of Ardscull.

At the end of October 1902, Jellinek and Vischer noted: "The German automobile club has to accept every submitted driver since it is impossible to entrust such machines to spoilt children. Nominated are Baron de Forest, Jenatzy, Werner or Fournier, as relief Baron de Caters, de Crawhez and Degrais." In the spring of 1903, the nominees were de Caters, Jenatzy, Werner and Hieronimus. The German club, an elitist combination of Kaiser's entourage, Prussian gentry, and military officers, did not agree. Of course the Belgian nobleman de Caters was of suitable rank. But the parvenu Jenatzy! Hadn't he made his money as a civil engi-

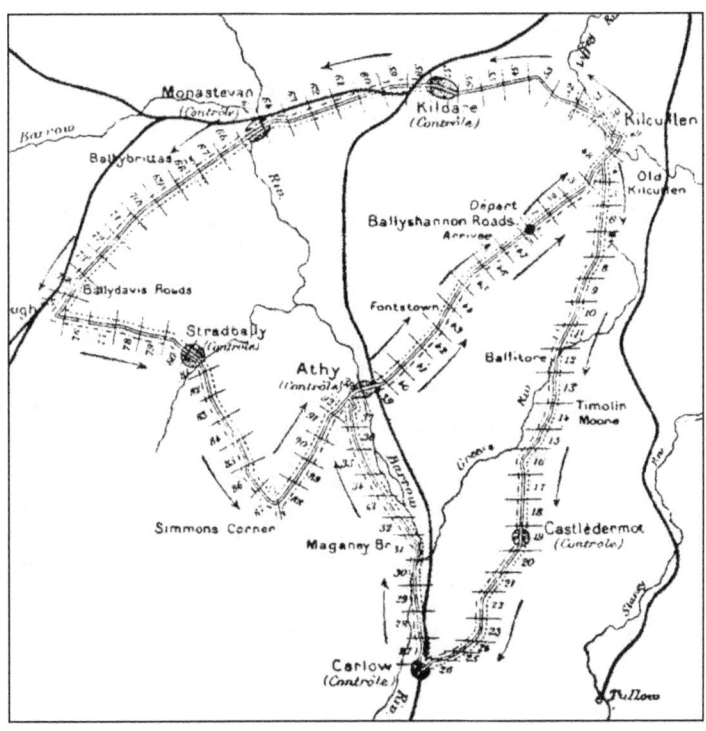

The Bennett course near Dublin, the Athy Circuit. Three laps of the 40-mile eastern circuit and four laps of the 51.9-mile western circuit had to be covered.

neer, before turning to motor manufacturing? Then the employee Hieronimus, not to mention the possibly social democratic mechanic Werner! In the face of this charade, Jellinek got in a temper and withdrew. In April, Willy Tischbein stepped in and wrote to the club's "Representative Board, to the attention of General Becker," pointing out the importance of the race for the German automobile industry and taking the side of the mechanics: "Concerning the personal situation of Hieronimus, I am not up to date, but his demeanor is in accordance with the better castes. I believe that inquiries about him would result in an acceptance as DAC member. Werner, on the other hand, is just *mécanicien*. But a man with the driving skills and the name of Werner would certainly be member of the French club." By the beginning of May, the DAC gave way, partially, creating a new category for "technical members" which continued to exclude simple mechanics. Cannstatt compromised by choosing de Caters, Keene and Hieronimus, with Jenatzy, Barrow and Degrais as reserves. And after Barrow's accident, Hermann Braun suddenly came into play: "Braun should immediately make an application for membership in the German Automobile Club."

Charley Lehmann was responsible for the organization. On 16 June, he came to Cannstatt to discuss further details: "Mister Charley receives 8000 francs to be shared by Mister Jellinek and the DMG. Engineer Balz and the mechanics are paid by Cannstatt. The drivers bring the cars to Paris. Charley assumes the travel expenses and the freight from Paris and back. If possible, one 60 hp should take part in the race. If a 60-hp is not available, three 80-hps should take part." On the early morning of 10 June, Jellinek arrived at Stuttgart. As usual, he went to the Hotel Marquardt, where he was just taking a bath when the servant knocked on the door: "Mister Jellinek, tonight a fire has destroyed the factory!" Jellinek, who normally hit the roof at the slightest provocation, kept calm: "Then I can take the bath at my leisure." The Seelberg assembly hall and its contents had gone up in smoke and flame, including the radiator and carburetor shop on the first floor and nearly one hundred cars, among them the three Nineties whose preparation had almost been completed.

What to do? With little time remaining, only Jenatzy's Madrid racer could be salvaged, if necessary. It was de Caters who took the initiative, on the same day:

> I have just received your telegram with the sad news that our beautiful cars burnt down. This is really unfortunate since I believe that it would have been easy game for us. Now my idea: With his 60 hp, Warden was able to beat all the Panhards. I believe that our 60 hps are able to win the Cup. They are mature and very homogeneous. Just one Mors will start in the Cup and we can forget it, you know why. The 60 hp Mercedes will beat the Panhards, and also the Americans. I have no information about the Napier, but Jarrott told me that they are very slow. I suggest to race, on one hand to win the Cup, on the other hand to make a huge fuss. We go to Ireland with three perfectly prepared cars, including coachwork to show clearly that we use touring cars. On site we strip the cars and remount the body just after the race.

10 June 1903—Cannstatt. The Seelberg factory after the fire: "Destroyed 80 hp racer and assembly hall."

## 11. La Coupe Bennett

In so doing de Caters, who not only owned a Ninety but also a Sixty racer, made sure that he was one of the Bennett drivers, at the same time paving the way for his friends Jenatzy and Keene, the latter of whom also had a Sixty in his stable. Cannstatt was quick in finding the missing 9-liter for Jenatzy. Duttenhofer cabled to Katzenstein: "Since the car belonging to Dinsmore is the only one which is able to win the Gordon Bennett race in Ireland, we ask you to intervene and to provide the car of your friend for us. We hope that your intervention will hold aloft the flag of Germany." Understandably Wilhelm Werner was obstructive. After all, it was only due to his missing club membership that he was not allowed to drive the Sixty. But his employer Dinsmore released the 9-liter. It was not until 15 June that the driver charade was definitively clarified. Staying at the Hotel Kaiserhof in Berlin, Duttenhofer reported to Jellinek: "I have met Count Sierstorpff and he agreed to mention again the question of Braun's membership. According to the telegram I received from Cannstatt, Braun drew back with your approval, and de Caters, Foxhall Keene and Jenatzy are nominated as drivers, Degrais and Hieronimus as reserve. Now, I have asked the Count to abstain from taking an additional step because of Braun."

On the other side of the Rhine, the French complained about the restrictive three-car rule, a handicap to their industry. The rebellious Alexandre Darracq asked for the nomination of a 650-kg voiture légère. But it was not without good reason that Chevalier de Knyff acted at the Concorde as president of the Commission

July 1903—Gordon Bennett Cup, Ireland. The Panhard team just before the scrutineering at Naas: On the left, the reserve racer with Maurice Farman, in the middle Henry Farman, on the right René de Knyff.

**July 1903—Gordon Bennett Cup, Ireland. The Mors of Fernand Gabriel.**

Sportive and, at the same time, at Ivry as director of the racing department. The Basque Darracq found the *marque doyenne* a tough nut to crack. The ACF cut it short, chose two Panhards and a Mors, René de Knyff, Henry Farman and, in view of the impressive showing towards Madrid, Fernand Gabriel, who was quickly elected ACF member and took the place of the originally nominated Henry Fournier. And why did de Caters write off the speedy Mors? The mechanical operation of the intake valves, which did not offer any advantage when racing at constant speed on the long straights towards Bordeaux, was necessary when engine flexibility was in demand for speeding up out of the corners, and a proper intake-valve timing was still missing. Nevertheless, nobody was in doubt about the recovery of the Cup. Panhard, Mors and the Frères Michelin chartered the two-thousand-ton steamer *Ferdinand de Lesseps* to bring their stable of racers to the port of Dublin, including spare parts, mechanics, prominent guests and the latest haute couture for the victory banquet.

Two places in the English team were allotted to Napier: Selwyn Edge in the brand-new 13-liter (165 mm × 152 mm) and Charles Jarrott in the well-tried 8-liter (140 mm × 127 mm). For third place the Napiers of Rolls, Mayhew and Stocks sprinted against the Star of John Lisle, in the private park of the Duke of Portland at Welbeck. The 8-liter Napier of J. W. Stocks won the race. The Automobile Club of America entered the "Bullet no. 2," the 8-cylinder Winton (133 mm × 152 mm) of Alexander Winton, a 17-liter dirt track special. The teammates were chosen on the basis of two burlesque trials between Westbury and Merrick on Long Island.

July 1903—Gordon Bennett Cup, Ireland. The 13-liter Napier of S.F. Edge and cousin Cecil.

Harry Harkness did not start. Percy Owen and Louis Mooers were alone, a Winton Baby Bullet and a T-headed Peerless. After hobbling six kilometers straight on, a few times back-and-forth, they were allowed to go aboard.

At Cannstatt, everything was going according to plan, when Charley cabled on 19 June: "Foxhall Keene, Jenatzy and de Caters refuse to start on Continental. They drive on German made Michelin. Have informed Jellinek yesterday. Advise if you are bound to Continental and if we risk a lawsuit. Since the cars are in the possession of the gentlemen, I cannot force them to use Conti." Tischbein contacted the DAC who replied on the next day: "We have just heard that the Gordon Bennett cars will run on Michelin which are reportedly manufactured in Germany. We point out that the tires, in all their components, from the mixing of the rubber to the finish, have to be made in Germany. Otherwise the cars will be disqualified." By the morning of 22 June, Conti director Seligmann came to Cannstatt "to discuss the tire question in detail." On one hand the Conti man had assured Katzenstein, before the banker's intervention, that Jenatzy "would be allowed to run on Michelin at all events," but on the other hand he now considered "the situation very serious" and suggested "an investigation by the DAC." Jellinek stayed at Baden: "Tell Director Seligmann that I did everything to convince the drivers to use Continental. They refused since the cars are not owned by us and since the drivers have not been chosen by us but by the DAC. Seligmann should meet Charley in Paris and talk to Katzenstein since he has Dinsmore's car at his disposal."

This was the straight tip. Banker Katzenstein sorted the affair out. On 28 June, he wrote from Dublin: "On the road from Paris, Jenatzy's experience with Continental has been most unfavorable once again. I agreed to fit German Michelins. My interest in the race was to use Michelin and you had to decide on the content of existing contracts. I have decided to make a compromise, de Caters and Jenatzy on Michelin, and Keene on Continental. Whether Keene will do so, is doubtful with this man until the last moment. Inform Jellinek who is away from the action, while others are pulling the chestnuts out of the fire for him. Neither Charley nor anybody else is here. Dinsmore and I have to help our men. Cars arrived in good condition. Prospects not hopeless. Weather bad. Roads badly drained."

Thirty-three-year-old Foxhall Parker Keene was the son of well-known Wall Street broker James R. Keene, and the "world's greatest amateur athlete." He disliked instructions. In 1901, *Automobile Magazine* had written: "This gentleman was previously associated with almost every kind of amateur sport, he in his younger days being a good runner, base ball and tennis player. Those interested in amateur sports well remember that it was only half a dozen years ago when Mr. Keene suddenly loomed up as a golf player by winning the amateur championship of this country. His favorite pastime is polo, which he still follows successfully, he being rated with several others as being in a class by themselves at this game. Mr. Keene is a medium height slender type of man, weighing 152 pounds. In automobiling he displays the same slow movements that have characterised him in sports requiring much physical activity."

On Sunday, 1 July, the weighing ceremony at Naas, a few kilometers southwest of Dublin, attracted a huge crowd, and the tire charade sorted itself out: "International Committee has rejected Michelin because of valves manufactured in France. Use old 1902 Continental." Meanwhile, to avoid dust clouds, the start area near Ballyshannon and the approaches of dangerous corners had been treated with Westrumite, a 5 percent aqueous solution of paraffin and ammonia. On Monday morning, 2 July, a few minutes past six, the competitors arrived at the starting area, for the first time a really balanced international field, the English Napiers in green, the French Panhards and the Mors in blue, the American Wintons and the Peerless in red, and the German Mercedes in matte white:

| *No.* | *Driver* | | |
|---|---|---|---|
| 1, 5, 9 | Edge | Jarrott | Stocks |
| 2, 6, 10 | de Knyff | Gabriel | Farman |
| 3, 7, 11 | Owen | Mooers | Winton |
| 4, 8, 12 | Jenatzy | de Caters | Keene |

Promptly at seven o'clock, Colonel Lindsay Lloyd fired the starting pistol for Edge. The field followed at seven-minute intervals, spacing the twelve racers all over the eastern circuit. Jenatzy and de Caters shot away "in great style." The Baron even found time to blow a kiss to his wife Axeline. Gabriel too displayed speed immediately. Farman's Panhard spluttered. Keene stalled his Mercedes. Mooers forgot to release the handbrake. And Winton, cleaning the Bullet's fuel line, lost 45 minutes. Near Castledermot, Stocks missed the fork leading to Carlow and went straight ahead into the pole of a wire fencing. Edge was the first to finish the opening lap,

July 1903—Gordon Bennett Cup, Ireland. The Mercedes of Foxhall Keene and mechanic Willy Lüttgen.

July 1903—Gordon Bennett Cup, Ireland. The Panhard of Henry Farman.

but it was Keene who was in the lead. Katzenstein was flabbergasted. With a first lap of 46 min 3 sec, Keene lay twenty seconds ahead of Edge, with Farman and Jarrott next in order, Jenatzy nearly three minutes back, then de Knyff, de Caters and Gabriel, whose Mors was swerving when approaching the angled corners. The speedy Gabriel had memorised the circuit for two weeks, leaving mysterious marks at every turn. It was all for nothing. At the Moat of Ardscull, he leaped out, checking the tires and axles. Red-bearded Jenatzy began to get warmed up. By the start line, he was on Owen's tail, waving furiously, nearly standing up in his car, ready to eat an American Winton driver. Fortunately the road widened so that the Belgian Barbarossa was able to shoot ahead.

At the beginning of lap two, on the longer western circuit, Edge's Napier began to overheat, having lost the radiator cap. Gabriel was flying: "He took Simmons corner on two wheels and on his descent to Athy, he had all four wheels in the air and flew like a projectile for twenty yards." With broken steering, Jarrott's Napier ran up a bank, rebounded back and overturned, with mechanic Cecil Bianchi lying pinned beneath. De Caters stopped, and Jarrott insisted: "Get on, we are all right." De Caters stopped again in front of the Ballyshannon grandstand, reassuring the Napier team and the race officials that the injuries were not fatal. The Peerless of Mooers lost a rear wheel, while Keene tore off a tire. Gabriel set the fastest lap time in 1 h 19 sec. But overall Jenatzy was in the lead now, with 1 h 49 min 17 sec. De Knyff followed three minutes back, then Edge, Gabriel, Farman, nearly twelve minutes back de Caters, and finally, twenty minutes back, Keene.

July 1903—Gordon Bennett Cup, Ireland. The Winton of Alexander Winton.

July 1903—Gordon Bennett Cup, Ireland. The Peerless of Louis Mooers: steel cylinders, T-head, 152 mm × 152 mm.

In lap three, the French put the screws on Jenatzy. Farman achieved the fastest time in 49 min 35 sec. But Jenatzy was only ten seconds back, increasing his lead over de Knyff. With the fourth-best time de Caters passed ahead of Gabriel; Keene was sixth, but not for long. In lap four the New Yorker retired his Sixty with a broken rear axle. Jenatzy continued to increase his lead, which was now ten minutes over de Knyff, twelve over Farman. Would the rear axle withstand the reckless treatment? De Caters, Gabriel, Edge, Winton and Owen were out of contention. In lap five, the Winton broke down. Farman was speeding up. With a lap time of 50 min 31 sec he squeezed up close to his teammate de Knyff. The Panhard duo lay eight minutes behind Jenatzy's leading Mercedes. But there was no end to the Belgian Barbarossa's forward surge. With a lap of 1 h 1 min 32 sec he dealt a further blow to the Frenchmen. Farman limited the loss to just 45 seconds, promoting him to second place. Dinsmore and Katzenstein were scared stiff. Would their Sixty reach the line?

Jenatzy kept at it. With 1 h 2 min 18 sec for the seventh and last lap on the short western circuit, his victory was in the bag. Jenatzy and the Sixty won in 6 h 39 min, averaging 79.162 km/h, 11 min 40 sec ahead of de Knyff, 12 min 44 sec ahead of Farman, more than one hour ahead of Gabriel, nearly three hours ahead of Edge, who was disqualified for having received a push at one of the controls. De Caters broke his rear axle, twenty kilometers from the finish. The Baron had to be content with a gold cigarette case, a reward for his sportsmanship in stopping to help Jarrott. Dinsmore immediately sent his congratulations to Jellinek: "Jenatzy drove a really marvellous race. He was happy, happy like a schoolboy. Without Keene's and de Caters'

July 1903—Gordon Bennett Cup, Ireland. The Panhard of René de Knyff finished second.

July 1903—Gordon Bennett Cup, Ireland. The winning Mercedes of Jenatzy.

axle failures, it would be first, second, third. Keene and de Caters too drove excellently and de Caters made sure to have the public on his side by helping Jarrott." And Braun assented: "Cannstatt owes this success only to you. The race was won through the genius of Maybach and the work of your friends. At Cannstatt, with the aid of Balz, I have meticulously prepared the car during two months until it was what it is." Of course, Fritz Walker and Willy Lüttgen, who served as mechanics for Jenatzy and Keene, had assisted from the outset as well. Both of them followed Keene to New York.

Jenatzy was entitled to choose a Mercedes, and Conti added 25,000 marks in cash. At the beginning of July, the Belgian wrote to Jellinek:

> I thank you again for your amiable telegram. As you have guessed right my choice falls on a 90-hp with removable rear tonneau. On 5 July, just after coming back to Brussels, I have sold the car to Monsieur Eugène Lefebvre, Avenue du Midi. By contract I have reserved the right to use the car in all meetings and record attempts in which I will take part during 1903. Hence, since 9 July, Monsieur Lefebvre is the new owner. I would appreciate if you could send him all documents. Concerning the Cup, the most absurd articles are being published day after day, and we cannot do anything about it. Our average of nearly 90 km/h will soon fall down to 60. You should rectify this once and for all by stating the following figures which are official. The effective race distance without neutralization was exactly 371 English miles, thus 597 km. My official racing time was 6 h 39', the average therefore 89.8 km/h, practically 90 km/h.

The Bennett Committee specified a distance of 524 km! Whether 80 or 90 km/h, the victory was the important point, not the average, the first victory of a foreign marque over the established French, in the first great race on foreign soil.

In *La France Automobile*, Jellinek commented:

> Jenatzy did not win the Bennett Cup because of better circuit knowledge. Quite the contrary. It was only a few days before the race that he drove on the circuit for the first time. Originally I suggested Werner, Jenatzy and de Caters to defend the German colours. The German Club refused. Jenatzy was not accepted until the Club appreciated that there was no substitute. Otherwise we could have been in Ireland at the beginning of June, and our 90-hp could have escaped the fire. With the revised racers we had all chances to take the first three places. But we were forced to enter three 60-hp touring cars. In order to push down their weight under the limit, we had to replace the too-heavy axles by lighter ones. This presented problems, but it left us no option. An independent observer would agree that it did not look too promising for us. But now I am very satisfied.

Jellinek forgot to add that, on 26 June, according to a decree of the municipality of Vienna, he was granted permission to change his name officially to Jellinek-Mercedes: "The first time that a father bears the name of his daughter!"

As usual the year closed with the hillclimb to the Semmering where Hermann Braun was allowed to drive Dinsmore's Sixty to victory, and the Salon in the Grand Palais. In Paris, the name Mercedes was now pronounced in one breath with Panhard and Mors. Charley displayed his entire range, the new T-head 18, 24 and 35 hp, three, four and one half, and six liters, 90 mm × 120 mm, 105 mm × 130 mm and 116 mm × 145 mm, for 30, 35, and 45,000 francs, and of course the F-head Sixty and Ninety, for 55 and 99,000 francs, bare chassis price. The neighbors were offering a 60-hp F.I.A.T. for 40,000, a 60-hp Napier and a 45-hp Panhard for

*Signatures: Gottlieb and Paul Daimler, Maybach, Jellinek, Duttenhofer, Degrais, Charley, Arthur de Rothschild, Stead, Braun, Barrow, Jenatzy, Hieronimus, de Caters.*

45,000, or a 40-hp Mors for 50,000, and these were the most expensive. In his illustrated magazine *La Vie Automobile*, Louis Baudry de Saunier described the shiny 90-hp racer that Köhler had driven towards Madrid: "It is exceptional work, as usual, and as usual the design is finished in pristine shape." By the turn of the year owner Willie Vanderbilt shipped the racer to Florida, took the wheel in February 1904 on the flat beach of Daytona, and covered the flying mile in 39 seconds: 148.5 km/h, good for a new absolute world record and a 50 percent discount on the next racer! Meanwhile, in Paris, the order books were filled to overflowing, so much that, in March 1904, Charley purchased no. 70 of the Champs-Élysées for one million francs, the future "Mercédès-Palace," with exhibition hall, *grand salon de réception*, French and foreign offices. As a result of the factory fire, Mercedes production had been rehoused in brand-new buildings, not far away from Cannstatt. The offices followed suit and, from 26 May 1904, the DMG headquartered at Untertürkheim.

# 12

## *Hot Favorite*

In order to keep the Bennett Cup within the Mercedes ranks, an opportunistic Jellinek had immediately three additional racers in mind, entered through the Austrian club, manufactured by the DMG branch at Wiener-Neustadt. Duttenhofer was reluctant, and wrote on 11 July 1903: "I disapprove that three 90-hp cars are made at Wiener-Neustadt. But at the same time I want to hear your opinion and I would be prepared to reconsider my resistance if the direction and the engineers are in favor of manufacturing in Austria. First and foremost, I consider the Wiener-Neustadt factory, the equipment and the personnel unsuitable to produce the cars so that there are chances of success." In any case a new, completely revised racer was on the agenda, maybe with steel cylinders. Willie Vanderbilt and his friend George Drexel had paid Jellinek a visit at Nice, proposing to finance a factory for the production of the Mercedes in America. Jellinek had to decline, but since the race towards Madrid Vanderbilt's 11-liter Mors had stayed at Cannstatt, having escaped the factory fire and served as a steel-cylinder sample. Duttenhofer urged Maybach and Brauner "to contact Lorenz since with his assistance it should be possible to make the 80 respective 90-hp cylinders of steel. Yesterday Mister Martin from the English Daimler Co. reported that the steel cylinders of Panhard & Levassor became deformed and oval after the race. These cylinders are made out of a steel billet, thus differently from our procedure at Ettlingen." Jellinek was heart and soul for the new lightweight engine. With steel cylinders his Mercedes would be unbeatable. On 21 July, Duttenhofer dampened the optimism: "Whether there is a possibility to push down the engine weight by 40 kilograms has to arise from the circumstances. I'll prompt Cannstatt to disclose in every weekly report how far the work on the 90-hp engine has got so that I am capable to estimate exactly how to proceed. Everything should be done to bring the project forward."

But Maybach and Brauner came up with a Swabian solution which respected the essential character of the Mercedes: they kept to cast iron pairs, reducing the bore from 170 to 165 mm and retaining the stroke of 140 mm, for a displacement of 12 liters. The valve operation was a synthesis of T- and F-head: The left-hand camshaft operated the standing exhaust valves, the Bosch magneto and the water pump, while its right-hand counterpart activated, via pushrods and rockers, the overhead intake valves and the wipe contacts of the ignition—in principle a T-head whose inlet had been turned upwards by 180°. At first glance, the second camshaft appeared to add unneeded ballast. But Maybach and Brauner mastered the distribution of the stresses, resulting in thinner wall thicknesses and saving the same amount of weight as cylinders made of steel! The intake valves were mounted in a detachable dome, for the purpose of quick access in case of a failure. The handicap of the

June 1904—Gordon Bennett Cup, Taunus. Camille Jenatzy and the new 95-hp Mercedes: Under the hood an entirely new engine, F-head operated via two camshafts.

new layout was the cost. A little brother for the speedy promenader was out of the question. The 12-liter produced 98 hp at 1150 rpm, 105 at 1380, but bore the designation of 95 hp. One part of the weight savings was necessary to avoid the usual trouble with the 1000-kg limit; the other part was invested in better brakes and a stiffer frame. The wheelbase and track were 260 and 145 cm, tires 870 or 910 mm × 90 mm front, 880 or 920 mm × 120 mm rear, and for extravagant customers the combination 920 mm × 120 mm front and huge 1000 mm × 150 mm rear. Upon the recommendation of Jenatzy and von Stern, the steering wheel lever for carburetor control was replaced by an accelerator pedal, between clutch and foot brake. As a result of the Bennett victory, not fewer than fifteen orders came in, from Henri de Rothschild, Dinsmore, Vanderbilt, de Caters, Jenatzy, Harmsworth, Warden and Ferdinand Spiegel. Landgrave Kees insisted on expensive shock absorbers from Truffault. Two racers were delivered to Italy, in July 1904 to Luigi Storero, Turin, Corso Valentino no. 37, and in October to Vincenzo Florio, Palermo. The Sultan of Jahore requested delivery to London, Wellington Court, and Prince Alexis Orloff, with the 1000 mm × 150 mm tires, to Paris, Rue Saint Dominique.

Vincenzo Florio was the initiator of the races of the same name, the Coppa for pure racers, and the Targa for stock chassis which was to be contested for the first time in 1906. Vincenzo was born in 1883 in Palermo, the younger brother of Ignazio who had inherited half of Sicily, a steamboat fleet, the Marsala vineyards,

## 12. Hot Favorite

Spring 1904—Untertürkheim. De Caters taking delivery of his 95 hp. In May, at Ostend, the Baron achieved 156 km/h, a new world record. On the left, Léon Desjoyeaux and Camille Jenatzy. Beyond the steering wheel, with pipe, Pierre de Caters. After the Bennett Cup, the racer was sold to Henri de Rothschild.

the Anglo-Sicilian Sulfur Company, the newspaper *L'Ora* and a chair in the Banca Nationale del Regno, and who was married to the Belle Époque beauty Franca Jacona di San Giuliano, the famous Donna Franca revered by Gabriele d'Annunzio. In 1903, Florio had purchased the Panhard driven by Georges Teste towards Madrid, for 70,000 francs, from Outhenin-Chalandre, a famous dealership located in Neuilly, rue de Chartres no. 4, and directed by Gaëtan de Knyff, René's brother. Felice Nazzaro drove the Panhard to victory in the Coppa della Consuma near Florence and a ten-kilometer sprint between Padua and Bovolenta, and until 1904 was looking after Florio's car collection.

Max von Duttenhofer was not able to enjoy the new racer. On 13 August 1903, he died of a heart attack. A late after-effect of the frictions with the old Daimler? Suddenly Alfred von Kaulla wanted to ascend the throne. But it was Lorenz who took the chair, and his protégé Brauner assumed the place of Maybach, who was feeling ill. On 18 March 1904, Jellinek wrote to him: "It is with the utmost regret that I heard about your sickness and cure. Your absence from Cannstatt is revealed by the infamous finish of the cars which are being delivered. The DMG without Maybach is like Russia without its fleet. I'll ask Spiegel to make enquiries about the doctor. The course of treatment seems very plausible since a neuropathy cannot be healed by medicine. You will be interested to know that the jesuitic DMG, stimulated by the benighted Kaulla and supported by Vischer, is trying to come to terms with a French factory behind my back. If, some years ago, you had accepted my proposal to work with me in France you could be not only a famous but also wealthy man."

On 28 March, the "infamous finish" came to light. At Nice the brand new 12-liters of Jenatzy, Werner, Braun and Warden started in the speed trials. The Gobron-Brilliés of Rigolly and Duray, and even the Napier of Mark Mayhew, ran them over. The Gobron was an oddity, having a frame made of tubes and an L-headed, vertically opposed double piston engine, the lower pistons being linked to the crankshaft in the usual way, the upper ones via long, external connecting rods. A bore of 140 mm and a stroke of twice 110 mm resulted in 13.5 liters and 100 hp at 1100 rpm. Rigolly covered the flying kilometer in 23⅗ sec, standing for 152.5 km/h and a new world record. The best Mercedes lost five seconds. Warden quickly packed up and left: "I return the 95-hp racing car and don't accept it because it is not up to the mark." The frame was unable to handle the power, the springs were too soft. On site Franzini & Ecclesia inserted additional leaves, and on 1 May de Caters was able to counterattack, on the seaside promenade between Ostend (Oostende) and Nieuport (Nieuwpoort), achieving 24.4 sec or 147 km/h, a new Belgian record. Two weeks later he knocked his time down to precisely 23 seconds, equaling 156.5 km/h. The world record was back in the Mercedes camp, a happy omen for a second Cup victory.

Originally, in August 1903, the German club suggested a 130-km circuit near Schwerin, going through Ludwigslust, Parchim, Lübz, Goldberg and Crivitz. But in mid–November, General Becker announced: "The Kaiser has taken a direct interest in the race on the Taunus circuit and the majority of the DAC committee will accept this circuit, despite the numerous blind bends which are typical for a mountain road. I have pointed out these shortcomings, requesting the appraisal of experienced drivers. René de Knyff pronounced himself in favor of the circuit." It was left at that. On Friday, 7 June 1904, four laps of the 141-km Taunus Circuit had to be covered, starting at seven in the morning at Saalburg, then going through seven neutralized control areas at Wehrheim, Usingen, Weilburg, Limburg, Idstein, Königstein and Oberursel, so that 13 km and 58 minutes per lap were not counted. Jellinek was actually able to push through the start of three additional racers, entered by the Austrian club. In return, he had to accept that an Opel, or more exactly a Darracq assembled under license at Rüsselsheim, joined the German team. This did not prevent Adam Opel from complaining and DAC's Baron von Brandenstein had to calm things down:

> By assigning two cars for the Gordon Bennett race to the DMG, the German club has merely taken into account the whole German industry. With regard to previous experiences no German factory except the DMG has built racing cars which ensure a promising representation of Germany. From the six factories which in 1903 announced their participation in a qualification for the 1904 Gordon Bennett race, three withdrew since they were so busy with the production of other cars that they had no opportunity to build racing cars. The intention of two other factories was obviously not honorable since by then they had never built cars of more than 24 hp. By awarding with the greatest willingness the third car to your factory, we intended to show that, apart from the DMG, there are other factories in Germany able to build racing cars and qualified to take part in the classical international contest. Concerning the remark that our present decision has been affected by special interests and unjustified favoritism, we think it is beneath our dignity to reply. An alteration of our statement concerning this year's race is excluded after the confirmations given to the DMG.

## 12. Hot Favorite

Young Fritz Opel was to drive the German Darracq, an F-head 11-liter (160 mm × 140 mm) with shaft drive. Jenatzy and de Caters were selected for the white Mercedes from Untertürkheim, Werner, Braun and Warden for the black-and-yellow racers from Wiener-Neustadt, with Hieronimus and Gastaud as substitute. Just for appearing at the start, the gentlemen drivers Jenatzy, de Caters and Warden collected "one car at choice." In case of a victory they would win an additional one, and for a second-place finish a 6-liter. The participation of Werner and Braun was included in their annual salary of 6000 marks, with a victory bonus of 10,000 francs, with 10 percent of the gentleman driver premium. After all, the DMG bore their insurance and accommodation. In order to become acquainted with the circuit, Untertürkheim made available a couple of 4-liters, which were not really the thing. Hieronimus contacted Jellinek: "For training I beg you for the Mors racing car standing at Cannstatt or for another fast car. It does not matter to you whether such an old car is rusting or in good hands with me."

The French could not avoid an elimination race. There were more than enough candidates to choose from. In the third week of May 1904, on the Circuit de l'Argonne, in the French Ardennes west of Reims, 29 racers competed for a ticket to the Taunus, the old marques against a pack of highly dangerous newcomers: Panhard, Mors, Serpollet, Darracq, Gobron, Turcat-Méry and De Dietrich against Richard-Brasier, Hotchkiss and Clément-Bayard. The barely known Léon Théry, formerly on the road at the wheel of a "voiturelle" from Decauville, drove the

May 1904—French Bennett elimination, Circuit de l'Argonne. J. T. Alexander Burton at the wheel of his Gobron-Brillié.

brand-new Brasier to victory, covering six laps of 94 km in 5 h 20 min 28 sec, ten minutes ahead of Marcel Salleron's Mors and fifteen minutes ahead of Henri Rougier's "Tarasque." Henri Brasier had drawn on his wealth of experience at Mors. His Brasier was perfectly fitted to the 1000-kg formula, combined a solid, chain-drive frame (wheelbase 260 cm, track 125 cm, tires 810 mm × 90 mm front, 820 mm × 120 mm rear) with a compact L-head 10-liter (150 mm × 140 mm) which delivered 80 hp, in principle an L-head *voiture légère* engine à la Renault or Darracq mounted in a chain drive chassis à la Mercedes Sixty. As could be expected, the Richard-Brasier was not among the fastest racers but was the most versatile: "From Théry's race we have learned that the winning car is the less powerful and the slowest over a flying kilometer." The latest Mors displaced 13.5 liters with the new dimensions of 170 mm × 150 mm.

The "Tarasque" was the latest Turcat-Méry (155 mm × 170 mm), sucking its mixture through four atmospheric intake valves—a dragon emerging from the Rhône near Tarascon to devour the young virgins. When the Turcat-Méry team, en route from Marseille to the Circuit de l'Argonne, stopped at Lyon to pass the night and to brush up the racers at the garage Ailloud-Dumont, rue Duhamel, a mechanic stained the hood with grease. Rougier was distraught. What now? A paint brush transformed the mark into the head of a dragon and the apprentice exclaimed in south–French patois: "Mais c'est la Tarasque!" The Turcat of the great Gabriel, entered under the name of licensee De Dietrich, the Serpollet steamers, the proud

May 1904—Ivry. The Richard-Brasier team about to leave for the elimination race on the Circuit de l'Argonne. On the left, Léon Théry; standing, Henri Brasier; in the middle, Gustave Caillois; on the right, E. T. Stead.

## 12. Hot Favorite

**May 1904—French Bennett elimination race, Circuit de l'Argonne. La Tarasque: the dragon-headed Turcat-Méry (155 mm × 170 mm) of Henri Rougier.**

Panhards, the Bayards, and the new racers of the gun company Hotchkiss and the Darracqs failed to qualify. (Since 1903, Adolphe Clément was allowed to use the name of the famous Chevalier Bayard.)

The English elimination took place in the Irish Sea, on the Isle of Man. Eleven racers, three Darracqs built by the Glasgow company of G. & J. Weir, three Wolseleys designed by a young Herbert Austin, and five Napiers turned up for a series of tests including a hillclimb. "On the basis of the judges' somewhat esoteric calculations," the first three places were awarded to the Napier (165 mm × 152 mm) of Edge and the Wolseleys (152 mm × 165 mm) of Sidney Girling and Jarrott, with the Napiers of Stocks and Hargreaves as reserves. F.I.A.T., the Fabbrica Italiana Automobili Torino, manned its team with Vincenzo Lancia, Luigi Storero and Alessandro Cagno. The time of the rear-engine designs of Aristide Faccioli was over. Giovanni Enrico and Cesare Momo charted the course now, relying on a big Simplex, a T-head 14-liter (165 mm × 165 mm) mounted in a rather bulky frame, wheelbase 288.5 cm, tires 910 mm × 90 mm front, 920 mm × 120 mm rear. But the gems came from Brussels, from the Compagnie Belge de Construction Automobile, three Pipes with Pierre de Crawhez, jeweler Auger and former champion cyclist Lucien Hautvast. The fine machinery arose from the board of Otto Pfänder, the one-time gearbox designer of the original Mercedes! Of course Pfänder used a T-head as his basis, but eliminated the bothersome pockets by turning the valves upwards, intake and exhaust inclined at 60° from the cylinder axis, operated by two side-mounted camshafts, pushrods and rockers. In the 13.5-liter

(175 mm × 140 mm) one-tonner, the OHV engine could not make full use of the advantages of its hemispherical combustion chamber. But the Pfänder idea caught on, in 1910 in a Prince Henry sprinter from Benz, in 1911 and 1913 in the racers from Delage, and later in the ERA and the Talbot-Lago. The Swiss Dufaux, with exotic eight cylinders and mysterious front wheel brakes, did not start; the steering broke on the eve of the race.

White was the color for Germany, green for England, black-and-yellow for Austria, black for Italy, blue for France and yellow for Belgium. The teams were:

| No. | Driver | | |
|---|---|---|---|
| 1, 8, 14 | Jenatzy | de Caters | Opel |
| 2, 9, 15 | Edge | Girling | Jarrott |
| 3, 10, 16 | Werner | Braun | Warden |
| 4, 11, 17 | Lancia | Storero | Cagno |
| 5, 12, 18 | Théry | Salleron | Rougier |
| 6, 13, 19 | de Crawhez | Augières | Hautvast |

It was seven o'clock when starter Molitor von Mühlfeld dispatched no. 1 Jenatzy. The Belgian shot away, as usual. His Majesty saluted. De Caters lost fifteen minutes, cleaning the oily wipe contacts of the ignition. The Austro-Mercedes misfired. Opel's Opel broke down, just a few kilometers after the start, with a fractured drive shaft. Jenatzy had carried out numberless training and practice laps, studying every pebble of the Taunus circuit. He drove like a demon through the pine forests. The crowd was enthused and quickly found a proper name for him: the Red Devil, since red was the beard and devilish the driving style. With a time of 1 h 26 min 56 sec for the opening lap, the Belgian Mephisto took the lead, though just one second ahead of the unknown Théry on the unknown Brasier, four minutes ahead of the surprisingly fast Edge, then the Wolseleys of Girling and Jarrott and the F.I.A.T. of Alessandro Cagno, the chauffeur of Queen Marguerita. De Caters and his Austrian confrères followed far away. The Court was

The Bennett course in the Taunus region near Frankfurt (from *La Vie Automobile*, 1904).

June 1904—Gordon Bennett Cup, Taunus. The black-and-yellow Austro-Mercedes of John B. Warden.

June 1904—Gordon Bennett Cup, Taunus. The Belgian Pipe of Lucien Hautvast.

unconcerned, the Kaiser joking and chatting with ACF president de Zuylen, Prince Henry attending the breakfast buffet, and Dinsmore, in correct formal attire of top hat and striped trousers, being much in evidence.

In the second lap, troubles assailed the English team. Near Limburg, Edge was fixing the steering of his Napier and Jarrott the governing gear of his Wolseley. The Mercedes of Werner was boiling. The Mors of Salleron lost a driving chain. The Red Devil opened up as never before. On the run down the long hill towards Limburg, *Der Motorwagen* clocked 180 km/h. That figure may have been exaggerated, but 160 was certainly possible. Anyhow, with 2 h 53 min 43 sec, the chubby Théry and his handy Brasier took the lead, 1 min 46 sec ahead of Jenatzy, then Girling, Cagno, Jarrott and de Caters. The Austro-Mercedes combo of Braun, Werner and Warden were without a chance in positions nine, 13 and 14. In round three, it was the turn of the leaders. At the Limburg control, Jenatzy's Mercedes refused to start, losing six minutes, and Théry had to remove a damaged cooling fan. De Caters overtook Jarrott, who was struggling with the gearbox and a leaky radiator, and Cagno. Théry increased his lead to 9 min 35 sec. Jenatzy was the first to cross the finish, shrouded in dust and oil, no trace of his red beard visible. The crowd waited for Théry. Was the Brasier unable to stand the pace? Would the Mercedes come off as winner after all? No! "Monsieur chronomètre" Théry and mechanic Muller gave the Red Devil the coup de grâce, set the lap record and won in 5 h 50 min 3 sec, defeating Jenatzy

June 1904—Gordon Bennett Cup, Taunus. The Mercedes of Pierre de Caters.

June 1904—Gordon Bennett Cup, Taunus. A horde of attendants swarming around Warden's Austro-Mercedes to change the tires.

June 1904—Gordon Bennett Cup, Taunus. The Austro-Mercedes of Wilhelm Werner, and a spiked helmet announcing his imminent restart.

June 1904—Gordon Bennett Cup, Taunus. The unknown Brasier of the unknown Théry.

June 1904—Gordon Bennett Cup, Taunus. The Mercedes of de Caters crossing the line for fourth place.

by 11 min 25 sec. Rougier took third place, de Caters fourth, Braun fifth, Werner eleventh. The *Frankfurter General-Anzeiger* wrote: "The Kaiser warmly congratulated the president of the ACF, Baron de Zuylen, the designer of the winning car, Monsieur Brasier, and the tire manufacturer Michelin."

On 25 July, the pack of the Cup losers let off steam in the third Circuit des Ardennes. Thirty-three racers had to cover five laps of 118 km, among them the Mercedes duo of Terry and Fletcher. Panhard, after mounting conventional radiators in order to avoid the cooling troubles encountered during the Argonne elimination, regained the leading position. Georges Heath, an American resident of Paris, took the victory for the *marque doyenne* in six and a half hours, with a narrow margin over his teammate, the popular tricycle star Georges Teste, who set a lap record in 1 h 10 min 23 sec. Terry's Mercedes broke down on the first lap. Scotsman Andrew Fletcher, handling the older Eighty driven by Hieronimus towards Madrid, made every effort and finished one and one half hours behind Heath.

In the meantime, the Jellinek squad had other things in mind. In August the focus was racing on the water. In the shipyard of Pitre & Cie., at Maisons-Laffitte, it was all about the *Mercedes III* and the *Mercedes IV*, entered for the power-boat race from Calais to Dover. The Compagnie du Nord provided a special train. The

August 1904—Calais–Dover. The *Mercedes IV* was manufactured by Pitre & Cie. at Maisons-Laffitte, with a hull design by A. Védrine. Powered by a 95-hp engine, she covered 22 sea miles in 1 h 7 sec.

German and the British admiralty sent observers. The 95-hp ran like clockwork. The *Mercedes IV* averaged 40 km/h and won, just as it did one week later in the great Paris-to-the-Sea race towards the estuary of the Seine, and at the end of the month in the Coupe Drexel between Trouville and Deauville.

In September the F.I.A.T. of Lancia took the first Coppa Florio near Brescia. The Panhard of Teste was second, the 95-hp Mercedes of cup sponsor Vincenzo Florio third. On Saturday, 8 October 1904, the "First International Competition for the William K. Vanderbilt Jr. Cup" was held on Long Island, ten laps of 48.4 km, including Jericho, Bethpage and Hempstead Turnpike, starting at Westbury. No fewer than five Mercedes were entered, four Sixties with A. L. Campbell, George Arents, Ed Hawley and Willy "William" Lüttgen, and the Dinsmore-owned 95-hp with Wilhelm Werner. Again it was a Panhard affair and again it was Heath who won the silver Tiffany cup, followed by young Albert Clément at the wheel of a Bayard and Herb Lytle on the American Pope-Toledo. Wilhelm Werner ran out of tires. Arents crashed. Hawley shattered the front springs at a railway crossing. When the race was stopped because of the feckless conduct of the crowd, Campbell was fifth and Lüttgen sixth, in his first race, at the wheel of Isidore Wormser's Sixty.

The competition got noticeably closer. On 29 October 1904, track specialist Willy Poege reported to Jellinek:

> It is certainly interesting for you that for the recent race at Hamburg Darracq has sent a 650-kg car with an engine of 150 mm bore and 145 mm stroke. Thus the engine was larger than the 60-hp Mercedes, the weight of the car 350 kg lighter. Although the car is certainly not suitable for longer distances, on a track it cannot be beaten anymore by the 60-hp since, due to the low weight, it can be slowed down very briskly and moreover does not sink in the soft track. If it is of particular

October 1904—Vanderbilt Cup, Long Island, New York. Willy Lüttgen and mechanic Kleinbeck in the Mercedes Sixty owned by banker Isidore Wormser, Jr..

## 12. Hot Favorite

**In June 1904, the Austrian DMG branch of Wiener-Neustadt delivered a 95-hp to Ferdinand Spiegel. During the course of the year, the racer received a red tonneau body.**

importance for you to win in the numerous track races which are held in Germany during the next year, the 60-hp would not suffice anymore. Since on the other hand these races are a good promotion it would perhaps be auspicious to build a car especially for this aim. Finally I am intending to buy a new touring car and in fact I wish to take again a 60-hp model but of current type and 1905 model. I inquire if you could give me such a car at a slightly lower price.

Poege had the new 70-hp in mind that Charley displayed in the Grand Palais at the end of the year, for the bargain price of 45,000 francs. Second place in the Bennett Cup was no disgrace but beat down the prices. Henri Brasier, who was just suing his associate Georges Richard for the future use of the factory at Ivry-Port and the name Richard, was bringing off the big deals now, selling on the spot two of the Bennett racers, each one for 70,000 francs, to Baron Fedor Nicolics and New York millionaire William Gould Brokaw who had purchased a Mercedes Eighty just one year before. Thereby, with the new Seventy for 45,000, the sportsmen were served as never before. In his luxury magazine *L'Automobile*, Gaston Sencier described a real mechanical marvel, "une vraie merveille de la mécanique." Josef Brauner had combined the 140 mm × 150 mm dimensions of the F-head Sixty with the more-accessible T-head of the Simplex, including the latest refinements. The cylinder pairs were more widely spaced allowing a larger center main bearing which was lubricated by a gear pump. The spur wheels spun at the front now, cleanly enclosed in an aluminum casing. By dint of a foot accelerator the sportsman was able to liberate 75 hp at 1400 rpm, making the 9-liter in the compact 215 or 250 cm frame now barely meeker than the pure racer!

# 13

# *Muscle Car*

In the spring of 1905, Untertürkheim could take its time since the meeting of Nice had definitively lost its status. The Riviera, however, was still in vogue. At the beginning of April, the sportsmen gathered at Monaco, the perfect place for a power-boat event. The Monte Carlo bay was teeming with Bennett engines. Charley came with the 12-meter racer *Mercedes VI*, Gustave Caillois with the Brasier-engined *Petit-Trèfle*, Maurice Farman with the *Palaisoto II*, Henry Fournier with the *Hotchkiss I*, Edge with the *Napier*, and Madame Camille du Gast with her *Turquoise*. Prince Albert de Monaco stayed aboard his *Physalie*. And a proud Jellinek displayed his *Mercedes-Mercedes*, an 18-meter yacht powered by two 95-hp engines. Paul Daimler recalled: "Jellinek complained about the work on his boat. But the men from Wiener-Neustadt were seasick. I suggested he go aboard himself, with the ulterior motive that he too would sicken. But he smelt the rat and slipped a few one-hundred-francs notes into my hands in order to cheer the men up." Monaco emerged as the perfect sales booth for racing cars: The Roman Demartini, Robert W. Graves and Alberto Santos-Dumont placed orders, in addition to the regular customers, Florio, Dinsmore, de Rothschild, de Caters, Keene and Warden.

In the absence of Maybach, who was taking the cure, Josef Brauner did not have any inhibitions about upgrading the 12-liter. Power was the keynote. Brauner took over the general layout of the previous year: the cylinders formed in pairs from iron castings, the F-head operated by two side mounted camshafts, and the chain-drive chassis. But, with the exception of the track, he stretched everything. The engine of 175 mm × 146 mm displaced 14 liters and developed 125 hp at 1300 rpm. The weight saved by a new compact gearbox was invested in the frame length: wheelbase 290 cm, track 140 cm, tires 870 mm × 90 mm front and 880 mm × 120 mm rear. "The DAC does not consider it necessary to organize an elimination race since none of the German factories is willing to compete against your cars and newspaper reports on this matter have to be regarded as mere advertising." Thus six racers were nominated to defend the Mercedes colors, three white ones from Untertürkheim and three black-and-yellow ones from Wiener-Neutstadt. It was all haywire. The Austrians forgot to order new axles at the Poldi ironworks and had to mount the old ones. Then the drawings of the differential castings were missing, and the brake shoes were too small. In the second week of April, the first engine was bench tested: "Compression only 36 percent. Have riveted seven-millimeter plates on the pistons. Engine output 90 hp at 1050 rpm."

Dirt track champion Willy Poege had hopes of getting a ride: "Baron von Brandenstein told me that you agree to leave the third car to me." But Jellinek declined at the last moment, suggesting Jenatzy, de Caters and Werner for the white

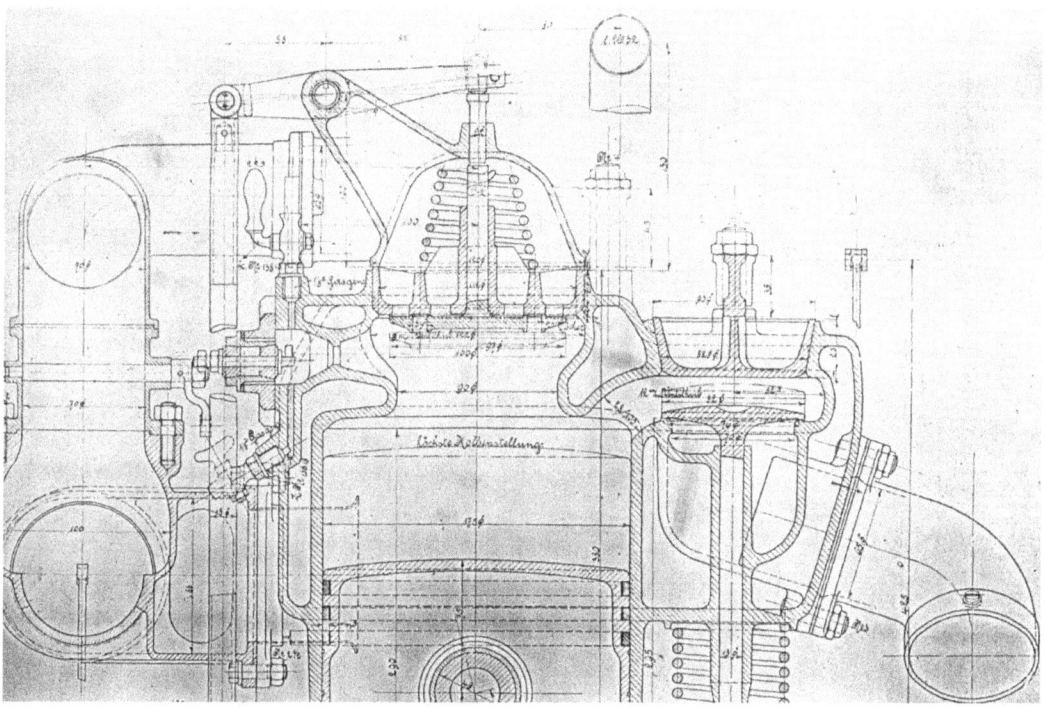

Cylinder head of the 1905 Mercedes: design by Josef Brauner, 175 mm × 146 mm, 14 liters, 125 hp at 1300 rpm, engine weight 440 kg.

team, Braun, Hieronimus and Burton for the black-and-yellow one. (J. T. Alexander Burton was a prominent customer from the power-boat scene, an exceedingly rich—and heavyweight—Englishman living in Cannes.) Hieronimus wrote to Jellinek: "I accept your conditions: 5000 marks for the start, 25,000 marks for a victory, 5000 marks for second place. Please arrange to take out an insurance for me. I would like to have mechanic Schloz as co-driver."

On 28 December 1904, the Commission Sportive of the ACF had decided in favor of a circuit near Clermont-Ferrand, in the sparsely populated volcanic region of the Auvergne: Four laps of 137.5 km, start in Laschamps, via the Col de la Moreno, through Rochefort, Bourg-Lastic, Herment, Pontaumur and Pontgibaud. Of course the French used the circuit for their *éliminatoires*, good for a lot of training. On 16 June, 24 racers lined up on the Plateau de Laschamps. Mors, Serpollet and Turcat-Méry were missing, but a CGV, an Automoto and three Renaults were present. Henri Brasier had increased the bore (160 mm × 140 mm) in order to counter the reborn Panhards. Théry drove cautiously, as was his habit. Panhard driver Maurice Farman missed a turn, and found himself engaged on a short cut through the woods to the valley below. He and co-driver Monge were thrown out, caught in the branches of the trees, Farman higher than his mechanic. He pulled out his cigarette case and, looking down, quietly remarked: "I wish you would pass me a match up, Tom." The Brasiers of Léon Théry and Gustave Caillois took first and second place. With the help of the elemental force of a T-head 17-liter (190 mm × 150 mm), the monumental De Dietrich of Arthur Duray, described as a Belgian

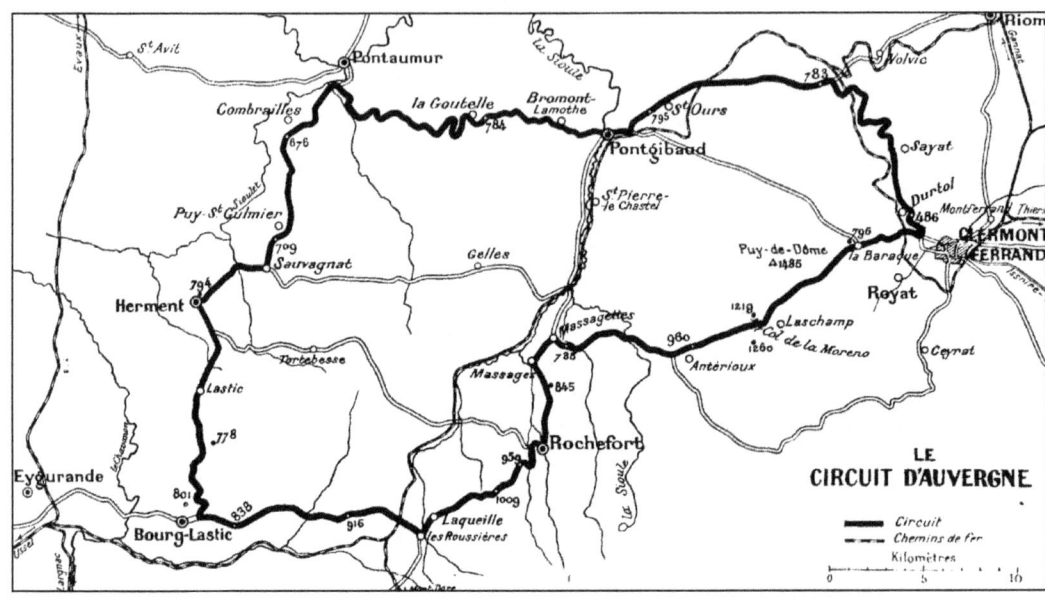

Le Circuit d'Auvergne, length 137.5 km (from *L'Automobile*, 1905).

June 1905—French GB elimination race, Auvergne. The Brasier of E. T. Stead passing through Laqueille. The Englishman missed the qualification. But his confrères Théry and Caillois finished first and second.

## 13. Muscle Car

July 1905—Gordon Bennett Cup, Auvergne. Third Frenchman: the De Dietrich of Arthur Duray.

born in New York and living in Paris, was third and completed the French Bennett team.

The Englishmen shipped their racers again to the Isle of Man, having selected two Wolseleys (152 mm × 152 mm) and a Napier (165 mm × 152 mm) to be handled by Rolls, Bianchi and Clifford Earp. The Automobile Club of America entered the well-tried Pope-Toledos (140 mm × 140 mm) of Herb Lytle and Bert Dingley, and the Locomobile of Joe Tracy, a huge T-head 17.7-liter (178 mm × 178 mm), almost an American De Dietrich. Relief driver was Carl Fisher, who would later found the Indianapolis speedway. Italy was represented by a trio of the latest F.I.A.T. racers driven by Lancia, Cagno and Florio protégé Felice Nazzaro. Turin had replaced the T-head by a more effective OHV arrangement, intake and exhaust each inclined at 30° from the cylinder axis, operated by push rods and rockers from a single side-mounted camshaft. Among the connoisseurs, 23-year-old Coppa Florio winner Lancia was the general favorite. Actually, Vincenzo was an accountant, having served his apprenticeship at the vélo and automobile factory of Giovanni Ceirano, but preferred to put his nose in the engines. When Giovanni Agnelli took over Ceirano & Cie. to establish his F.I.A.T., Lancia was promoted to chief tester. The contest between the typical Latin racer Lancia, the Red Devil Jenatzy, the speedy mechanic Werner and the "chronometer" Théry promised a great race. Charles Jarrott predicted a "titanic struggle between the Brasier and Mercedes teams," Dinsmore was, as usual, predisposed towards Jenatzy, and Henri de Rothschild saw a battle between

Baron de Caters and Signor Lancia. One very good reason for the probable success of the Mercedes was "that as they are so much faster than the Brasier machines they can afford to lose time on the curves, thus sparing their tires and relying on straight pieces of road to make up their average."

Wiener-Neustadt dispatched one of the 14-liters at the very last minute. The "docile giant" Burton was forced to take the wheel of an older 95-hp for practice, while Jenatzy had mounted a cinematograph on the radiator in order to record the intricacies of the Auvergne circuit. On Tuesday, 4 July, the racers were pushed to the holy *pesage*. "Weighing in was conducted in a manner similar to that previous to the elimination race, with the exception that members of foreign clubs were permitted to enter the tent. The press was rigorously excluded for some reason or other. Mr. Gray Dinsmore did not like the method at all, and believed the only just method was to hold the weighing-in in the presence of the whole public who might if it liked raise objections to various points." Several machines were found to be overweight, but all were reduced in the traditional manner. The 1006 kilos of Jenatzy's Mercedes could not be closer to the limit while the 984 of Dingley's Pope-Toledo were ticked off on the spot. F.I.A.T. tried by every means to strip unnecessary components. And had the Italian Michelins really been made in Italy? Right in the middle of it the sportsmen went to dinner, execrating the cuisine of the Auvergne. The discussions dragged on. Cagno's F.I.A.T. was on the scales and Dinsmore was snoring in a quiet nook when a thunderstorm blew away the marquee. The Mercedes had already been driven back to their camp at Royat. On Wednesday, 5 July, promptly at six in the morning, starter Tampier dispatched the racers at five-minute intervals:

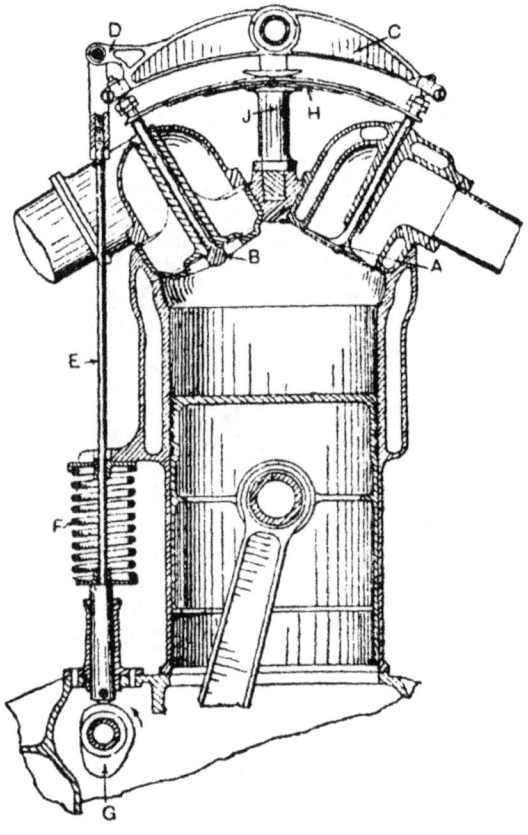

**OHV-head of the Fiat (from *La France Automobile*, 1906).**

| *No.* | *Driver* | | |
|---|---|---|---|
| 1, 7, 13 | Théry | Caillois | Duray |
| 2, 8, 14 | Earp | Rolls | Bianchi |
| 3, 9, 15 | Jenatzy | de Caters | Werner |
| 4, 10, 16 | Lancia | Cagno | Nazzaro |
| 5, 11, 17 | Braun | Hieronimus | Burton |
| 6, 12, 18 | Lytle | Dingley | Tracy |

July 1905—Gordon Bennett Cup, Auvergne. The hoodless Pope-Toledo of Herb Lytle at the Rochefort control. The stiff hills and sharp turns required constant mixture adjustments, which had not been necessary during the trials on a three-mile straight near the factory!

July 1905—Gordon Bennett Cup, Auvergne. The Locomobile of Joe Tracy broke down.

July 1905—Gordon Bennett Cup, Auvergne. Mercedes camp at Royat, a few kilometers to the southwest of Clermont-Ferrand. The racers of Werner, Hieronimus and Burton.

July 1905—Gordon Bennett Cup, Auvergne. Coming out of the hairpin at Rochefort, Hermann Braun tried hard to avoid excessive wheel spin.

Werner had a fine start, covering the first 1850 meters to the hairpin at the foot of the Col de la Moreno in 57 seconds, Jenatzy in 59, Burton in 60, de Caters in 63, Braun and Théry in 64, Hieronimus in 72. Halfway up the Col, the no. 3 Mercedes ran out of steam because of oily ignition contacts. At Rochefort, a tire valve unscrewed. And at Pontgibaud, a leaf spring broke. It was a bad day for the Red Devil. Théry was the first to finish the opening lap, but Lancia secured the lead in 1 h 34 min 57 sec. Monsieur chronomètre followed nine minutes back, Werner in position six, Braun eighth, de Caters ninth, Hieronimus tenth, Jenatzy on twelfth, Burton sixteenth. The weight distribution of the Mercedes was unsuited to the mountain circuit. The combination of long straights, switchbacks and hairpins resulted in constant tire trouble. All the racers used clincher-type soft-bead tires, pumped up at five bars (72.5 psi) front and seven bars (101.5 psi) rear, properly held on by several bolts placed at intervals around the rim. In the case of the Mercedes, the interaction of inappropriate set-up and high speeds quickly generated so much heat that the tires were overvulcanised. The casings gradually disintegrated and wore out, separating the fabric layers and causing the threads to cut each other, with the consequence of a blow-out. Most of the time, the bang was innocuous, and the racer was able to reach a neutralized section where it was not necessary that the driver and the mechanic should do all the work.

July 1905—Gordon Bennett Cup, Auvergne. The Austro-Mercedes of Hermann Braun at the Rochefort control.

July 1905—Gordon Bennett Cup, Auvergne. The Fiat of Felice Nazzaro about to start. (Fiat)

July 1905—Gordon Bennett Cup, Auvergne. Wilhelm Werner changing the right hand front tire of his Mercedes. In the background the Brasier of Théry.

## 13. Muscle Car

A horde of attendants would swarm down on the car. There was no time to lever the tires off; they were simply cut off the rims by the use of suitable knives. But, when a blow-out or a puncture came away from the controls, precious minutes were lost. Théry had all four of his tires changed in an amazing five and one-half minutes:

> The men in charge, some twenty perhaps in number, rush upon the machine in a mass as it arrives and with patent jacks have it off the ground in an instant. A gang sets to work on each cover. Two strokes of a knife are given and the worn envelope is off. The bolts are unscrewed and the rim is free for the new tube and cover. One bead is slipped beneath the rim, and with a handy instrument the other is forced into place. There is no struggling, all goes as mechanically as the action of the motor itself. Each wheel is receiving individual attention. At last the cover is in place, the bolts are screwed up, and, as they are being screwed, another man places on the valve a tube connected with a cylinder in which compressed air is stored. All this done, the captain of the gang shouts "ready!," a turn of a handle is given, and the whole four tyres are inflated.

It was just while Théry's Brasier was undergoing this operation that Lancia swept past: "Yes, he is going fast, faster than I am, in fact, but I think we shall see him again before the end."

Lancia continued to increase his lead. The Frenchmen became worried. For

July 1905—Gordon Bennett Cup, Auvergne. The Austro-Mercedes of Otto Hieronimus at the *virage de Rochefort,* the Rochefort hairpin.

July 1905—Gordon Bennett Cup, Auvergne. The Mercedes of Jenatzy entering the Rochefort hairpin.

July 1905—Gordon Bennett Cup, Auvergne. Léon Théry, mechanic Muller, and their Brasier: four victories in succession.

July 1905—Gordon Bennett Cup, Auvergne. Wilhelm Werner at work in the Mercedes, in the middle of the *Grand Tournant*, in his last race. He became the personal chauffeur of the Kaiser, His Majesty's *Oberwagenführer*.

the third time Théry crossed the line at Laschamps. Henri Brasier was chewing up his cigar. The F.I.A.T. was faster. Suddenly a message came from the mountains that a stone had penetrated the F.I.A.T.'s radiator, causing a piston to seize up. Théry drove his Brasier to victory in 7 h 2 min 42 sec. Nazzaro and Cagno took second and third place for Italy and F.I.A.T., more than fifteen minutes back. The Brasier of Caillois finished fourth, the De Dietrich of Duray sixth, and the Mercedes trio Werner, de Caters and Braun fifth, seventh and tenth. Jenatzy withdrew with another broken spring. Brasier was the heir of the *marque doyenne*. The Italians too had put on a fine performance, and team manager Enrico Marchesi was carried on the shoulders of his countrymen. Herb Lytle finished twelfth and last: "At the very first round the main oil-pipe from my reservoir was punctured by stones from the route. Oil was shot out on me and my machinist in streams and my goggles were clouded so that I could not see before me. My machinist with his hand kept in as much of the oil as possible, and, despite our speed and the necessity of following the route, he managed to keep up the strain until the end." Paris–Berlin winner Henry Fournier said "that he considered Théry not merely a clever driver, but positively miraculous. His automobile was perfectly 'au point', and he is of opinion that all four of Théry's great victories were won in advance by reason of Brasier's sound technical knowledge. The Brasier machines are put on the road months before any of the others, and drivers practice with them until they make, so to speak, part and parcel of the same vehicle. The revelation of the race has been the wonderful F.I.A.T. performance. The F. I.A.T. team was the finest in the field, and under normal conditions they cannot be beaten."

One month later, on 7 August, the muscle cars of Jenatzy and de Caters encountered the Darracqs of Hémery, Wagner and Montjoie, the De Dietrichs of Gabriel, Rougier and Duray, the Panhards of Teste, Tart, Heath and Le Blon, the CGV of Behr and the dewy Itala of Maurice Fabry. In the fourth Circuit des Ardennes, five laps of 120 km had to be covered. The CGV did not survive the start, as the drive shaft flew away. Teste changed a tire, losing three minutes. Gabriel overturned, escaping serious injury. Wagner was in the lead, ahead of Rougier, Tart and Jenatzy. De Caters was off form because of rheumatism. In lap two, the brand-new Itala broke down. Jenatzy worked up into second place, closely behind Rougier, ahead of Hémery. But in lap four, the Red Devil caught a nail. By the time his Mercedes came to a standstill the rim was destroyed. Victor Hémery came in the victor for Darracq while de Caters finished sixth, 42 minutes back. The Darracq (150 mm × 140 mm) was the first OHV engined racer to win a main event. Devised by Paul Ribeyrolles, it had vertical valves operated by one side-mounted camshaft, pushrods and rockers, producing 85 hp at 1250 rpm in a rather short frame: wheelbase 240 cm, tires 810 mm × 90 mm front, 820 mm × 120 mm rear.

August 1905—Circuit des Ardennes: *Pesage*. The Mercedes of Jenatzy weighed in at 1005 kg. On lap four, the Red Devil caught a nail and retired with a twisted rim.

On 10 September 1905, 21 racers battled for the second Coppa Florio near Brescia, including five Mercedes, Florio himself, his friend Cortese, newcomer Marieaux, Gastaud and Terry. To the delight of the Tifosi, Vincenzo Florio had painted the family crest on the tank! Hubert Le Blon turned up at the wheel of an enormous Isotta-Fraschini, an OHC 17-liter (185 mm × 160 mm) designed by a young Giustino Cattaneo. But the Isotta was ahead of the times; it did not run properly, quickly broke down and disappeared from the scene. The race was left to Hémery in a Darracq, Rougier and Duray in De Dietrichs, Lancia in a F.I.A.T. and, to the surprise of all, Ceirano and Raggio in an Itala. And, after three laps of 167 km and 4 h 46 min 47 sec, Giovan Battista Raggio won, averaging 105.3 km/h, ahead of Duray, Lancia and Hémery. The Mercedes brigade badly disappointed. Florio was just able to secure ninth place, Terry eleventh; the others broke down. Untertürkheim was glum. Hadn't Conte Carletto Raggio purchased a Sixty? At Turin, Via Petrarca, future general manager Guido Bigio, technical director Alberto Ballocco and—although he was to leave the company in the course of the year—co-founder Matteo Ceirano got down to work immediately, adopted the F-head, and within one year designed a flawless, updated 180 mm × 145 mm copy of the German Eighty. Should Josef Brauner have continued to develop the original one-camshaft layout? The Itala shot to fame, became the *voiture chic*. Cagno and de Caters switched sides. Queen Marguerita placed an order, as did even Jellinek, wanting to make a close inspection.

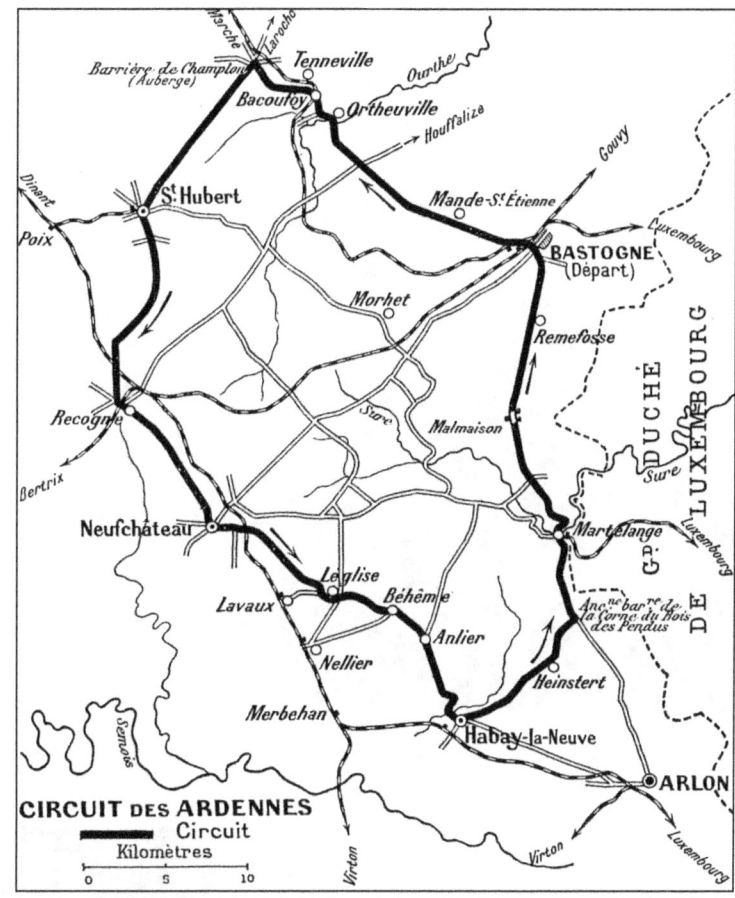

The Circuit des Ardennes: five laps of 120 km, starting in Bastogne (from *L'Automobile*, 1905).

On 14 October, it was time for the second Vanderbilt Cup on Long Island, a distance of ten laps of 45.6 km. The 125-hps of Jenatzy, Keene, Warden and Campbell competed against the De Dietrich of Duray, the Pope-Toledos of Dingley and

August 1905—Circuit des Ardennes. The Mercedes of Pierre de Caters just after the start.

September 1905—Coppa Florio, Brescia. Giovan Battista Raggio at the wheel of the winning Itala.

August 1905—Circuit des Ardennes. The Darracq of Victor Hémery leading the Panhard of Hubert Le Blon.

Lytle, the F.I.A.T. quartet of Lancia, Cedrino, Chevrolet and Sartori, the Darracqs of Wagner and Hémery, the Locomobile of Tracy, the Renault of Szisz, the Panhard of Heath, the front-drive Christie of Christie and the White steamer of White. The racers of Warden and Keene came directly from the factory, with extended stroke, 175 mm × 150 mm, 14.4 liters, good for better torque. Latin racer Lancia jumped into the lead, ahead of Jenatzy and Szisz. Keene was eighth, Warden tenth, and Campbell far back by reason of gearbox trouble. Jenatzy went out with a broken wheel. Suddenly Warden pressed Lancia and Keene speeded up. When getting under way after a fuel stop, Lancia was struck by Christie. Hémery took first place and won in 4 h 36 min 8 sec, ahead of Heath, Tracy and Lancia, who had repaired his racer.

In November, sad news came from New York, when sportsman Clarence Gray Dinsmore died of pneumonia, aged 58. Henceforth Wilhelm Werner drove for Kaiser Wilhelm; the reaction of DAC's highborn Ratibor remained unpublished. The days of Panhard and Mors were definitively numbered. The great sport had gradually become an international spectacle and a commercial rivalry. In 1905, for the first time, American car production was in the lead. The French position was shaky. It was high time for the Grand Prix.

# 14

# *Grand Prix*

Despite the Brasier victories, Paris rebelled against the Coupe Bennett, the three-car-to-a-nation rule being unacceptable. What about the 20 non-qualified racers in an elimination which was hardly of a lower level than the main event itself? Far too many manufacturers were left on the sidelines. In the autumn of 1904, on the occasion of the Salon, the French manufacturers began to get their club moving, requested a merging of elimination and Cup, a race for all, a "Grand Prix de l'Automobile Club de France." On 18 January 1905, the Commission Sportive agreed to a first set of rules governing the Grand Prix, drawn up by Louis de Chasseloup-Laubat. Clause no. 3 stated that the first 15 in the French elimination were qualified to start in the Grand Prix, the first three in both the Cup and the Grand Prix. Clauses no. 5, 6 and 7 defined the number of cars from other nations, six from Germany and Great Britain, three from Italy, Switzerland, Austria, the United States of America and Belgium, including the Bennett racers. Actually even odds for all parties—for all *French* parties. Unsurprisingly there was a storm of protest and not a single consent from non–French countries. Thus the club invited all the high priests to the Hôtel Pastoret: de Zuylen, de Dion, de Knyff, de Vogüé, Julian Orde, Adalbert Sierstorpff, Mario Monta, Prince von Solms-Braunfels, de Crawhez and Baron von Sulzer, of course each one in company of his servant. On 20 February 1905, in the late afternoon, the parties agreed to run the Coupe Bennett under the existing rules, with the Grand Prix to follow two weeks later. But the French manufacturers demanded a single main race per year, a "championnat du monde." At the beginning of March, the ACF cancelled the Grand Prix for 1905, and in June, it announced that it would not organize the Coupe Bennett in 1906, no matter what the outcome of the 1905 race, but the Grand Prix instead. It was left at that.

When, in January 1906, a meeting was held to choose the circuit, the Commission Sportive was still wavering between the Circuit de la Brie near Melun and the Circuit de la Sarthe to the west of Le Mans, since no one was able to submit the requested 100,000 francs! Sarthe was more effective in collecting money. The mayors of Sceaux-sur-Huisne, Champagné and Montaillé insisted on contributing the surplus of their borough fund. Conneré postponed the market day, for the first time since the 1789 revolution! The Western Railway Company subscribed 5000 francs. The popular newspaper *L'Auto* put on several special trains. On 21 April, the Comédie Française produced a special performance of "Ruy Blas" starring Mademoiselle Delvair, Albert Lambert and Paul Monnet. The circuit was a flat and fast triangle between Le Mans, Saint-Calais and La Ferté-Bernard, with wooden tracks by-passing Saint-Calais and Vibraye, over a length of 103.18 km, certainly two-thirds of which would

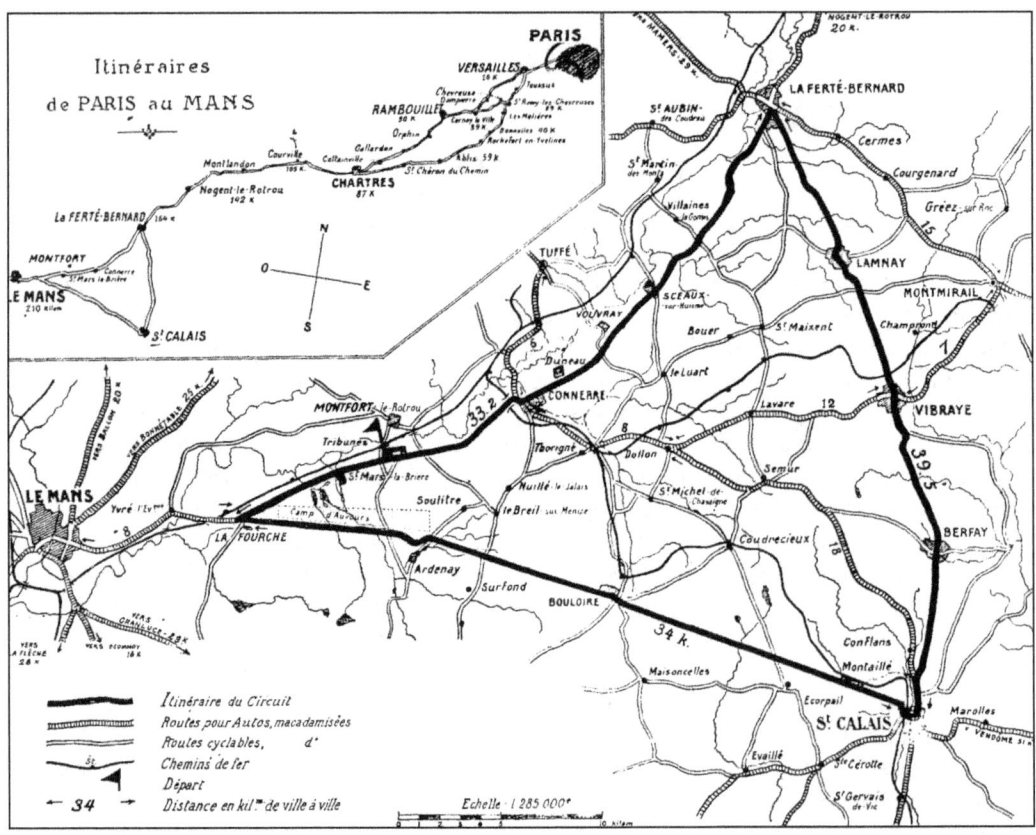

The Circuit de la Sarthe, run counter-clockwise, was 103.18 km including the by-pass near Vibraye which was added later (from *Omnia*, 1906).

see full throttle. The standard distance of the Ardennes, Brescia or Long Island seemed too short for a Grand Prize. The ACF decided on a two-day affair, six laps on each day, on Tuesday and Wednesday, 26 and 27 June 1906. The final regulations permitted three cars per marque, no matter what the nationality. The entry fee was 5000 francs until the end of April, doubled from then until mid–May.

Untertürkheim entered three revamped 125-hps to be handled by Jenatzy, Marieaux and Florio. The stretched dimensions of 185 mm × 150 mm resulted in 16.1 liters and 130 hp at 1300 rpm. No completely new racer was ready, the development of a six-cylinder having stagnated since the sparks were flying at all levels. By the end of 1905 Jellinek's personal supply contract expired. While Monsieur Mercedes by no means wanted to abandon his gold mine, for the DMG a prolongation of the old monopoly was out of the question. Already in June 1903, "it was decided after exhaustive discussion to create a sales company." Just before his death, Duttenhofer purchased on his own account the plot number six, Quai National in Puteaux, which, in March 1904, turned into the Ateliers Mercédès-Daimler, a repair shop and showroom for utility vehicles managed by Edmond de Weisweiler—a cousin of Mathilde de Rothschild, the wife of Henri. Jellinek fought tooth-and-nail, but was not able to prevent the formation of the Mercédès Société Française d'Automobiles.

On 1 January 1906 it took over the foreign distribution; Jellinek continued to hold 40 percent of the five million francs capital stock and in future acted as "a delegate of the supervisory board with appropriate compensation."

But his direct influence on the engineering was lost. A recovered Maybach was not able to establish himself again. In November 1905 Paul Daimler returned to port from his guest performance at Wiener-Neutstadt and rigorously cut him off. Lorenz and Kaulla gave Maybach the advice "to abstain from any intrusion in current construction work in order to concede the office directors Paul Daimler and Moewes more independence." Josef Brauner respected Maybach's know-how but had to follow the orders of his patron Lorenz and thus followed suit. Only the former railway engineer Friedrich Nallinger, who was a member of the board since 1904, backed the new OHC six. On 6 November 1905, Vischer wrote to Jellinek: "In Maybach's designs, provision is made for plug ignition and it cannot be replaced by a low-tension system. This factor as well as the position of the camshaft and different other details created considerable concerns among all members of our directorate." Desjoyeaux suggested adopting at least the new frame. Untertürkheim declined because of technical reasons, but proposed as an alternative solution "five cars, also with six cylinders, but with low-tension ignition and low-mounted camshaft, in accordance with the design of director Paul Daimler." One week later, Maybach wrote: "As a result of your telegram that you want only cars with low-tension ignition, the supervisory board has decided that now my construction on which a low-tension ignition cannot be fitted anymore may be built as a test car." With the dimensions of 140 mm × 120 mm the six-cylinder displaced 11 liters, and had an inverted T-head: The valves were still located in pockets, operated by an overhead camshaft and rockers. During first tests the six delivered 105 hp at 1300 rpm and weighed 350 kg: "The 1906 model was not built with higher power in mind. The car was to be more docile, lighter and lower, able to use its output." Maybach had cancelled the low-tension ignition since he planned 1600 rpm from the outset whereby 130 hp was possible, as much as the rebored muscle car. It was a pity that only a prototype was built.

It was nine o'clock on Sunday morning, 24 June 1906, when the first racer was pushed into the scrutineering area, vis-à-vis the grandstand at Pont-de-Gennes. With the exception of the diminutive 8-liter Grégoire, the queue was composed of refined Bennett racers, the cream of the one-tonner era, with displacement in bucketfuls packed into a little bit of frame. All of them were four-cylinders—steel singles in the case of Panhard and Bayard, otherwise cast-iron pairs, the heads being either welded into position or cast integrally, in no case detachable, thus avoiding the gasket problem and ensuring a good coolant flow around the valve seats. Distinctive were the 165 mm × 150 mm bore and stroke of the compact 12-liters from Brasier and Renault, in comparison to the 180 mm × 150 mm, 185 mm × 150 mm, 180 mm × 160 mm or 185 mm × 160 mm power plants from Darracq, Mercedes, F.I.A.T. or Lorraine-Dietrich, the new name of the cars manufactured by the Société Lorraine des anciens Établissements De Dietrich & Cie. Henri Brasier and Paul Viet considered a solid chassis important, accepting a smaller engine, whereas Paul Ribeyrolles, Josef Brauner, Cesare Momo and Léon Turcat relied on power. The two-piece crankcases were made of light alloy. With two exceptions, the un-counterbalanced crankshafts were carried in three white-metal bearings, Panhard preferring five

June 1906—GP de l'ACF, Le Mans. The Mercedes of Vincenzo Florio on the way to the scrutineering, the *pesage* at Pont-de-Gennes.

Darracq OHV engine: 180 mm × 150 mm, 15 liters, 125 hp at 1200 rpm, design by Paul Ribeyrolles. The OHV head set a fashion, becoming the 1908 standard. The Conti tires were unusual for a French racer. Was Darracq's relationship to the Frères Michelin recently disturbed?

plain bearings and Hotchkiss five ball bearings, in conjunction with a four-piece bolted-up shaft. The pistons were made of cast iron, resembling a Swiss cheese to save weight; the compression ratio was between 4.5 and 5 to 1. The automatic intake valve was a thing of the past: Lorraine, Panhard and Bayard used T-heads; Itala, Hotchkiss and Vulpès F-heads, Sixty-fashion; Mercedes a two-camshaft F-head; Renault and Brasier L-heads; F.I.A.T. an inclined OHV-head, Darracq and Grégoire vertical OHV-heads.

All used carburetors of their own. Many still had throttle control via sliding camshaft. Around 150 liters of fuel were placed behind the rear axle, pressed forward by the exhaust gases or by means of a hand pump. Bosch, Eisemann and Nilmélior were the specialized suppliers of the magnetos. Renault, Panhard and Gobron used high-tension plug ignition, the rest low-tension systems. The mechanic watched over a whole set of adjustable drip-feed lubricators mounted on the dashboard, which delivered oil to the main bearings, the camshafts and sometimes to the cylinder walls, and varied the supply in accordance with the load. In the crankcase of the Renault, a gutter system collected splash oil, delivering it back to the main bearings. There, the oil was collected in rings in the crankshaft and fed by centrifugal force into the big ends. Full pressure lubrication would come later, when engine speeds of 2000 rpm became normal practice. The coolant flow was assisted by a centrifugal or a gear-type pump although Renault relied, at least partially, on the thermosiphon principle. The giants had a specific output of eight horsepower per liter of swept volume, delivered useful power between 300 and 1400 rpm, fuel consumption between 25 and 30 liters per 100 km, between 9.4 and 7.85 miles per gallon. The engine of the Bayard weighed 380 kg, the bigger Mercedes 440, the colossal Lorraine 480 kg, not overweight given the shape: length 90 cm, height 80, width 35 cm.

The scroll clutch of the Mercedes was an exception. The competitors preferred a leather cone or a multiple-plate clutch. Three or four speeds were considered sufficient. Was the chain drive now obsolete? In principle it was a variation of the De Dion system: The chains fed the wheels instead of the half shafts; the heavy differential was chassis-mounted, the axle lighter, minimizing unsprung weight and employing the soft springing to best effect; and the axle was free of the torque which tended to lift up one wheel when accelerating. But the chains absorbed 3 percent of the power and were sometimes thrown off, so that half the field opted for the propeller shaft drive, the torque being transmitted through radius arms, a torque tube, or, in the Hotchkiss system, through the rear spring leaves. Renault and Darracq saved weight and by-passed the lift-up effect by canceling the differential. The frames were light constructions of straight-sided channel steel, the four-point engine and gearbox mountings providing additional stiffness. The girder-type tubular frame of the Gobron was the exception. Semi-elliptic springs, fore and aft, and friction dampers were standard. The internal expanding brake drums on the rear wheels were controlled via hand lever, the external contracting band brake on the gearbox shaft via foot pedal. The fixed wood wheels (non-detachable wire wheels were found only on the Darracq and Hotchkiss) were regarded as an integral part of the car and sealed, a wheel change being prohibited. The so-called racing body consisted of the hood and two high-built seats. Despite the un-streamlined shape, huge radiator and a frontal area of 1.5 m², the one-tonners could expect a top speed of

160 km/h. At sunrise on Tuesday, 26 June, 32 racers lined up at Pont-de-Gennes. The Vulpès of Barriaux and the Grégoire of Taveneaux were missing. Xavier Civelli de Bosch, manager of the Parisian Grégoire agency in the Rue Villaret-Joyeuse, was all on his own in wearing the colors of the small factory located at Poissy. It was just one year since Grégoire stepped into the limelight when Taveneaux took second place in the voiturette class of the Ardennes race. Admittedly, beside him and winner Wagner in his Darracq, nobody reached the finish.

Twenty-three French racers were facing three Germans and six Italians, but there was no trace of Belgium, Great Britain and America, no Pipe, Wolseley, Napier, Pope-Toledo or Locomobile. The favorites were the victors of the previous year, Brasier, Darracq and Itala, but also F.I.A.T., Lorraine and the *marque doyenne* Panhard. The numbering of the cars was unusual, each make being allocated a number and the driver a letter. Starts were at 90 second intervals, beginning with the A series, then B and C:

|  |  | *Driver* |  |  |
|---|---|---|---|---|
| *No.* | *Make* | *A* | *B* | *C* |
| 1 | Lorraine-Dietrich | Gabriel | Rougier | Duray |
| 2 | F.I.A.T. | Lancia | Nazzaro | Weill-Schott |
| 3 | Renault | Szisz | Edmond | Richez |
| 4 | Darracq | Hémery | Wagner | Hanriot |
| 5 | Brasier | Baras | Barillier | Pierry |
| 6 | Mercedes | Jenatzy | Marieaux | Florio |
| 7 | Gobron-Brillié | Rigolly |  |  |
| 8 | Itala | Cagno | Fabry | de Caters |
| 9 | Grégoire | Taveneaux | Civelli de Bosch |  |
| 10 | Panhard & Levassor | Heath | Tart | Teste |
| 11 | Vulpès | Barriaux |  |  |
| 12 | Hotchkiss | Le Blon | Salleron | Shepard |
| 13 | Clément-Bayard | Clément | Villemain | de La Touloubre |

Promptly at six, Chevalier de Knyff dispatched the Lorraine of the great Gabriel. Who else should start first in the first Grand Prix? When de La Touloubre, pseudonym of the artillery officer and popular balloonist Genty, disappeared with his Bayard on the horizon, the sportsmen were eagerly waiting for the first to finish the opening lap. In any case it would not be Gabriel, since his Lorraine could already be cancelled from the official time-keeping of Messieurs Riguelle, Salomon, Audistère and Gaudichard, having suffered a broken radius arm. The F.I.A.T. of Latin racer Lancia was the first to cross the line, having covered the 103 km in 53 min 42 sec, followed by the red Renault of Szisz and the blue Brasier of Baras who turned a lap in 52 min 19 sec, a definitive lap record. Despite the standing start, in most of the races the first lap remained the fastest of the day, thanks to fresh tires and pistons which were not overheated. Fabry turned over at Vibraye. Fernand Charron, recently married to a daughter of Adolphe Clément, was nearby and managed to release the crew from underneath the Itala. René Hanriot went out with a broken cylinder, Civelli de Bosch with a leaky radiator. The Mercedes trio of Jenatzy, Marieaux and Florio, in positions 17, 21 and 22, struggled with the rear tires. Vincenzo Florio came directly from Sicily where he had just organized his first Targa, for stock chassis not exceeding 20,000 francs, over three laps of the long 148-km course through

June 1906—GP de l'ACF, Le Mans. The Renault of Szisz at speed through Connerré. The neutralized sections of the Bennett era were a thing of the past. (Renault)

June 1906—GP de l'ACF, Le Mans. The Clément-Bayard of Capitaine Genty alias de La Touloubre.

the Madonie massif. The route was guarded by three thousand carabinieri of General Marza, since the Sicilian robbers were notorious and the cars should preferably pass without forced stops. Marieaux and Florio drove their Mercedes calmly and without fuss, having to change one tire during this first lap. But the Red Devil had his usual series of "incidents" so that two tires whistled past his head, causing 23 minutes' delay.

As the field finished the lap, Baras led Duray by 13 seconds, then Szisz, Weill-Schott—whose driving skills proved to be a surprise—and Lancia. After two laps Baras was still in the lead while his teammate Pierry, the *nom de course* of Huguet and second pseudonym of the vélo star "Gaby," climbed to second with a lap time of 52 min 31 sec, ahead of Weill-Schott, Szisz, Hémery and Teste. It went like clockwork for Henri Brasier who cherished the fond belief that he was back in Gordon Bennett times and was enjoying his inevitable cigar. Itala lost a second car when de Caters matched his team colleague Fabry in turning an inelegant somersault. Jenatzy's and Florio's tires held up. The Red Devil achieved 55 min 23 sec, the fourth best time in lap two, made good three positions. With 58 min 35 sec, Florio climbed to position 15. Marieaux fell back; at the front the Contis held up, at the rear they burst one after the other.

Michelin had supplied special high-speed tires made of extra-strong fabric and extra-fine tread. But the 26th of June was a baking-hot day. In lap three Baras lost 20 minutes and fell back to third behind Szisz and Barillier, ahead of Teste,

June 1906—GP de l'ACF, Le Mans. The F.I.A.T. of Aldo Weill-Schott at the start.

June 1906—GP de l'ACF, Le Mans. The Darracq of Louis Wagner in Conneré.

Shepard and Clément. Weill-Schott even lost 11 positions. Wagner parked his Darracq with a broken valve, Cagno his Itala with a leaky radiator, when he poured cold water in the radiator, a cylinder seized. Salleron, director of the Auto Générale in the Rue Saint Ferdinand, was repairing his Hotchkiss after a crash. Hotchkiss used non-detachable wire wheels like Darracq and Renault for pre-race tests, certainly not the best idea since Hubert Le Blon—who had contested the Targa in company of his wife!—was spending three hours in straightening a rim. But Elliott Fitch Shepard held position five, proving wrong the wicked tongues saying that he turned up at Le Mans to kill time and that the drive for Hotchkiss was due to his relationship to the Vanderbilts. At the end of the third lap, Szisz stopped at his depot. The 33-year-old Hungarian Ferenc Szisz had joined Renault in 1900 as chief tester and had been the riding mechanic for Louis Renault in the races towards Vienna and Madrid. The Grand Prix regulations permitted only the driver and his mechanic to work on the car. Nevertheless Szisz and his mechanic Marteau changed tires in less than four minutes! The neighbors from Panhard, having done the same job in 20 minutes, were completely baffled. How was it possible?

Despite the use of special high-speed tires, the Frères Michelin were convinced that the stress limit would be exceeded on the fast Le Mans circuit and hence focused on quick changeability via the *jante amovible*, the detachable rim. But one of these new rims weighed eight kilograms. F.I.A.T. had enough margin to adopt the novelty on all four wheels, Renault on the rear wheels only, while Itala abstained entirely. Renault chauffeur Edmond changed a tire in 75 seconds, saving four minutes over

June 1906—GP de l'ACF, Le Mans. At the depot: Jenatzy changing a tire on his Mercedes.

June 1906—GP de l'ACF, Le Mans. Elliott Fitch Shepard, mechanic Charles "Baby" Lehman (no relation to Charley Lehmann) and their Hotchkiss at the depot.

the cut-off method and thus gaining an enormous advantage. It was general practice to stop at the depot every lap and replace as many as four spare tires which had been changed during the preceding circuit. Only Renault and F.I.A.T. had a chance to win. And it was Nazzaro who climbed to fifth in the fourth lap, behind Szisz, Teste, Shepard, Baras and Tart. However it was only a question of time before the former tricycle stars Teste and Tart would park their Panhards with flat tires. During lap five and six, Szisz continued to increase his lead. Edmond and Jenatzy withdrew, their goggles having broken letting tar and dust into their eyes. Jenatzy handed over no. 6A Mercedes to relief driver Burton, who was the owner of their car. Florio retired with a buckled wheel after a tire burst at full speed, Tart with a broken chassis arm, Weill-Schott after running off the wooden section at Vibraye. It was a pity that banker Aldo Weill-Schott intended to abandon the great sport, joining F.I.A.T. in the position of a director. With four circuits below 57 minutes, he was considerably faster than Nazzaro. The crowd missed him.

Szisz finished the first day in the lead, 26 minutes ahead of Clément and 41 minutes ahead of Nazzaro. Marieaux was twelfth and Burton seventeenth, more than two hours back. On Wednesday, the grandstand remained quite empty, a consequence of the prices, a seat costing 20 francs, a box 200. Only the Grand Duchess of Mecklenburg provided some elegance, making her appearance in company of Minister Louis Barthou. After a night in the *parc fermé*, 17 survivors out of 32 were dragged

June 1906—GP de l'ACF, Le Mans. The Mercedes of Marieaux passing through Conneré.

June 1906—GP de l'ACF, Le Mans. On the second day, J. T. Alexander Burton drove the Mercedes no. 6A. No wonder, he was the owner of the racer.

by horses up to the start, and were sent off in the order and at the intervals in time that they had finished the previous day. Szisz lost 11 min 30 sec to refuel his Renault and to change the tires, Shepard half an hour. Teste turned over near the *fourche* as a spring broke; he escaped with a broken leg, mechanic Artaud with a fright. Hémery withdrew with a broken valve, Rigolly with a leaky radiator, Shepard and Richez after leaving the road near the troublesome *fourche*. Young Albert Clément was gradually dropping back with tire trouble. Szisz kept resolutely ahead, completed the 12 laps in 12 h 14 min 7 sec, averaging 101.2 km/h. Nazzaro followed 32 min 19 sec back, Clément 35 min 39 sec back, then Barillier, Lancia and Heath. Burton and Marieaux were tenth and eleventh.

For Paul Daimler the Grand Prix disgrace arrived just at the right moment. Now he was in a good position to ditch the gentlemen drivers of the Jellinek squad, and without problems he was able to place a man from the factory's own ranks, the 32-year-old Otto Salzer. A mechanic through and through, and no mean driver, Salzer had entered the DMG in 1896 as locksmith, was promoted foreman at the turn of the century, and was heading the racing preparation department. On 13 August, Salzer was allowed to start alongside Jenatzy and Marieaux in the Circuit des Ardennes, at the wheel of the 125-hp owned by Florio, preferring it to the new six-cylinder prototype after longer comparison tests. The race was to be over seven laps of 85.714 km. Renault and F.I.A.T. did not enter, but Darracq, Brasier and Lorraine-Dietrich each appeared with four cars, Bayard with three, and Corre, the largest Parisian De Dion dealer, with a prototype made to the order of Comte

August 1906—Circuit des Ardennes. Left to right: Christian Lautenschlager, Otto Salzer, Paul Daimler, Friedrich Nallinger and unidentified man.

d'Hespel. Detachable rims were standard now. Conti had quickly bought a Vinet license but supplied tires only for Marieaux and Salzer, since the Red Devil promoted himself by running on Jenatzy tires.

Straight off Otto Salzer showed a world-class performance. On the first lap he was second, behind Wagner, in front of Duray, Rougier, Clément, Hanriot and the great Gabriel! Marieaux was tenth, in front of the Lorraine of Englishman Sorel

August 1906—Circuit des Ardennes. The Mercedes of Otto Salzer.

August 1906—Circuit des Ardennes. Long-overdue victory for the Lorraine-Dietrich of Arthur Duray.

**August 1906—Circuit des Ardennes. The Brasier of Pierry being serviced. The exhaust manifold combined cylinders one with four, and two with three.**

who, during the twenties, was to manage the London Bugatti agency in the Brixton Road. Jenatzy was struggling with his own tires, ahead of the light 650-kg Darracq of Victor Demogeot who had won the Cuba race in February, and the Bayard of the popular rugby player Pierre Garcet. The Corre started and never reappeared. After the second lap Duray was in the lead, in front of Salzer and the Darracq trio Hémery, Hanriot, Wagner. Marieaux withdrew with gearbox trouble, the first mechanical defect since the introduction of the 125-hp. Jenatzy was cursing at his rubber supplier. But the Contis too were bursting—Salzer lost seven minutes. Arthur Duray drove his Lorraine to victory in 5 h 38 min 39 sec, 12 minutes ahead of Hanriot; Salzer finished ninth, Jenatzy tenth. With a best lap of 46 min 39 sec, Salzer was 40 seconds slower than the winner Duray but one minute faster than the second-place Hanriot, and one minute faster than the Red Devil. Was it due to the Jenatzy tires?

On 6 October 1906, the third Vanderbilt Cup was held on Long Island, ten laps of 47.8 km. There was talk of 600,000 spectators, and "fifty million dollars worth of motor vehicles concentrated in a ten-mile circle around the grandstand." America was represented by five cars. The spade-bearded Hubert Le Blon drove a Thomas Flyer, Lawell an air-cooled six-cylinder Frayer Miller, the emigrated Irishman Joe Tracy as usual a Locomobile, Harding a Haynes and Walter Christie his front-drive Christie. Europe had shipped three 125-hps for Jenatzy, Lüttgen and Keene, a Panhard for Heath, three F.I.A.T.s for Lancia, Nazzaro and Weill-Schott, a Hotchkiss for Shepard, a Darracq for Wagner, an Itala for Cagno, a Bayard

**October 1906—Vanderbilt Cup, Long Island, New York. The Itala of Alessandro Cagno broke down on lap eight. (Fiat)**

for Clément and a Lorraine for Duray. The Red Devil was in fine form, all dressed up in red overalls at the wheel of his red-painted Mercedes, the talk of the town. Tracy set the lap record in 26 min 37 sec in a Locomobile prepared by Fritz Walker, Jenatzy's riding mechanic in Ireland. Wagner won, ahead of Lancia, Duray, Clément and Jenatzy.

The 1906 Vanderbilt was the farewell performance of the one-tonners. The 1000-kg formula lasted for five seasons, from 1902 until 1906. In the eyes of the ACF, the one-tonners had reached the planned target, the use of new metals, of thin-walled cast iron, of nickel steels and light alloys. There were two recipes for success, on one hand the large-capacity option of F.I.A.T. or Lorraine, on the other hand the L-head solution of Brasier or Renault, whose smaller displacement and simpler engine layout left plenty of margin for chassis refinement. The most consistent formula adaptation was symbolized by the unequalled stripping of the Darracq. Paul Ribeyrolles simply omitted every unnecessary component, from the hood to the differential, while the efficient OHV engine and the filigree wire wheels fulfilled predefined functions at minimal weight.

# 15

# *Italian Supremacy*

The French manufacturers were rather pleased by the 1906 season, by the Le Mans victory of Renault over the strong F.I.A.T., by the third place showing by Bayard, by the team result of Brasier, by the victories of Lorraine in the Ardennes and of Darracq on Long Island. They accepted the Grand Prix as the new main event of the year. A majority however asked for a one-day affair and a restriction on the engine output since the tires exerted too much influence. After all, the Grand Prix was meant as a contest for automobiles and not for tires! The ACF did not encroach directly upon bore or displacement; instead, at the beginning of 1907, it replaced the weight limit of 1000 kg with a fuel-consumption limit of 30 liters per 100 kilometers, or 9.41 miles per gallon. In Le Mans the front-placed Renault and F.I.A.T. had consumed 28 liters. Why should the builders redraft *any* engine feature? Thus it was no surprise that in 1907 a pack of one-tonners reappeared, with reinforced frames, on a new course twistier and shorter than the previous year's: the 76.983-km Circuit de la Seine Inférieure between Dieppe, Londinières and Eu. Renault, F.I.A.T. (from 1907, Fiat), Bayard and Brasier just polished their engines and shortened the wheelbase for the purpose of better handling in the corners. Lorraine turned up with the revised dimensions of 180 mm × 170 mm. Alexandre Darracq was increasing his foreign interests; wanting a complete championship and no decisive single event, he planned only a private commitment under the entry of Messieurs d'Arnaud and Hériot. The ACF refused. Hence works racers were entered, with the older crankshaft and 180 mm × 140 mm. Panhard relied on its traditional dimensions of 170 mm × 170 mm, but relocated the radiator rearwards, à la Renault. Unbelievable what the *marque doyenne* was copying now!

It was on 15 February 1907 that the bombshell was dropped at Untertürkheim: Wilhelm Maybach left his DMG, frozen out by Lorenz, Kaulla and the Daimler brothers.

> When, after 24 years of work with Daimler and the DMG, I had finally succeeded to make money with the business, a few members of the board, Lorenz and von Kaulla, incited by the sons of Gottlieb Daimler, were not afraid, after the death of privy councillor Duttenhofer, of pushing me out of my position as technical director in the most crude way and appointing the Daimler sons. Jealousy was the motive, they would have preferred that I disappear from the world. The supervisory board had the goodness to accept me as a member but I declined, so that I was left stranded without any compensation for all the valuable, fee-bringing inventions that I left. I don't want, and according to the contract with the DMG I am not free, to do something in the automobile sector.

164  Mercedes and Auto Racing in the Belle Epoque, 1895–1915

As a stopgap Maybach designed gas ovens and lubricators for Eisemann & Cie. In 1909, with Count Zeppelin, he founded an aero-engine factory at Bissingen. His son Karl carried on and was to construct the proud Maybach automobiles.

In view of the Grand Prix, Paul Daimler and Josef Brauner reduced the bore from 185 to 180 mm and the wheelbase from 290 to 285 cm. More was out of the question because of the precarious situation. The strategy of Jellinek, Desjoyeaux and Charley to leave the racers only to gentlemen drivers who disposed of the Mercedes within their wealthy coterie during the social season was to be cancelled. The gentlemen were headstrong and overpaid, did not sell enough cars, and sometimes drove like lame ducks. From 1907, a working-class background was no longer an obstacle to handling a Mercedes. The Société Mercédès took over the organization. Jenatzy was the only survivor of the old guard. He was approaching forty and calming down but he was still one of the fastest drivers of his time. Furthermore Otto Salzer was appointed works driver, after his fine performance in the Ardennes. And for the third racer, the Société Mercédès borrowed the 31-year-old former Darracq star Victor Hémery—from Benz!

A whole regiment of neophytes tried to squeeze up close to the established marques. The shaky Corre could be forgotten even if it started as Corre-La Licorne

Untertürkheim—Spring 1907. The 1907 Mercedes racer: 180 mm × 150 mm, wheelbase 285 cm, altogether more compact than the predecessor.

15. Italian Supremacy 165

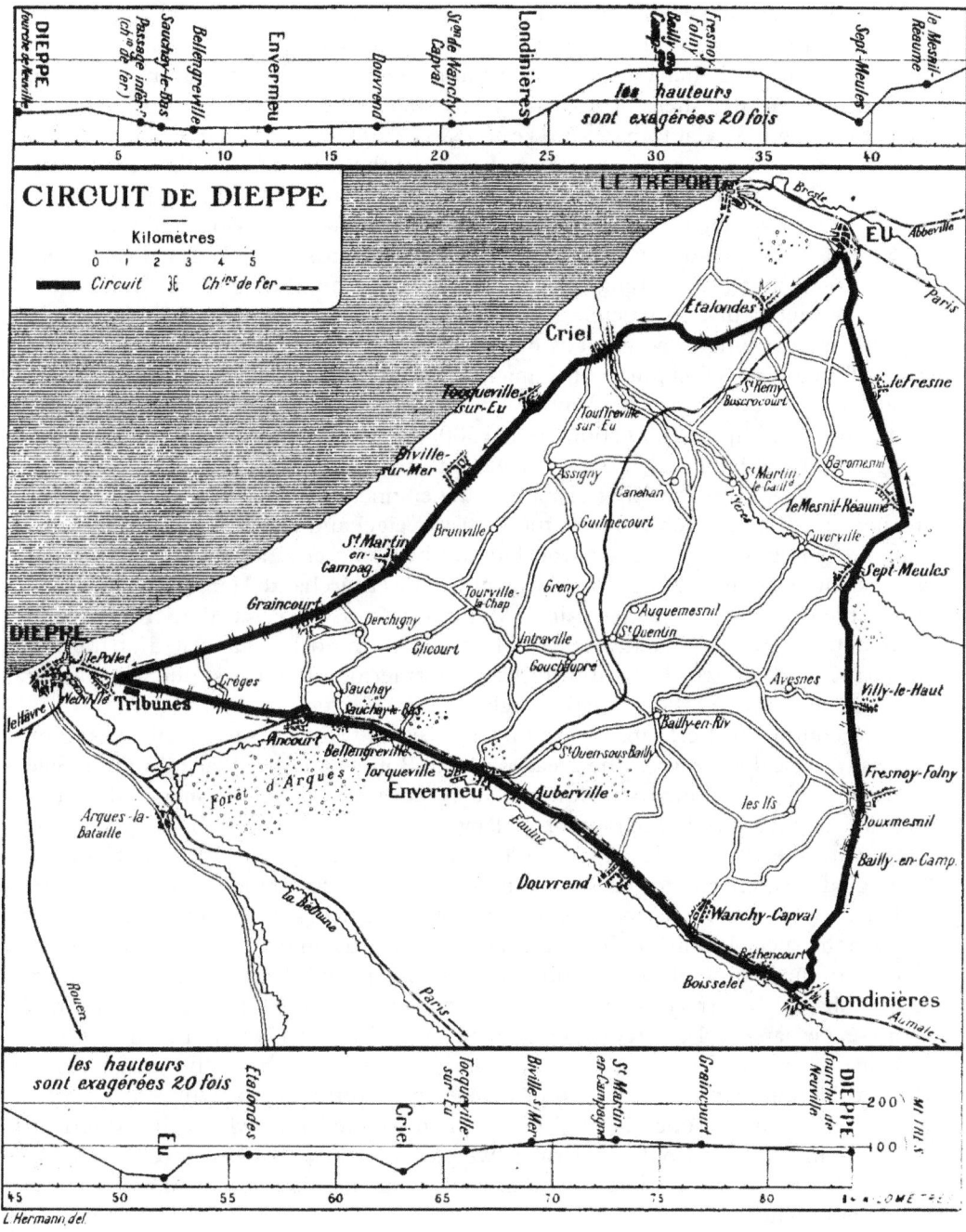

In 1907, 1908 and 1912, the Grand Prix was run on the 77-km Circuit de la Seine Inférieure near Dieppe (from *L'Automobile*, 1908).

with relocated radiator in front of the L-head 10.5-liter (150 mm × 150 mm). From Bordeaux the brothers Charles and Émile Dombret sent off their inventive Motobloc, an F-head 12-liter (165 mm × 140 mm) whose crankshaft ran in four plain bearings, because of the centric-mounted flywheel. The American Christie was out of the ordinary. The automatic-intake V-4 swept 20 liters (184 mm × 184 mm) and was placed crosswise at front axle level to drive the front wheels via a two-speed gearbox. The front-wheel-drive on a racing car was a novelty, the V-arrangement old hat. Unforgotten were the V-2 from Daimler, the V-4 from Mors and the filigree V-8s that Clément Ader had entered in the race towards Bordeaux. Unusual were the Antoinette engines, a range of lightweight V-8s from the specialist "Léon Levavasseur, ingénieur-constructeur, 10, rue des Bas-Roger, Puteaux": 90° V-8s made up of cast iron singles with heads of aluminum and water jackets of brass, using no carburetor but a fuel pump injecting into the intake ports, available in the dimensions of 65 mm × 65 mm, 80 mm × 80 mm, 100 mm × 100 mm and 130 mm × 130 mm, output 25 hp at 2800 rpm, 40 at 2500, 60 at 1800 and 100 hp at 1400 rpm, weight 25 kg, 40, 72 and 150 kg. Perfect for use in power boats, like Madame du Gast's *Turquoise*, and the first airplanes, the engines were not flexible enough for racing cars. The French Porthos, the British Weigel and the Swiss Dufaux turned up with straight-eight engines, the Dufaux being entered as Dufaux-Marchand after an agreement with the Parisian agent Charles Marchand. Henri Sarazin, director of the Belgian Ateliers Germain at Monceau-sur-Sambre, relied upon a stripped production type. Aquila Italiana too had this in mind but cancelled at the last moment. With no weight limit in force the former one-tonners suddenly weighed 1050 or 1100 kg, and the longish straight-eights 1200 kg.

In contrast to Le Mans where the enthusiasm was limited, Dieppe was to be a feast. The cafés between the arcades of the Bourse and the Place du Puits-Salé were open all night long to welcome the constantly arriving sportsmen and sportswomen. A never-ending parade of beflagged cars roamed through the town: blue flags with the cross of Lorraine for Lorraine-Dietrich, green for Motobloc, red with golden stitcheries for HISA which had good chances in the Coupe de la Commission Sportive. Admission was just six francs, enticing thousands of spectators to take the special trains to Dieppe. The Englishmen came by steamer from Newhaven. In the betting office Renault and Fiat were given 2:1, Lorraine 2.5:1, Brasier 3:1, Panhard 5:1, Mercedes only 8:1, the newcomer Motobloc 12:1. Messieurs Lumet, Périssé, Fernand and Georges Longuemare supervised the filling of the fuel rations, 231 liters per car. Henri Deutsch and the Desmarais brothers, the producers of "Moto-Naphta" and "Automobiline," kept an eye on the procedure. The racers were painted in national colors, the German Mercedes in white, the American Christie in white and red, the British Weigels in green, the Belgian Germains in yellow, the Swiss Dufaux in yellow-and-red, the Italian Fiats in red, and the French armada in blue.

On Tuesday, 2 July 1907, ten laps were to be completed, a total distance of 769.83 km, starting as usual at six in the morning. The Coupe de la Commission Sportive, for cars consuming a maximum of 15 liters per 100 km, was run concurrently, over six laps, starting at nine. The ACF tried out a new numbering, letters for the cars, numbers for the drivers:

## 15. Italian Supremacy

July 1907—GP de l'ACF, Dieppe. The Renault team: Szisz, Edmond and Richez. In the race, Dimitriévitch took the place of Szisz' mechanic Marteau who was injured, and Henry Farman the place of Edmond who was sick. (Renault)

| Make | | Driver Series 1 | Series 2 | Series 3 |
|---|---|---|---|---|
| F  | Fiat               | Lancia                    | Nazzaro      | Wagner       |
| C  | Corre-La Licorne   | d'Hespel (replaced by Collomb) | | |
| D  | Darracq            | Hanriot                   | Rigal        | Caillois     |
| LD | Lorraine-Dietrich  | Duray                     | Rougier      | Gabriel      |
| P  | Porthos            | Stricker                  |              |              |
| DM | Dufaux-Marchand    | Dufaux                    |              |              |
| BC | Bayard-Clément     | Garcet                    | Alézy        | Shepard      |
| MB | Motobloc           | Pierron                   | Page         | Courtade     |
| R  | Renault            | Szisz                     | Henry Farman | Richez       |
| GE | Germain            | Perpère                   | Degrais      | Roch-Brault  |
| PL | Panhard & Levassor | Heath                     | Le Blon      | Dutemple     |
| WC | Christie           | Christie                  |              |              |
| M  | Mercedes           | Jenatzy                   | Salzer       | Hémery       |
| W  | Weigel             | Guinness                  | Weigel (replaced by Harrison and Laxen) | |
| GB | Gobron-Brillié     | Rigolly                   |              |              |
| A  | Aquila-Italiana    | Pichat (did not start)    |              |              |
| B  | Brasier            | Barillier                 | Baras        | Bablot       |

Starting order: F 1, C 1, D 1, ... , B 1, F 2, D 2, ... , B 2, F 3, D 3, ... , B 3.

The racers passed the night in their compound and were released half an hour before the start. The steel-studded anti-skid tires were quickly replaced by flat-tread ones since on race day the sun was shining. Much admired in the grandstand booths were the Brazilian balloonist Alberto Santos-Dumont, turn-of-the-century stars like Giraud, Pinson and Girardot, prominent sportsmen like Robert de Vogüé, Alexander Burton, Aldo Weill-Schott, de Caters and de Crawhez. Monsieur Mercédès was discussing with Giovanni Agnelli and minister Louis Barthou the bad market situation. Among the crowd, the incredibly long Weigel and the unusual Christie caused a flurry of excitement. Among the manufacturers and their guests, it was more a matter of subtleties. Robert Gallien, Louis Sarda, Alphonse Tellier and Louis Kriéger represented the motorcycle, boat and electro scene, and marveled at the springs of the Fiats, tautly wrapped for the purpose of better damping.

Latin racer Lancia was the first to start. In November 1906, he had established his own company at Turin, Via Ormia.

Victor Hémery, born in 1876 in Le Mans, drove the Grand Prix for Mercedes, switched over to Benz during the 1907 season.

The neighbors from Fiat continued to place a Grand Prix racer at his disposal. Lancia finished lap one in sixth place. Another Fiat was in the lead, the former Darracq star Louis Wagner with a lap in 39 min 53 sec, ahead of Duray, Szisz, Salzer and Gabriel. Hémery was fifteenth, Jenatzy twentieth. For many the fourth rank of Otto Salzer was a surprise. Didn't he keep up with the front-runners one year ago in the Ardennes? The Panhards of Heath and Le Blon clattered like harvesters and refused to speed up, just the beginning of the débacle. Barely started, Collomb, who replaced the originally entered d'Hespel on the Corre, was much too fast when approaching the left hand fork at Londinières. Fortunately the ACF had not closed the road straight on so that the Corre was able to slow down safely. As the Corre re-entered the course, Garcet's Bayard was just arriving. Collomb darted sideways and ran down the official's tent.

Wagner continued to step on it. In the second lap he was one minute faster than Duray despite an acrobatic maneuver at Londinières to avoid the spinning Brasier of Paul Baras. With 38 min 22 sec, the second-fastest lap of the race, Barillier made up ten places, climbed to third, ahead of Lancia, Szisz, Gabriel, Hanriot, Rougier, Caillois, Nazzaro and Hémery, the best Mercedes driver. Salzer fell back to sixteenth, struggling with the tires. Heath retired his Panhard with a defective

July 1907—GP de l'ACF, Dieppe. *Pesage* and allocation of the fuel ration: The Fiat of Vincenzo Lancia received exactly 231 liters.

July 1907—GP de l'ACF, Dieppe. The Mercedes of Salzer passing through Eu.

July 1907—GP de l'ACF, Dieppe. The Christie of Walter Christie was not able to keep pace.

July 1907—GP de l'ACF, Dieppe. The Clément-Bayard of Alézy.

water pump. Richez and Bablot had a tough slipstream duel, but the experience for such an action was missing. The Renault as well as the Brasier paid for it by turning over. Both crews managed to restart, the Renault without its hood. The best newcomer, the Motobloc of Courtade, lay 22 minutes behind Wagner and was losing five seconds per kilometer.

Lap three did not change anything between the leaders Wagner and Duray. But Gabriel took third ahead of Lancia, Szisz, Hanriot and Nazzaro who got his Fiat up to speed. Hémery fell back to fifteenth, Salzer to eighteenth, while Jenatzy relapsed into old habits and, with 39 min 16 sec, his second best time, moved forward to nineteenth. Between three Fiats, two Lorraines, one Renault and three Darracqs, everything remained open. The former motorcycle star Victor Rigal lay 17 minutes behind Wagner. In lap four, Wagner pulled out with engine trouble. Duray inherited the lead, one minute ahead of Lancia, two minutes ahead of the patient and methodical Nazzaro who began to move forward according to his usual strategy. Gabriel's Lorraine covered the leading trio, ahead of Callois, Barillier, who caught up, Rigal, Baras, Szisz and Rougier. Shepard followed further back, then Garcet, Hémery, Pierron, Courtade, Salzer, Dutemple and Jenatzy. Laxen, replacement for Weigel, parked his long Weigel, and Le Blon his Panhard.

At half distance the fight for the lead had stabilized. A few stragglers fell out: Stricker's eight-cylinder Porthos, Alézy's Bayard, Christie's Christie and Page's Motobloc. It was on the second lap that Walter Christie achieved his best time of 48 min 19 sec, ten minutes behind the fastest. The Bayard team was still in a state of

July 1907—GP de l'ACF, Dieppe. The Panhard of Dutemple had cooling problems.

shock: While carrying out trials in the morning of 17 May, Albert Clément had lost control of his Bayard in the fast right-hand bend of Saint-Martin-en-Campagne and succumbed to a skull fracture, mechanic Gauderman escaping severe injuries. Meanwhile, the nine racers competing for the Coupe de la Commission Sportive had been dispatched: a Gillet-Forest, two Darracqs, two HISAs, three La Buires and a Porthos. After six laps Duray lay three minutes ahead of Lancia and four minutes ahead of Nazzaro, who was speeding up with a lap under 39 minutes. Szisz followed eight minutes back, then Gabriel, Caillois, Rigal, Barillier, Baras and Garcet, the Mercedes trio Hémery, Jenatzy and Salzer in twelfth, thirteenth and fourteenth. The best lap times were impressive: Hémery achieved 39 min 9 sec, Jenatzy 39 min 8 sec. The detachable rims dashed all hopes, as they were difficult to fit. Rougier's Lorraine, Rigolly's Gobron and Harrison's Weigel fell out.

The pressure of the Turin roller was increasing. On lap seven Nazzaro took second place in front of his confrère Lancia, 2 min 47 sec behind Duray. Lap eight gave Duray some margin since Nazzaro and Lancia changed tires. Even Szisz moved forward. Pierron, Dufaux and Farman withdrew, as well as Jenatzy who was unable to attach a rim. On lap nine came a bolt from the blue: With a lead of six minutes Duray had the victory in view when a ball bearing in the gearbox gave up the ghost. Duray and mechanic Henry Matthys came back on foot to the depot, to the thundering applause of the grandstand. Of course Nazzaro took the lead, confirming his position with 38 min 16 sec. Dutemple, elsewhere known as manufacturer of the

July 1907—GP de l'ACF, Dieppe. The Darracq of the former tricycle champion Victor Rigal and the Mercedes of Victor Hémery at Eu.

July 1907—GP de l'ACF, Dieppe. The Fiat of Lancia in the S-bend near Londinières. (Fiat)

Dutemple motorcycles, parked the remaining Panhard. In the last lap poor Lancia pulled out at Criel with clutch failure, and Salzer because of a rim. Nazzaro drove his Fiat to victory in 6 h 46 min 33 sec, averaging 113.621 km/h, 6 min 37 sec ahead of Szisz, 18 min 32 sec ahead of Baras, then Gabriel, Rigal and Caillois, Hémery in tenth. At the finish, Nazzaro had still eleven liters of fuel in his tank, Szisz 30, Caillois 36, Baras 38, Barillier and Rigal 42. Nazzaro and Fiat had made the most of the fuel limit. The Coupe de la Commission Sportive was won by de Langhe in a Darracq.

After the Fiat victory Paris was deeply shocked. Felice Nazzaro, just like his friend Lancia, was born in 1881, the son of a Turin coal merchant. At the beginning of the year he had already gained the Targa Florio and the Kaiserpreis for Fiat and now had put a third damper on the French superiority spirit. He became the first *campionissimo*, and with the simple address "Nazzaro, Italy" every letter was certain to reach its goal.

What was the speedy Hémery doing at Mannheim, when Karl Benz did not want to know anything about races? "Fifty kilometers per hour are enough," he had preached again and again, at least until the turn of the century, until the sales dropped by one-third within three years and his Benz & Cie. almost went bankrupt. Marketing director Julius Ganss quickly changed the strategy. In October 1902 he engaged the young Clément engineer Marius Barbarou and six of his colleagues, relying on a front engine and styling à la Mercedes. Benz & Cie. kept alive, even dared to enter a racer in the race to Madrid, a T-head 11-liter (160 mm × 140 mm), Clément fashion.

July 1907—GP de l'ACF, Dieppe. The spectacular Duray, his Lorraine and the railway bridge near Ancourt.

July 1907—GP de l'ACF, Dieppe. Felice Nazzaro, mechanic Antonio Fagnano and the winning Fiat.

Barbarou himself took the wheel and reached Bordeaux in twenty-eighth place, three and one-half hours behind Gabriel. Barbarou was born in 1876 in Moissac, in the département Tarn et Garonne, learned his trade in Paris under Gustave Chauveau and Aimé Witz, and devised a V-2 which was exhibited at the 1900 Exposition Universelle. Adolphe Clément was interested and engaged him as technical director. Barbarou left Benz in May 1904 and returned to Paris, or more exactly to Saint-Denis, where he designed a marvelous luxury car for Delaunay-Belleville which instantly entered the limelight. Georg Diehl and Fritz Erle took over the technical direction, and a new organization, created in October 1905, handled the distribution and the promotion through sporting events. Since their experience was limited to national reliability events, the 1907 season was run as an apprenticeship year, with stripped stock types.

The overture took place by the beginning of April 1907, far to the south, in Sicily, on the occasion of the second Targa Florio. After three long 148-km circuits across the Madonie massif, Fritz Erle, Paul Spamann and the local nobleman Clemente De Boiano finished fifteenth, seventeenth, and twenty-third with their reliable but still-too-slow Benzes, one hour behind the speedy Fiat of Felice Nazarro. Nothing outstanding. The Mediterranean trip bore fruit at a different level. Just behind De Boiano none other than Victor Hémery struggled towards the finish, not at the wheel of a Darracq but in an exotic Deluca, a British Daimler license from Naples. Hémery had just resigned from his job as chief tester at Suresnes and was free. Mannheim seized the opportunity with both hands and gave him a contract on the spot.

June 1907—Kaiserpreis, Taunus. Second place for the Pipe of Lucien Hautvast.

It was in June that Hémery handled a Benz for the first time. The Kaiserpreis was to be run in the Taunus forests, with displacement not exceeding eight liters, wheelbase at least three meters, weight at least 1175 kg. Not fewer than 77 cars started in two preliminary heats, over two laps of 120 km on the slightly modified 1904 Bennett circuit: the Benzes of Hémery, Spamann and De Boiano; the Mercedes of Jenatzy, Salzer and Poege; the Mercedes *mixte* of Burton and Gastaud against a pack of Dürkopp, Opel, Protos, Adler and NAG from Germany, of Minerva, Pipe, Métallurgique and Imperia from Belgium, of Martini from Switzerland, of Fiat, Bianchi and Isotta-Fraschini from Italy. Two cars were outstanding: the Fiat (140 mm × 129.9 mm) designed by Cesare Momo and Guido Fornaca, with vertical OHV head à la Darracq, and the Pipe (140 mm × 128 mm) devised by Otto Pfänder. Hémery qualified his Benz for the four lap final, as well as Jenatzy, Salzer and Poege their Mercedes. Nazzaro won in 5 h 34 min 26 sec, five minutes ahead of the Pipe driven by Hautvast, then the Opels of Joerns and Michel ahead of the Fiats of Wagner and Lancia. Poege broke down on lap one, Hémery on lap two, Salzer finished ninth, Jenatzy fourteenth.

By July, René Hanriot too had switched over to Benz, making his debut by the end of the month in the Ardennes meeting. The 8-liters were sent away first—Hémery, Hanriot and Spamann in Benzes, Théo Pilette in a Mercedes, Jenatzy in a Pipe. Of note were the OHC engines of the two newcomers from Ariès (160 mm

June 1907—Kaiserpreis, Taunus. The Isotta-Fraschini of Nando Minoia finished eighth in the second heat and seventh in the final. By the end of the season, the Isotta and Minoia won the Coppa Florio at Brescia.

April 1907—Targa Florio, Sicily. Nazzaro's Fiat, a pepped-up 7.3-liter stock chassis (125 mm × 150 mm, T-head), passing through the village of Petralia Sottana. Nineteen seven was the year of Felice Nazarro and Fiat: They won the Targa, the Kaiserpreis and the Grand Prix.

× 98 mm) which were too much ahead of their time since they did not run properly. The Minervas of Moore Brabazon, Koolhoven and Algernon Lee Guinness took the first three places, ahead of Hanriot. It was a small success for Benz but a great success for Sylvain de Jong, his Minervas and the tires of Oscar Englebert. Two days later just six cars lined up in the race for Grand Prix-type cars, Jenatzy and de Caters in Mercedes, Harrison and Laxen in Weigels, Algernon Lee Guinness in a Darracq and Chevalier de Lammine in a Duchesne, a tarted-up stock chassis. Jenatzy was slowed down by valve problems so that Pierre de Caters struggled with Algy Guinness for the lead, and was able to put through his Mercedes. Jenatzy crept to the finish third, ahead of de Lammine. The Weigels fell out.

The 1907 season closed in September near Brescia where the Itala of Cagno won the Coppa della Velocita, ahead of the Darracq of Demogeot and the Lorraines of Rougier and Gabriel. Concurrently the 8-liters contested the Coppa Florio. Ferdinando Minoia won in an Isotta-Fraschini ahead of the Benzes of Hémery and Hanriot while Erle finished tenth behind the Bianchi of Carlo Maserati. "The Isotta is the Italian De Dietrich license" could be read in the French papers. Did De Dietrich built the Isotta under license or Isotta the De Dietrich? Whichever

July 1907—Circuit des Ardennes: GP class. Of course Pierre de Caters concluded his career at the wheel of a Mercedes, with a victory in the Circuit des Ardennes. Standing beyond the dashboard is Théo Pilette.

way it was convenient. Altogether 1907 turned out as the year of the Italians. Fiat, Itala and Isotta took nearly everything which could be taken to Turin and Milan. In the meantime the Mannheim racing department had reached top level, with the help of Hémery's and Hanriot's savoir-faire. The planned Grand Prix entry stood under a lucky star.

# 16

## *Apotheosis*

For Paris, London and Brussels the triangular course of Dieppe was perfectly located and thus was retained in 1908. But apart from the old circuit a new spirit was making itself felt. The new regulations were not elaborated in the Hôtel Pastoret under the aegis of the Commission Sportive and the pro forma presence of the others, but in Belgium with international participation, at Ostend, on 14 July 1907. Germany proposed a minimum weight of 1175 kg and a maximum bore of 150 mm for four cylinders; France preferred 1100 kg and 160 mm, England 1300 kg. The parties agreed on 1100 kg and 155 mm, equaling a maximum piston area of 755 $cm^2$, or 127 mm in case of a six-cylinder. At least 1100 kg implied "en ordre de marche," without coolant, fuel, spare tires and mudguards, but including lubricant. In addition the Ostend formula prescribed a maximum width of 175 cm, a functioning reverse gear and a horizontal exhaust pipe at the back to prevent deliberate dust raising. The next day, Untertürkheim decided "to construct a new model and to find out the most auspicious stroke by making trials with 150, 155 and 160 mm. The choice of the correct relation between bore and stroke should result in around 110 hp and we hope that the minimal weight of 1100 kg will not be exceeded again." Upon Vischer's request "the 150 hp six-cylinder in process was shelved for the time being."

The clubs did not come up with the bore limit out of thin air. Since 1906 the newspaper *L'Auto* had set the fashion with its "Coupe des Voiturettes." On one hand many national taxing authorities made their calculations on a bore basis; on the other hand experts deemed a piston speed of ten meters per second insuperable. Limiting the bore instead of the swept volume gave the imagination fuller scope, promising diversity, from the low-speed long-stroke engine to the high-speed short-stroke engine—in any case more possibilities than the simple encroachment upon fuel consumption or air supply. Moreover bore and engine speed were closely connected since a mysterious phenomenon was up to no good in the midst of the huge cylinders. At full load and top speed on the long straights, the gigantic pistons were glowing, unable to dissipate the heat quickly enough to the cylinder walls. The geometry bore the blame! The swept volume had grown cubically with the diameter, but the cooling surface only quadratically. What could be done against the evil genius, against "the misfiring due to self-ignition of the mixture"? Over-lubrication was the standard remedy. Every decent racer smoked like a chimney, a delicious aroma for every sportsman. Drivers and mechanics, however, were not brimming over with enthusiasm; they grappled with a deteriorated mixture, with incomplete combustion, with incrustations and oily plugs. The Ostend formula cured the monsters' ills, at least partly.

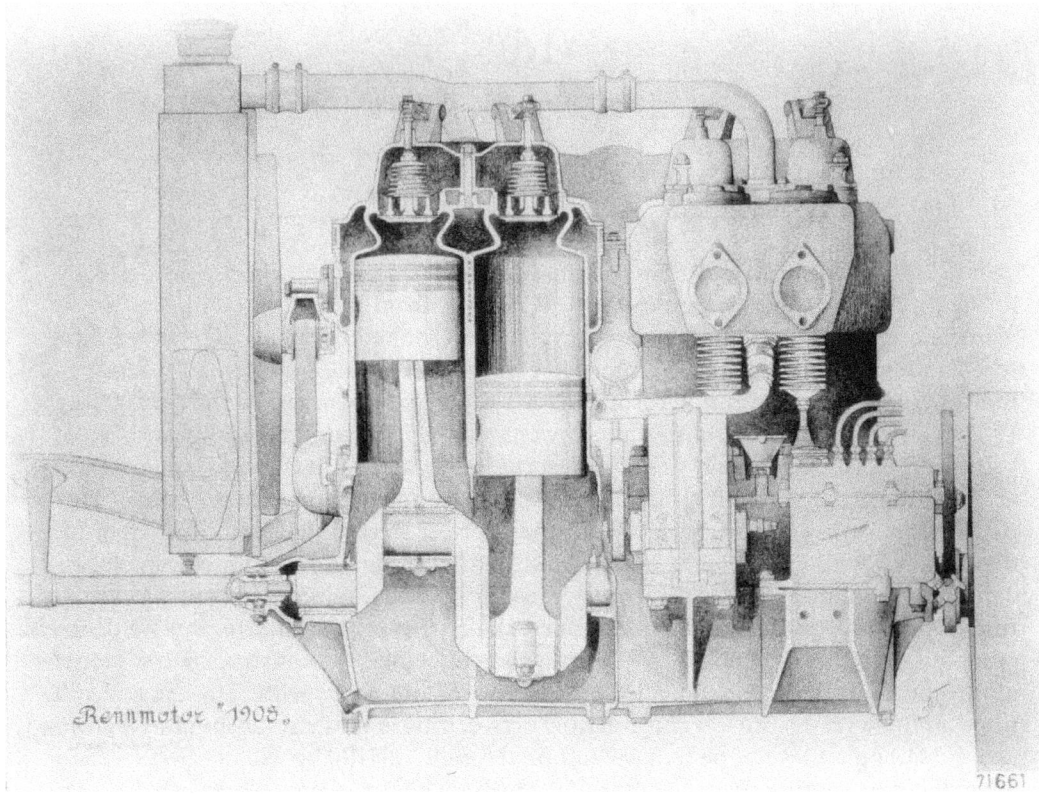

**Mercedes engine of 1908, originally in the dimensions of 155 mm × 160 mm, as compact as possible, with the help of offset connecting rods.**

Untertürkheim quickly discovered that a stroke of 160 mm provided better results than the shorter 150- or 155-mm options. Josef Brauner packed the finding into the well-established four-cylinder, as usual with F-head and two camshafts but as compact as possible with the help of offset connecting rods. Otto Salzer tried out the new 12-liter in the previous year's frame. Did the output disappoint? Disagreements with Paul Daimler, who focused on 170 or even 180 mm, were bound to happen. By the end of March 1908, Josef Brauner left the DMG, switched to Berlin, to the Bergmann Electricity Works, where his former colleague Ernst Lehmann was working on the Bergmann-Métallurgique. Eugen Link was more acquiescent, and stretched the stroke to 170 and 180 mm, resulting in 12.8 and 13.6 liters, 135 and 138 hp at 1400 rpm. Daimler was satisfied. Optimum weight distribution had top priority. Karl Schnaitmann devised the appropriate frame, radically shortening the wheelbase to 270 cm with track of 140 cm. Engine and gearbox were moved back, improving the handling. Michelin supplied the tires, 875 mm × 105 mm front, 895 mm × 135 mm rear, including the latest rims which could be removed and refitted by 22 turns of a single lock screw. The Mercedes weighed in at 1120 kg; to that 250 kg coolant and fuel, 80 kg spare tires and 50 kg tools were added before the start. The drivers? De Caters applied for a place but got no chance with Paul Daimler and definitively gave himself over to the airplane. The Red Devil Jenatzy,

## 16. Apotheosis

July 1908—GP de l'ACF, Dieppe. The Mercedes team at Dieppe: in the foreground are Salzer and Stegmaier; in the middle are Poege and Bott; in the background are Lautenschlager and Mäckle.

as a precaution, had signed at Mors. Otto Salzer stood firm. He recommended his friend from the assembly plant, the 31-year-old Christian Lautenschlager. The third car was committed to track specialist Willy Poege. Stegmaier, Mäckle and Bott were the mechanics. Salzer and Poege opted for a stroke of 180 mm, Lautenschlager for 170. One short- and one long-stroke racer stood by with Lorenz and Burton.

In contrast to the Mercedes which retained its very own character even without Maybach, the first Grand Prix racer from Benz was made up of successful features from the outside. After all, in the same manner Henri Brasier had taken two Bennett Cups! At Mannheim, however, the direction was provided by Hémery and Hanriot. This was a minor revolution since normally the technical director reigned as absolute monarch and did not accept any meddling. Georg Diehl, his right-hand-man Fritz Erle and the young Hans Nibel were soon convinced, and combined a chain-drive chassis, Mercedes fashion, with a four-cylinder engine, Darracq fashion, including the vertical OHV head and dual ignition. The former Barbarou assistant Louis de Groulart put the lot down on paper. Conservative Mannheim had a stroke of 160 mm in mind, but Hémery and Hanriot were aware of the French voiturette scene's approach and suggested a long 200 mm. Or was it exactly the reverse? In any case both options were built. The short-stroke 12-liter was brisker in speeding up, developed 130 hp at 1600 rpm; the long-stroke 15-liter vibrated but achieved 158 hp at 1500 rpm. The engines were mounted on classic chain-drive frames, wheelbase 275 cm, track 135 cm, tires from Michelin, 870 mm × 90 mm or 875 mm × 105 mm front, 895 mm × 135 mm rear, on fast courses also huge 935 mm × 135 mm. They weighed 1240 kg, 100 kg more than the Mercedes. On 31 May 1908, Hémery tested a short-stroke car in the 606-km road race between St. Petersburg and Moscow and won in 8 h 30 min 48 sec, 51 minutes under the previous year's record of Duray in Lorraine, beating Demogeot's Darracq and Pope's Itala. Suddenly the Benzes were joint favorites. By early summer, Mannheim had not cured the vibrations of the long-stroke engine so that Hémery and Hanriot decided in favor of two smoother short-stroke 12-liters while Erle handled a rough 200-mm racer. Gilli, Heim and Gass acted as oil pumpers.

Not only Benz but also Lorraine, Fiat and Mors relied upon the OHV head à la Darracq with its vertical valves. Since, at the higher engine speeds, the valve springs did not get along with the long pushrods, Bayard and Weigel opted for an overhead camshaft. Sabathier and Guillelmon, the engineers responsible for the Bayard, inclined the valves at 30° and found enough room to house a 100-mm intake, a lot more than the 80 mm of the Mercedes or the 90 mm of the Benz. On average, the cylinder dimensions changed from the previous year's 170 mm × 155 mm to 155 mm × 175 mm, whereby the 170 and 180 of the Mercedes lay in the middle and the 200 of the Benz took the cake. As for the height of the engines, the new buzzword was *désaxé*: The block was mounted offset in order to shorten the connecting rods; the crankshaft ran beside the cylinder axis, offset between 10 and 20 percent of the stroke.

Just as two years before at Le Mans, 23 French cars turned up. But now they faced 25 foreigners, more than half the field! Seventeen marques made a grandiose spectacle, maybe the greatest motoring battle of all times, since the Channel coast in July 1908 was the last time that the representatives of a whole industry struggled for its highest award, the Grand Prix. Of course the Renaults, the Brasiers, the new Lorraines and the Bayards were among the favorites, as were foreigners Fiat and even Benz, but not Mercedes. The ACF scheduled the start on Wednesday, 7 July 1908; the distance was ten laps of 77 km. The cars were numbered from 1 to 49, according to the starting minute after six:

| No. | Make | Driver | | | |
|---|---|---|---|---|---|
| 1, 18, 34 | Austin | Resta | Moore Brabazon | Wright | |
| 2, 19, 35 | Mercedes | Poege | Salzer | Lautenschlager | |
| 3, 20, 36 | Motobloc | Pierron | Garcet | Courtade | |
| 4, 21, 37 | Renault | Szisz | Caillois | Dimitriévitch | |
| 5, 22, 38 | Lorraine-Dietrich | Duray | Rougier | Minoia | |
| 6, 23, 39 | Benz | Hémery | Hanriot | Erle | |
| 7, 24, 40 | Fiat | Lancia | Nazzaro | Wagner | |
| 8, 25, 41 | Brasier | Théry | Baras | Bablot | |
| 9, 26, 42 | Porthos | Stricker | Gaubert | Simon | |
| 10, 27, 43 | Opel | Opel | Joerns | Michel | |
| 11, 28, 44 | Clément-Bayard | Rigal | Gabriel | Hautvast | |
| 12, 29, 45 | Itala | Cagno | Fournier | Piacenza | |
| 13, 30, 46 | Weigel | Harrison | Laxen | Shannon | |
| 14, 31 | Mors | Jenatzy | Landon | | |
| 15 | Thomas | Strang | | | |
| 16, 32, 48 | Panhard | Heath | Farman | Cissac | |
| 17, 33, 49 | Germain | Degrais | Roch-Brault | Perpère | |

## 16. Apotheosis

As usual Chevalier de Knyff dispatched the field. Two newcomers had drawn no. 1, Dario Resta and the six-cylinder from Austin. Resta was born in Livorno (or Leghorn), but grew up in London and served his apprenticeship at the Panhard agency and on the new Brooklands track driving the Mercedes racer of F. R. Fry, a wealthy chocolate manufacturer from Bristol and prominent British turfman. Bablot and mechanic Lausson were waiting for the signal to start as Willy Poege in the Mercedes no. 2 passed at prodigious speed. An omen? Certainly, since, as the lap time of Salzer was announced, it was beyond doubt that the Mercedes were fast, much faster than anticipated. Salzer played the part of the baiter. Of course he did things in style, establishing a new lap record of 36 min 31 sec, more than two minutes under the best Mercedes time of the previous year—and this with a car of nearly the same power and higher (but redistributed) weight! Only the Brasier of Bablot was close to that pace, nine seconds slower. Szisz, the resurrected Léon Théry, Wagner, Baras and Nazzaro lost more than 30 seconds. First to retire was the Porthos of Gaubert which was not quite as strong as the musketeer of the same name.

During the second lap Salzer dropped to position 34, having overstrained the engine and the tires. But he had rendered good service. The opposition too was getting into difficulties so that Lautenschlager came up to second place, one minute behind Nazzaro. The Brasier of *monsieur chronomètre* Théry followed in third, then the Fiat of Louis Wagner, the Lorraines of Arthur Duray and Nando Minoia, the Benzes of René Hanriot and Victor Hémery, the Brasier of Paul Bablot and the Panhard of Georges Heath, just six minutes back. The Belgians, the Englishmen

July 1908—GP de l'ACF, Dieppe. The Benz of Hémery arriving at Dieppe.

July 1908—GP de l'ACF, Dieppe. René Hanriot was born in 1876 in Reims, made his money with champagne and began his driving career at Darracq. By his side: Franz Heim, who was born in 1882 in Wiesbaden and entered Benz in 1897 as an apprentice.

July 1908—GP de l'ACF, Dieppe. The Benz trio: no. 6 (Hémery and Gilli), no. 23 (Hanriot and Heim), and no. 39, the slightly taller long-stroke car of Erle and Gass. The scales showed 1237, 1243 and 1240 kg, more than 100 kg above the 1121, 1118 and 1125 of the Mercedes trio.

July 1908—GP de l'ACF, Dieppe. The Fiat team: no. 40 (Wagner and Ferro), no. 24 (Nazzaro and Fagnano), and no. 7 (Lancia and Bordino). (Fiat)

and the lone American were hanging behind. Nevertheless Lewis Strang, Christie's co-driver in 1907, provided amusement, for he had seated his mechanic on the spare tires of the Thomas, in hopes of better traction. The crammed grandstand rolled up with laughter. Two leading actors, a supporting role and a walk-on fell out: the Lorraine of Rougier with a broken gearbox, the Fiat of Lancia with a defective water pump, the Itala of Giovanni Piacenza and the Weigel of Shannon.

By the end of the third lap Lautenschlager changed his tires, dropping to third. Wagner and Hémery took first and second place. But fitted with the latest rims, the Mercedes did not stop for long. Now finally the skeptics who had considered the Benz victory in the race to Moscow as a piece of good fortune were waking up. It was not only Hémery who lay in front; Hanriot in fifth place held the glorious Théry at bay, and in eighth Erle kept the speedy Bablot under control. That no French car was involved in the struggle for the lead, and that the Benz newcomers ground the venerable Brasiers down, was very strange. Blessedly the Bayards came up, Hautvast eleventh, Rigal twentieth, after four blowouts in the first lap. Straight on, the Bayard was the fastest, being timed at 168 km/h; a Mercedes was clocked at 166, a Benz, a Lorraine, a Fiat and a Brasier at 162, a Renault at 158. Salzer withdrew his Mercedes, Baras his Brasier, Szisz his Renault with a twisted front axle. Jules Simon parked his Porthos, Duray his Lorraine after a somersault at Mouchy, Nazzaro and Wagner their Fiats with broken crankshafts, obviously a material defect. Hémery led at the end of the fourth lap, 1 min 38 sec ahead of Lautenschlager, four and one half minutes ahead of Hanriot, then Heath, Théry, Bablot, Cissac, Hautvast, Joerns and Poege who had hit a garden fence. Panhard was celebrating a real comeback, the

July 1908—GP de l'ACF, Dieppe. The Bayard team: no. 11 (Rigal and Gilbert), no. 28 (Gabriel and Alézy), no. 44 (Hautvast and Chassagne).

July 1908—GP de l'ACF, Dieppe. The Belgian Germain team: no. 33 (Roch-Brault and Jargot), no. 49 (Perpère and Ghide), no. 17 (Degrais and Salvator).

fourth place of Georges Heath and the seventh of the motorcycle star Henri Cissac rehabilitated the *marque doyenne*. The Lorraine of Nando Minoia fell out with a defective magneto, the Thomas of Lewis Strang with clutch trouble. Pierron used his Motobloc to cut a small tree; one of the tires flew away and slightly injured a woman spectator. After an amazing lap of 40 min 29 sec, the Weigel of Laxen ran into a sand bank. With 40 min 20 sec for the fifth lap Lautenschlager passed Hémery who stopped at the depot to brush his Benz up and to receive medical treatment, a stone having broken his goggles. Lautenschlager led Hémery by three and Hanriot by five minutes. Carl Joerns, lying fifth, showed an outstanding performance. Wasn't his Opel described as a hanger-on? Rigal climbed to ninth, ahead of Poege. Bablot lost ten places, Hautvast 22. Strang fell out with his Thomas, as well as Warwick Wright with his Austin after having struggled forward to fourteenth.

No changes occurred among the leaders during lap six. Cissac passed Joerns for fifth, and Erle dropped back to tenth. Hauvast retired because of a broken rim. The Italas did not make any progress; Alessandro Cagno and Henry Fournier were twenty-fourth and twenty-seventh, constantly afflicted by tire defects. However Fournier set a pace as in olden days, achieving his first lap in 38 min 55 sec. At the end of lap seven Lautenschlager stopped at the depot. Hémery reduced the gap to 51 sec. Joerns repassed Cissac, Poege took seventh, Courtade position tenth, his Motobloc showing a good performance. Christian Michel parked his Opel, the radiator letting

July 1908—GP de l'ACF, Dieppe. The Fiat of Latin racer Lancia and mechanic Pietro Bordino at the depot with a defective water pump.

July 1908—GP de l'ACF, Dieppe. The six-cylinder Austin of Dario Resta finished nineteenth.

July 1908—GP de l'ACF, Dieppe. After a sensational lap in 40 min 29 sec, the Weigel of Laxen let off steam.

July 1908—GP de l'ACF, Dieppe. New *roi du volant*: Lautenschlager in the Mercedes.

off steam. When arriving at the market square in Eu, Harrison thought that he was passing through Criel. Coming in much too fast, he rolled over; both Harrison and the Weigel escaped with scratches and dents. Outstanding in lap eight was Rigal in his elegant Bayard: a time of 37 min 28 sec resulted in sixth place. Lautenschlager increased his lead over Hémery by three minutes. The German racers kept the lead, a quarter of an hour in front of Théry, 25 minutes in front of Cissac. Dimitri in the best Renault held eleventh place.

After a penultimate lap in 38 min 42 sec, Lautenschlager stopped again; with more than ten minutes to the good he added 20 liters of fuel as a precaution. Hémery lay more than ten minutes back. Mors was not able to renew its old performances. Already in practice a mechanic had destroyed Jarrott's car. Jenatzy lay eighteenth, in front of his colleague Landon, hardly honorable for a marque which was unbeatable at the turn of the century. When touching down after a bump near Sept-Meules, Cissac crashed into a tree because of a tire defect, the tube being caught up in the sprocket and the Panhard out of control. Mechanic Schaube died on the spot, Cissac in a nearby barnyard. Théry and Bablot withdrew because of defective rims. Lautenschlager won in 6 h 55 min 44 sec, averaging 111.107 km/h. The Benz of Hémery followed 8 min 41 sec back, Hanriot 9 min 30 sec back, Rigal as best Frenchman 35 minutes back. Then came Poege, Joerns, Erle, Dimitri, Heath, and Perpère in the Belgian Germain. The best English finishes were the Austins of Brabazon and Resta, eighteenth and nineteenth. Twenty-three cars crossed the finish. After the debacle Louis Renault complained about the latest Michelin rims which did not grip the wheels

July 1908—GP de l'ACF, Dieppe. The Benz of Hémery on the start-finish straight. De Dion was already advertising the voiturette victory of the previous day.

if the tires were not pumped up at 8 bars: "In the face of the appalling state of the roads we could not go up to 8 kilos." Mercedes and Benz pumped up at 6.5 bars, most of the French teams at 4.5. Hadn't Renault won at Le Mans thanks to the rims? Couldn't he suffer defeat in 1908? The track had effectively gone to pieces, had been improperly rolled and was broken up by the voiturette race of the previous day.

While the Mercedes were resting on their laurels, the Fiats called for revenge in their homeland. The Coppa Florio was run on Sunday, 6 September, near Bologna, over ten laps of a 53-km circuit through Borgo-Panigale, Castelfranco, Sant'Agata and San Giovanni, partially over the dead-straight Via Emilia on which the Roman legions had once marched. Bologna, the Plazza Vittorio-Emmanuele, the Via Garibaldi, and the Café San Pietro were bursting with enthusiasm, in the middle of which was a ten-year-old Enzo Ferrari. At six o'clock starter Gregorini Bingham dispatched 17 racers at one-minute intervals:

| No. | Make | Driver | | |
|---|---|---|---|---|
| 1, 7, 13 | Lorraine-Dietrich | Duray | Minoia | Trucco |
| 2, 8, | Motobloc | Gauderman | Faroux | |
| 3, 9, 14 | Mors | Demogeot | Garcet | Landon |
| 4, 10, 15 | Fiat | Lancia | Nazzaro | Wagner |
| 5, 11, 16 | Clément-Bayard | Gabriel | Hautvast | Shepard |
| 6, 12, 17 | Itala | Cagno | Fournier | Piacenza |

July 1908—GP de l'ACF, Dieppe. The Panhard of Henri Cissac at the depot, in the last Grand Prix of the *marque doyenne*.

July 1908—GP de l'ACF, Dieppe. The Benz of René Hanriot at Criel.

The Dombret brothers had committed one of their Motoblocs to the well-known journalist Charles Faroux, expecting a lot of promotion. Faroux started but did not appear on the scoreboard; the field was too fast. It was Nando Minoia who jumped into the lead, ahead of Lancia, Wagner, Gabriel, Duray, Shepard, Piacenza, Nazzaro and Fournier. But the leading Lorraine was soon slowed down by mechanical troubles. Minoia and mechanic Cinotti disappeared under the hood for three minutes, while Duray broke down near San Giovanni and Trucco's racer did not run properly. Who should hold back Latin racer Lancia? With 23 min 24 sec he set a lap record and took the lead, ahead of Wagner, Fournier, Minoia and Nazzaro. Lancia's tires were the first to complain. The Fiat hobbled to the depot. The *tifosi* had been waiting for it! They greeted their favorite with loud applause and bunches of flowers. The tire was changed in a flash. The Latin racer stayed in front, three and one half minutes in front of Fournier, five minutes in front of Nazzaro who came up as usual, and Wagner who had made repairs on the road. Fournier was only able to hold his position by driving at the limit. Near Borgo he was too fast and set his Itala into the ditch. Nazzaro moved forward to second place. The Lorraines of Trucco and Minoia went like clockwork now, keenly making up for the lost time. Then the engine of Lancia's Fiat began to complain about the all-too-heavy foot of its guide. Mechanic Bordino spent ten minutes to rearrange the pushrods. Teammate Nazzaro took the lead. In lap six poor Lancia again lost half an hour, dropping back to eighth, while Wagner retired because of a broken front axle and

September 1908—Coppa Florio, Bologna. Vincenzo Trucco and mechanic Alfieri Maserati took second place for Lorraine-Dietrich.

Landon flew off the road. Vincenzo Trucco and his Lorraine got faster and faster, lying just two minutes behind Nazzaro in lap eight. The *tifosi* were amazed. But hadn't he to stop for refueling? His colleague Minoia collided with the grandstand at Castelfranco, fortunately without injuring anybody. Hautvast skidded into a moat. Finally Nazzaro secured the victory in 4 h 25 min 21 sec, equaling a fabulous 119.6 km/h. The Lorraine of Vincenzo Trucco followed nine minutes back, the Itala of Cagno half an hour back, then Lancia and an anonymous Garcet. All Bayards and Motoblocs had retired. The presentation ceremony was very elegant, a happy Nazzaro being congratulated by Principessa Laetitia and the Duchess of Aosta.

The year closed with the first Grand Prize of the Automobile Club of America, on Thanksgiving Day, Thursday, 26 November. Under the palms of Savannah, Georgia, fifteen laps of an angular 43-km course had to be completed. An excellent field had been obtained: three Fiats, Italas and Benzes, two Bayards and Renaults, and one Lorraine facing six American racers by the name of Lozier, Simplex, Buick, Chadwick, Acme and National.

November 1908—GP of America, Savannah, Georgia. Erle and mechanic Müller in the long-stroke Benz.

November 1908—GP of America, Savannah, Georgia. Last Grand Prix for Renault. (Renault)

| No. | Make | Driver | | |
|---|---|---|---|---|
| 1, 13 | Clément-Bayard | Rigal | Hautvast | |
| 2 | Lozier | Mulford | | |
| 3 | Simplex | Seymour | | |
| 4 | Buick | Burman | | |
| 5 | Chadwick | Haupt | | |
| 6, 14, 18 | Fiat | Nazzaro | Wagner | DePalma |
| 7 | Acme | Zengle | | |
| 8, 15, 19 | Benz | Hémery | Hanriot | Erle |
| 9 | Lorraine-Dietrich | Duray | | |
| 10, 16 | Renault | Szisz | Strang | |
| 11 | National | Harding | | |
| 12, 17, 20 | Itala | Cagno | Fournier | Piacenza |

Keene had entered his Mercedes for Fritz Walker but at the last moment the block broke. "Mercedes Fritz" did not remain jobless for long, as Hémery took him along in the Benz. The start was scheduled at a late nine o'clock but had to be postponed to ten because of thick fog. The race became a contest between the Fiat and Benz teams. During the first two laps the Fiat of the young, barely known Ralph DePalma lay in front, ahead of Hanriot's Benz. On lap six DePalma fell back. Erle left the road after a tire tread flew away and hurt his head. Finally Wagner drove his Fiat to victory in 6 h 10 min 31 sec, a mere 56 seconds ahead of Hémery, eight minutes ahead of Nazzaro. The great sport was going strong. The sportsmen looked forward to the next Grand Prix. By the end of the year they pilgrimaged to the Grand Palais—where the manufacturers got into a dispute. The Grand Prix hibernated until 1912, according to legend the consequence of an arranged abstinence longed for by all parties.

# 17

# *Depression*

In 1909 the ACF intended to transfer its Grand Prix to the Circuit de l'Anjou, a 74-km course west of Angers. Of course the great victors of 1908, Mercedes and Fiat, promised an entry, as well as Opel and Isotta and the French newcomers Cottin-Desgouttes, Rolland-Pilain and Le Gui, but among the old marques only Mors. The old established Parisian factories did not make a sound, considered a respectable showing impossible. With a certain Mercedes or Fiat success in view, the ACF was in trouble and had to cancel its Grand Prix. This was only the tip of the iceberg. The magnificent races of Dieppe had sealed the fate of an already foundered era. The real uproar followed by the end of 1908, in the elitistly subdivided Grand Palais, where the age of the company and the number of the victories determined the best location. For many years Panhard, Peugeot, Mors, De Dion and their friends had constantly been in the limelight, since the first great motorcar show in the Jardin des Tuileries, in 1898 when Félix Faure, then president of France, declared: "Messieurs, it is true that your efforts are commendable but your cars are stinking to high heaven!" Again and again it was the Basque Darracq who got things moving, confederated the parvenus bit by bit, gave the signal to attack the crown and demanded position selection by lot. The old guard was wrought up and planned an exhibition with the pilots. Darracq and his following cancelled their ACF membership. The Grand Palais would have been empty in 1909! Thus the Salon also fell through.

A slump in sales was behind it. Even the Jellinek squad was suffering its full weight. On 30 September 1907, Untertürkheim notified: "The Société Mercédès has unsold cars on stock. The DMG proposes to reduce the 1200 chassis which have to be delivered on 1 October to 800 if the Société Mercédès turns down an extension of contract per 1909." Automobile pomp had turned into a non-seller. Jellinek, Desjoyeaux and Charley couldn't do anything about it. In the showrooms of the Avenue de la Grande Armée, in the Agence Générale des Automobiles of Charron, Girardot & Voigt, in the Automobilium, in the Auto-Palace, even in the Grand Palais, beating down the prices was suddenly *de bon ton*. On the occasion of the Salon, a fully resolved client paid a visit to the fine stand of the *marque doyenne* Panhard, the widely-known symbol for arrogance, fixed price and year-long delivery time:

"How much do you ask for the 15-hp?"

"Twelve thousand."

"Twelve thousand! What do you make of the crisis? Do you take me for a fool? Here are ten thousand. They are yours if you give me the chassis right away."

The seller complied, in former times unthinkable. All the wealthy dandies and sportsmen had been served. Even the ladies of the world and the demimonde socializing at Maxim's, even Liane de Pougy, the attraction of the Folies-Bergère, and the beautiful Caroline Otero, who learned to drive by the side of Abyssin Zélélé, Albert de Dion's black chauffeur, were promenading at the wheel of a motor carriage between the Place Vendôme and the Bois. The luxury market at the Seine was saturated.

In the meantime the peewees named voiturettes sold like hotcakes. In 1909 De Dion and Peugeot-Frères scored the unbelievable profit of one and one half million francs with their one-cylinder midgets. In 1899 France had registered 1672 four-seaters, in 1900 the number rose to 2937, in 1903 to nearly 13,000, in 1905 to more than 20,000 for the first time, and in 1907 to 31,286. Before the turn of the century, just 14 percent were used for business-related purposes, the rest for pleasure. The early clientele was made up almost entirely of extravagant dandies, since the motorcar remained an expensive and crazy substitute for the horse-drawn carriage. But the proportion changed quickly; in 1903 the original 14 percent used for business rose to one-quarter, in 1905 to one-third, in 1907 to nearly half, the two-seater part being even higher. The emerging middle class was behind it—commercial travelers, doctors, notaries and clergymen. The new clientele was not able to afford art nouveau on wheels. Somehow the automobile investment had to be worthwhile. In 1906 a workman with his monthly 200 francs could only dream of a 3800-francs Peugeot voiturette, not to mention the cheapest Renault for 7650, whereas speedy salesmen and doctors increased their revenues thanks to the mobility of the small cars. Superior makes for 50,000 and more were left to a small upper-class, the target by 1908 being a Mercedes, a Fiat, maybe a Benz or Lorraine, but not a Panhard, a Mors or a Brasier.

After the Grand Prix success, Untertürkheim breathed a sigh of relief. Things were looking up. The actual winner of Dieppe was Paul Daimler. Who was able to blame him for the Maybach affair? Since he was missing Maybach's intuition the only option left was chassis tuning. With the aid of Schnaitmann, he adjusted the old but fully developed features so accurately to the Dieppe course that an original gamble turned out as a victory. This could only be successful within a real factory team, without gentlemen drivers, without Charley's organization. Paul Daimler proved that Untertürkheim was absolutely able to win by itself, justifying his position as technical director. Indirectly his triumph caused the downfall of the Société Mercédès: The great loser of Dieppe was Emil Jellinek. On 7 August 1908, the board of directors confirmed that "all business relations with Mister Jellinek have been terminated and that process-related claims are still undecided." The Société Mercédès was unable to sell the minimum quota and refused deposit for an overstock of several hundred cars. The consequence followed by the end of September 1908: "I wish to inform you that I am retiring from the DMG supervisory board and that I don't stand for re-election." Thus a chapter of the Mercedes era came to an abrupt end. Jellinek accepted the position of Mexican consul at Nice with four French départements as district, took charge of the Austrian consulate at Monaco, and got the 145-ton dual-propeller steam yacht *Mercedes II* built by Simpson & Strickland at Dartmouth. He continued to be on good terms with his old friends. On 14 October 1910 he wrote to James Gordon Bennett: "I have learned that through Mess. Caraccio's recommendation you are about to engage

1908—Untertürkheim: Mercedes Street. After the victory of Dieppe, the DMG was again fully booked with orders.

on board your S. Y. *Lysistrata* two stokers I have employed for several years. I consider it of utmost interest for you to know that after having kept those two men during the summer season whilst my yacht was laid up at Cannes, one day about a week ago, they threatened me for an increase of salary of 25 percent. I have therefore discharged them notwithstanding their wish to remain on duty." Bennett replied two days later: "You may rest assured that I shall not engage the stokers in question and if they have been engaged by my chief engineer I shall order them to be dismissed at once." Besides, Jellinek managed several hotels, Grand Hotels of course, the Royal and the Scribe in Nice, and together with Charley the Astoria in Paris. In future the DMG sold abroad directly and the Société Mercédès was relegated to an ordinary French agency.

And how did the old marques survive without the great sport? With quality, just like Delaunay-Belleville or Rolls-Royce. Panhard relied on whispering luxury with its Knight sleeve-valve engine, Renault on a complete model range, Mors, since 1907 under the direction of André Citroën, on efficient production. Henri Brasier hoped in vain for fresh Rothschild money, having frozen out Georges Richard by 1905. Richard for his part built the popular Unic, a T-head two-cylinder. Adolphe Clément and Alexandre Darracq slowly drew back, preferring to collect license fees, Clément from Diatto in Turin and Talbot in London, Darracq from Opel in Rüsselsheim and A.L.F.A. in Milan. The ACF never recovered and was reduced to the rank of a simple association. By the end of 1910, the club issued invitations to the

The grand salon in the Villa Mercedes at the Promenade des Anglais where Jellinek enjoyed his pension.

Salon, indeed together with the confederations, to a democratic and uniformly decorated Salon. Promptly sparks were flying as the up-and-coming Rolland-Pilain Co. displayed a chassis with a new sleeve-valve engine. Knight & Kilbourne and the British Daimler Co. took legal proceedings. But the confiscated chassis quickly came back since the engine was not made according to the Knight system. Now Rolland-Pilain filed a damage suit.

The withdrawal of some old French marques barely made an impact on the other side of the Rhine. Why shouldn't the Grand Prix have a break? After all Germany had the Prince Henry tour, a reliability trial focusing on the "sporting-social field." It was in 1905 that a long reliability contest was held for the first time, called "Herkomer-Fahrt," Herkomer run, after the donor of the challenge cup. The Mercedes of Ladenburg, Weingard and Poege took the first places. Prince Henry, who had already made the automobile attractive to His Majesty, started himself in a Benz, as well as in 1906 when he won a golden badge for a penalty-free arrival. As Hubert von Herkomer did not want to go on, the Prince stepped in and donated his own cup in 1908. The distance of 2200 km led through the entire Kaiserreich, starting in Berlin and finishing in Frankfurt am Main. Fritz Erle in a Benz took this first Prince Henry tour, ahead of Willy Poege's Mercedes and Paul Geller's Adler.

In 1909 "the most important automobile sporting contest of the year" went over 1857 km from Berlin via Breslau, Lomnicz, Budapest, Vienna and Salzburg to Munich. Two special stages were included, a "flat stage" near Guben, and another one in the Forstenried Park near Munich. "The Opel factory provided the largest contingent, in the middle and above all in the small category. The Adler cars deserved admiration for their sleek and at the same time touring appearance. But the closest attention was given to the Mercedes and Benz cars which wanted again to struggle for the hegemony in the automobile industry. "Here Poege, here Erle" was the slogan. Many manufacturers took the wheel themselves, the 28-year-old Ettore Bugatti in a Deutz, Dr. Ludwig Opel and councilor of commerce Wilhelm Opel in Opels, Richard Benz in a Karl Benz & Sons, Karl Reichstein, the junior director of Brennabor, in a Brennabor. August Horch competed in a Horch, indeed in company of his chauffeur, Ferdinand Porsche in an Austrian Daimler, Emil and Bernhard Stoewer in a Stoewer. Much-admired Lilli Sternberg entered a Protos. The engines turned up with long strokes, according to the times, Gaggenau and Presto with 100 mm × 200 mm, Horch with 85 mm × 170 mm, Puch with 86 mm × 172 mm: a bore/stroke ratio of 1/2, the maximum allowed by the regulations. Kommerzienrat Opel won with an Opel, ahead of Alfred Vischer, the son of Gustav Vischer, in a Mercedes. An almost perfect rendez-vous for sport and society:

> Prince Henry and the other German sportsmen, especially Professor Herkomer, who were responsible for the Herkomer and Prince Henry tours, never can be thanked enough for what they have done for the German motor industry. These tours have done more than all the Bennett, Emperor and other cup road races and speed contests held in Germany. It is only since these annual tours have been started that the class of people which really makes it possible for motor car manufacturers to exist has started to buy cars. Until then the motor car was in every respect a luxury. People who then had cars were the wealthiest, the sportiest or the highest in the country. Just like in France, it was a case of having a big racing car to drive about at record speed whether one knew anything about the car or not. The man who had the money and could afford a 60- or 70-horsepower car simply bought one if he found out that his friend or some one else he knew had bought one. Since the tours have taken the place of the road races the demand for racing cars naturally has decreased and I doubt if today there is a single order during a whole season for a racing car except by professional drivers who make a living that way. This turn or change in public taste has been all for the good of the industry.

In 1910, a 1944-km tour led from Berlin via Braunschweig, Kassel, Nürnberg, Strassburg and Metz to Bad Homburg. The two special stages were decisive in the results: "The first flat race is run near Genthin, to the west of Berlin. On a straight road 500 meters are used for speeding-up, then 5.5 kilometers are timed. The second flat race near Heiligkreuz in Alsace leads over a relatively straight stretch where likewise 5.5 kilometers are timed after 500 meters speeding-up." Cars with a tax horsepower between 8 and 25 hp were admitted; the stroke was allowed to be 60 mm longer than the diameter of the bore, hence the frequent dimensions of 100 mm × 160 mm, 105 mm × 165 mm or 115 mm × 175 mm. Coachwork with mudguards was prescribed, and staged minimum weights. Austrian Daimlers under Ferdinand Porsche, Eduard Fischer and Heinrich Count von Schönfeld took the first three places, ahead of Herbert Ephraim (Opel), Fritz Erle (Benz), Adam Paul (Adler), Théo Pilette (Mercedes) and Arthur Henney (Benz). Apart from a few Berliets and Delaunay-Bellevilles in private hands there were no French cars.

Porsche, since 1906 technical director and successor of Paul Daimler at Wiener-Neustadt, relied on four steel singles of 105 mm × 165 mm, 5.7 liters . The

OHC head was welded into position, the 75-mm valves being inclined at 45°, camshaft drive à la Bayard via vertical shaft, output 32 hp at 1000 rpm, 86 hp at 1900, and 95 hp at 2100 rpm. On the special stage near Genthin, it achieved 130 km/h. From 1911 the Austrian Daimler was officially named Austro-Daimler and the Prince Henry model was offered as type 22/86 hp until the beginning of 1914. Wiener-Neustadt produced nearly three hundred units, exporting two hundred to England and America. One of the last, a spectacular boat-shaped torpédo with four elegantly swung exhaust pipes and cycle-type mudguards, specially made to the order of Prince Ely of Parma, created a great stir at the 1914 Prague salon.

The Benz, designed by Georg Diehl and Hans Nibel, was available in two dimensions, 105 mm × 165 mm and 115 mm × 175 mm, 5.7 and 7.25 liters. It had four valves per cylinder and thus a pent-roof combustion chamber, the 57-mm intake being inclined at 25°, the 42-mm exhaust at 20°, the valves operating à la Pipe via two camshafts mounted on crankcase level, with pushrods and rockers. The output of the 7-liter was 104 hp at 2050 rpm and its compression ratio 4.7:1. Since the special stages were run on straight roads with a flying start, chain drive was not necessary, and a torque-tube axle saved weight. A streamlined body in tulip form was standard. Wheelbase was 300 cm, track 125 cm, weight 1340 kg. In the American 450-cubic-inch formula the 7-liter Benz engine survived until 1913, with magnalium pistons in the Bergdoll brothers' Erwin special.

The OHV four-valve engine of the 1910 Prince Henry Benz: valve operation à la Pipe, 115 mm × 175 mm, 7.25 liters, 104 hp at 2050 rpm.

In 1911 the Prince Henry tour was run for the last time, a pure excursion without real competition character, "a friendly and social match between the Imperial Automobile Club of Germany and the Royal Automobile Club of Great Britain," starting in Hamburg, running through Cologne, Bremerhaven, Southampton, Edinburgh, and finishing in London. The British club won. A few years later, Paul Daimler combined the steel singles and the shaft-driven overhead camshaft of the Austro-Daimler with the four-valve combustion chamber of the Benz: the characteristic features of the 1914 Mercedes racer, an Austro-Daimler-Benz, a Daimler-Benz, years before the merger.

# 18

# *Blitzen Benz*

Smaller and lighter racers were to compete in the 1909 Grand Prix on the Circuit de l'Anjou. The clubs had agreed on a maximum piston area of 530 cm$^2$ and a minimum weight of 900 kg, in short, on 130-mm four cylinders. After the withdrawal of the French marques, Mercedes, Fiat and Isotta put the further development of suitable racers on ice for the time being. But abstinence was not the point, neither at Untertürkheim nor at Turin. Didn't the numerous sprints and hillclimbs provide a perfect field of activity for hotted-up Dieppe veterans? Already in the summer of 1908, Paul Daimler and Eugen Link had combined the old Bennett bore with the long stroke used at Dieppe, and got such a 17.3-liter (175 mm × 180 mm) colossus mounted into Willy Poege's Grand Prix frame: output 170 hp at 1400 rpm. In the spring of 1909, Théodore Pilette, the Mercedes agent in Brussels, took delivery of two cars, for himself and the Red Devil. At Ostend, in mid–July, Jenatzy achieved 34.1 sec over the standing kilometer, despite rain, and 9 min 8.2 sec in a 20-km sprint, while Pilette covered the flying kilometer in 23.4 sec.

The neighbors from Mannheim got on with it even more vigorously. Hans Nibel granted the long-stroke Benz bigger pistons and five main bearings. With 185 mm × 200 mm the new powerplant displaced not less than 21 liters, weighed 400 kg and delivered 184 hp at 1500 rpm during first bench tests, increasing after short development to 200 hp at 1600. The barely reinforced Grand Prix chassis had its work cut out for it. Chief tester Fritz Erle put the finishing touches in August 1909, winning the kilometer race at Frankfurt. And on 19 September, the speedy society came together at Schottwien, at the foot of the Semmering, the big Benz of Erle and the two 17-liter Mercedes of Salzer and Poege. Salzer pushed his Mercedes to the new record time of 7 min 7 sec on the pass, six seconds ahead of Willy Poege, 22 seconds ahead of Fritz Erle, 30 seconds ahead of Carl Joerns in an Opel. Thus the combination of Salzer and agile Mercedes gave Erle and the Benz a thrashing of more than two seconds per kilometer!

One month later, Victor Hémery drove the big Benz to Belgium where a kilometer race took place on 17 October, in the castle grounds of Tervueren, 30 km east of Brussels. The Benz ran on elegant wire wheels and competed against the two 17-liter Mercedes of Jenatzy and Pilette and the 10.5-liter Opel (130 mm × 200 mm) of Carl Joerns which was actually intended for the cancelled Grand Prix. It was raining at Tervueren. Hémery fitted steel-studded tires and achieved 31⅓ sec over the standing kilometer, two seconds ahead of Pilette, three ahead of Jenatzy, seven ahead of Joerns and eight ahead of Gasté in a stripped six-cylinder Rossel. Hémery was satisfied with the Benz and continued his trip across the Channel to Brooklands. One year earlier, Nazzaro and his Fiat "Mephisto" had averaged 173 km/h

*Top:* The 21-liter power plant of the Benz: 185 mm × 200 mm, 200 hp at 1600 rpm, OHV head à la Darracq, five main bearings, dual ignition. *Bottom:* Cross-section of the 21-liter Benz.

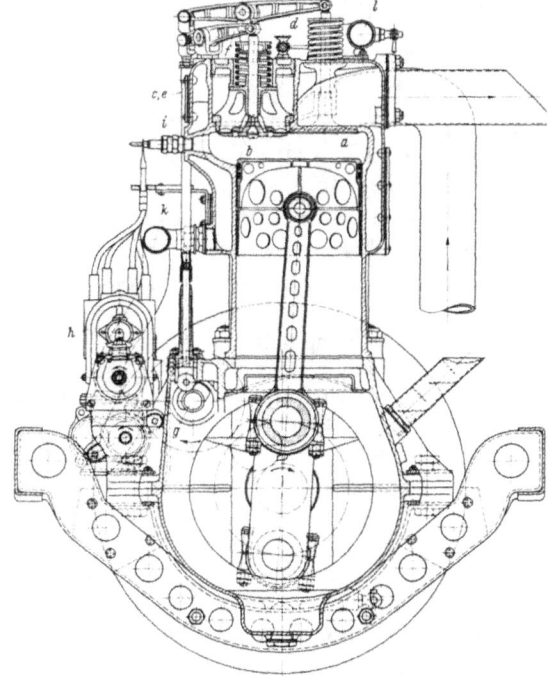

over one lap of the concrete oval, in a match race against Frank Newton's Napier "Samson." The Mephisto was a heavy 18-liter Fiat (190 mm × 160 mm), with vertical OHV head, one 108-mm intake valve and two 66-mm exhaust valves. The Samson, a six-cylinder Napier, stretched from 127 mm × 152 mm to 155 mm × 178 mm, had not been allowed to start at Dieppe because of the detachable Rudge Whitworth wheels, it was said. The match race was to cover nine laps, forty kilometers in top gear with wide-open throttle, man against man. Somehow Newton assumed the lead. Did the Italian rely on his usual tactics? He

September 1909—Semmering hillclimb. Salzer (at the wheel) and Stegmaier in the 17-liter Mercedes. Holding the cup, beer brewer Theodor Dreher (left), the owner of the sprint racer, and Willy Vogel; pictured between Dreher and Vogel is Gustav Vischer; standing to the driver's immediate right is Friedrich Nallinger; and seated on the left front tire is Hermann Braun.

was steadily creeping up and after three laps the Napier pulled out with a broken big-end bolt. Nazzaro collected the nice sum of £500. The devilish Fiat remained in England, finishing up in the hands of Brooklands habitué Ernest Eldridge who implanted a Fiat aircraft engine, a 300-hp six-cylinder A12bis (160 mm × 180 mm). In this form Mephisto took the world record, in 1924, on the dead-straight *chaussée* of Arpajon south of Paris. But by the end of 1909, it was the turn of Hémery and the Benz, this time at Brooklands. On the 4.5-km colosseum southwest of London, he set up six records on 8 November 1909:

| | |
|---|---|
| the flying half mile | in 14.076" (127.877 mph = 204.6 km/h), |
| the flying kilometer | in 17.761" (125.947 mph = 201.5 km/h), |
| the flying mile | in 31.055" (115.923 mph = 185.5 km/h), |
| the standing half mile | in 25.566" (70.406 mph = 112.65 km/h), |
| the standing kilometer | in 31.326" (71.409 mph = 114.25 km/h), |
| the standing mile | in 41.268" (87.233 mph = 139.6 km/h). |

The flying mile proved to be rather slow since the audacious Hémery had difficulties in taking the banking. And when Hémery throttled down there was a reason for it. This did not really bother Barney Oldfield who had an eye on the big Benz. Oldfield had bought the ex–Hémery short-stroke GP racer and, at Dallas, on 9 December, 1909, set a 50-mile record in 47 min 18 sec. The New York Benz Auto Import

Co. under the direction of Jesse Froehlich took the GP Benz back, and Oldfield added $6000 cash for the record racer. Berna Eli Oldfield was born on 3 June 1878, near Wauseon, Ohio, the son of a farmer. He began his career as a bicycle champion, and from 1903 was a dirt-track star at the wheel of the Ford "999," the Winton "Bullet no. 2" and the Peerless "Green Dragon." The organizers of these hippodrome shows were Alex Sloan and Ernie Moross. It was the Moross Amusement Co. and the manager of the Benz Auto Import racing department, the former Buick team manager William Hickman Pickens, who attended to the promotion of the Benz, planning as a first step record attempts in Florida. The racer's usual Grand Prix dress looked too common. By the end of the year, Mannheim tailored a high-speed robe for it, including a prominent "bird beak" on the

By the end of 1909, Mannheim adapted a streamlined dress to the big Benz, including a "beak" on the radiator and a long tail.

radiator and a streamlined tail. Pickens was not wrong since now, even when standing still, the Benz looked like a record breaker. By the beginning of 1910, Mannheim shipped the racer to New York where the Benz Auto Import took over towards the beaches of Ormond and Daytona.

The promotion of the Benz went like clockwork. Until the 21-liter colossus arrived at Daytona, the "Lightning Benz" was the talk of the town. On 16 March 1910, the Benz turned up on the beach, on Firestone tires, 32 × 4 front, 34 × 5 rear. The Fiat importers Hollander & Joseph entered Ralph DePalma on a twin brother of Mephisto, but a broken piston prevented the interesting match. The Moross squad was left alone, George Robertson with a front-drive Christie and the bold Ben Kerscher with an old Darracq (170 mm × 140 mm) "in which Hémery won the 1906 Vanderbilt." Since 1906 the absolute flying mile record was held by Fred Marriott and the Stanley steamer in 28⅕ sec (127.66 mph = 204.25 km/h), the gasoline-engine record by Louis Chevrolet and the Darracq V-8 in 30⅗ sec. The Darracq was an old warrior: Already by the end of December 1905, Victor Hémery had covered the kilometer in 20⅗ sec, at 174.75 km/h, in the South of France, between Arles and Salon. The 90° V-8 was made up of two of the well-known OHV blocks (170 mm × 140 mm) and passed its 230 hp on via a two-speed gearbox.

Oldfield and the Lightning Benz set new standards, covering the flying mile in 27.33 sec (131.72 mph = 210.75 km/h) and the standing mile in 40.53 sec (88.18 mph = 141.09 km/h), both new absolute world records although the runs were timed in one direction only. On 23 March, Oldfield achieved 17.04 sec (131.28 mph = 210.05 km/h) over the flying kilometer and 55.87 sec (128.88 mph = 206.2 km/h) over the two-mile distance. Later he tried to improve his mile times but had to be content with 28.40 sec and 27.88 sec, while Robertson sent the Christie

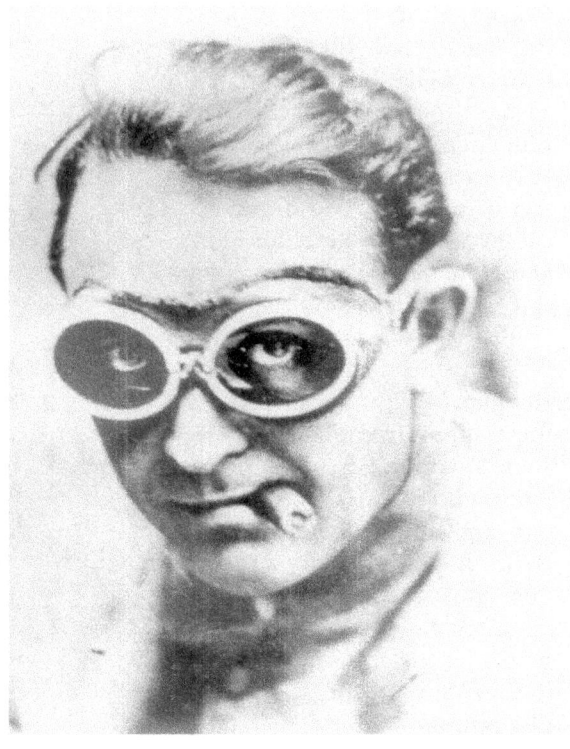

*At right:* Barney Oldfield campaigned the dirt tracks of America, "with or without official sanction wherever he got the sugar."

March 1910—Daytona Beach, Florida. 27.33 sec was Oldfield's time for the flying mile, meaning 131.72 mph, 210.75 km/h and the world record.

December 1905—Arles–Salon. On the dead-straight road between Arles and Salon, Victor Hémery and the Darracq V-8 covered the flying kilometer in 20³⁄₅ sec, averaging 174.75 km/h.

The record Darracq: 90° V-8, 170 mm × 140 mm, OHV head, 230 hp, two-speed gearbox.

over the beach in 30.29 sec and Ben Kerscher the old Darracq in 37.34 sec. Oldfield was credited with four new records:

| | |
|---|---|
| the flying kilometer | in 17.04" (131.28 mph = 210.05 km/h), |
| the flying mile | in 27.33" (131.72 mph = 210.75 km/h), |
| the flying two miles | in 55.87" (128.88 mph = 206.20 km/h), |
| the standing mile | in 40.53" ( 88.18 mph = 141.09 km/h). |

The Kaiser cabled: "I congratulate a daring Yankee on so remarkable a performance in a German car." And Oldfield described his run as "the sensation of riding a rocket through space." Reason enough for the Red Devil Jenatzy to postpone his retirement: On the seaside promenade of Ostend, he sped his 17-liter Mercedes in 16⅘ sec over the flying kilometer, a speed of 212.95 km/h, faster than the Benz! But the international body required two runs in opposing directions and refused recognition. On 8 April 1910 the "one-mile board motordrome" was opened at Playa del Rey, just outside the city gates of Los Angeles. Oldfield and the Lightning circled the pie pan in 36.22 sec (99.39 mph = 159.02 km/h). Caleb Bragg and his brand-new 130-mm Fiat achieved 37.56 sec, DePalma and his Mephisto Number Two 38.76 sec.

Thereafter speed king Oldfield traveled eastwards, demonstrating the Benz on the new brickyard of Indianapolis and setting up new hippodrome records. The state fairs were the big event of the year. Farmers packed their wives and children, friends and neighbors, into their buggies to see Oldfield and the Benz. Bill Pickens came up with a new name: "Blitzen Benz" brought the proper glamour into it. Pickens, Oldfield and the Blitzen gave the public what they wanted to see, a great show, a thrilling display of speed, circus-style racing. The speed king developed an unmatched flair for close finishes, beating the "Flying Dutchman" Kerscher by less than the width of a tire. Beforehand, Pickens provided the "sugar," met the fair manager, and announced a new mile record, good for an adequate bonus. The barbers and the barkeepers posted bills: "Oldfield is coming in the Blitzen!" The fans pilgrimaged to the Union Pacific siding where the white Benz was enthroned in its own railcar. Wherever Barney passed the night was written: "Oldfield sleeps here!" After a few warm-up races, Oldfield and the Blitzen made their appearance. Barney fiddled with ignition and mixture, the Benz backfiring like a mortar—to the farmers, pure magic. Barney adjusted goggles and cigar, and shot away. He became a legend. But Oldfield was not only a publicity-conscious dirt-track star. In Indianapolis and other races, he gave proof of his top-class skill again and again. Moreover Barney and manager Bill Pickens, "prince of hecklers," never lost their sense of humor. It was in the 1910 Elgin road race that Barney was running next to last. As he crawled past his pit Barney shouted to Pickens: "What's my position, Bill?" "Most embarrassing," Pickens megaphoned through his hands. And Pickens played to a full house, for there was hardly a person in the stands that did not hear him.

In October 1910, Oldfield was suspended by the AAA, the American Automobile Association. Barney had started at Readville in a race without official sanction. There was also the matter of a series of three five-mile match races at Sheepshead Bay against heavyweight boxing champion Jack Johnson in a Renault. Of course Barney won them all, but Johnson had no license. Oldfield was suspended until 30 April 1912 and

**April 1911—Daytona Beach, Florida. "Wild" Bob Burman and the Blitzen pushed the mark for the mile and the kilometer to 226 km/h.**

sold the Blitzen to Ernie Moross for $13,500. The Moross Amusement Co. was managing "wild" Bob Burman and it was he who, by the end of March 1911, took the wheel of the Blitzen for the first trials on the beach of Jacksonville, achieving 30.25 sec over the mile. On 24 April, at Daytona, Burman gave free rein to the Blitzen. After 16.28 sec over the kilometer and 26.12 sec over the mile, he set new marks for:

| | |
|---|---|
| the flying kilometer | in 15.88" (141.42 mph = 226.27 km/h), |
| the flying mile | in 25.40" (141.73 mph = 226.76 km/h), |
| the flying two miles | in 51.28" (140.4l mph = 224.65 km/h). |

By the end of May, Burman established four new brickyard records at Indianapolis: the quarter-mile in 8.16 sec, the half-mile in 16.80 sec, the kilometer in 21.40 sec, the mile in 35.35 sec. Then he went on tour. Beside the new superstar Burman and the Blitzen, the Moross Amusement Co. employed alternately Louis Disbrow and Billy Knipper in a sprint Mercedes (175 mm × 180 mm) and H. J. Kilpatrick in a 1906 Grand Prix Hotchkiss (180 mm × 160 mm). Whether in the Electric Park Meet at Baltimore, in the presence of 15,000 spectators at Brighton Beach, at Minneapolis or Syracuse, wild Bob Burman and the Blitzen beat all track records. On 9 September 1912, Burman turned up at Brighton Beach with a freshly imported 300-hp "Jumbo" Benz, with 200 mm × 250 mm and 31 liters, good for 47.85 sec,

*The Burman record certificate.*

a new dirt track record over the mile. Had Mannheim really shipped a bloated racer? Or was it promotion à la Moross? After a successful 1913 season with Burman, Disbrow and the Endicott brothers, the Moross Co. engaged the popular Californian Teddy Tetzlaff. In 1914, Tetzlaff took the wheel of the renamed Jumbo, "Blitzen Benz no. 2" being written in angular letters on its flank, and thundered over the Bonneville Salt Flats in Utah. He covered the half-mile in 12⅗ sec equaling 142.8 mph or 228.5 km/h, the highest speed achieved by a big Benz.

In Europe, already in 1910, a second 21-liter Benz had turned up, in the traditional hillclimb of Gaillon, near Sainte Barbe, on the main road between Paris and Rouen. Since the stone age, one kilometer was timed there, uphill at an average gradient of 9 percent, from a flying start after a short run-up. In 1901, Edge and his Napier achieved 1 min 3⅗ sec but fastest time of the day was set by young Victor Rigal and his Buchet engined Darracq tricycle, a two-cylinder 1.4 liter producing 20 hp at 2500 rpm, beating the Napier by 13 seconds. In 1910, Fritz Erle and the Benz covered the kilometer in 23 seconds, and in 1912 he came back, this time with streamlined body and the Jumbo dimensions of 200 mm × 250 mm, good for 22 seconds. Erle started in many sprints and hillclimbs west of Mannheim, in Belgium, France and Spain, while, with an additional Blitzen, his confrères Franz Heim and Franz Hörner attended to the eastern side, setting new records at Graz, Königssaal and St. Petersburg. Fiat replied with the *tipo* S 76, a wild combination

October 1910—Gaillon hillclimb. Fritz Erle and his 21-liter Benz covered the flying and ascending kilometer in 23 seconds, 157 km/h. Erle was born in 1875 in Mannheim and entered Benz in 1894 as a locksmith.

October 1912—Gaillon hillclimb. During the winter of 1911–1912, the record Benz of Erle received the same streamlined bodywork as the Blitzen, then improved to 22 seconds.

Like his friend de Caters, the Red Devil Jenatzy concluded his career with Mercedes. In July 1910, at Ostend, he squeezed 212.95 km/h out of his sprint racer.

January 1914—Brooklands. Two men lined up to swing the big Benz of Cupid Hornsted into action. A tire disintegrated and stopped the record attempt. In June the tires held up: 124.10 mph or 198.56 km/h, an official mile record timed in two directions.

## 18. Blitzen Benz

May 1913—Whitsun Meeting, Brooklands. Start of the 100-mph short handicap. On the left are the faster cars, the old Kaiserpreis Isotta of Henderson, the big Benz of Eric Loder and the 4.5-liter Vauxhall of Hancock. The Benz is the dark blue Grand Prix racer that Hornsted casually lent out. Loder was unable to keep the pace. The Singer of Lambert won.

of head-high 300 hp aircraft engine (190 mm × 250 mm) and chain-drive frame à la Mephisto. Pietro Bordino was unable to tame the beast at Brooklands. The Russian nobleman Boris Soukhanoff bought the big Fiat. In December 1913, Arthur Duray, with Soukhanoff himself acting as mechanic, achieved 211.66 km/h at Ostend before being forced to abandon the assault on the Benz records due to bad weather.

The last record Benz was delivered in October 1913, just before the Olympia Show, to Brooklands artist L. G. "Cupid" Hornsted, the London counterpart of Barney Oldfield. In 1911, Hornsted had reached 165 km/h with his small Prince Henry Benz (105 mm × 165 mm). In 1912, Mannheim shipped a white Grand Prix racer (155 mm × 200 mm) for him. Hornsted had it painted dark blue, but to the Brooklands crowd it was the "big black Benz." It was obvious that the 21-liter record version would follow in 1913. As usual, Hornsted fitted Rudge Whitworth wheels, Palmer cord tires and Houdaille shock absorbers. In January 1914, he experienced one of his classic Brooklands pirouettes. Mechanic J. A. Toop reported:

> We were taking the railway straight and I was pumping to keep up pressure when I heard a tyre go. I estimate that at the time we were doing just about 119 miles an hour. Directly the tyre went the car skidded sideways in spite of all Hornsted's

January 1914—Brooklands. The 21-liter Benz of Cupid Hornsted ran on Palmer cord tires, 35 × 5 rear.

efforts to keep it straight. We continued broadside for about 80 yards, and then turned two complete backward loops in quick succession. Then the car made a dash backwards up the banking, and it seemed as though we should go over, but Hornsted, who had declutched at the start of the skid, accelerated the engine when we were within 6 inches of the edge, and let in the clutch with a bang. Strips of the tyre had wound around the chain and locked the right-hand wheel; with the sudden acceleration these gave way, and the car shot down the banking in a cloud of smoke, turned another loop, this time bonnet first, and then dashed off the track into the sewage farm grounds, where we pulled up. Somewhere on the track there is an edge of cement which cuts the tyres at high speed.

In June, the tires lasted, even when run in two directions, enabling an official mile record: 29.93 sec and 28.09 sec averaged 29.01 sec and 124.10 mph or 198.56 km/h. Was this the end of the big Benzes? By the end of the twenties, a 21-liter turned up at Brooklands, a long-chassis four-seater, "used by Hindenburg to inspect the front near Verdun." A Blitzen was always good for a legend.

# 19

# *Voiturettes*

The nice designation "voiturette" came from Léon Bollée, the brother of Amédée Junior. In 1896 Léon had the name protected for his tricycle, so that Decauville called their little jobs "voiturelles" and Cottereau "voiturines." Later voiturette became widely accepted. The original 400 kg regulation quickly provided a distinctive character and accounted for the success of Renault and Darracq, but lost its attractiveness over the years since at the turn of the century only a few manufacturers were able to build an interesting car under 400 kg. In 1905, when the Ardennes race was the only event for the 400-kg speedsters, the sports paper *L'Auto*, which later became *L'Équipe*, imagined a more suitable competition: the Coupe des Voiturettes. Of course, the ACF and the two largest voiturette manufacturers, De Dion and Peugeot-Frères, acted in the background. Publicity through sport was to benefit everyone, including the midgets. The Marquis not only provided the standard engine for nearly all newcomers, but held a share in the largest daily newspaper of its kind. The house of Peugeot was split since the launch in 1896 of its two-cylinder, which was a thorn in Monsieur Eugène's side. Cousin Armand did not waste time, but founded in nearby Audincourt his autonomous Société Anonyme which was to build automobiles of Peugeot make. In the meantime, in 1899, the parent house, under the direction of Eugène and his three sons Pierre, Robert and Jules, began production of motorcycles and quickly realized the huge potential of the voiturette market. Armand was open to discussion and from 1906 admitted four-wheeled lightweights, not exceeding 345 kg without body, under the name "Lion-Peugeot." With the small Lions, the parent house soon left the Société Anonyme behind so that the dissidents reunited in 1910.

In 1905, *L'Auto* restricted the displacement to one liter. By the end of November, 13 voiturettes went on a six-day reliability tour: three Lacoste & Battmanns, Grégoires and De Dion-Boutons, a Gladiator, a Demeester, a Hugot and a Vulpès. The caravan struggled round Paris, through sticky snow, until someone scattered bent nails over the road near Poissy. The ACF did not acknowledge the results. In 1906 the rules became more lively and more complicated. Only one- and two-cylinders were allowed to start, with touring body in "ready to travel" condition, maximum bore 120 and 90 mm. Graduated minimum weights ensured equality: for singles 578 kg at 94 mm up to 905 kg at 120 mm, for twins 792 kg at 70 mm up to 963 kg at 90 mm. Nearly one-tonners! By the beginning of November, 15 voiturettes with mudguards rattled to the south of Paris, to Rambouillet, among them many newcomers: three Sizaire et Naudins and Lion-Peugeots, two Delages and Alcyons, one Auto-Stand, Le Métais, Vulpès, Fouillaron and Bailleau. Did the 707-kg Lions carry along lead plates? Six 200-km stages had to be covered at a

June 1903—Circuit des Ardennes: Voiturette class. Originally the midget racers had to weigh between 250 and 400 kg, leading to wild constructions with no bodywork and filigree wire wheels. Denis de Boisse had self-made his De Boisse, with a hotted-up two-cylinder from De Dion. The driver's ducked posture was typical, particularly in the small class as it reduced air resistance, improving speed on the straights. After two long laps of 136 km and 4 h 39 min 26 sec, de Boisse in his De Boisse finished third, averaging 58.45 km/h.

November 1905—Coupe de l'Auto: *Pesage* near the Darracq factory at Suresnes. Gachet and mechanic Duclos were bundled up in thick furs. It had snowed. Their single-cylinder Lacoste & Battmann (100 mm × 120 mm) kept pace and finished fourth after six days and 1200 km. Then the ACF nullified the results. On the level, the Lacoste covered the flying kilometer in 1 min 42.3 sec; uphill it managed 4 min 29.1 sec!

minimum of 30 km/h, then 233 km as fast as possible. Georges Sizaire put through his Sizaire in 4 h 7 sec, 5 min 33 sec ahead of Ménard in a Delage, 14 min 34 sec ahead of the popular motorcycle champion Giuppone in a Lion. The rest followed far behind. In 1907, *L'Auto* changed all figures: the minimum weight for singles became 450 kg at 85 mm up to 670 kg at 100 mm, for twins 687 kg at 71 mm up to 850 kg at 80 mm. The course and the winning make remained unchanged. Louis Naudin won the Coupe ahead of his confrère Georges Sizaire and Jules Goux in a Lion. Many current and future Grand Prix drivers were on the starting line: Rigal, de Langhe and Molon in Werners, Barriaux and Laly in a Vulpès, Thomas in a Prima, Cissac in an Alcyon. Champoiseau drove a Demeester, de la Touloubre a Guillemin-Le Gui, Collomb a Corre, Anzani a Le Métais and de Marne a Grégoire.

The sensational field of 64 voiturettes gave the ACF food for thought. In 1908 the club organized a Grand Prix des Voiturettes! One day before the big cars, a pack of genuine midget racers was allowed to let off steam, over seven laps of the 77-km Grand Prix course: 100-mm singles, 78-mm twins, 68-mm three- and 62-mm four-cylinders, the minimum weight for all being 600 kg. With the exception of the three-cylinder, every option turned up. The trend was set by the brothers Maurice and Georges Sizaire and their partner Louis Naudin at their small workshop in Paris, Rue de Lourmel. Maurice Sizaire was a former architectural draftsman, the younger Georges a saddler, and only Naudin came from the automotive scene, having handled a lathe at De Dion. From the outset Maurice Sizaire relied

October 1906—Coupe de l'Auto, Rambouillet. The Autostand-De Dion of Pellegrin rounding the *fourche* near Rambouillet.

October 1906—Coupe de l'Auto, Rambouillet. Georges Sizaire in his Sizaire et Naudin passing through La Hunière.

October 1907—Coupe de l'Auto, Rambouillet. Two Werners: Victor Rigal in front of Léon Molon.

October 1907—Coupe de l'Auto, Rambouillet. The Vulpès of Barriaux.

on an F-head single, the valves being superimposed in the external pocket and hence able to grow with the stroke. In 1906 the Sizaire ran with the dimensions of 120 mm × 150 mm, output 18 hp at 2000 rpm, in 1907 with 100 mm × 170 mm and 22 hp at 2400 rpm, and at Dieppe with the funnel dimensions of 100 mm × 250 mm, 30 hp at 2400 rpm, 75-mm valves, engine height 105 cm. The crankshaft ran in two ball bearings, and the piston was machined out of a steel bar, with one compression ring. Throttle control was by variable intake valve lift: The intake cam could be moved on a squared shaft by the operation of the steering wheel lever or the foot accelerator. The intake opened 35° after TDC, closed 20° after BDC; the exhaust opened 60° before BDC, closed 20°–30° after TDC. Lubrication was via pure castor oil supplied by a specialist from Marseille; a few years later even private owners who had trouble with smoky exhausts used castor oil for service in Paris. As the law only made it a crime to smoke but was silent about disagreeable smells, castor oil users were satisfied.

Gratien Michaux, the freelance long-stroke artist from Peugeot-Frères, did not go beyond a stroke of 170 mm in his Lion voiturette expérimentale no. 2, in short VX 2. The L-head single had difficulties in breathing! Conventional L-heads from Aster (100 mm × 150 mm) or De Dion (100 mm × 160 mm) powered the remaining single armada by the names of Le Métais, Bailleau, Jean de La Roulière, Taine, Truffault, Thieulin and Werner. Of the Delages, only Thomas and Lucas started with De Dion engines, a new L-head twin (78 mm × 130 mm). The third Delage was propelled by an evil prototype, a Causan (100 mm × 160 mm) with

October 1907—Coupe de l'Auto, Rambouillet. The Sizaire of Louis Naudin.

July 1908—GP des Voiturettes, Dieppe. The Sizaire of Georges Sizaire and mechanic Rochette. The radiator was made of copper tubes, with flow by thermosiphon. Power transmission was via single plate clutch and three-speed gearbox. Independent front suspension. Wheelbase 225 cm, track 117 cm, tires 760 × 90, on fast courses 810 × 90, dry weight 680 kg.

four horizontal valves and dual ignition, good for 28 hp at 2800 rpm. Things almost turned out differently. The 25-year-old Némorin Causan was constantly modifying and improving. Louis Delage hit the roof! Only the intervention of Albert Guyot, since 1906 Delage and Gladiator agent at Orléans, Boulevard Alexandre Martin, released the high-speed four-valve single. Concerning handsome equipment, the Ariès (100 mm × 180 mm) came off best, with an overhead camshaft, four vertical valves and four plugs. A blower and desmo-operation were employed as an experiment in one of the Ariès.

While the long-stroke supporters passed sleepless nights to find space for the numerous and expanding valves, the higher piston area of the four-cylinders provided a simple solution to the breathing problem. The Swiss Martini (62 mm × 90 mm) from Saint-Blaise at Lake Neuchâtel and the Italian Isotta-Fraschini (62 mm × 100 mm) from Milan were outstanding. They brought not only international flair, but also an elegant two-valve OHC four-cylinder with camshaft driven by a vertical shaft, in the Martini via helical gears, in the Isotta (devised by a young Giuseppe Coda) via more conventional bevel gears. Coda was born in Biella, 50 kilometers to the northeast of Turin, in 1883. He had worked for Züst at Brescia and Rapid and Scat at Turin, and was about to switch back to Turin where he was to be responsible for the future Fiat racers. The Martini, with its crankshaft

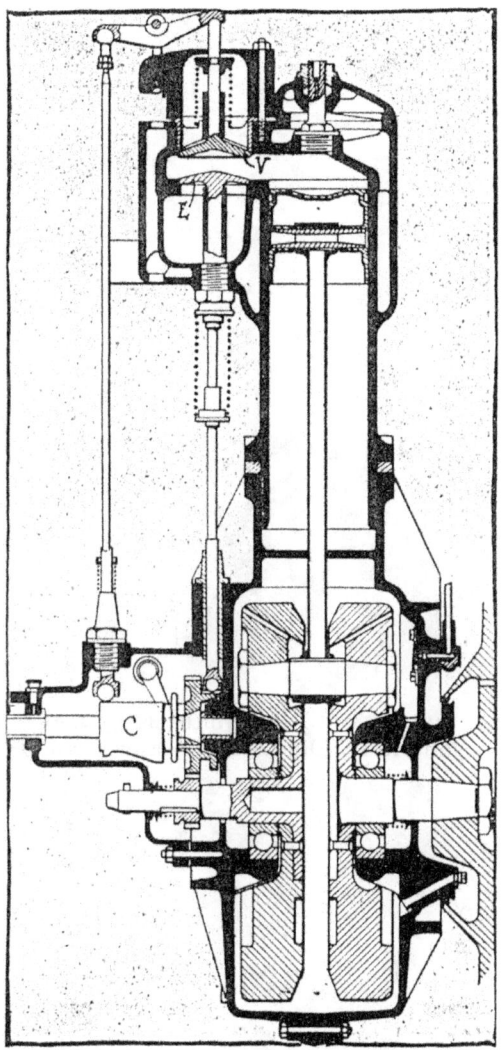

The 1908 *monocylindre* Sizaire et Naudin: 100 mm × 250 mm, F-head, 75-mm valves, crankshaft in two ball bearings.

running in only two ball bearings, briskly speeded up to 3000 rpm, producing 12 hp at 1300 rpm, 17 at 2000 and 26 hp at 3000 rpm. Both cars were available in barely tamed form as serial vehicles and the Isotta in particular served as a model at Alsacian Molsheim for the small Bugatti which became known as type 13.

On 6 July 1908, at six in the morning, they hammered away, at minute intervals. Albert Guyot and mechanic Reyrol took the lead with a 57-minute lap, two minutes ahead of Louis Naudin. Despite the Sizaire's 130-kg weight disadvantage, on lap two Naudin speeded up and passed. In standby position were the Lions of Jules Goux and Georges Boillot, the Martini of Beck and the Thieulin of

July 1908—GP des Voiturettes, Dieppe. The Isotta-Fraschini team: on the left Trucco and Rossi; then Alfieri Maserati and Pontiroli; on the right Buzio and Butti.

July 1908—GP des Voiturettes, Dieppe. The Swiss Martinis: on the left Boris, the marque's agent at Argenteuil; on the right Beck, who, in the twenties, built his own Becks.

July 1908—GP des Voiturettes, Dieppe. The Grégoire of Gasté leading the Werner of Vallée.

Thieulin. After four laps Guyot regained the lead; Naudin was changing a tire. Martin used his Demeester to knock down a bridge pillar. Charlas turned over with his Truffault, Hamilton with his Guillemin, Sonvico with his Martini. The Ariès of Perrot lost a wheel, and Beck twenty minutes because of a leaky radiator. The speed of the midgets left the sportsmen flabbergasted. Guyot was averaging 80 km/h! Albert de Dion and his marketing director Charles Lecoeur rushed up to Louis Delage. Wasn't the Causan in front and running like clockwork? A clever de Dion seized the opportunity: "My dear Louis, should Guyot win, leave Causan out of it! Then we'll give you an additional 5 percent discount on our engines." And Guyot won in 5 h 45 min 30 sec, equaling 80.3 km/h, six minutes ahead of Naudin; then came the Lions of Goux and Boillot, the two-cylinder Delage of Thomas and the Thieulin of Thieulin. As for the four-cylinders, the Isotta of Felice Buzio finished eighth, the Martini of Beck despite radiator trouble tenth, and the Isotta of Alfieri Maserati fourteenth. Delage was well on his way right to the top. In 1903 he worked for Peugeot at Levallois-Perret; in 1905 he established his own shop, supplying components for the Helbé voiturettes of Levecque & Bodenreider and, by the end of the year, displaying his own two-seater whose distinctive style instantly attracted *Tout Paris'* self-driving ladies. After the victory at Dieppe, the sportsmen too bought Delage. And the inventive Causan? He looked for a new employer.

The Coupe des Voiturettes followed suit by the end of September 1908 and was run as a pure race, over eight laps of a new 50-km circuit south-west of Compiègne.

**July 1908—GP des Voiturettes, Dieppe. Albert Guyot and mechanic Reyrol in the Causan engined Delage.**

*L'Auto* more-or-less took over the ACF rules with bores of 100, 80 and 65 mm at minimum weights of 500, 600 and 650 kg. Suddenly the Martinis were 50 kg underweight! Improvements included F-head De Dion singles (100 mm × 200 mm) in the Corre and the three Werners and a De Dion type axle in unit with a three-speed gearbox in the De Bazelaire. Delage and Isotta stayed at home. The finish was in accordance with the usual Coupe de l'Auto order: Naudin ahead of Sizaire and Goux. Voiturette races enjoyed increasing popularity. Giuppone drove his Lion to victory at Turin and in the small Targa Florio on Sicily over two laps of the 148-km Madonie circuit while Barriaux and his L-head twin from Alcyon (78 mm × 150 mm) took the Coupe de Normandie.

*L'Auto* did not give the midgets a moment's peace, as usual changing the rules for 1909, permitting by way of variety graduated maximum values for the bore/stroke dimensions: 100 mm × 250 mm to 120 mm × 120 mm for singles, 80 mm × 192 mm to 95 mm × 95 mm for twins and 65 mm × 140 mm to 75 mm × 75 mm for fours, at a standardized minimum weight of 600 kg. As the Coupe became overnight the "course de l'année," the race of the year, the Lion racing department laid it on thick. By the end of April, Georges Boillot tested the first of the new racers in Sicily. Originally the *monocylindre* VX 3 (100 mm × 250 mm), supplied by Boudreaux-Verdet, pounded away in a power boat. Normally Louis Boudreaux, a leading member of the Hélice Club de France (the ACF for motorboats), and his partner Louis Verdet, a former railway engineer, made their money with reliable, rather conventional boat and stationary engines. Thus the racing world was speechless at the first appearance of the racing single. Operated through a mysterious system of rockers and eccentrics, three 45-mm intake and exhaust valves cared for the breathing and no less than three plugs for the ignition. Clearly the output was higher than in the Sizaire, namely 33 hp at 2400 rpm. At the beginning of May, Jules Goux started in the Copa Catalunya near Barcelona on the next Lion number, the VX 4, a combination of the familiar chain-drive frame with the latest Gratien Michaux design, a 20° V-2 (80 mm × 192 mm) with bland L-head. After all, the V-2 delivered a reliable 30 hp at 2500 rpm, enough for the victory ahead of Georges Sizaire. Wasn't Barcelona the home town of Hispano-Suiza? In the Copa they made their voiturette debut, with T-head four-cylinder (65 mm × 140 mm) and 27 hp at 2400 rpm. The latest Coupe regulation seemed successful;, one-, two- and four-cylinders were equal, at least on paper.

Since the Grand Prix was cancelled the Coupe was run in June, on a new course at Boulogne-sur-Mer, for a distance of twelve laps of 37.9 km. In addition to the Lions and the Hispanos, there were three Crespelles with L-head single from Aster (108 mm × 183 mm), a Le Gui (104 mm × 213 mm) and a Werner (100 mm × 250 mm) with F-head De Dions and finally six fours, three Calthorpes from Birmingham and three Belgian FIFs. Giuppone won at the wheel of the Lion *monocylindre*, averaging 75 km/h, in front of Goux in the V-2 and Thomas in the Le Gui. Although the wicked tongues were saying that the Lion single contented itself with

April 1909—Targa Florio voiturette race, Sicily. Georges Boillot in the Boudreaux-Verdet-engined Lion-Peugeot VX 3.

June 1909—Coupe de l'Auto, Boulogne. The Le Gui of René Thomas.

June 1909—Coupe de l'Auto, Boulogne. The Lion-Peugeot of Giuppone.

one ignition per telegraph pole, there was no stopping it: Near Caen, in the Coupe de Normandie over six laps of 56 km, Georges Boillot scored his first victory and in the Circuit d'Ostend over 12 laps of 33.3 km it was again Giuppone's turn. In the 20-km race between Ostend and Wenduyne, the Lion competed against heavier contenders:

| | | |
|---|---|---|
| 1. Jenatzy | record Mercedes (175 mm × 180 mm) | 8' 52" |
| 2. Hörner | Prince Henry Benz (115 mm × 175 mm) | 10' 16" |
| 3. Boillot | six-valve Lion (100 mm × 250 mm) | 10' 21" |
| 4. Joerns | Prince Henry Opel (115 mm × 175 mm) | 10' 49" |
| 5. Mathis | Prince Henry Fiat (95 mm × 155 mm) | 11' 15" |

*L'Auto* was not swayed by the critics and, in 1910, permitted even more extreme dimensions: 100 mm × 300 mm, 80 mm × 280 mm and 65 mm × 260 mm, minimum weight 650 kg. Had Boudreaux and Verdet lost their vivid imagination? Their single disappeared from the scene. Michaux supplied the Lion numbers five and six. The VX 5 was based on the previous year's 20° V-2, now with the dimensions of 80 mm × 280 mm and new three-valve head, a vertical 60 mm intake being operated by a high-mounted camshaft running between the two cylinders and two horizontal exhaust valves by the vertical camshaft drive. Output was 40 hp at 2200 rpm. Each cylinder had its own carburetor, a Claudel, projecting through the sides of the hood, and its own high-tension magneto. The fuel tank was carried on the floor boards, behind the engine and in front of the mechanic. Tires were 810 mm × 90 mm on non-demountable wire wheels; total weight was 800 kg. And the VX 6 was a 20° V-4 (65 mm × 260 mm) which was content with only one exhaust valve and delivered 50 hp at 2200 rpm. The racers were brought to the circuit at night. While they were being weighed-in a big screen was placed round them, and before the mechanics would disassemble the cylinders the hall had to be cleared of all but officials: Information was most jealously guarded. Tribet (65 mm × 180 mm, two-camshaft OHV-head), De Bazelaire (65 mm × 160 mm, F-head) and Calthorpe (65 mm × 170 mm, L-head) relied on straight-fours, output 35 hp in all cases. This was also the output of the current De Dion singles, with 100 mm × 250 mm and dual F-head, or 100 mm × 300 mm and dual L-head.

Hispano turned up with a T-head four as in the previous year and, with 65 mm × 200 mm, deliberately stayed under the maximum dimensions, with output of 45 hp at 2500 rpm. How could the Spaniards, in 1910, rely on the archaic T-head? Just like Peugeot-Frères they received their racing engines from a specialist. At Geneva, the brothers Charles and Lucien Picker had squeezed the last drop out of the old Maybach idea. A young Ernest Henry worked at the drawing board of their shop, the same Henry who switched to Peugeot in 1911 and was to be celebrated as the father of the DOHC head. The connection to Barcelona? Marc Birkigt, the Hispano director born in Geneva, still had close business contacts with C. Jules Mégevet and his Société de Constructions Mécaniques de Genève. Mégevet not only copied the Mercedes radiators but supplied everything the new industry could use, from the tire to the vélo, to the motorcycle, to the services of the Picker brothers. A T-head long-stroke engine resolved two major problems from the outset: The narrow bore of 65 mm prevented the piston from glowing, while the valves could expand freely on both sides of the combustion chamber and supply enough mixture

September 1910—Coupe de l'Auto, Boulogne. Standing behind the Hispano engine, mechanic Ernesto Fanelli; behind the dashboard Paolo Zuccarelli; behind Zuccarelli with cap, Ernest Henry. The short T-head four from the workshop of the Picker brothers was mounted as far back as possible. The crankshaft ran in three ball bearings. Dimensions of 65 mm × 200 mm resulted in 2.65 liters and 45 hp at 2500 rpm. The shaping of the spur wheel housing was typical for Henry.

September 1910—Coupe de l'Auto, Boulogne. The Hispano of Zuccarelli revealed the way into the future.

despite a bore and stroke ratio of nearly 1:3. But the glow problem was not completely cured. At high engine speeds, the outer edge of the exhaust valve pocket overheated, resulting in misfiring. The Picker brothers addressed the problem by giving the combustion chamber above the exhaust pocket a hemispherical form and the valves a slight inclination of eight degrees, scavenging the exhaust pocket and blowing away the heat concentration. The engine could speed up to 3000 rpm. In Paris, Labor manufactured the Picker under license, as boat and aero engines in the dimensions of 65 mm × 210 mm, 90 mm × 210 mm and 100 mm × 210 mm. The 5.3-liter produced 62 hp at 1350 rpm, the big 6.6-liter, not least thanks to its 70-mm valves, 80 hp at 1330 rpm, equaling a mean effective pressure of 8.21 bars, 30 percent more than a good 1908 Grand Prix racer. In 1909 the Swiss T-head made the breakthrough, on one hand in the power-boat races at Monaco, on the other hand when Picker agent Guillaume Busson demonstrated it in his Blériot monoplane. In 1910, in view of a voiturette use in the Hispano, Ernest Henry devised a 65 mm × 200 mm version of the Labor-Picker, with 55 mm valves, two-piece crankshaft running in three ball bearings, tubular connecting rods and steel pistons. Only the new "BND" steel from the Dérihon brothers, a special brand of chrome-nickel steel, made possible the realization of such details. Everyone bought from Dérihon, either from the Loncin factory, in the suburbs of Liège, or from the Jeumont branch, in North-France.

With only 14 starters the Coupe des Voiturettes was run on Sunday, 18 September 1910, as in the previous year over 12 laps of the narrow circuit of Boulogne.

September 1910—Coupe de l'Auto, Boulogne. Stroke record under the hood of Collomb's Corre: a De Dion single in the dimensions of 100 mm × 300 mm!

Tragically, Giuppone was not among the starters. When testing the V-4 the friendly Italian tried to avoid a cyclist and was thrown out of the car, landing on the back of his head and sustaining such injuries that he died a few minutes later. A Tribet broke its clutch coming to the starting line, and the De Dion-engined Saint-Lanne-Martinet quietly disappeared. Starting second, Zuccarelli finished first after an initial lap in 25 min 35 sec, easily beating the 1909 record of 29 min 28 sec over the same course. There was a surprise when the next car to roar by was Boillot's four-cylinder Lion which had started twelfth and passed a Hispano, a Calthorpe, a D.S.P.L., a Corre and a De Bazelaire. But there was still faster work, Goux coming round on his two-cylinder Lion in 24 min 33 sec, or 17 seconds faster than his teammate. With a third lap in 24 min 2 sec, the record for the day, Goux increased his lead. On lap seven Goux punctured two tires and had to change with fixed rims, allowing Zuccarelli to get a lead of six minutes. Boillot was a frantic sprinter unable to make up the time lost through his frequent but brief stops, and Chassagne was a dangerous runner-up. On lap eleven Goux lost the race when he punctured three more tires, losing 14 minutes. Zuccarelli, who never once lost time to a puncture but was held up by reason of a leak in the Hispano's fuel tank, won in 5 h 4 min 50 sec, averaging 89.5 km/h, 17 minutes ahead of Goux in the two-cylinder Lion, 26 minutes ahead of Jean Chassagne in another Hispano, 33 minutes ahead of Boillot in the four-cylinder Lion. On the spot a telegram was sent to the thirteenth Alfonso: "The Coupe des Voiturettes organizers appreciate the first international victory of the Spanish automobile industry."

September 1910—Coupe de l'Auto, Boulogne. No fear! The Lion VX 5 of Jules Goux did not turn over.

In the ensuing year a civilized street version (80 mm × 180 mm) of the Boulogne racer appeared: the Hispano "Alfonso." "The race for the sixth annual voiturette cup was one of the finest exhibitions of speed we have seen in France, and was particularly welcome after a monotonous series of aviation meetings. It is doubtful if Szisz could have held his own on the straightaway Sarthe course against these terrible pigmies."

Were the hurdles not high enough? Or was there not enough competition? In any case *L'Auto* put the long-stroke midgets on early retirement and revived the *voitures légères*, the light cars. In 1911 *voiture légère* meant a maximum displacement of three liters with a bore and stroke ratio between 1:1 and 1:2, at least four cylinders and weight of at least 800 kg! Didn't the old 1901 regulation set a maximum of 650 kg? Obviously *L'Auto*'s naming was wide of the mark. Nevertheless the 3-liters were interesting. The new Lion, which was shortly called Peugeot after the 1910 reunification, was the hot favorite, a V-4 (78 mm × 156 mm) with OHV four-valve head and 55 hp at 2500 rpm. Louis Delage was back, having obviously come to the conclusion that his 1908 laurels were becoming a bit tarnished and needed refurbishing, with his new designer Arthur "Léon" Michelat and the type X (80 mm × 149 mm). Michelat relied on two side-mounted camshafts operating horizontal 60-mm valves, à la Pipe. To allow timing variations, the cams were keyed on their shafts. The tubular connecting rods were made of BND steel; the pistons were too at first but were later changed for a set made of fine-grade cast iron. The four-piece crankshaft, as well as the two camshafts, ran in five ball bearings from Malicet & Blin. Output was 60 hp at 2600 rpm. During first tests the Delages were equipped with five speeds, the fifth speed being geared up for the long straightaway downgrades and the other speeds carefully proportioned for the hilly, winding roads. However better results were obtained with four speeds with direct drive on the fourth. The shaft-drive frame followed standard practice, using distance rods having a slight downward push on the rear axle and provided with universal joints to prevent any breaking effect on the springs. Wheelbase was 275 cm, track 130 cm, tires 815 mm × 105 mm front, 820 mm × 120 mm rear, total weight "without spares" 1100 kg.

The Boulogne circuit was lengthened to 52 km, 12 laps of which were to be run on 25 June 1911. After the initial lap Burgess, with his Calthorpe, secured second position only 31 seconds slower than Boillot with the Peugeot. Hancock's Vauxhall, "a magnificently prepared car, with much of its equipment recalling Brooklands practice," went out with a broken piston head. Zuccarelli's Peugeot dashed into a tree, ripping the bark off for a height of five meters from the ground and shooting the mechanic over a hedge three meters in height. Zuccarelli escaped without a scratch; the mechanic suffered the loss of a tooth. The old guard disappointed the public: Wagner retired his Alcyon, Hémery's Grégoire and Duray's Excelsior failed to figure, and Hanriot parked his Peugeot at the depot, allowing his mechanic to tie up a broken mudguard with wire while he wiped up spilled oil with a piece of rag, the onlookers remarking "polish the brasses next" and "why don't you wash the car down?" Up to the midpoint the race was between Boillot and Goux for Peugeot, the full Delage team, and Porporato and de Marne for Grégoire. Against the advice of Louis Delage, Bablot had started the race with only half the quantity of fuel and oil necessary to finish the distance. Filling up cost him three and one half minutes.

June 1911—Coupe de l'Auto, Boulogne. The three-liter Peugeot of Georges Boillot at the depot.

June 1911—Coupe de l'Auto, Boulogne. René Thomas at work in the Delage.

Nevertheless, at the beginning of the twelfth and last lap, Bablot had an advantage of 1 min 24 sec on Boillot's Peugeot. Then, ten kilometers from home, a back tire of the Delage went flat. Bablot decided to run on the rim. At 120 km/h on the straightaway, down the hill through Baincthun, over the rough pavé of the village, swinging around the sharp turn on the outskirts of the hamlet, then up the 12 percent grade and along the winding descending road to the grandstands, Bablot roared without a slackening of speed, and was rewarded by winning the race in 7 h 2 min 52 sec, with a margin of 1 min 11 sec over Georges Boillot in a Peugeot, then René Thomas and Albert Guyot both in Delages and Jean Porporato in a Grégoire. In 1912 the Coupe was run concurrently with the resurrected Grand Prix. With their bizarre architecture the long-stroke midgets put all previous achievements in the shade. They supplied all the components for the birth of the modern racer, from the mechanical layout to the protagonists. It would be a question of months until the appearance of the DOHC engine.

# 20

# *Savannah*

While the ACF was in a mood of crisis, while the Coupe des Voiturettes degenerated into a meeting for long-stroke fetishists, while "Prince Henry acted as pacemaker in German tour," in America the great sport began to flourish, and the Benz Auto Import was ubiquitous. At the end of August 1910, Eddie Hearne and his stripped 3.5-liter stock Benz (90 mm × 140 mm) won the Fox River Cup, the 230-cubic-inch class of the "national stock chassis road races" at Elgin, near Chicago. On 2 October, the Benz Auto Import had a home match, the sixth Vanderbilt Cup, "Long Island's greatest Speed Carnival," open to class C, to "any gasoline car or chassis made by a factory that has during the last twelve months produced at least fifty cars, not necessarily of the same model," displacement between 301 and 600 cubic inches (4.92 and 9.83 liters). The race would consist of 22 laps of 12.64 miles (20.22 km). Bill Pickens, Jesse Froehlich and the Benz Auto Import entered three stripped stock chassis, T-head 8-liters (130 mm × 150 mm), for gold mine heir Eddie Hearne, 23-year-old David Bruce-Brown and experienced George Robertson, who had won the 1908 Vanderbilt on the Bennett Locomobile "Old 16." But it was the experienced Robertson who sustained injuries when he took New York journalist Stephen Reynolds around the course at speed, the Benz going over the edge of the slightly banked Massapequa turn and rolling over. The Benz looked to be a wreck but mechanic Franz Heim was able to put it back in racing condition and took the wheel. The main competition came from the Marmons of Joe Dawson and Ray Harroun, the Marquette-Buicks of Bob Burman and the Chevrolet brothers, the Alco "Bête Noire" of Harry Grant, the Nationals of Johnny Aitken, Al Livingstone and Louis Disbrow, and maybe from the 9-liter Mercedes of Spencer Wishart.

At 5:55, just as dawn was breaking, starter Fred Wagner began to dispatch the 30 cars. Despite a slight drizzle, there were 300,000 spectators. As had been anticipated the Buicks of Louis Chevrolet and Bob Burman ran flat-out from the first lap on. Heim pulled out when his Benz broke a fuel line and caught fire, and Wishart withdrew his Mercedes by reason of valve trouble. In lap 18 Chevrolet's Buick plunged off the road, hit a touring car and turned over, pinning mechanic Charles Miller beneath it and injuring him so that he died shortly after. Chevrolet himself, outside of several bruises, came out in fairly good shape. A lot of spectators were injured by venturing onto the course and being struck by the cars. The course was so poorly guarded that the back stretch was overrun with people who greatly handicapped the drivers. Dawson, Disbrow and Mulford slowed down, as did Hearne and Brown. Harry Grant, mechanic Frank Lee and the big black Alco were following the same tactics that won the cup for them in the previous year. Grant moved to the lead and won in 4 h 15 min 58 sec, ahead of Joe Dawson in a Marmon and Johnny Aitken in a National, with Hearne eighth and Brown twelfth, one lap back. "Harry Grant is the most phlegmatic driver. Once he decides on a certain plan of action, no one can make him change it. If he thinks a 60-mile-an-hour pace will win, Harry maintains that rate of speed from starting bomb to finishing flag, although the other cars may be hitting around 70 miles an hour and drawing farther away from him on every lap turned." The American Locomotive Co., maker of the Alco, had started with licensed production of the American Berliet at Providence, Rhode Island, and now had mounted a T-head six (4.75" × 5.5", 121 mm × 140 mm) in the shorter and lighter four-cylinder chassis, wheelbase 126", 320 cm.

Froehlich and Pickens sharply criticized the organization. The Motor Cup Holding Co. of Willie Vanderbilt rejected the Benz entry for the Grand Prize which was to be held two weeks later on the same course: "In view of the criticism you make of the management of the race, which we consider to be absolutely uncalled for and unwarranted, we do not think it wise that the cars under your management should compete." This did not sit well with Froehlich and Pickens, who urged the other contestants to cooperate in an effort to send the race to Savannah. Vanderbilt was left empty-handed! Long Island was cancelled. The second American Grand Prize was to be run on Saturday, 12 November 1910, over 24 laps around a slightly changed 17.3 mile (27.8 km) circuit at Savannah, Georgia. The only restriction was an overall width of 175 cm. In addition to the gold trophy of the Automobile Club of America for the winning entrant, there were cash prizes of $4000, $2000 and $1000 awarded to the first three drivers while Bosch offered $500, $250 and $150 as bonuses.

The Benz Auto Import turned up with a trio of Dieppe-type OHV racers. Victor Hémery and David Bruce-Brown drove two new long-stroke cars (155 mm × 200 mm), Willie Haupt a reconditioned 1908 short-stroke racer (155 mm × 160 mm). Franz Heim, Fritz Craemer and Harris Feyhle acted as mechanics. The Fiat Automobile Co. of Hollander & Joseph entered three brand-new S 61s, Fiat's 130-mm racer for the 1909 formula. It was fortunate the racers could be removed from the steamer *Moltke* which was quarantined with cholera cases on board! The S 61 was

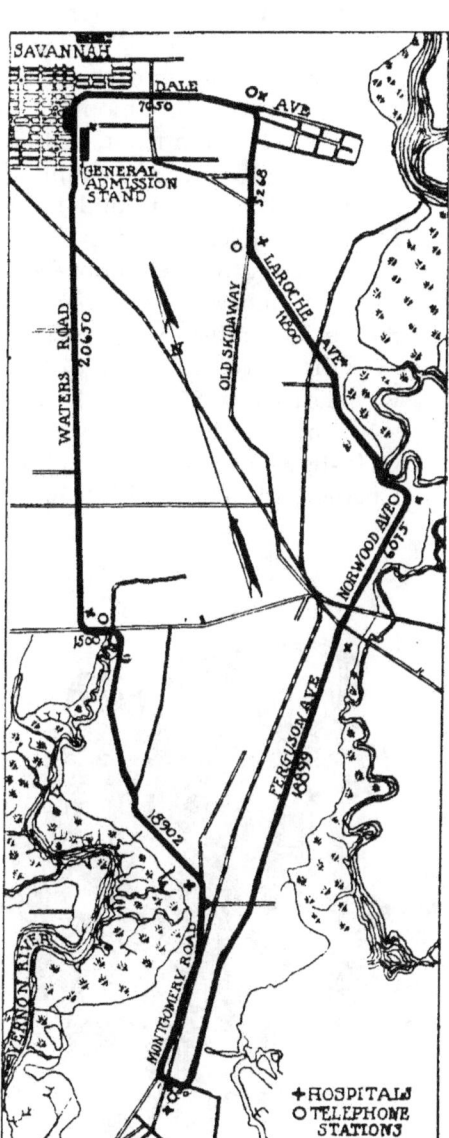

The 17.3-mile (27.8 km) course at Savannah, Georgia (from *Motor Age*, 1910).

devised by Giuseppe Coda who left Milan in 1908 to introduce the overhead camshaft to Turin. In the first act, Coda delivered, on the initiative of Émile Mathis, the well-known Fiat importer at Strassburg and friend of Bugatti, an OHC four-valve sprinter (95 mm × 155 mm) for the Prince Henry tour. The Grand Prix car (130 mm × 190 mm) followed in the second act. As in his Isotta voiturette racer, a vertical shaft drove the overhead camshaft via bevel gears. It was typical of Coda's four-valve engines that the intake and exhaust pairs were placed transversely. Each cam engaged with a roller centrally disposed on a bridge piece connecting two vertical 57-mm valves, good for a simple valve gear and heat balance across the head. The 10-liter delivered 115 hp at 1650 rpm, 130 at 1900, and could be speeded up to more than 2000 rpm thanks to a fully forced lubrication. The new engine was mounted in a slightly modified 1908 chain-drive frame, wheelbase 275 cm, tires 875 mm × 105 mm front, 880 mm × 120 mm rear. The drivers were Felice Nazzaro, Louis Wagner and Ralph DePalma with their mechanics Antonio Fagnano, Antonio "Tony" Ferro and Joe Pozzo. The main opposition came from the two Marquette-Buick 100s of Arthur Chevrolet and Bob Burman, two pure racers which had appeared by the end of May at Indianapolis with OHV four-cylinders (6" × 5.25", 152 mm × 134 mm), Darracq or Benz or Fiat fashion. T-heads were used in the Loziers, in the four (5.375" × 6", 135 mm × 152 mm) of Ralph Mulford as well as in the six (4.625" × 5.5", 118 mm × 140 mm) of Joe Horan, in the Marmons of Ray Harroun (4.5" × 5", 114 mm × 127 mm) and Joe Dawson (4.5" × 6.5", 114 mm × 165 mm) and in the Alco six (4.75" × 5.5", 121 mm × 140 mm) of Harry Grant. OHV-heads were used in the Pope-Hartfords (4.75" × 5.5", 121 mm × 140 mm) of Charlie Basle and Louis Disbrow. The whole field started on Michelin tires.

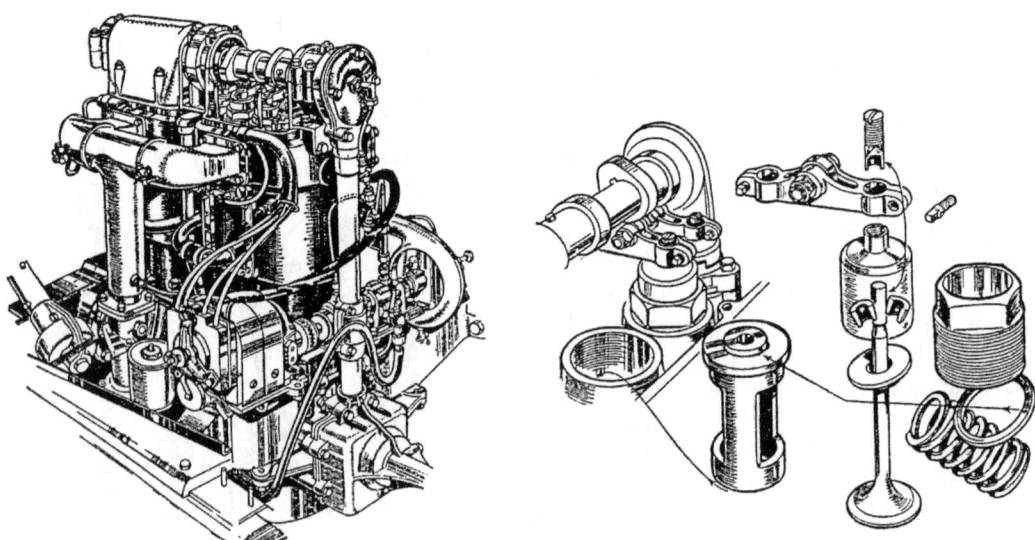

Fiat tipo S 61: 130 mm × 190 mm, OHC four-valve head, devised by Giuseppe Coda (from Pomeroy, *The Grand Prix Car*).

| No. | | | Make | Driver | | | |
|---|---|---|---|---|---|---|---|
| 3, | 17 | | Marquette-Buick | A. Chevrolet | Burman | | |
| 4, | 12 | | Lozier | Mulford | Horan | | |
| 6, | 13 | | Pope-Hartford | Basle | L. Disbrow | | |
| 7 | | | Alco | Grant | | | |
| 8, | 14 | | Marmon | Dawson | Harroun-Dawson | | |
| 9, | 15, | 18 | Benz | Hémery | Bruce-Brown | Haupt | |
| 10, | 16, | 19 | Fiat | Nazzaro | Wagner | DePalma | |

Louis Wagner, 1908 victor, said in an interview:

> This year I expect to break my record for the Savannah course which stands at 65.2 miles an hour, chiefly because I learn that there are to be fewer turns in the course than that of 1908. I believe that I, or any other driver for that matter, would have a hard time lowering that record on the old course with its 260 turns to negotiate during the 402 miles. There is, of course, no chance of my equalling the world's road race record of 74.5 miles an hour, made by my team-mate Nazzaro in the Florio cup race. This was on a smooth quadrilateral course with only four turns and four long stretches. However, the record was most remarkable. You ask me if it is difficult to keep my 90-horsepower car on the turns and narrow sections of the course going at the speed I expect to attain. No, I do not fear that at all, knowing my car as I do. It is a mistaken impression that it becomes highly difficult for a skilled driver to steer correctly at a speed of 80 miles an hour. I have been driving cars for years and keep my racer on the road as if by instinct. Of course an amateur with but little experience cannot appreciate what this means. When going at this speed it is wind resistance with its tendency to flatten you out against the seat back and tear you apart, against which a driver has to contend. Tyres, however, are an element that have to be taken into consideration most seriously, for they have much to do with the average speed attained. Taking the turns is hard, indeed, on tyres. Even though the curve or angle is rounded perfectly by a car there is a big strain on the tubes.

With a lap time of 14 min 18 sec, Victor Hémery and his heavy Benz took the lead, one second ahead of Arthur Chevrolet in the agile Buick. Art replaced his elder brother Louis who was suffering from arm injuries since the bad accident on Long Island. Louis Wagner followed three seconds back, then David Bruce-Brown in his strange gray cloth mask through which peered a pair of ghostly-looking eyes. For eight laps the speedy Hémery fought against the Fiat gang that was closing the gap. In the front line was Nazzaro, who else? On the seventh lap the Italian sped in 13 min 42 sec through the avenues, achieving 122 km/h and a lap record. Concerning power-to-weight ratio the big Benzes and the smaller but more modern Fiats were on the same level; the Benzes, however, had to maneuver an additional 200 kg around the course. Hence it was no surprise that, in the ninth lap, Hémery had to change both rear tires, which gave him the circuit in 19 min 13 sec and dropped him into fifth place. The Fiat trio—Wagner, Nazzaro, DePalma—were now in front. Art Chevrolet and Joe Dawson were out with broken crankshafts, Louis Disbrow with a cracked cylinder, Harry Grant with stripped high gears. On lap ten Willie Haupt and the short-stroke Benz suddenly appeared in the lead. But not for long! Haupt was too fast in the right-angle corner at Montgomery crossroads and struck a tree broadside. The Benz turned over and over, throwing Haupt and mechanic Feyhle clear of the wreckage. Neither was hurt to speak of. But the Benz was a total wreck.

November 1910—GP of America, Savannah, Georgia. Victor Hémery and Franz Heim in their Benz, entries from the American representation, the New York Benz Auto Import Co. of Jesse Froehlich.

Brown and mechanic Fritz Craemer had their big moment at the depot, leaping out simultaneously as soon as the Benz stopped. Brown seized the ten-gallon cans of fuel from the pit and dumped them into the big funnel, handling the cans as if they were trifles. Meanwhile Craemer swung out the used tires from the rear and rolled the new ones in. Brown vaulted into his seat from the steering-wheel side, and while the Benz was moving, Craemer scrambled up over the tires to his place and fastened down the filler cap as the car accelerated. Brown and Hémery were hot on the red brigade's trail, with a gap of three minutes. At the first opportunity the Benz duo would move up. The opportunity was not long in coming. Early in the race Wagner broke the right front spring clip. During a stop the technical committee and Caleb Bragg, in charge of the Fiat team, suggested installing a new clip. But Wagner insisted that there was ample clamping power remaining and flatly refused to make the change. On lap 17 Wagner hit a soft spot near La Roche Avenue, tearing away the rest of the spring clip, the Fiat turning end-for-end into the ditch. Wagner was bruised about the abdomen from being jammed against the steering wheel and Ferro obtained a big black eye when striking a branch of a bush into which he was hurled. The Fiat was completely wrecked. Brown and Hémery forced the pace. Even Nazzaro began to lose his cool and skidded off into the ditch at the Burnside corner, bending the Fiat's rear axle. During the following laps the left chain broke three times and, in lap 19, Nazzaro was forced to quit the race. Now DePalma assumed the lead, two minutes ahead of the Benz duo. But he was in trouble. Vibration had

November 1910—GP of America, Savannah, Georgia. 23-year-old David Bruce-Brown (born 13 August 1887 in New York City) and the Benz crossing the finish, "winner by a second and less than a half of the greatest race ever held in any country."

broken a water connection and the Fiat's radiator was running dry. On the penultimate lap a rear cylinder cracked.

When it was seen that one of the two Benz drivers would win, the thousands in the stands worked themselves into a veritable frenzy from nervous excitement. After a lap in 13 min 54 sec, Hémery was the first to cross the wire. For a moment the cheering crowd thought that the Frenchman had won. Then came the announcement that Brown had a starting handicap of three minutes. The announcers began to toll off the seconds and then "no. 15 car is on the home stretch!" "Men yelled and jumped and coaxed, women screamed and waved handkerchiefs and umbrellas, all, everybody, begging him to come. Would he make it? A throb went through everybody as he neared the corner at Dale Avenue and Waters Road. He was playing safe, shut down to a mere crawl until half around, then opening his giant engine wide, he fairly flew across the finish in 5 h 53' 5.35", winner by 1.42"." The crowds settled back to watch the other four finish, the Marquette-Buick of Bob Burman, the Loziers of Ralph Mulford and Joe Horan, and finally the Marmon driven by Ray Harroun and Joe Dawson. The Benz Auto Import firm had every reason to be satisfied: after the records of speed king Oldfield, now a double victory at Savannah. Brown's mother was the first to leave her box and to congratulate Davey. Starter Fred Wagner remembered: "I could not help but recall her opposition of less than a year previous when her son ran away from preparatory school to make his debut as a racing driver. The first time I saw Bruce-Brown was early one morning in March 1909. He was sleeping with a bunch of Italian mechanics over a garage at Daytona. Two days before he had borrowed the month's wages of his boxing instructor and left the classic shades of New Haven for the sandy beaches of Florida." Later that same morning, Hollander, the American agent for the Fiat, and Robert Morrell, referee of the races, each received telegrams from Mrs. Bruce-Brown in which she warned them that she would hold them responsible for anything that might happen to her son should they allow him to compete. For two days Brown was a disgruntled spectator. Whenever he came near a racing car, either Hollander or Morrell shooed him away. Finally he called Wagner aside: "Wag, I've got it all fixed with Joe," pointing to Cedrino's mechanic. "At the start of the five-mile race he's going to jump out of the car and I'm going to take his place just [as] you send them away. You'll go through with it, won't you, Wag? I didn't come clear down to Florida for my health." When Morrell and Hollander first caught a glimpse of Brown riding in the disappearing car they acted like maniacs. "Call them back, I'll lose Mrs. Brown's trade," shrieked Hollander. Cedrino won the race and Brown rode across the line as healthy and whole as when he started. "Wag, I'm in for it when I get home, anyway, so I might as well make the most of it. Let me take the Benz and go after the one-mile amateur record." Brown took the Benz, drove a mile in 33 seconds and clipped six seconds off Willie Vanderbilt's record.

November 1910—GP of America, Savannah, Georgia. David Bruce-Brown and Benz, the winners of the second Grand Prize of America.

By the end of May 1911, the 500-mile race of Indianapolis was held for the first time, the Indy 500. The Indy speedway owed its origin to "a promoter of things worth while," a Hoosier by the name of Carl Graham Fisher, the father of the Lincoln Highway and Miami. Fisher began his career before the turn of the century on the bicycle: "I never was a champion although I've taken the dust of the best of them, Eddie Bald, Earl Cooper, Fred Titus and Arthur Zimmerman. I was only a second-rater, but I made money at the game and designed, manufactured and sold the wheel that I rode." In 1898 Fisher purchased at a cost of $650 the second De Dion tricycle imported into America and, in 1901, made his debut in a four-cylinder Winton at the county fair of Dallas, covering the mile in 1 min 43 sec. His summer campaign of 1901 was a tremendous success. He pitted the Winton against race horses, charging from $600 to $1500 for each exhibition, taking adventurers around the track for $10 per mile, clearing $20,000 at the end of the year. In 1902 he took the Indiana state agency for Oldsmobile and Winton, discarded the Winton for an eight-cylinder Premier and formed a dirt-track alliance with Walter Winchester, Earl Kiser, Barney Oldfield, Tom Cooper and Louis Chevrolet. Fisher drove his last race in 1905, and started the Prest-O-Lite Co., manufacturing acetylene gas headlights.

Did Fisher really hit upon the idea of a decent track when he was in the Auvergne for the last Bennett Cup? He was relief driver for Dingley and Lytle, had worked on the Pope-Toledos and was confident that they would be serious contenders. But the crude carburetors refused to function properly. The racers had never been worked out on bends, the testing having been confined solely to a three-mile straightaway near the factory where the drivers practiced secretly to evade antagonistic police officials. Dingley and Lytle had no way to regulate the fuel mixture except to stop, raise the hood and make carburetor adjustments directly: "America don't need drivers. What we need are cars and a place to prepare them for such a race as this." Back at Indianapolis, he interested his friends James A. Allison, his partner in the Prest-O-Lite Co., F. H. Wheeler, the carburetor manufacturer, and A. C. Newby, builder of the National cars and, in the heyday of the bicycle, maker of the Diamond chains, in the project to construct a speedway on the outskirts of Indianapolis. They bought 350 acres of the Presley farm situated northwest of Indianapolis and work was started early in the spring of 1909. By August, $460,000 had been expended and the 2.5-mile track made of macadam with slightly banked turns was ready, including grandstands, garages, a large aerodrome, aviation sheds and office buildings. Eighty thousand spectators came to the first meeting, but after three days of racing, the course was an oval of deep furrows. The macadam had failed to withstand the tires' pounding and a new surface was imperative. Fisher and his associates invested an additional $180,000 to reconstruct the track with vitrified brick and cement. When the 3,500,000 bricks had been laid, it was discovered that the track was too rough for high-speed work, cutting tires to pieces after four laps. For three weeks heavy cement blocks were dragged by a fleet of test cars. Then the track was as smooth as glass. Another meet was held in the summer of 1910 and then Fisher conceived the idea of an international 500-mile race to be run annually.

In 1911 the race was opened for the popular class C, with maximum displacement of 600 cubic inches (9.83 liters). Forty-three racers pilgrimaged to Indianapolis:

Case, Westcott, Firestone-Columbus, Velie and Cole with L-heads, Interstate, National, Stutz, Alco, Cutting, Marmon, Lozier, Apperson, Mercer and Simplex (which had nothing in common with the Mercedes Simplex) with T-heads, Pope-Hartford, Knox, Buick, McFarlan and Jackson with OHV-heads, finally Amplex with a two-cycle engine. Three Fiats, two Benzes and a brand-new Mercedes came from Europe. Hollander & Joseph had mounted new 128-mm blocks in their S 61 Fiats in order to comply with the displacement limit. The driver team was rather wealthy: Caleb Bragg, Eddie Hearne and David Bruce-Brown. The Benz Auto Import Co. entered two OHV stock chassis, a 65-hp (130 mm × 160 mm) for Bob Burman and a 45-hp (110 mm × 135 mm) for Billy Knipper. The Mercedes? Young Spencer Wishart had just imported a 130-mm racer from Untertürkheim. In the presence of 80,000 spectators, the Marmon Wasp of Harroun, the Lozier of Mulford, the Simplex of DePalma, the Fiat of Brown and the Mercedes of Wishart struggled for the lead. The Mercedes was able to stay in front for 20 miles, but dropped back because of tire trouble. Then it was the turn of Brown in the Fiat. But after 180 miles the long yellow Marmon six (4.5" × 5", 114 mm × 127 mm) driven by Ray Harroun, relieved for 100 miles by Cyrus Patschke, definitively took the lead and won in 6 h 42 min 8 sec, ahead of Mulford, Brown and Wishart. The performance of the Mercedes appealed to the driver of the Simplex. Hadn't his sponsor placed an order with Untertürkheim?

# 21

## *Grey Ghost*

Paul Daimler was not a pioneer anymore. He acted first and foremost as technical manager and not as flamboyant and revolutionary drawing-board artist. Arrangement and tuning of well-tried elements was his motto, if possible without risk, without the intuitive flash of genius of a Maybach, without the Mediterranean vein of a Coda, without the puzzling play instinct of a Causan, Verdet or Michaux. In view of the 130-mm formula, which did not take effect in 1909, his engine and chassis specialists Link and Schnaitmann combined the successful chain-drive frame of Dieppe with a new OHV engine. As usual the four-cylinder was made up of two cast-iron pairs; dimensions were 130 mm × 180 mm, displacement was 9.5 liters, and the engine was designated M 1384 for Motor 130 mm × 180 mm 4-cylinder. One camshaft, driven by a train of gears placed between the two cylinder blocks, ran on the exhaust side and operated, via pushrods and rockers, a huge intake and two smaller exhaust valves measuring 86 and 50 mm. With increasing engine speed, the lubrication became more elaborate: A piston pump sucked oil from the sump and fed the four main bearings and the big ends. A second, smaller pump maintained a constant level in the sump. The mechanic was not jobless, though as he still looked after the valve gear. The cast iron pistons were fitted with two rings, with clearance at the top 0.075 mm, at the middle 0.05, and at the bottom 0.04 mm. A Bosch high-tension magneto provided power to two plugs per cylinder. The three-valve engine weighed 300 kg and delivered 37 hp at 400 rpm, 90 at 1350, 110 at 1600 and 130 hp at 2000 rpm, with possible peaks of 2500 rpm. Concerning the chassis, Schnaitmann changed only details; wheelbase was 270 cm, track 140 cm, tires 880 mm × 120 mm front, 895 mm × 135 mm rear. The unloaded weight of 1000 kg provided a better power-to-weight ratio than the 1908 forerunner. And weight distribution was first-class, with the weight nicely balanced over the front and the rear wheels, the rear axle carrying 20 kg more than the front, due to a separately mounted gearbox and now-archaic chain drive. From 1911 the sportsman could order the 9.5-liter as a grand tourer, as type 37/90, with a wheelbase of 338, 358 or 374.5 cm, tires of 915 mm × 105 mm front, 935 mm × 135 mm rear, and a chassis price of 22,500 marks. By 1914 Untertürkheim produced two hundred units.

It was in the autumn of 1911 that Untertürkheim shipped the three-valve racer for DePalma, painted in battleship gray, the "grey ghost," in due time for the great Savannah meeting, the seventh Vanderbilt Cup and the third Grand Prize. DePalma was born in 1883, in Biccari, between Foggia and Naples in southern Italy, emigrated with his parents to Brooklyn in 1892, made his debut as a bicycle rider in 1898 and finished second in the 1901 Madison Square Garden race for the one-mile amateur championship. During 1902 he began to race for money and won

The new 9.5-liter Mercedes three-valve engine could be ordered in combination with a long chassis and elegant body. On the right-hand rear seat Paul Daimler; by his side Eugen Link; at the wheel chassis specialist Karl Schnaitmann.

the twelve-hour race at Rochester, defeating such stars as Nat Butler, Ray Duer and Floyd Krebs. Between 1903 and 1905 he campaigned the eastern tracks with one of the first Indian motorcycles ever turned out by George Hendee. By the end of 1907 DePalma began to work for Allen-Kingston, assembling three cars for the 1908 Briarcliff road race. Al Campbell, the former Mercedes driver, made him his mechanic. After Campbell sustained a broken leg in a practice crash, DePalma was chosen as substitute. He crashed the racer but his skills impressed so that he was given the Allen-Kingston for dirt track sprints, defeating Barney Oldfield and Harry Grant at Boston, capturing the 25- and 50-mile races at Elkwood Park, and the 5-, 10- and 25-mile races at St. Paul. After the fatal accident of Emanuele Cedrino on 29 May 1908, Hollander & Joseph wooed him away from Allen-Kingston to drive the Fiat "Cyclone" (165 mm × 165 mm), a dirt-track special based on the 1904 Bennett racer. In autumn of 1908 DePalma was awarded the circular-track championship of the AAA and the diamond-studded medal for turning the three fastest laps in the Savannah Grand Prize. At the wheel of the Cyclone, DePalma continued to reign over the dirt tracks, but in 1911 he decided to go freelance and bought a Simplex, the same car that Louis Disbrow campaigned as the "Zip." The sponsor for the following year, 1912, was Edward J. Schroeder, the Jersey City sportsman and former commodore of the Motor Boat Club of America who had entered his gray Mercedes racer in the Vanderbilt Cup and Grand Prize, but he lacked a driver.

The Cup was to be run on Monday, 27 November 1911. Maximum displacement

21. *Grey Ghost*

The 9.5-liter Mercedes: three valve OHV head, 130 mm × 180 mm, 90 hp at 1350 rpm, 130 at 2000, engine weight 300 kg.

October 1911—Fairmount Park, Philadelphia. Erwin Bergdoll, mechanic Frank "Raz" Johnson and the privately entered short-stroke Benz won the "Fourth Annual 200 Mile Race of the Quaker City Motor Club." After 25 laps of 8.1 miles and 3 h 18 min 41 sec, he lay 1 min 30 sec ahead of Wishart's Mercedes and two minutes ahead of Mulford's Lozier.

was 600 cubic inches; distance was 17 laps of 17.41 miles (27.9 km). DePalma joined the Mercedes of his friend Wishart and the Fiat S 61 trio of Brown, E. H. Parker and Joe Matson, the T-head Loziers (5.375" × 6", 137 mm × 152 mm) of Ralph Mulford and Harry Grant, and a pack of Marmon, Abbott-Detroit, Pope-Hartford, Mercer and Jackson. DePalma took the lead for the first four laps, but had to change a tire on the course and to stop at the depot for two minutes to put tires in the rack and take on oil and water. As a result Mulford and his Lozier had a lead of 2 min 6 sec at the end of lap six. "Smiling Ralph" was in top form, showed remarkable regularity and won in 3 h 56 min, 2 min 11 sec ahead of DePalma and 10 min 10 sec ahead of Wishart, with Grant, Parker and Louis Disbrow in a Pope-Hartford far back. DePalma made fourteen laps under the 14-minute mark, his best lap being 13 min 14 sec, as compared with Mulford's thirteen laps under the 14-minute mark and 13 min 25 sec. "Ralph Mulford is the most modest of drivers. He nurses his car along and yields more to the whims of his machine than any pilot now racing for fame and fortune. His mechanics say that he talks to his car as if it were a family horse or household pet, but they may be guilty of exaggerations. At all events, Ralph treats his machine as if it had human qualities. He never is impatient. If the motor seems a trifle temperamental, he waits awhile before raising the hood and chastising it."

The Grand Prize followed on Thursday, on Thanksgiving, over 24 laps, a distance of 418 miles or 669 km. DePalma and Wishart reconditioned their Mercedes. Hollander & Joseph turned up with the brand-new Fiat S 74. Giuseppe Coda had taken over all details of the fine S 61 and simply increased the bore by 20 mm, the stroke by 10 mm and the valves by 3 mm. The new dimensions of 150 mm × 200 mm resulted in 14 liters and 160 hp at 1600 rpm. The drivers were Wagner, Brown and newcomer Caleb Bragg, the son of a wealthy Cincinnati publisher. The Moross Amusement Co. entered the Prince Henry Benz (115 mm × 175 mm) that wild Bob Burman had bought from Barney Oldfield, but replaced it in the last moment with a Marmon. The Benz Auto Import Co. appeared with an older 1910 Savannah car (155 mm × 200 mm) for Eddie Hearne, Erwin Bergdoll's short-stroke car, and a freshly imported long-stroke racer for Victor Hémery. The American Buicks, Marmons, Popes, Abbotts and Loziers were fighting a losing battle. The complete field:

| No. | Make | Driver | | |
|---|---|---|---|---|
| 41, 48, 53 | Fiat | Wagner | Bruce-Brown | Bragg |
| 42 | Pope-Hartford | L. Disbrow | | |
| 43, 49 | Buick Hundred | Basle | Cole | |
| 44, 50 | Abbott-Detroit | Mitchell | Limberg | |
| 45 | Lozier | Mulford | | |
| 46 | Marmon | Burman | | |
| 47, 52, 56 | Benz | Hearne | Bergdoll | Hémery |
| 51 | Marmon | Patschke | | |
| 54, 55 | Mercedes | Wishart | DePalma | |

The European racers set out to win everything in the first lap. Fiat, Fiat, Mercedes, Benz was the order, Bragg in the lead with 13 min 1 sec, 6 seconds ahead of Brown, 14 seconds ahead of DePalma, 16 seconds ahead of Hémery. But on lap three Mulford and Patschke broke into the foreign phalanx. Hémery was repairing a broken valve somewhere on the course. The enormous speed of the Fiats and the

## 21. Grey Ghost

November 1911—GP of America, Savannah, Georgia. The Benz Team: Hémery, Bergdoll, and Hearne on the right.

Benzes began to show its results. Wagner had to change both rear tires. The "grey ghost" of DePalma gained first place with the Benzes of Hearne and Bergdoll second and third. Burman fell out with a broken magneto shaft sprocket. Hémery set a new lap record, but 12 min 36 sec proved too much for his Benz, which swallowed a second exhaust valve. The Wishart Mercedes was steaming like a locomotive, with a cracked cylinder jacket.

By the end of lap eight the Fiat trio, DePalma and Hearne changed tires. Bergdoll went out with carburetor trouble. Cyrus Patschke put his Marmon to the front, but only for a few miles until the cylinders loosened from the crankcase. Lap twelve saw Hearne running steadily in the lead, three minutes ahead of Wagner and Brown, four minutes ahead of DePalma and Mulford. On lap 15 Wagner ran off the road, putting the steering out of commission. Brown made laps 18 and 19 in 30 seconds under the other drivers and so found himself but 43 seconds from Hearne. At the end of lap 22 the leading trio stopped at the depot, the Fiat of Brown, the Benz of Hearne and the Lozier of Mulford. Brown and Hearne changed a rear tire. Mulford took on some fuel only to break a gearbox shaft on the next lap. Brown took the lead and held it, winning in 5 h 31 min 29 sec, 2 min 4 sec ahead of Hearne, 3 min 11 sec ahead of DePalma, then Bragg and Disbrow. It was astonishing that the Benz, already in its fourth season, and the relatively small 9.5-liter Mercedes were able to keep up with the strong Fiat.

By the beginning of May 1912, the spectacular Fiat was in full flow. Teddy Tetzlaff won the "Pacific coast classic" at Santa Monica, 36 laps of 8.4 miles at an average of 78.7 mph (126 km/h): a new road race record. The Fiat of Bragg and the Benz of Brown finished second and third. The Fiat of the resurrected Barney Oldfield and the Stutzes of Dave Lewis and Earl Cooper fell out. The Fiat S 74 was too large for the second Indy 500 held at the end of the month, restricted as in the previous year to 600-cubic-inch racers. DePalma and Wishart turned up with their Mercedes, Tetzlaff with a Fiat S 61, Len Ormsby with a Prince Henry Opel (115 mm × 175 mm). The Opel broke down on lap six, the Wishart Mercedes on lap 92. DePalma led from the start, smashing records at every milestone, and was eleven minutes ahead of Dawson's National when a connecting rod broke and saw the light of day, five miles from the finish. Joe Dawson won in front of Tetzlaff. At the beginning of July, the same Tetzlaff and his Fiat S 61 took the 250-mile free-for-all and the 200-mile heavy car race at Tacoma, Washington.

"DePalma star of the Elgin road races" was the headline by the end of August. The Italian-American scored a double victory in the Elgin trophy over 30 laps of 8.46 miles, beating the Knox six of Ralph Mulford, and the free-for-all run concurrently over six additional laps, beating the short-stroke Benz of Erwin Bergdoll. The Mercedes consumed 29 gallons of fuel for the 305-mile free-for-all, an average of 10.5 miles to the gallon. There was to be no race at Savannah. In 1912 the traditional meeting took place on a new 7.8-mile (12.6 km) circuit at Wauwatosa, Milwaukee County, Wisconsin. The Milwaukee Automobile Dealers' Association set up four races: the Wisconsin Challenge Trophy open to cars of 161 to 230 cubic inches; the Colonel Gustave Pabst Blue Ribbon Trophy, up to 300 cubic inches;

May 1912—Indy 500. In this line-up of the cars before the start; no. 7 is the Mercedes of Spencer Wishart and no. 8 the winning National of Joe Dawson. (Fiat)

## 21. Grey Ghost

July 1912—Tacoma, Washington. Teddy Tetzlaff and the Fiat S 61 won the 200-mile "heavy car event" in 2 h 54 min 31 sec, "despite extremely cold weather," in front of Mulford's Knox. Next day Tetzlaff won the 250-mile free-for-all in front of Bergdoll's Benz. In the background the Mercer of Pollem. (Fiat)

the Vanderbilt Cup, up to 600 cubic inches; and the unlimited Grand Prize. The Vanderbilt, with only eight starters, far fewer than the preceding classics, was scheduled for 2 October, over 38 laps, 299 miles. Teddy Tetzlaff in his red Fiat S 61, Ralph DePalma in his "grey ghost" and Hughie Hughes in his yellow T-head Mercer (4.39" × 5", 112 mm × 127 mm) were the favorites of the 50,000 spectators. Tetzlaff set the lap record in 6 min 15 sec and looked like a sure winner until the driveshaft of the Fiat broke on lap 26. DePalma took the lead and won in 4 h 20 min 31 sec, 43 seconds ahead of Hughes and 16 min 4 sec ahead of Wishart in a second 9.5-liter Mercedes, then Gil Anderson in his white Stutz (4.75" × 5.5", 121 mm × 140 mm) and George Clark in a third 9.5-liter Mercedes. Two days later Fred and Augie Duesenberg celebrated their first great victories when Mortimer Roberts and Harry Endicott drove their Mason specials to victory in the Pabst and Wisconsin trophies. With his light Mason-Duesenberg (3.875" × 5", 97 mm × 127 mm), Roberts achieved a lap time of seven minutes flat, just half a minute slower than DePalma in the Mercedes. The Mason featured horizontal valves operated by long rocker arms, vertical rockers so large they were usually called walking beams, crankshaft in two large plain bearings, output of 58 hp at 2300 rpm, a three-speed gearbox mounted at the rear axle, a wheelbase of 104 inches (264 cm), tires 32" × 3.5", and weight of 930 kg.

During practice for the Grand Prix, a rear tire of Brown's Fiat exploded at 130 km/h causing the car to lurch into the ditch. Brown and mechanic Anthony

Schudelare were picked up unconscious by farmers who had witnessed the accident and were rushed to Trinity Hospital at Milwaukee. David Bruce-Brown never regained consciousness. Nevertheless a complete Fiat S 74 trio lined up for the start: Tetzlaff, Bragg and Barney Oldfield, who stood in for Brown on the S 74 owned by E. H. Hewlett, "without even driving a practice lap over the dangerous road course." Ernie Moross entered a long-stroke Benz (155 mm × 200 mm) for Bob Burman, the Benz Auto Import Co. a similar model for the former Mulford mechanic Joe Horan, and Erwin Bergdoll his private short-stroke racer (155 mm × 160 mm). The rest of the field came from the Cup:

| *No.* | *Make* | *Driver* | | |
|---|---|---|---|---|
| 31, 40, 42 | Benz | Burman | Bergdoll | Horan-Burman |
| 32 | Lozier | Fountaine | | |
| 33, 41, 44 | Fiat | Tetzlaff | Bragg | Oldfield |
| 34 | Mercer | Hughes | | |
| 35, 36, 39 | Mercedes | DePalma | Wishart | Clark |
| 43 | Stutz | Anderson | | |

Fifty-two laps, 409 miles, were to be run. Tetzlaff, "demon driver of them all," jumped into the lead, ahead of Bragg, Bergdoll, Wishart and DePalma, while Oldfield stopped at the pits to change a rear tire. Burman was adjusting the valves of his Benz. Tetzlaff continued to drive in his terrific, slam-bang style. Burman fell out with a broken piston, Wishart with a broken crankshaft. On lap seven DePalma snatched third place from Bergdoll who stopped for fuel and an extra supply of tires. At the end of lap eleven Tetzlaff changed a right rear tire, thus giving his lead to Bragg. Horan, who had been running seventh, passed Anderson, Bergdoll and Fountaine, and took fourth position only to drop back again. Lap 14 was Tetzlaff's best and the fastest of the race: 6 min 7 sec. Another record followed on lap 25 when DePalma and mechanic Tom Alley replaced a tire in 37 seconds. Fifteen miles later the Mercedes crew lost nearly four minutes, adjusting the valves and removing a magneto wire that had caught on the carburetor lever. When Tetzlaff withdrew on lap 31 because of a broken radius rod, the race was between Bragg and DePalma. With four laps to go, DePalma was 4 min 19 sec to the bad. He made a lap in 6 min 28 sec to Bragg's 7 min 21 sec and cut the margin to 3 min 26 sec, then to 2 min 36 sec when starter Wagner waved his green flag for both of them. Upon receiving a signal from his pits to "beat it," DePalma stepped on the throttle when he swung into the North Fond du Lac road. He came up to the Fiat with great leaps and bounds and tried to pass. Bragg swung over a trifle and the gray Mercedes ran into the rear of the red car. The Mercedes turned over, throwing out its crew. DePalma suffered abdominal injuries which confined him to bed for a week. After 5 h 59 min 27 sec Bragg crossed the finish as winner, 15 min 29 sec ahead of Bergdoll, 15 min 53 sec ahead of Anderson, nearly 40 min ahead of Oldfield. Bragg made only two stops, the first one after 165 miles when he changed both rear tires and took on fuel and oil, the second after 290 miles when he refilled his supply tanks and changed the left rear tire. After this race the dinosaurs from Benz and Fiat were retired, since in 1913 a 450-cubic-inch limit was adopted in America. In July 1912, at Dieppe, they had fought out their last battle in Europe—the Fiats as original, the Benzes as copy.

# 22

## *Modern Times*

The fine Hôtel Pastoret was bored to death. Only the great sport could save the Automobile Club de France from a true collapse. In 1911 the humbled club invited racers once again to its Grand Prix, according to the style of the times by limiting the bore/stroke dimensions to a maximum of 110 mm × 200 mm. But the expected entry flood failed to appear and the specifications were just used for a corresponding class in the Grand Prix de France. The sportsmen quickly forgot this first Grand Prix de France which took place on a new course near Le Mans. Hémery won in a stripped Fiat which had been intended for the proprietor of a fashionable café in Paris and was to have received a limousine body; owing to delay, delivery was refused, and by arrangement with Michelin it was put in the race. Ernest Friderich finished second in a 1.3-liter Bugatti (65 mm × 100 mm). Not a bit of great sport! Then formula-free and concurrently with the successful Coupe de l'Auto! Anything else was out of the question at the moment. On the old course of Dieppe, two races were run together on two consecutive days, ten 77-km laps on Tuesday and Wednesday, July 25 and 26, 1912, starting at half-past five, at half-minute intervals. A novelty was the acceptance of five racers per manufacturer. Except for a maximum width of 175 cm, the Grand Prix class was unlimited while the 3-liters had to weigh at least 800 kg. The entries for the Coupe de l'Auto were automatically eligible for the Grand Prix.

In the unlimited Grand Prix class, four development levels lined up: L-heads borrowed from stock chassis ran against the OHV fashion of 1908, the current OHC four-valve standard against the trend-setting DOHC head. From Saventhem in Belgium, Arthur de Coninck sent an L-head Excelsior, a stripped six-cylinder (110 mm × 160 mm) stock chassis, with the well-known aero-engine tuner Josef Christiaens at the wheel. The Mathis "Baby," a 1.8-liter midget (70 mm × 120 mm) playing in the big class by reason of underweight, came from Strassburg in Alsace and hence from Germany. Thirty-two-year-old Emil Mathis, whose parents managed the "Ville de Paris" hotel at Strassburg, had a meteoric career that began ten years before at nearby Niederbronn, at the parent plant of De Dietrich, where he was responsible for the marketing of a Bugatti design. In 1904 Mathis established his Auto-Mathis-Palace at Strassburg which soon acted as German agency for De Dietrich, Panhard, Fiat, Minerva and Rochet-Schneider, selling no fewer than 500 cars in 1906. But its own production, the Mathis "Hermes," devised by Ettore Bugatti, was a non-seller. Bugatti switched to Deutz and Mathis engaged the experienced De Dietrich engineer Heinrich Esser and his son Willy. In 1911 production of the Baby started in a new plant south of Strassburg. Willy Esser picked one of the Babies out, prepared it with an eye toward the Grand Prix and took the wheel.

Lorraine-Dietrich surprisingly presented a flawless copy of the 1908 long-stroke Benz. The Savannah successes of the Benz Auto Import Co. quickly reached the noble desk of Adrien de Turckheim. The Baron did not waste time and engaged the complete Benz squad, from Victor Hémery, to René Hanriot, Franz Heim and Louis de Groulart. Did de Turckheim, after the good experiences with Bollée, Turcat-Méry and Isotta-Fraschini, consider a Benz license? At Argenteuil, the renegades built four new Benzes, of course with the typical art nouveau feature above the front axle, the curved Lorraine radiator. Otherwise nothing was changed, neither the dimensions of 155 mm × 200 mm nor the output of 160 hp at 1500. The fourth driver was Paul Bablot. Fiat relied upon an S 74 trio with Brown, Wagner and DePalma. Nazzaro was focusing on his own Nazzaro. From Tours in the Loire valley, François Rolland and Émile Pilain sent two OHC four-valve racers (110 mm × 165 mm) for Albert Guyot and the Parisian banker Jacques Fauquet. Despite a start in the 1911 Grand Prix de France, the two Rolland-Pilains still suffered from numerous teething troubles. At Tours financial support was lacking. The elegant racer was even offered via catalogue, but found few customers, if any.

In mid–June, Boillot turned a practice lap in 35 min 55 sec at the wheel of a new Peugeot. The sportsmen knew that Boillot was a top-notch driver, but 36 seconds under the record of Otto Salzer! The Peugeot looked like an inflated Hispano. And that was just the point. When, in 1910, Robert Peugeot took over the direction of the united Société Anonyme, he not only adhered to publicity through sport in the Coupe de l'Auto but planned the leap into the Grand Prix class. Of course Goux and Boillot were heart and soul for it, but not Gratien Michaux since the clever Robert Peugeot put him under pressure with top-class engineering from the outside, as in 1909 when his V-2 had to compete against the angry six-valve single from Boudreaux and Verdet. Michaux continued to concentrate on his bizarre Lion racers, fighting tooth-and-nail against the new trouble-makers. There was nothing for it. Who was producing the best racers during the 1910 season? The Picker brothers. Peugeot was not interested in them, as they were too conspicuous. He needed the technical people from the background. At first, in November 1910, just after his victory in the Coupe de l'Auto, Paolo Zuccarelli switched to the Peugeot racing department at Levallois, of course in company of his shadow Ernesto Fanelli. Nobody smelled a rat, since somehow Peugeot had to replace Giuppone. Why not with Zuccarelli? Drawing-board artist Ernest Henry followed in 1911, officially as "directeur du bureau de dessin et des ateliers," as director of the drawing office and the workshop. The merry Zuccarelli, who was born in Brescia, and the rather dry Henry, who came from Geneva, immediately felt at home at Levallois-Perret since they knew the suburb from many visits and from their work at the Parisian Picker agency, the actual racing-car shop of Hispano. Their first project was a racer for the 1911 Grand Prix, an inflated Hispano, with slightly modified Labor-Picker engine in the dimensions of 110 mm × 200 mm, of course still with T-head. When the Grand Prix was cancelled once again, there was enough time for a radical engine conversion. Henry, Zuccarelli, Goux and Boillot, all of them born in 1885 or 1886, got a revolution under way, without being aware of it at the time.

The Picker revved up so briskly that it misfired in spite of the hemispherical exhaust pockets. Somehow the pockets had to disappear! The solution seemed rather simple: The valve gear of the T-head was turned upwards. The plug remained in the middle of the combustion chamber, which became a pent roof since Henry had to settle on four inclined overhead valves to provide for the breathing of the long-stroke cylinders. Thus a combination of Prince Henry Benz and a power-boat engine from Delahaye. "Titan" was the name of the Delahaye, rightly: The 62-liter (300 mm × 220 mm), devised by Amédée Varlet, propelled the *Dubonnet* of liqueur magnate Marius Dubonnet during the 1905 Monaco power-boat races, later also the *Trident* of M. Pabanel. The two overhead camshafts of the Delahaye were driven via bevel gears and a vertical shaft and operated three vertical intake and exhaust valves. It was an outstanding solution in 1905, although the whole complexity primarily served the purpose of by-passing the huge distance to the head. The Picker brothers, under whose wings Ernest Henry was acting at that time, were also represented with some engines at Monaco. The Delahaye design must have been in the back of Henry's mind when he came to Peugeot.

The cast-iron block of the *étude expérimentale* number one retained the old dimensions of 110 mm × 200 mm: the first Grand Prix Peugeot was named EX 1 or L 76 for 7.6-liter displacement. In all his racers for Peugeot, Henry set the valves at an angle of 30° to the vertical, and the tappet guide was his hobby. In the EX 1, a ring in the form of a semicircle or stirrup surrounded the cams, connecting the tappet guides above and below the camshaft. A small return spring, located at the upper guide outside the camshaft housing, kept the clearance between tappet and valve shaft. Desmo operation? A legend from the sixties. Small bulges in the combustion chamber made possible the use of 60-mm valves. The two camshafts ran within separately mounted aluminum housings for quick disassembly in case of a damaged valve. The detachable cages of the intake valves gave access to the inside, while the exhaust valves were seated directly in the head for the purpose of better cooling. Further features of the number one were the vertical shaft driving the

The block of the Peugeot EX 1/L 76: 110 mm × 200 mm, two overhead camshafts driven by a vertical shaft, four valves, semicircle tappets, camshaft housings easily removable in view of quick access in case of a valve failure, 135 hp at 2200 rpm (from Pomeroy, *The Grand Prix Car*).

camshafts and the pressure-lubricated crankshaft running in five plain bearings. Not the cleverest solutions: Both the crankshaft and the vertical shaft got too long, causing vibrations in the crankcase and a deranged valve timing further upwards. The 7.6-liter delivered 135 hp at 2200 and a compression of 5.5:1, briefly also 148 at 2500 or even 175 at 2900, but only momentarily since the vibrations of the very primitive crankshaft prevented sustained output. A pity, the head tolerated more.

Nevertheless the EX 1/L 76 was a fine engine. Including the multiplate clutch and the separately mounted four-speed gearbox, it was carried in a U-shaped subframe, attached by ball-and-socket joints to the main frame. The chassis was free to warp and twist as much as it wanted so that the road-holding of the Peugeot came close to a wild jig, a behavior that the *rois du volant* promptly turned into agility, into fine handling. Too-extreme reactions were mitigated by simple but effective tricks. In a state of rest the rear springs were more or less straight. When cornering, the outer spring, with the help of the flexible frame, pulled the Hotchkiss-type axle forward and reduced the oversteering tendency while the front spring shackle stop provided a progressive rate. The combination of three-point mounting of the engine-gearbox complex with a simple Hotchkiss axle, itself just as revolutionary as the new head, helped the famous 1.5-liter Delages to triumph in 1927. Meanwhile the ACF permitted the use of detachable wheels so that Peugeot fitted Rudge-Whitworth units and tires from Continental, 875 mm × 105 mm front, 880 mm × 120 mm rear. With 275 and 135 cm, the wheelbase and the track of the EX 1 matched the dimensions of the 1908 Benz. The unloaded weight of 1000 kg was acceptable, slightly more than the 130-mm Mercedes, 150 kg less than the Fiat S 74. First tests showed promise. Wasn't it magic? The old-established drawing office quickly found a matching name for the Levallois quartet: Henry, Zuccarelli, Goux and Boillot were nothing else than "charlatans"! Moreover Henry was allowed to devise a little brother for the 3-liter class, the EX 2/L 3 (78 mm × 156 mm), wheelbase 256 cm. Did Michaux feel hoodwinked? He quit Peugeot and henceforth acted for Théophile Schneider at Besançon. Louis Verdet? He had left Lion-Peugeot already by the end of 1909 to found the Société des Moteurs Le Rhône which was to built the famous nine-cylinder radial aero engines.

With the name Lion on the radiator, the solitary EX 2 under René Thomas started against a strong 3-liter armada from France and England. The Sizaire brothers and Louis Naudin were back. The inventive trio had not forgotten anything since 1908: they relied on four steel singles (78 mm × 156 mm) which were bolted together, with triple ignition and four horizontal 45-mm valves operated à la Pipe by means of vertical push rods and forked rockers and crankshaft in five plain bearings, altogether good for 80 hp at 2800 rpm. The gearbox gave direct drive on all speeds, and the differential was abolished allowing independent brakes on each wheel, the foot brake on one wheel and the hand brake on the opposite one. Lucien Picker had devised something similar for Grégoire, but at the moment it lacked development, a four-carburetor four-valve engine that produced 85 hp at 2950 rpm ... eight years later, when entered in the 1920 Indianapolis 500. As a precaution Grégoire turned up with conventional T-heads (80 mm × 149 mm) derived from the stock chassis. However, the drivetrain stepped out of line: The three-speed gearbox was combined with a dual-crown-wheel rear axle, giving six speeds. Alcyon appeared with the OHV four-valve racers (85 mm × 132 mm) of the previous year. The valve

July 1911—GP de France, Le Mans. The Rolland-Pilain of Victor Rigal fell out with a broken front axle.

July 1912—GP de l'ACF, Dieppe. The Sunbeam of Gustave Caillois. Sunbeam started with a simple L-head, the valves being inclined at 6° to the vertical in view of a reduced pocket volume and better scavenging. The nice coil above the radiator is a condenser.

July 1912—GP de l'ACF, Dieppe: *Pesage*. The Belgian six-cylinder Excelsior of Josef Christiaens.

operation was unusual: Instead of opening the valves on the upward push of the rods, they were operated on the downward pull against the compression of very stiff helical springs, there being a reversing mechanism within the enlarged camshaft housing. Vinot-Deguingand started with an F-head (89 mm × 120 mm) and a streamlined tail containing the tank in its center with two spare wheels to the left and right. Singer sent unusual F-heads (85 mm × 132 mm) with two exhaust valves from Coventry, Sunbeam fully developed L-heads (80 mm × 149 mm) from Wolverhampton, and Vauxhall almost-short-stroke L-heads (90 mm × 118 mm) from Luton. Hispano intended to start with four supercharged racers but withdrew after having entered at double fees. Were some engineers missing? The Ford entry of the French representative Henri Depasse was pulled out because of illness.

Grand Prix class:

| No. | Make | Driver | | | |
|---|---|---|---|---|---|
| 11, 31, 34, 57 | Lorraine-Dietrich | Hémery | Bablot | Hanriot | Heim |
| 12 | Mathis | Esser | | | |
| 13, 22, 45 | Peugeot | Goux | Boillot | Zuccarelli | |
| 23, 37, 42 | Fiat | Wagner | Bruce-Brown | DePalma | |
| 30, 49 | Rolland-Pilain | Guyot | Fauquet | | |
| 50 | Excelsior | Christiaens | | | |

Three-liter voiture légère class:

| | | | | |
|---|---|---|---|---|
| 3, 16, 17, 52 | Sunbeam | Rigal | Caillois Resta | Medinger |
| 4, 27, 40 | Alcyon | | Barriaux Page | Duray |
| 7, 19, 38 | Sizaire | Sizaire | Naudin | Schweitzer |
| 8, 32, 56 | Vinot | Léon Molon | Vonlatum Lucien Molon | |
| 9, 20 | Schneider | Champoiseau | Croquet | |
| 10, 18, 21, 24 | Grégoire | de Marne | Collinet Romano | Renaux |
| 14, 26, 43 | Calthorpe | Garcet | Hornsted Burgess | |
| 25, 39 | Singer | Rollason | Haywood | |
| 28, 36, 55 | Arrol-Johnston | Reid | Crossman Wyse | |
| 29, 41 | Côte | Gabriel | de Vère | |
| 33, 51, 54 | Vauxhall | Lambert | Hancock Watson | |
| 47 | Lion-Peugeot | Thomas | | |

The popular Victor Rigal in his slim Sunbeam no. 3 was the first to start. By his side was Jean Chassagne, a former submarine mechanic, flying instructor of the école Hanriot, pilot of the Bayard monoplane and Hispano driver. The grim Barriaux followed in his earsplitting Alcyon, then Georges Sizaire in his solid-looking Sizaire, and Léon Molon, the aviator, in his egg-shaped Vinot. The Peugeot of Goux sounded healthy. Anfort, pseudonym of the banker Fauquet, was unable to speed up his

July 1912—GP de l'ACF, Dieppe. *Pesage* of the two-cycle Côtes of de Vère and Gabriel: 1045 and 1050 kg.

July 1912—GP de l'ACF, Dieppe. Brown refueling his Fiat with cans.

July 1912—GP de l'ACF, Dieppe. The Fiat of Wagner catching the Vinot of Lucien Molon. The big Fiat went at 180 km/h, the three-liter Vinot at 120.

Rolland-Pilain. Hémery's Lorraine was the first to reappear, having overtaken six 3-liters. But it was the phenomenal Brown who led with 37 min 18 sec, a minute ahead of Boillot and Hémery. In lap two Boillot had to make a short stop near Londinières in order to sort out his brake cables. Hémery and Heim left their Lorraines by the roadside with cracked cylinders. Guyot parked his Pilain near the *fourche* of Neuville with big-end failure. Goux worked up into third place and Christiaens into fifth, right behind Wagner who struggled with a slipping clutch. Christiaens, a former racing mechanic at Darracq, foreman at Vivinus, Claudel carburetor expert and assembler of the aero engines of Moore Brabazon and Henry Farman, had prepared the Excelsior himself. But during lap three his precision work was of no use as he fell back by reason of tire trouble, while Goux was repairing a punctured fuel tank. Brown and Boillot were struggling for first place, Wagner and DePalma for third, with Resta fifth, the best 3-liter. Watson retired his Vauxhall with a broken wrist pin. Collinet, who replaced Porporato, ditched his Grégoire trying to pass Garcet; mechanic Passagnet was killed and Collinet suffered a broken wrist. In lap four Boillot and mechanic Prévost had to change two wheels after both rear tires burst at the same moment when approaching the *fourche* at Neuville. Brown led ahead of Wagner, Boillot, Bablot, DePalma and A. J. Hancock, the director of the Vauxhall racing department at Luton. René Thomas struggled with ignition problems, Paolo Zuccarelli with a coolant pipe. Léon Molon lost the oil plug of the crankcase. Haywood skidded into a tree. Cupid Hornsted pulled out with a broken gearbox.

July 1912—GP de l'ACF, Dieppe. Bustling depot stop for Barriaux and his Alcyon.

July 1912—GP de l'ACF, Dieppe. The Sizaire of Sizaire lost a wheel on lap 18.

July 1912—GP de l'ACF, Dieppe. The Sunbeam of Ernst Medinger, a former Puch motorcycle star from Vienna.

The Fiat drivers had decided to fit Michelin detachable rims instead of the wire wheels used in practice, declaring that the former enabled the cars to hold the road better and also to go faster. In fact Brown made changes in 40 and 45 seconds while other drivers with wire wheels occupied between 60 and 90 seconds. During the second half of the first day's racing Brown, Wagner and Boillot formed a compact trio, with Hancock, Resta and the former Puch motorcycle star Ernst Medinger close behind. Wagner made a short stop to fix a stuck valve. Rollason went out with a broken connecting rod, de Marne with defective steering, Thomas with ignition trouble, Zuccarelli with a broken gasoline pipe. Caillois withdrew with engine trouble, Bablot and Barriaux with valve defects, and Lucien Molon with yet another lost oil plug. Brown came in the victor of the first day in 6 h 36 min 37 sec, with an advantage of 2 min 1 sec on Boillot and nearly half an hour on Wagner. Resta led the 3-liters. As usual the ACF had timed the cars over a level kilometer: Brown's Fiat sped by at 164 km/h, Boillot's Peugeot at 161, Christiaens' Excelsior at 155, Hémery's Lorraine at 152, Resta's Sunbeam at 136, Hancock's Vauxhall at 127 km/h. Twenty-seven of 47 starters passed the night in the *parc fermé*.

Twenty-two racers lined up for the start of the second stage. Goux and DePalma were disqualified because they had accepted fuel away from the depot, a result of fractured fuel lines. Grégoire withdrew after Collinet's accident. Hanriot's Lorraine caught fire while running to the official garage. Brown took on fuel, changed the tires and was the first to get under way. Boillot lost nine minutes when the Peugeot had difficulties starting. During the night the racer had been housed in a rather flimsy shed; rain water had passed through the hinge of the hood and got

July 1912—GP de l'ACF, Dieppe. The Fiats of Brown and Wagner at the start for the second stage.

July 1912—GP de l'ACF, Dieppe. Boillot and the Peugeot accelerating after the *fourche* at Neuville.

July 1912—GP de l'ACF, Dieppe. Start of Hanriot in the Lorraine no. 34. In the background Brown's Fiat no. 37, on the right Crossman's Arrol-Johnston no. 36, in front of Robert Schweitzer's Sizaire.

on and around the plugs. While Schweitzer parked his Sizaire with a broken crankshaft, Boillot ran all-out and pulled his initial disadvantage down to 1 min 25 sec since Brown suffered from tire trouble. Then, on lap thirteen, Brown was forced to stop at Criel with a broken fuel pipe. He connected the spare line, obtained fuel from outside and was promptly disqualified. Brown talked it over with the Fiat team manager and then decided to finish the race although his time was no longer recorded. After 13 laps Boillot lay 27 minutes ahead of Wagner, around 40 minutes ahead of Resta and Rigal, two hours ahead of Christiaens, three hours ahead of Émile Pilain, who was replacing Anford, and nearly five hours ahead of Willy Esser's Mathis which struggled at 95 km/h over the long straights.

Hancock withdrew with engine trouble, Sizaire lost a wheel, and Percy Lambert lost coolant. On lap 18 it looked as if Boillot might lose the race. He had been changing gears without declutching, owing to a slipping clutch. Now the selector rods were bent. Prévost straightened them out with a lever. Meanwhile Boillot repaired the aluminum housing of the rear universal joint, which had been broken by a flying stone, and filled it with grease. The work occupied 20 minutes. Boillot finished with the use of practically only his high gear and won in 13 h 58 min 2 sec (110.256 km/h), 13 min 6 sec ahead of Wagner, then the Sunbeam trio of Rigal, who took the Coupe de l'Auto, Resta and Medinger, Christiaens' Excelsior and Croquet's Schneider. With luck seven liters defeated fourteen: modern times at Dieppe. Boillot declared: "Brown is extraordinary, he is the finest race driver I ever have seen. I know of no man who can approach him. He also is one of the squarest, most honest and loyal competitors I ever met. When he saw that an accident had put him out of the race he just

July 1912—GP de l'ACF, Dieppe. The Vauxhall of Hancock at the depot.

July 1912—GP de l'ACF, Dieppe. The Peugeot of Boillot at the depot.

August 1912—Mont Ventoux hillclimb. Best time for Georges Boillot and the Peugeot: 23.6 km in 17 min 46 sec.

urged me on to win in an open, generous manner, although one of his own teammates still was in the race. On the road he drove fiercely, but he was full of consideration for the little fellows. He gave them plenty of room; he did not try to hound them off the course. I should have liked to have seen him win the race." Boillot took the fresh car of Goux, transferred the fuel tank and the hood bearing the number 22 and started off to Paris, home and honors. Victor Rigal, Sunbeam agent for France, was highly satisfied: "I shall be able to sell every car I can get. We obtained 80 hp at 2800 revolutions on a bore and stroke of 80 by 148.5. We ran between 2000 and 3000 revolutions. When our speed dropped to 2000 as shown on our indicator we changed gear. Down the gradients by Sept Meules we were doing 155 km/h and we always closed throttle then so that we should not make the engine go faster than 3000 revolutions."

One of the 7.6-liter Peugeots should have been shipped to the American races at Elgin and Milwaukee, but at the last moment was kept back owing to some misunderstanding between the American backers and Peugeot. Once again the Grand Prix de France for 3-liters and the Coupe de la Sarthe for Grand Prix-racers, which were run on 9 September near Le Mans, were quickly forgotten. Wagner's Fiat, which was to have been driven by an amateur, failed to turn up. Boillot covered five laps, was forced to park his Peugeot with a seized engine and returned to the depot in the mechanic's seat of Duray's Alcyon, wearing a happy smile which dispelled the sinister rumor that he had killed a spectator and overturned into the ditch. Goux won the Coupe for Peugeot in front of Leduc in a standard stripped SPA

September 1912—GP de France, Le Mans. The three-liter Peugeot of René Thomas started as a Lion.

**September 1912—Coupe de la Sarthe, Le Mans. The 7.6-liter Peugeot of Jules Goux.**

and Crespelle in his De Dion-engined Crespelle, Zuccarelli the Grand Prix for Lion in front of Champoiseau in a Schneider and Léon Molon in a Vinot.

But the Peugeots were not ready for retirement. Henri Boissy, the London Peugeot manager, asked for a record attempt at Brooklands. At the end of March 1913, Goux and Boillot crossed the Channel with a 7.6-liter, chassis no. 2 with engine no. L 76/01 in high-speed bodywork, with radiator cowl and pointed tail. The Brooklands scales quoted 3220 lbs, 1458 kg. But the axle was bounding more than anticipated and a shock absorber arm touched and slightly damaged the tank. The hour record was postponed and Goux decided to cover ten laps from a standing start, averaging 103.23 mph, 166 km/h. By the second week of April, the Peugeot was repaired. Goux and Boillot aimed at the six-hour record of the 8-liter class. Tire trouble caused two stops, then a big-end went which rendered the Peugeot hors de combat. The last attempt was made on 13 April. Goux covered 106.22 miles (170 km) in the first hour, handed over to Boillot after 41 laps. A carburetor fire stopped the fast run. Later Malcolm Campbell purchased the Peugeot, named it "Bluebird" and, in the early twenties, turned fast laps at Brooklands. In 1923 he lent the fast bird to a brave lady, Mrs. O. S. Menzies; she achieved many successes in club races.

While Goux and Boillot chased records, Levallois was preparing the other two Grand Prix Peugeots for a transatlantic expedition. The goal was the Indianapolis 500. In 1913 the regulations there allowed a maximum of 450 cubic inches (7.374 liters) so that Peugeot mounted new 108 mm blocks (108 mm × 200 mm). The two racers were shipped on the North-German Lloyd steamer *Kronprinzessin Cecilie*, sailing from Cherbourg on 30 April. The drivers and their mechanics, Jules Goux and Émile Begin, Paolo Zuccarelli and Ernesto Fanelli, sailed on the French liner *La France* from Le Havre on 3 May, in company of team manager Charles Faroux, in his other life editor of *La Vie Automobile*. The Indy officials gave every assistance. Two weeks before the start the Peugeot squad took up headquarters in a nice all-wood cottage belonging to one of the gardeners; Zuccarelli immediately called it "mia casa." C. G. Sedwick placed his private car and chauffeur at their disposal, and A. C. Newby, president of the National Motor Car Co., his entire factory! Johnny Aitken looked after the organization. Begin and Fanelli fitted Firestones, 35 × 4 front, 34 × 4.5 rear. The promotion was soon in full swing:

> Paul Zuccarelli is the antithesis of Goux, large and powerful, inclined to be frivolous, laughs, sings and jokes all through the busy, nerve-racking day, and wears two-franc overalls, with broad bib to protect his obese tummy from spattering grease, when he thunders over the bricks of the red oval in his blue car. Goux's moustache is sparse and neatly trimmed, the moustache of a dandy. Zuccarelli's hirsute adornment is almost terrifying and sprouts untamed and uncut on his upper lip, the moustache of a warrior. Goux knits his brow in serious determination. Zuccarelli's blue eyes twinkle with merriment. They are a strange combination, Goux, the scheming, daring Napoleon; Zuccarelli, the powerful, good-natured Garibaldi.

Spring 1913—Untertürkheim. Before the shipment to Indianapolis: Théo Pilette and mechanic Barthélémy Bruyère in the Mercedes-Knight.

The strange combination and the blue Peugeots encountered an angry competition. Three T-head Mercers came from Trenton, New Jersey, two 7.4-liters (4.8" × 6.19", 122 mm × 157 mm, 445 cubic inches) for Caleb "Caley" Bragg and Ralph DePalma, and a 4.9-liter (4.37" × 5", 111 mm × 127 mm, 300 cubic inches) for Spencer Wishart. No mean team! In America the T-head was far from being finished, either in the yellow Mercers, the white Stutzes (4.8" × 5.5", 122 mm × 134 mm) of Charley Merz, Gil Anderson and Don Herr, or in the Keeton (5.09" × 5.5", 123 mm × 134 mm) of wild Bob Burman, which was distinctive by reason of the dashboard location of the radiator, Renault fashion. The former Mercer engineer E. H. Delling and his partner W. Hecketal relied upon the L-head in their Deltal (4" × 5.3", 102 mm × 151 mm), with previous year's winner Joe Dawson at the wheel. The Fox special (4.75" × 5.5", 124 mm × 134 mm, OHV-head), built by Frank Fox and driven by Howard "Howdy" Wilcox, was not to be underrated. The Mercedes of E. J. Schroeder was compelled to start with a new 114 mm block (114 mm × 180 mm) and a new driver: smiling Ralph Mulford. Another sponsor came from Chicago: E. C. Patterson, who entered the Belgian Théo Pilette in a Mercedes Knight, a sleeve-valve 4-liter (100 mm × 130 mm) producing 65 hp at 2500, mounted in a 250-cm shaft-drive frame. Mechanic Barthélémy Bruyère fitted American Diamond tires, 34 × 4.5 front and rear. With 130 liters of fuel and 65 liters of oil the little Knight weighed 970 kg: "Pilette relies on continuous running rather than high speed to make a showing in the race." Wolverhampton sent a six-cylinder Sunbeam (90 mm × 160 mm, L-head) for Albert Guyot, Milan three Isotta-Fraschinis (120 mm × 160 mm, OHC four-valve head) for Vincenzo Trucco, Harry Grant and Teddy Tetzlaff. The race started as usual on Memorial Day, Friday morning, 30 May, at half-past ten.

American race critics admitted the French cars to be fast and the drivers efficient but prophesied that the blue machines would not be able to sustain the grind of 500 miles. In fact Zuccarelli limped to the pits in lap 21 when a fuel line gave way and the carburetor caught fire. After 100 miles Bob Burman assumed the lead, in front of Goux, Anderson and Mulford, Pilette in position ten. After 250 miles the order was Anderson, Mulford, Goux, and after 400 miles it was Goux, Wishart, Mulford. Everything remained open. Mulford's Mercedes began to splutter on the backstretch. The tank had run dry! The Mercedes had consumed 60 gallons in 440 miles, 39 liters per 100 km, much more than expected. Mechanic Paul Stevens ran a mile to the pits for a fresh supply. Anderson's Stutz refused to restart after a tire stop, having suffered a broken camshaft gear. Finally Goux drove the Peugeot to victory in 6 h 35 min 5 sec, followed by the Mercer of Wishart, the Stutz of Charley Merz and the Sunbeam of Guyot. Charles Faroux after the race:

> For Goux all went well and at the end he was sailing along tranquilly. Burman who was way behind tried his best to engage Goux in a battle of speed, but Goux knowing all the ins and outs of his profession left Burman to amuse himself alone. I much admire the construction of the Stutz and Mercer cars and the lines of the Keeton. You have excellent drivers over here, DePalma, Merz, Anderson, Burman, Wishart and Bragg knew the track as well as they did their cars. It would require our Boillot to beat them. I want to rectify some common mistakes made about our Peugeot racing team. The Peugeot cars were completely designed according to contract with Zuccarelli and Boillot by an engineer of very great ability named Henry. These three men, Goux, Zuccarelli and Boillot, traveled together from one year's

end to the next. Zuccarelli is a mechanical genius; Boillot is without superior when it comes to carrying out orders of others; Goux is likewise a driver of the very first order. I want to add that Zuccarelli and Goux treat their mechanics like comrades, not like servants.

And the little Mercedes Knight of Pilette? It finished just behind Guyot and came very close to finishing without difficulty, but on its last few laps had a stuck float valve. The little Mercedes used eight gallons of oil and 25 gallons of fuel in the 500 miles, getting 20 miles to the gallon, 14 liters per 100 km, averaging 68.14 mph (110 km/h). This did not impress E. J. Schroeder, who preferred to purchase the winning Peugeot while the racer driven by Zuccarelli finished up in the hands of amateur driver Armour Ferguson. Thus the revolutionary cylinder head remained, in duplicate, in America. At Levallois this did not disconcert anyone. Ernest Henry had continued designing....

# 23

## *Rivals in Blue*

After their victory in the Indianapolis 500, the Charlatans from Peugeot had just five weeks to prepare their new cars for the Grand Prix de l'ACF. In 1913 the club got going again and granted the sportsmen not only a new course but also a new regulation. On Wednesday, 12 July, 29 laps of the 31.6-km Circuit de la Picardie, a few kilometers south-east of Amiens, had to be covered for a total distance of 916 km. Maximum fuel consumption was 20 liters per 100 km, 14.12 miles per gallon, and weight was to be between 800 and 1100 kg without fuel and oil, coolant, tools and spare parts. The Commission Sportive imposed standard tanks of circular section placed at the rear of the driver's seat, banned streamlined tails, and sealed all filler caps, fuel lines, connections and carburetors. Each racer was given an amount of 183.3 liters (40.3 gallons) of fuel, measured at 15°C. Nine leading commercial brands were available, density between 0.715 and 0.720, filled in the usual 5-liter cans. Peugeot decided in favor of "Motricine."

Of course the Charlatans remained true to their concept, eliminating the previous weak points and adjusting the cars to the new regulations. The cylinder dimensions were reduced from 110 mm × 200 mm to 100 mm × 180 mm, resulting in a swept volume of 5.6 liters, for a consumption in accordance with the fuel allowance and in the new designation EX 3/L 56. Concerning the valve mechanism, the vertical shaft with bevel gearing was replaced by a train of spur pinions running in ball bearings and enclosed in an aluminum housing, and the rather frail semicircles by stronger L-shaped tappets. The vertical member of the L acted as an upper guide and the small return spring was located below, inside the camshaft housing. Nothing major was changed, but the details were simplified and the method of guiding improved. In the bottom half Ernest Henry returned to the old Hispano recipe: Two-piece bolted-up crankshaft running in three ball bearings, the front and central ones being single, the rear one double, within a one-piece barrel-type crankcase. This was shorter, stiffer and lighter than the side trip of 1912, but required a lot of exactitude from the assembler. To support the ball bearings, which came from SRO, the Usine de Roulements à Billes Schmid-Roost at Oerlikon near Zürich, Levallois manufactured three plates serving as closure and stiffening elements. The crankshaft including its ball bearings and plates was inserted endwise and bolted through inspection holes. The inventive dry sump of the Peugeot used only one oil pump, a plunger pump, which drew either oil or air from the sump and delivered it to an air-tight tank under the driver's seat. By reason of the pressure, the lubricant was driven to six sight-feeds on the dash and then to the various lubrication points, to the two camshafts, the spur pinions and the three ball bearings of the crankshaft. The oil splashing out of the ball bearings was collected

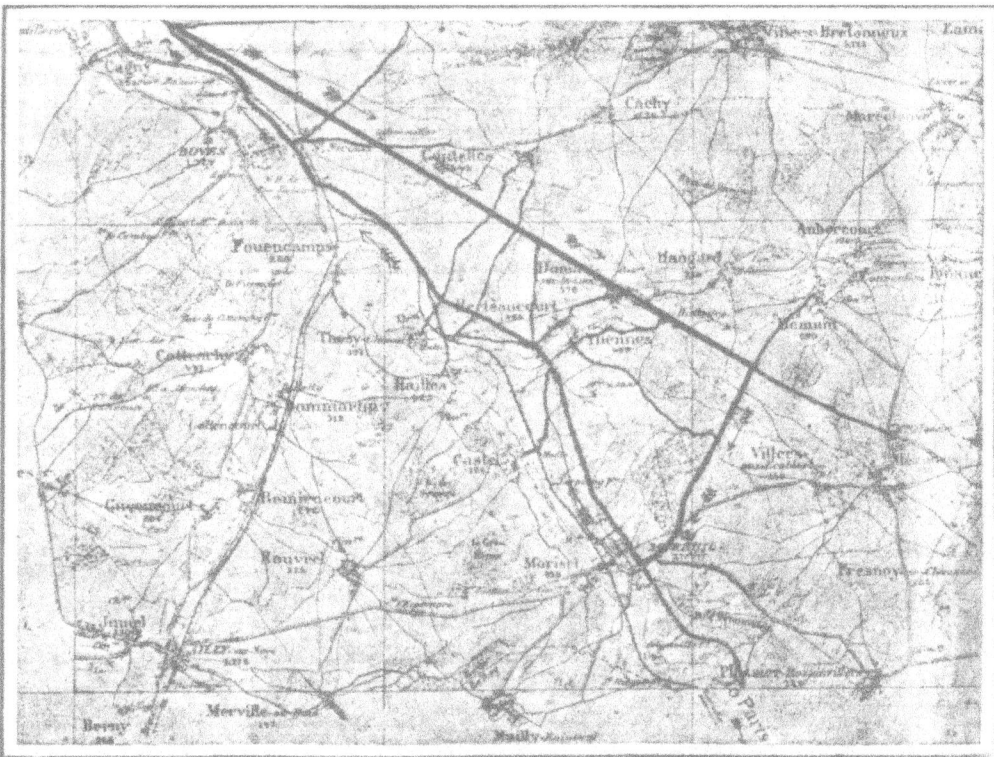

The Circuit de la Picardie, to the south east of Amiens, length 31.6 km (from *Motor Age*, 1913).

in catcher rings placed on the webs, and fed by centrifugal force through oilways in the shaft to the big ends, 1906 Renault fashion. An improvement over the Hispano was that the hollow big ends acted as small tanks and assured a constant oil flow. Herewith all lubrication problems were resolved for the moment. The carburetor was supplied by the specialist Claudel as in the previous year; the plugs by Oléo, a new French make founded by Léo Ripault; the magneto not by Bosch anymore but by MEA, the Fabrik Magnet-Elektrischer Apparate at Stuttgart-Feuerbach. The 5.6-liter delivered 110 hp at 2500 rpm, or, according to contemporary bench tests, an exaggerated 138 hp at 2150 rpm, with a fuel consumption of 0.274 liters per horse-power hour.

A Ferodo-lined cone replaced the multiplate clutch. To reduce weight transfer, the rear springs were mounted just under the main frame members instead of outboard, and also under the rear axle. As a result of trials in the wind tunnel of Gustave Eiffel, the Peugeot was given a radiator with rounded edges, a clean-cut underpan and enclosed sides for the seats, while one EX 3 was equipped with a wood-lined front axle and transverse connecting bar. The wheelbase was shortened by 5 cm to 270 cm, the track was 135 cm, and tires were 875 mm × 105 mm front, 880 mm × 120 mm rear, from Pirelli since the Italians offered the best contract. As usual Henry devised a little 3-liter brother for the Coupe de l'Auto, the EX 4/L 3 (78 mm × 156 mm) producing 92 hp at 2870 rpm.

July 1913—GP de l'ACF, Amiens. Georges Boillot and mechanic Prévost in the 5.6-liter Peugeot EX 3.

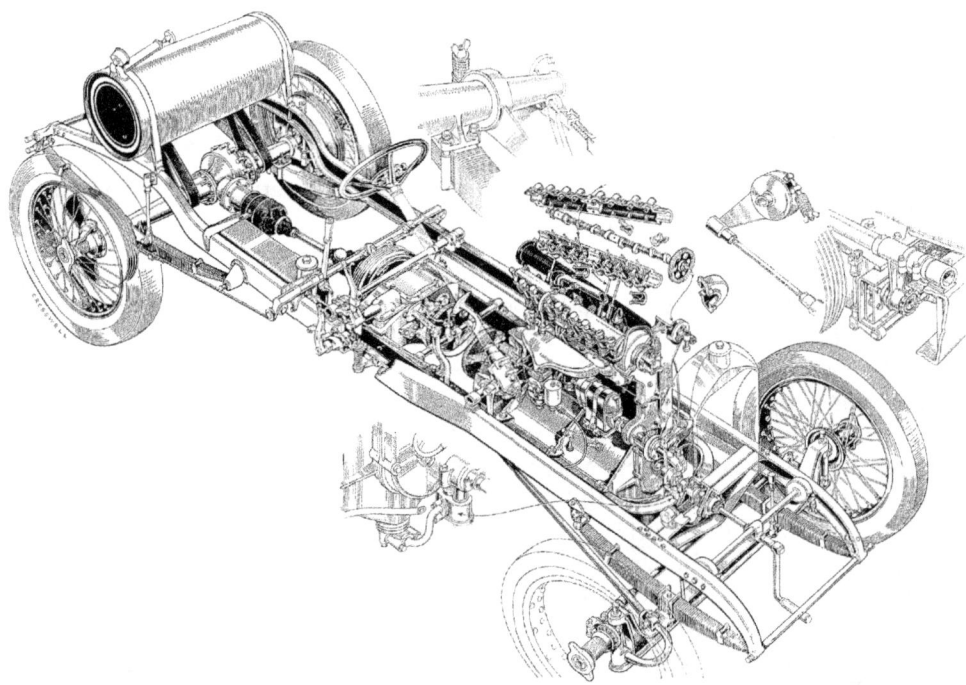

Under Boillot, the three-liter Peugeot EX 4/L 3 took first place in the 1913 Coupe de l'Auto; under Duray, it captured second place in the 1914 Indy 500. Characteristic for all Peugeot racers was the three-point mounting of the engine-gearbox complex in combination with the Hotchkiss-type rear axle. In the racers of 1913 and 1914 spur pinions drove the camshafts. In 1913 the valves were closed by two springs. The intake opened 12° after TDC, closed 45° after BDC; the exhaust opened 45° before BDC, closed 18° after TDC (from Pomeroy, *The Grand Prix Car*).

## 23. Rivals in Blue

Delage had moved from the small workshop at Levallois to a large, newly-built plant at Courbevoie, just on the other side of the Seine. Meanwhile Monsieur Louis was aged 35, high time for great sport. After X came Y. And that was the designation of the first Grand Prix Delage. X stood for expérimental, Y for nothing. Chief engineer Arthur Michelat was hardly influenced by Henry, but relied on a big brother of his 1911 Coupe de l'Auto winner. Why not? 105 mm × 180 mm meant 6.2 liters and the two low-mounted camshafts operated four horizontal 55-mm valves via hollow pushrods and forked rockers made of BND steel. The camshafts and the four-piece crankshaft ran in five ball bearings, the big ends in plain bearings. Two Bosch magnetos delivered high tension for the dual ignition. Output was 115 hp at 2500 rpm, transmitted through a five-speed gearbox, as in one of the 1911 3-liters. The torque-tube axle of the X gave way to a Hotchkiss axle in the Y, not à la Peugeot but in combination with a more conventional front: rigid four-point mounting of the engine and flexible three-point suspension of the gearbox, good for a tamer road holding than the Peugeot.

Opel started with an OHC two-valve head (90 mm × 156 mm), Itala with rotary valves (125 mm × 150 mm). After the overwhelming success in the 1912 Coupe de l'Auto, the rest of the field relied upon the simple L-head, Sunbeam (80 mm × 150 mm) and Excelsior (90 mm × 160 mm) in their six-cylinders, Théophile Schneider in a long-stroke four-cylinder (96 mm × 190 mm) and Mathis in an inflated Baby (70 mm × 140 mm). The Grand Prix performance of the Baby had

July 1913—GP de l'ACF, Amiens. Paul Bablot and mechanic Lausson in the 6.2-liter Delage Y.

July 1913—GP de l'ACF, Amiens. Dashboard of Guyot's Delage.

July 1913—GP de l'ACF, Amiens. The Opel of Carl Joerns, the sole German competitor.

a quick result: Already the Princess of Hohenlohe, Joachim of Prussia and Prince Albert of Greece drove Mathises. Chain drive and wooden artillery wheels did not appear at Amiens. But Excelsior fitted modern Palmer cord tires. Instead of woven fabric, the cord tires used large or fine cords placed diagonally, reducing friction and thus heat development. Two great engineers had died in crashes. Guido Bigio, technical director at Itala, skidded off the road in a fast bend near Eu when practicing on the old Dieppe course. While carrying out speed tests with the 5.6-liter Peugeot on the 20-km straight between Nonancourt and Évreux, 90 km west of Paris, Paolo Zuccarelli collided with a hay cart driven by a deaf farmer who had not heard the racer and suddenly emerged from a side road. The collision cut the horse and the shafts away from the cart. Zuccarelli was torn from his seat and killed on the spot, while mechanic Fanelli was thrown on the road where he suffered a broken arm and severe flesh wounds. "Zuccarelli was more than a race driver," wrote Charles Faroux, editor of *La Vie Automobile*. "In conjunction with Boillot and engineer Henry he was largely responsible for the design of the successful racing cars produced by Peugeot during the last three years."

Twenty racers from eight marques and five nations lined up for the start:

| No. | Make | Driver | | | |
|---|---|---|---|---|---|
| 1, 9, 15, 19 | Sunbeam | Caillois | Resta | Chassagne | Guinness |
| 2, 10 | Delage | Bablot | Guyot | | |
| 3 | Opel | Joerns | | | |
| 4 | Mathis | Esser | | | |
| 5, 11 | Excelsior | Christiaens | Hornsted | | |
| 6, 12, 16, 20 | Schneider | Croquet | Gabriel | Champoiseau | Thomas |
| 7, 13, 17 | Itala | Nazzaro | Pope | Moriondo | |
| 8, 14, 18 | Peugeot | Boillot | Goux | Delpierre | |

July 1913—GP de l'ACF, Amiens. The Schneider of Croquet.

The start, which was scheduled for five o'clock, was delayed by 30 minutes until a dense fog lifted. Gustave Caillois was waiting in his long Sunbeam for the signal. Mechanic Smith cranked up the six-cylinder at the last moment, fuel economy being the order of the day. The Sunbeam had not been warmed up in advance, and it misfired and went away slowly. No trace of a Grand Prix start! One minute later it was the turn of Paul Bablot, the phlegmatic from Marseille: "He started in a race as if it really did not matter whether he got there or not." Bablot was so careful not to use a spoonful of fuel more than necessary that he stalled the Delage twice. Mechanic Lausson cranked like the devil. Suddenly the Delage began to fire, not on all cylinders, but it ran, until it reached the first stiff rise. Then the Delage stalled again. Lausson was exhausted. Bablot was unable to give any help, being partially paralyzed in one arm. Finally he put the car in reverse gear and let it run backwards. He had lost an additional five minutes. Nazzaro made a nice start. The dashing Boillot hesitated before his engine got into its stride. The others had learned the lesson and warmed up their engines.

Boillot set the pace with 16 min 39 sec, four seconds ahead of Goux, then Chassagne, Guyot, Guinness, Resta and Moriondo. Delpierre turned the third Peugeot over in the S-bend under the railway bridge just after Boves. How Delpierre won a spot at the wheel of the Peugeot remained a mystery; certainly his anonymous starts in the Coupe de l'Auto and some hillclimbs were not adequate credentials

July 1913—GP de l'ACF, Amiens. The Delage of Paul Bablot at Moreuil.

when aces like Wagner, Hémery and Duray were free. Was his father playing cards with Robert Peugeot? Or were the Charlatans anxious about disclosing technical details to competitors? H. R. Pope, the London agent for Itala, withdrew with a damaged main bearing, Joerns with a burned-out big-end. Croquet was too fast when entering the slightly banked grandstand track and shot straight ahead down the escape road. In the same corner, Moriondo had a bad skid, threw his Itala into the cinder wall and turned turtle amidst a cloud of earth. Moriondo and mechanic Giulio Foresti sprang up in a second, lifted the car up on its wheels and within four minutes were off again, to hearty applause. In front, sky blue struggled against royal blue, Peugeot against Delage, Boillot against Guyot, Goux against Bablot, although Chassagne, replacing the injured Rigal, was able to keep up. After four laps the order was Goux, Chassagne, Boillot (who had changed the attachments of the ignition wires), Guyot and Resta. Gabriel retired with a broken piston. The short stub exhaust pipes of the Excelsiors blew directly into the faces of the crews and before very long the spectators made fun of the "black-and-white brigade," of the "niggers," of the "chimney sweeps." In lap five Bablot moved forward to position six. Caillois overlooked and hit a culvert at the exit of Boves. The torque member of the Sunbeam broke and cut the gasoline tank open. Moriondo withdrew with broken steering.

During lap seven a glass sight-feed tube broke on Boillot's Peugeot. It had been screwed up too tightly and under expansion gave way. Mechanic Prévost made

July 1913—GP de l'ACF, Amiens. The duel, blue against blue in front of the grandstand: Peugeot ahead of Delage, Boillot ahead of Guyot.

July 1913—GP de l'ACF, Amiens. The Excelsior of Hornsted at Moreuil.

the repair while the Peugeot was in motion. In lap nine, after 285 km, Guyot took the lead in 2 h 27 min 28 sec, 58 seconds ahead of Goux, 2 min 7 sec ahead of Boillot, then Chassagne, Bablot and Kenelm Lee Guinness. The Mathis was held up by engine trouble. Guyot, in typical composure and armchair contentment, and the royal blue Delage were 20 seconds per lap faster than Goux and the sky-blue Peugeot. This could not go on forever. Boillot forced the pace and passed his tender teammate in lap 13. Bablot lost ten minutes by reason of tire trouble. The Schneider of René Thomas was boiling. Dario Resta had to stop every two laps to pour oil into the crankcase, the Sunbeam's leaking oil tank losing all its lubricant. Felice Nazzaro, who in May had won the Targa in his own Nazzaro, withdrew the last Itala with a broken spring. At Boves, Guinness felt a front tire go. The Sunbeam swayed from side to side of the road, touched the palisade, swept away half a dozen huge boulders, shot its crew out, caught a spectator and fell into the river Avre. Guinness and mechanic Cook escaped with injuries but the spectator died the same night. In lap 17 the right rear tire burst on Guyot's Delage. In his excitement, mechanic Achille Secuws jumped out of his seat while the racer was running at a fairly high speed and was knocked down, the car passing over him. No bones were broken, but he suffered flesh wounds, was injured in the head, and fainted with pain. Guyot had his hands full to lift the strong and powerfully-built mechanic back into the seat. Guyot drove slowly back to the stands, passed him over to the pit attendants and took on a relief mechanic. This was Guyot's only stop but it proved a costly one: The Delage had dropped to fourth place, 16 minutes behind Boillot, 13

July 1913—GP de l'ACF, Amiens. The Itala of Nazzaro coming out of the right-angled corner at Moreuil.

July 1913—GP de l'ACF, Amiens. The Peugeot of Goux at Moreuil.

minutes behind Goux and nine minutes behind Chassagne. As consolation Bablot completed a lap in 15 min 17 sec, the fastest of the day.

The sportsmen were faced with the question of which Peugeot would win. Suddenly the number eight was overheating and began to knock. Boillot stopped at the depot, took off the hood and found that a water-pump connection had burst. Prévost bound it up with rags and adhesive tape and added some water. Then the radiator cap was mislaid and the Peugeot had difficulties in starting up. The lead was reduced to six seconds: "Boillot, although the most skillful race driver in France, and probably in the world, does not show at his best in pit work, being rather resentful of the expenditure of the minutes. His strong feature is the way he handles a car at speed on a difficult road." Boillot got cracking now: "It was during the last three rounds that I had to make the call for all the power the motor was capable of developing. I realized that I had plenty of gasoline and could race my motor and use my gears without any danger of falling by the roadside. During the earlier portion of the race I had been doing nearly all my driving on top gear, with the use of my second for quick get-away, and employing third for the grandstand track. By using third on the hills and getting into second on the grandstand stretch, it was possible to gain a certain amount of time." His time of 15 min 24 sec was the best Peugeot lap and 1 min 18 sec less than Goux. "Just at the end my ignition lever broke, leaving the magneto in fully-advanced position, which was too much for constant use. It was with this handicap that I finished." Boillot won in 7 h 53 min 57 sec (116.19 km/h), 2 min 15 sec ahead of Goux, twelve minutes ahead of Chassagne. The Delages of Bablot and Guyot lay twenty minutes back, the Sunbeam of Resta nearly half an hour. The Schneiders or Excelsiors never had a chance. The Peugeots and the Delages finished with 20 to 23 liters of fuel in reserve.

**July 1913—GP de l'ACF, Amiens. The Sunbeam of Jean Chassagne in front of the grandstand.**

July 1913—GP de l'ACF, Amiens. The Peugeot of Georges Boillot at Moreuil.

"Peugeot the invincible!" In August Boillot won the Mont Ventoux hillclimb in 17 min 38 sec clipping eight seconds off his own 1912 record, and in September, on the old Boulogne course, he drove the 3-liter to victory in the Coupe de l'Auto, 620 km in 6 h 7 min 40 sec: "It was the hardest race I have ever driven in, immeasurably more difficult than the Grand Prix at Amiens." Goux came second, nine minutes back, "for it appears impossible for him to come in first when his team-mate is in the neighborhood." Kenelm Lee Guinness in a Sunbeam was 12 minutes back, then Hancock's Vauxhall, Rigal in the third Peugeot, Tabuteau's Alda and d'Avaray in an Anasagasti seventh and last. The latter, representing Argentina, was an old, renamed Picker-engined racer built and driven by Guyot in 1912. Georges Boillot said in an interview: "The racing cars were produced by a special staff, of which Ernest Henry, my late friend Zuccarelli, my companion driver Goux, and myself are the leading members. In Zuccarelli's sad and untimely death we lost not only a close friend, but an engineer of considerable ability. There is only one sad feature about my victory in the Grand Prix—it is that Zuccarelli is not here to share the honor with us. Zuccarelli and I supplied the main idea for the car. Henry was responsible for the drawings, and it is to him that we owe the beautiful lines of these cars." The meteoric Georges Boillot became the d'Artagnan of the Belle Époque. In the cafés of the Avenue de la Grande Armée, the sportsmen celebrated him as the worthy successor of Léon Théry, Victor Hémery and Louis Wagner. "Slightly below average height, somewhat heavily built, of ruddy complexion, having black hair and moustache, well developed physically, Georges Boillot, the winner of the Grand Prix, is the ideal type of race driver. He is of a frank, open, generous nature, which has naturally made him a favorite with all who have been brought in contact with him." Like Barney Oldfield in America, Boillot combined steering-wheel artistry with charisma and a nose for publicity: "Boillot turns the wheel against all ethics of good driving. He crosses his arms. The writer witnessed Boillot driving a touring car and when taking a corner, it was done with a quick turn of the wheel with the arms crossed. This is not approved by most of the good drivers." As soon as the races approached the great Georges monopolized all headlines. There was barely a demoiselle between Lille and Marseille who did not dream about him.

# 24

## Test Run

The victory of Dieppe had increased the turnover at Untertürkheim: Whereas in 1908 the DMG was just able to sell 109 Mercedes, one year later the number rose to 671, topping the result of 1904, the year after the Bennett victory, Jellinek's second best season. And the rosy situation was continuing. Through 1912 the numbers rose to 1106, 1490 and finally 1866. The supposition of Messrs. Lorenz and Kaulla was confirmed; despite abstinence in the great sport, things were looking up. Did the resurrection of the Grand Prix change the situation? In 1913 the DMG was again in the doldrums. The wealthy clientele tended towards Fiat and Peugeot. The successes of DePalma got only the American representation going. Moreover the future 4.5-liter formula promised good sport. Thus, in the spring of 1913, the board gave the go-ahead, and Paul Daimler immediately planned a test run, in August, in the Grand Prix de France at Le Mans.

It was no surprise that Daimler had a racer with an aircraft engine in mind. In 1912 the second Wilhelm had organized his Kaiserpreis for the pilots whereby power-to-weight ratio and low fuel consumption decided the classification. An overhead-valve Benz (130 mm × 180 mm) collected the 50,000 goldmarks from the Kaiser's coffer, followed by DMG with a six-cylinder, ahead of the NAG, the New Automobile Co. in Berlin, a subsidiary of the AEG, then again the DMG with a four-cylinder and finally Argus, the Argus Motor Co. in Berlin-Johannisthal. For the Grand Prix de France, Paul Daimler had two sixes (105 mm × 140 mm, 7.2 liters) and a four (140 mm × 150 mm, 9.2 liters) mounted in the well-known chain drive frame of Dieppe, wheelbase 270 cm. An older 9.5-liter (130 mm × 180 mm) served as a benchmark. The Brussels agency of Théo Pilette took care of the entries.

Untertürkheim saved weight according to the old Panhard recipe: The six-cylinder was made up of three steel pairs, the heads and water jackets being welded on. An overhead camshaft operated two 51-mm valves set at 15° to the vertical, driven via vertical shaft. During the bench tests of the Kaiserpreis at Berlin-Adlershof, the 7.2-liter delivered 90 hp at 1350 rpm, good for 120 at 2000 in the racing car. The weight in comparison to the 130 mm cast-iron engine was astonishing: 142 kg, about half! Christian Lautenschlager and Otto Salzer were the drivers. Later the six-cylinder finished up in a sports car, in the 28/95, the successor to the 37/90. Pilette started on the four-cylinder which had the same buildup, output and weight. His friend Leon Elskamp, a former Minerva motorcycle racer, took the wheel of the 9.5-liter. The newcomers weighed just 850 kg. Conti supplied the tires, 875 mm × 105 mm front, 895 mm × 135 mm rear. "The finish of the cars and their detail equipment was a credit even to Mercedes. Why Mercedes reserved such a powerful team for a provincial race, it was impossible to understand."

August 1913—GP de France, Le Mans. The Mercedes team: on the left the well-tried 9.5-liter of Elskamp; in the middle the two OHC sixes (105 mm × 140 mm) of Lautenschlager and Salzer; on the right the OHC four (140 mm × 150 mm) of Pilette.

August 1913—GP de France, Le Mans. The four-cylinder Mercedes of Théo Pilette waiting for the start. In the background a Schneider and the 9.5-liter of Leon Elskamp.

## 24. Test Run

Three Delages for Bablot, Guyot and Duray came from Courbevoie, four Théo Schneiders from Besançon and a pair of Excelsiors from Saventhem. An older 155-mm Benz should have been driven by Hémery but finished up at the last minute in the hands of its owner, the Marquis de Moraes. A picturesque note was added by the "Brasier with which Léon Théry won the Bennett Cup in 1905," handled by an attaché of the Russian embassy in Paris named Basil Soldatenkow. The Coupe de la Sarthe for 3-liters was run concurrently. As for Peugeot, with the Delages being extremely fast and the Mercedes unpredictable, the Charlatans could lose face and preferred to conclude their season in the Coupe de l'Auto at Boulogne. The 54-km course south of Le Mans, via Pontlieu, Parigné-l'Evêque, Le Grand-Lucé and Ecommoy, had nothing in common with the Grand Prix circuit of 1906, but included part of the famous Hunaudières straight of the 24-hour course. The race would be run on 7 August 1913 over ten laps.

The Delage trio took the lead. After two laps the order was Guyot, Bablot, Duray, then Lautenschlager, Hornsted's Excelsior, Salzer, and Croquet's Schneider. On the long straights, at top speed, Lautenschlager and Salzer were hardly able to hold their steering wheels because of the vibrations of the six-cylinders. In lap six Duray fell back after a puncture. Pilette moved to position three, nine minutes behind Bablot. Lautenschlager lay fourth despite having lost his hood and the side-mounted

August 1913—GP de France, Le Mans. Théo Pilette at the wheel of the Mercedes; leaning over the mechanic's seat, Alfred Vischer.

August 1913—GP de France, Le Mans. Two views of Pilette rounding the hairpin at Pontlieue. The Mercedes lost 1.5 seconds per kilometer in comparison to the fastest Delage.

spare wheel. Salzer was fifth, with Elskamp far back. In lap seven, Pilette passed Guyot. Before starting for his last lap with a lead of six minutes, Bablot pulled in to change tires. Then the Delage refused to fire. The mechanic put every ounce of strength into a few more pulls. The Delage remained silent. Utterly exhausted, the mechanic leaned for support against the wheel. "A new mechanic!" A man vaulted over the rails, a slim youth with more enthusiasm than brawn. "No, not you. Get back!" A second man, a red-faced, muscular fellow, grabbed the handle. "Put some life into it," shouted Louis Delage. Again and again the fellow tugged the handle up with not a fraction of a second's interval between the pulls. The engine remained dead. Pilette was rapidly closing up. A lady in the grandstand, unable to contain herself any longer, cried out in a shrill voice: "Ah mais c'est énervant!" Intense silence reigned. "C'est à moi!" The words came from a powerful frame leaping from the pits on to the road: Léon Molon, the aviator and Vinot agent at Le Havre, whose 3-liter Vinot-Deguingand had been forced out by lubrication troubles. "Can we have a third mechanic?" "Yes, but not two at once." Molon gripped the starting handle and with utter disdain of a backfire spun that stubborn Delage engine as if it had been a taxicab. There was an answering roar. Molon leaped up beside Bablot, without goggles, with a happy grin. Then they were off, and won in 4 h 21 min 50 sec, 4 min 40 sec ahead of Guyot, 6 min 3 sec ahead of Pilette, 13 min 2 sec ahead of Salzer, 13 min 13 sec ahead of Duray, a quarter of an hour ahead of Lautenschlager. Elskamp finished nearly one hour back. After the victory the clever Adolphe Clément promptly offered his friend

August 1913—GP de France, Le Mans. The six-cylinder Mercedes of Salzer on the start-finish straight at Hunaudières.

August 1913—GP de France, Le Mans. The 9.5-liter Mercedes of Elskamp in front of the Delage of Bablot.

August 1913—GP de France, Le Mans. The six-cylinder Mercedes of Lautenschlager just before losing its hood.

Delage a favorable loan. Monsieur Louis did not invest it in his factory but in a fine château at Le Pecq!

From Untertürkheim's standpoint, the test was a success since now Paul Daimler knew how a perfect 4.5-liter for the 1914 season had to be built up: with four cylinders, aero-engine fashion. At the same time, this meant the end for the chain drive, the end of a whole era. The lower engine weight, saving 150 kg, upset the ideal mass distribution of 50/50. The ratio in the racers of Lautenschlager, Salzer and Pilette was 43/57, 370 kg at the front, 480 at the rear. The gearbox could, even had to, move forward, not only restoring the old balance but reducing the polar moment of inertia, the best way for better agility. But with a centrally mounted gearbox, the chain drive was suddenly superfluous since overall a shaft-drive axle saved weight. With this knowledge in mind, Daimler, Link and Schnaitmann devised the 4.5-liter, the first Mercedes racer of a new generation. Until the new creation found its feet, the "grey ghost" of E. J. Schroeder kept the Mercedes flag flying.

On 26 February 1914, the ninth Vanderbilt Cup was held at Santa Monica, California. The displacement limit was 450 cubic inches, 7.4 liters, and the distance was 35 laps of the fast 8.4-miler. The gray Schroeder Mercedes appeared with fresh bearings, Miller carburetor, Braender tires and an old driver: Ralph DePalma. The main competition came from the T-head Mercers (4.8" × 6.2", 122 mm × 157 mm) of Spencer Wishart, Eddie Pullen and Barney Oldfield, and the Stutzes (4.8" × 6", 122 mm × 152 mm) of Gil Anderson and Earl Cooper. Promising outsiders were the two Mason-Duesenbergs (4.4" × 6", 110 mm × 152 mm) under Dave Lewis and Billy Carlson. William Ziegler, a baking-powder manufacturer from Boston, entered an Isotta (120 mm × 160 mm) for Harry Grant and a six-cylinder Sunbeam (80 mm × 150 mm) for Johnny Marquis. In the autumn of 1913, at the Olympia Show in London, Grant and Marquis had purchased two ex–Amiens Sunbeams for Ziegler; only one of them was entered. But the talk of the day was the 6.2-liter Delage that Mrs. Leotia Northam had bought for her chauffeur Omer Toft. Then the local papers published the story that Toft, displaced at the eleventh hour by Bert Dingley, had stopped the car in New York because he was not going to be at the wheel. Barney Oldfield intimated that Toft never went to France to get the car and offered a reward of $100 for proof that the purchase was made. In fact the Delage did not turn up, but had been entered. Among the new drivers were many former mechanics: Pullen had learned beside Wishart, Lewis beside Tetzlaff, Marquis beside Strang.

| No. | Make | Driver | | |
|---|---|---|---|---|
| 1 | Isotta | Grant | | |
| 2, 4, 7 | Mercer | Wishart | Pullen | Oldfield |
| 3, 8 | Stutz | Anderson | Cooper | |
| 6, 10 | Duesenberg | Lewis | Carlson | |
| 9 | Fiat | Verbeck | | |
| 11 | Apperson | Frank Goode | | |
| 12 | Mercedes | DePalma | | |
| 14 | Sunbeam | Marquis | | |
| 15 | Marmon | Guy Ball | | |
| 16 | Touraine | George Joeriman | | |
| 17 | Alco | Tony Janette | | |

In the presence of 120,000 spectators, Eddie Pullen's Mercer set a lap record in 6 min 3 sec and led from lap two to lap 13 when the Mercer blew a tire in the "death curve" and collided with the protective fence. Then it was the turn of Gil Anderson in the white Stutz to set the pace, until the driveshaft broke. Now DePalma crept up, passed Oldfield who had clung tenaciously to the leaders, and drove the old Mercedes to victory in 3 h 53 min 41 sec. DePalma never stopped from the time starter Fred Wagner patted him on the back, but nursed the Mercedes along, turning his fastest lap in 6 min 20 sec, his slowest in 6 min 42 sec. The Mercedes consumed 32 gallons of fuel (154 liters), or 9.18 miles per gallon, and seven gallons of oil (34 liters). Barney Oldfield, in the yellow Stutz owned by George F. Settle, lost the race by just 1 min 20 sec, after changing three tires and being handicapped in the last few laps by a broken plug and piston ring. Two other cars got the checkered flag, the Mason of Billy Carlson, nine minutes back, and the Stutz of Earl Cooper, ten minutes back. Two days later, the formula free Grand Prize was run over 48 laps. The Fiats of Teddy Tetzlaff and Frank Verbeck completed the nearly unaltered Cup field, the last great start of the S 74.

| *No.* | *Make* | *Driver* | | | |
|---|---|---|---|---|---|
| 1, 18 | Fiat | Tetzlaff | Verbeck | | |
| 2, 4, 7, 9 | Mercer | Wishart | Pullen | Oldfield | Gordon |
| 3, 8 | Stutz | Anderson | Cooper | | |
| 5 | Mason | Rickenbacher | | | |
| 6, 19 | Alco | Bill Taylor | Tony Janette | | |
| 11 | Apperson | Frank Goode | | | |
| 12 | Mercedes | DePalma | | | |
| 14 | Sunbeam | Marquis | | | |
| 17 | Marmon | Guy Ball | | | |

February 1914—Vanderbilt Cup, Santa Monica, California. Ralph DePalma and the gray Schroeder Mercedes winning their second Vanderbilt Cup.

Spencer Wishart shot to the front and remained there for 22 laps until being stopped by a burned-out bearing. DePalma took over the lead until lap 29 when the Mercedes swallowed an intake valve. Having no replacement, DePalma continued on three cylinders for the rest of the race. Now Johnny Marquis in the Sunbeam was in front, for three laps, until he took a hand off the steering wheel to wave to the crowd at "death curve." The Sunbeam turned over three times and landed against the fence, with driver and mechanic buried under the debris. Both escaped with injuries. Pullen assumed the lead. Tetzlaff set a new lap record in 5 min 49 sec but went out with a broken connecting rod. Pullen won in 5 h 13 min 23 sec—40 minutes ahead of Ball, 55 minutes ahead of Taylor, nearly one hour ahead of the limping Mercedes of DePalma. In April 1914, Mercer designer Finley Porter read a paper at the New York meeting of the Society of Automobile Engineers: "The Mercer that won the Grand Prize weighed 782 pounds (361 kg) and developed 150 horsepower."

Then it was time for the Memorial Day classic, the 500-mile race at Indianapolis. Levallois shipped a pair of improved 5.6-liters for Boillot and Goux: A Zenith carburetor replaced the Claudel instrument; the chassis was set several inches lower, the front as well as the rear springs being mounted below the axles; the left-hand frame member was filled with lead; and Hartford shock absorbers and French Palmer tires, 4.5 × 34 front (inflated at 5.5 bars), 6 × 35 rear (6 bars), were fitted. William Bradley, a well-known journalist and Paris representative of the Indianapolis Motor Speedway, found six additional racers: Two 6.2-liter Delages with Guyot and Thomas, a 3-liter Peugeot with Duray, an Amiens Excelsior with Christiaens, a Sunbeam with Chassagne and finally a Bugatti with Friderich. The small Peugeot came from the brimming garage of Gaston Menier and his sons Georges and Jacques. Backed by the sugar-cane plantations of half of Central America and a huge chocolate factory at Noisiel near Paris, they were easily able to afford a Coupe de l'Auto racer ... and the Château de Chenonceau, the former love nest of Diane de Poitiers, bought by Gaston's brother Henri in 1913. The Sunbeam six crossed over with shortened wheelbase (211 cm, 83 inches) and two-speed gearbox. The Bugatti was a pepped-up Prince Henry Deutz with new radiator badge and an OHC three-valve four-cylinder (100 mm × 180 mm) with rather unconventional gas flow: The two smaller intake valves provided far less area than the big exhaust valve! Such expermentation was typical for the engine mystic Bugatti. The famous pilot Roland Garros, who was the first to fly over the Mediterranean, purchased such a Bugatti, in the original dimensions of 100 mm × 160 mm; hence the name, type Garros. The Bradley squad started on English made Palmers. E. C. Patterson had again imported a Mercedes, the former Le Mans six-cylinder of Salzer. DePalma took the wheel, but only during practice, the excessive vibrations being unbearable. E. J. Schroeder entered his 7.4-liter Peugeot, the 1913 winner, for Ralph Mulford. But the entry was declined because of the rule forbidding more than three cars of one make. Wasn't Schroeder the owner of the gray Mercedes which had just won the Vanderbilt Cup? Thus the Peugeot engine (with the slightly changed dimensions of 112 mm × 183 mm) finished up in the Mercedes chain-drive frame and the singular combination started as "Mercedes special"! That European purists were appalled was not reported.

The cars of the Bradley squad sailed on 22 April on the *Oceanic* from Cherbourg, the drivers on 9 May on the *Provence* from Le Havre. No surprise that

Thomas was seasick: "he was born in a workshop, was suckled on gasoline and had tire irons for playthings," as *Motor Age* put it in May. In other respects everything turned out all right. In New York, nobody knew where to go. A passer-by sent them to the restaurant of Pierre Chevalier, the meeting place of French artists and bicycle racers who were competing in the six-day race at the Madison Square Garden. They dropped in on the banquet of the former bicycle champion Constant Huret and had to promise to defeat the Americans. By sleeping car they went on to Indianapolis. Robert Laly, Thomas' old friend and mechanic, was immensely proud of his two-tone shoes, black and dark yellow. During the night he left them in front of the door for brushing. When he woke up he could not believe his eyes. They shone in uniform black, like the shoeshine boy who beamed from ear to ear! At Indianapolis, Boillot and Goux had appropriated the reserved cottage. The Bradley squad moved to a disused farm, and checked the racers which had already arrived. Laly, Secuws, Matthys, Dills and Mitchell were fitting the Palmers on the wheels and pumping them up by hand when a man with a bowler hat turned up; everybody took him for Buster Keaton, but he was the fitter of the Hartford shock absorbers. He looked for a socket for his drill, but did not find anything and wanted to leave. Thus the holes were drilled by hand according to the indications of the fitter who fixed the hole pitch by rule of thumb, in the literal sense of the phrase.

In addition to the T-head Mercers and Stutzes, two American racers of a completely new wave started for the first time, the two Maxwells of Teddy Tetzlaff and Billy Carlson, a sophisticated cocktail of speedway experience and imported long-stroke technology. Ray Harroun, the first Indy 500 victor, was behind it. In Detroit, on Milwaukee Avenue, he found a receptive ear in the office of Walter E. Flanders, the president of the Maxwell Motor Co. The contract of 20 December 1913 called for the production of three racers. Since Harroun knew exactly where he was going, the construction work began in March: An OHC two-valve four (4.2" × 8", 107 mm × 204 mm) and a three-speed gearbox were mounted without differential in a Hotchkiss-type frame, drive and torque through the rear springs. The camshaft, driven by a vertical shaft via spiral gears, was carried on three plain bearings and operated the 70-mm valves through rockers. The counterbalanced crankshaft ran in three main bearings, double row ball bearings from Rhineland at the outer ends, a plain bearing in the center, with lubrication under pressure. Output was 140 hp at 2400 rpm; weight was 950 kg.

After the usual preliminary lap behind the pace car of Carl Fisher, thirty drivers stepped on as many throttles, promptly at ten o'clock. Howdy Wilcox in the Gray Fox shot into the lead, followed by Christiaens, Carlson, Tetzlaff and Chassagne. In lap 22 Duray and the tiny Peugeot went to the front, ahead of Christiaens, Bragg's Mercer, Goux, and Wishart's Mercer. Boillot lay fifteenth, struggling with the French Palmers. Chassagne's Sunbeam blew a tire and turned over. After 96 laps Boillot moved to fifth, behind Duray, Thomas, Wishart and Goux. Wishart sped up and took the lead on lap 122 but was pushing the Mercer too hard and broke a camshaft. Duray changed tires. Suddenly Thomas was first. A desperately driving Boillot passed him after 320 miles. Thomas restrained himself, and it was the Peugeot which blew a tire and pulled out with a broken frame member. Thomas had the race as good as won when the attachment of the exhaust pipe broke. Laly repaired it with a belt. At the pits the Delage was whipped into shape for the last laps. Thomas and Laly asked

Bradley for a strap. Bradley did not understand: "A black or a yellow one?" Laly cut it short: "A black one!" The Delage stayed the course and won, six minutes ahead of Duray's small Peugeot. Thomas and Laly, exhausted, were given a can of grape juice and a cigar. Guyot finished third in the second Delage, then Goux in the works Peugeot, speed king Oldfield in a Stutz, Christiaens and then Grant, "wearing black jersey and black driver's helmet and driving the black Sunbeam as if he were cast for the role of death in a morality play." Against the current Grand Prix racers the Bugatti had no chance. Many years later Ernest Friderich related: "After 425 miles I was third. Everything remained open when a ball bearing of the driving pinion broke..." The Bugatti fell out on lap 134, after 345 miles, in position 13, losing ground steadily. The performance of the small Peugeot was remarkable, so remarkable that many believed in a test run of the new 4.5-liter engine. The New York Peugeot agent Kaufman and the wealthy L. C. Erbes took over the two 5.6-liters, for Mulford and Burman.

The succesful Bradley squad sailed home on the German *Imperator*. From Cherbourg the drivers were allowed to take first-class compartments to Paris, the mechanics second-class, in separate trains. Monsieur Louis, his wife, Arthur Michelat and a huge crowd of racing fans were waiting at the Gare Saint-Lazare. Flowers were presented, flags were waved, and men and women alike struggled to kiss the somewhat bashful and embarrassed Thomas. Louis Delage took him by his side in the latest Grand Prix racer and drove to the showrooms at the Boulevard Pereire where champagne flowed freely. Laly joined later: "You were lucky to be on the winning car in your first race for me." On the recommendation of Monsieur Louis, Thomas invested the better part of his $20,000 prize money in an insider's tip; Delage knew for certain that without the introduced money the company was unable to settle his open accounts. In the meantime war was raging in Paris between Delage and Peugeot partisans: "An inferior grade of tire was sold to Boillot and Goux, and had they been given the same high quality as supplied to Thomas, one of the Peugeots would have won the race." The Palmer Tyre Co. kept out of the discussion, stating that Delage was supplied from the London stock and the two Peugeot drivers bought privately from the French factory, but that the English and the French tires were identical. Tire experts explained the failure of the Peugeots by defective fitting. But in its heart Paris was content since blue had won.

# 25

## *Tactics*

The early summer of 1914 was exceptionally nice. In the evenings, the "Picadilly," the most fashionable café in Berlin, was at its busiest. The dances were American now, instead of waltz, polka or rhinelander it was maxixe, la furlana, boston or tango. And the younger generation liked to dance and was good at dancing. The Kaiser stayed at Potsdam, occupied with his Corfu excavations. The bourgeoisie ordered holiday accommodations in Venice and Tuscany. Business circles were concerned about the unemployment figures, but the stock market was quiet, even rosy. Then, on 28 June, it was reported that the Austro-Hungarian heir to the throne, Archduke Franz Ferdinand, and his wife, the Duchess of Hohenberg, had been killed by a member of a Serbian conspirator gang. Would Austria invade Serbia and bring Russia onto the scene? Would three mad monarchs, Emperor, Czar and Kaiser, plunge all Europe into a war?

It was in a hot atmosphere that the ACF issued invitations to its sixth Grand Prix. On Saturday, 4 July, 20 laps of 37.6 km would be covered, on a new course near Givors, a few kilometers south of Lyon. Maximum displacement was 4.5 liters, and maximum weight was 1100 kg. The race would start at eight o'clock in the morning, with the cars being sent away in pairs for the first time, at intervals of 30 seconds. *Pesage* was on 3 July, at Brignais, a village a stone's-throw away from the *fourche* at Les Sept-Chemins. France's motoring classic attracted 41 entries, 14 makes from six nations. France had 12 cars, Italy 11, Germany 8, England 6, Belgium and Switzerland 2, a topnotch field promising amazing sport. The *rois du volant* turned up in their entirety, from Fernand Gabriel to Ferenc Szisz, Felice Nazzaro, Christian Lautenschlager, Ralph DePalma, Alessandro Cagno, Louis Wagner, Otto Salzer, Paul Bablot and Georges Boillot. Ten days before the race "no money could secure a box seat in the grandstands and ordinary reserved seats were as scarce as roses in November." Three days before the race Lyon and Givors were filled with motorists. Hotel proprietors were not slow to take advantage of the influx, asking a price for a night's accommodation equivalent to the value of all the furniture in the room. The local authorities were doing their best by putting visitors in touch with landlords having rooms to let. An electric tramway service was maintained from the center of Lyon to Les Sept-Chemins. Concerning the favorites, Louis Delage stated: "I give Peugeot a 48 percent chance of victory, myself 48, and Mercedes 4 percent!"

Favorite Peugeot started with the EX 5/L 45, the fifth model of the new generation with a displacement of 4.5 liters (92 mm × 169 mm). The intake valves were larger than the exhaust valves, 52 mm compared to 46. Of course Ernest Henry was faithful to his hobby: The L-shaped tappets of 1913 were simplified and condensed so that just cups remained of them, the large diameter of the cups securing their

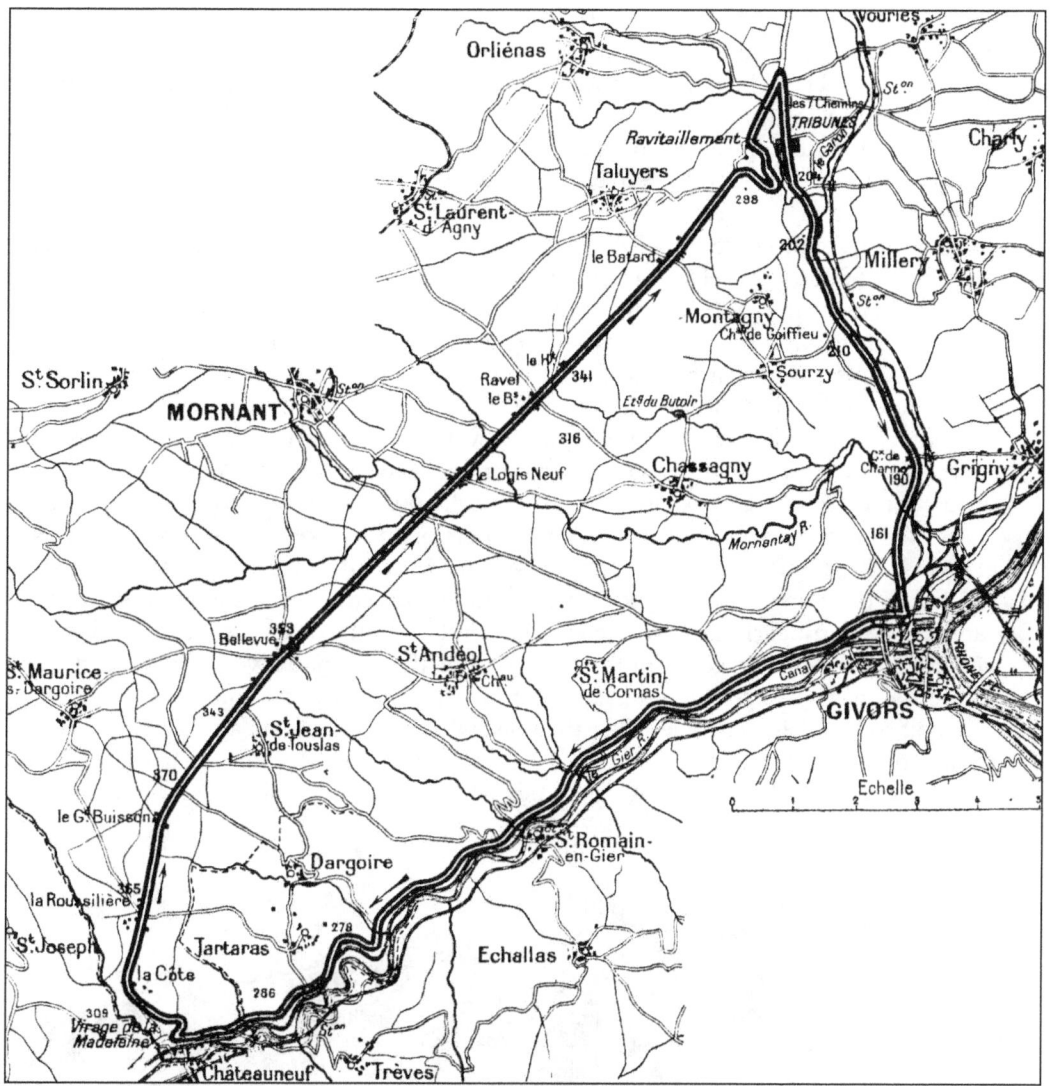

The 37.6-km course of Givors, near Lyon (from *Omnia*, 1914).

guide. Only the stars Boillot and Goux enjoyed the benefits of this new arrangement. In the 4.5-liter of Victor Rigal and in the reserve racer that André Boillot, the younger brother of Georges, was allowed to demonstrate, the valves were still operated through the older L-shaped tappets. In April, Boillot had tested an Isotta with four-wheel brakes, and was delighted. The physical characteristics of the course, comprising a hilly and winding part, a stretch of 13 kilometers with eighty curves, made additional front wheel brakes a necessity, not only on the Peugeots, but also on the Delages, Fiats and Piccard-Pictets. On the Peugeot, the wheel brakes, front and rear, were operated as usual by hand lever, the transmission brake by foot pedal. In view of the endless 12-km straight of "les Montagnes Russes," Peugeot added an elongated, streamlined tail carrying a locker for a couple of spare wheels, like the 1912 3-liter Vinot. The top of the tail was hinged, with an eyebolt in the end so that the mechanic could pull up the lid from his seat while the car was coming to a stop. The wheelbase remained unchanged at 270 cm, track 135 cm, tires from Dunlop 875 mm × 105 mm front, 880 mm × 120 mm rear. The little brother for the Coupe de l'Auto was named EX 6/L 25 (73 mm × 146 mm). In 1914 the Coupe was to be run in the Auvergne under a 2.5-liter maximum, but was cancelled because of the war.

Untertürkheim entered a full five-car team with the Swabians Lautenschlager, Salzer and Sailer, the Belgian Pilette and the Frenchman Louis Wagner. The 4.5-liter with the designation M 93654 (93 mm × 165 mm) was made up of four steel singles with welded on periphery, whereby Daimler and Link, in contrast to the 1913 Le Mans engines, arranged for a four-valve head. This was necessary to provide proper breathing for the slimmer cylinders. The camshaft was driven by a vertical shaft at the rear of the engine, via bevel gears. Due to forked intake valve rockers, there were only three cams per cylinder. Valve sizes were 43 and 40.5 mm; inclination for intake and exhaust was 30°. For the purpose of better cooling and easy access for valve-clearance check, the outer part of the rockers and the springs was exposed. Was the Peugeot head better? Not in 1914. Didn't one overhead camshaft resolve all problems? The crankshaft was only rudimentarily counterbalanced and ran in five plain bearings. A whole arsenal of piston pumps took care of the lubrication: A first one sucked from the front end of the sump, delivering rearwards to the actual main pump which pressurized only the crankshaft; a third one delivered fresh oil from a 12-liter tank under the cowl while the mechanic attended by a foot pump to the head and the cylinder walls. To avoid a steel-to-steel bearing surface with a correspondingly short life, Daimler relied on the well-tried cast iron pistons.

The 4.5-liter Mercedes: 93 mm × 165 mm, four valves, in contrast to Peugeot only one overhead camshaft, steel cylinders, crankshaft in five plain bearings, double cone clutch, four-speed gearbox (from Pomeroy, *The Grand Prix Car*).

A pair of double Bosch magnetos provided high tension for three plugs, two below the intake and one on the exhaust side, special constructions from Ernst Eisemann, with mica insulator and platinum electrode. The 4.5-liter produced 81 hp at 2000 rpm, 115 at 2800, 105 hp at 3100 rpm. Paul Daimler a few years later said, "The 1914 4.5-liter was intended to serve as a model for aero engines. It could be pushed up to 5340 revolutions. One of them blew up at this speed. To avoid injuries during these tests, wire nettings had been disposed around the engine." The power was transmitted to the separately mounted four-speed gearbox by a double cone clutch which combined the grip, the reliability and simplicity of a cone clutch with the lower spinning mass of a plate unit. Two separated crown-wheel-and-pinion sets permitted a slight kink in the rear axle, good for a negative camber of 1° 20 min and consequently less tire stress in the bends. Concerning the chassis layout, the Mercedes represented the exact opposite of the flexible Peugeot: rigid four-point attachment of the engine and the gearbox in combination with an X-bracing member and a torque-tube axle. A wheelbase of 285 cm resulted in the desired mass distribution of 50/50. Track was 135 cm; tires from Conti were 815 mm × 105 mm front and 835 mm × 135 mm rear; unloaded weight was 900 kg, starting-line weight 1200 kg. The front-wheel brakes were a touch-and-go affair. Two additional drums with the corresponding operating mechanism and necessary reinforcement of the front axle meant a lot of weight; even worse, it increased the unsprung mass and demanded stiffer springs and shocks in order to keep the lot under control. Certainly not good for the tires. Did the better deceleration make up for it? At Dieppe or Amiens, where the aces applied the brakes only every three kilometers on average, certainly not; on the other hand, the difference may have been felt at Lyon, over two or three laps. Daimler and Schnaitmann did without front brakes deliberately, saving unsprung weight with small and hence light wheels, and mounted soft springs for additional lightening. The sportsmen were on tenterhooks waiting for the confrontation with the avant-garde.

Delage was part of the avant-garde. The new 4.5-liter (94 mm × 160 mm) from Courbevoie was designated type S, for sport. Arthur Michelat relocated the camshafts of the 1913 type Y to the top of the head, where they were driven by a vertical shaft. Intake and exhaust valves were set at 45°. It might have seemed a Peugeot copy at first glance, but under the fine aluminum housing was hidden a desmo operation. Apart from the spectacular head, the four-wheel brakes, the more pleasant radiator and other only cosmetic retouching, the type S resembled its precursor. Bablot, Guyot and Duray were the drivers. Besançon, too, sent positively operated 4.5-liters, fine works of art from the shop of Théophile Schneider. The former V-2 artist Gratien Michaux had them on his mind. In contrast to the Delage, the Schneider (94 mm × 160 mm) had only one overhead camshaft which opened and closed two 60-mm valves. Drive was by spur pinions, and the intake and exhaust were inclined at 10° from the vertical. By using only two valves per cylinder Michaux was able to place oversized valve stems of 12-mm diameter. The light valve springs, provided to give a final seating to the valves, were not necessary: After the race, a broken spring was only discovered when the engine was entirely dismantled. The one-piece crankshaft ran on three two-piece roller bearings of RBF make, the first time that such roller bearings were used within the crankcase. Fernand Gabriel started with a five-speed gearbox; his colleagues Champoiseau and Henri Juvanon, the Schneider agent at Lyon, had four speeds.

May 1914—Courbevoie. Paul Bablot testing the unpainted desmo Delage. Delage, Peugeot, Fiat and Pic-Pic mounted additional brake drums for the front wheels.

July 1914—GP de l'ACF, Lyon. Delage trio: Arthur Duray, Albert Guyot and Paul Bablot. Indianapolis victor Thomas was reserve driver.

The latest Fiat design from Giuseppe Coda, the S 57, was rather conventional, a short-stroke OHC two-valve four (100 mm × 143 mm). The cast bell housing around the clutch joining engine and gearbox was remarkable, as well as the elegant Grand Prix body with the spare wheels mounted on the side. Wolverhampton copied. Victor Rigal, at the same time works driver of Peugeot and Sunbeam agent in Paris, supplied a 3-liter Coupe de l'Auto Peugeot to Sunbeam director Louis Coatalen. The result of the disassembly was a DOHC 3.3-liter Sunbeam (81 mm × 160 mm) which, by the beginning of the season, promptly won the Tourist Trophy on the Isle of Man. For the Grand Prix, Wolverhampton simply stretched the dimensions to 94 mm × 160 mm and replaced, as on one of the 3.3-liters, the L-shaped tappets with cam followers. Another DOHC four-valve engine à la Peugeot sat in the Belgian Nagant (94.5 mm × 158 mm), a design of the former Mathis engineer Willy Esser. OHC four-valve engines appeared in the Alda, the latest company of Fernand Charron, in the Nazzaro and the Opel, all in the dimensions of 94 mm × 160 mm. Unconventional was the DOHC head of the Vauxhall (101 mm × 140 mm) in which Laurence Pomeroy, by means of diminutive rockers, restricted the inclination of the intake and the exhaust to just 9°. The OHC six-cylinder Aquila (85 mm × 132 mm), devised by Cesare Cappa (later to be a Fiat engineer), was derived from a stock model. And the Piccard-Pictet ("Pic-Pic") (97 mm × 150 mm) from Geneva was off-beat, relying on a single-sleeve engine, an idea of Peter Burt used in the Argyl touring cars built at Alexandria, near Glasgow. The single sleeve had a double movement, a reciprocating one and a part-rotating one.

July 1914—GP de l'ACF, Lyon. The Fiat team: Jack Scales, Antonio Fagnano and Alessandro Cagno.

July 1914—GP de l'ACF, Lyon. Belgian Nagant duo: Willy Esser and Leon Elskamp.

In detail, a lot had changed since 1906. Four-cylinders still dominated the scene, cast-iron monoblocs, except the Mercedes. The division of 4.5 liters in the rather long-stroke ratio of 1:1.8 brought into line the existing limit values, a piston speed of 20 meters per second and an engine speed of 3200 rpm, with output of circa 110 hp. The current quality of the valve springs, plugs and magnetos prevented the realization of a 4.5-liter in the dimensions of 110 mm × 117 mm: With its piston area of 380 cm$^2$, this fictive short-stroke four would have delivered 160 hp at 4100 rpm and a piston speed of 16 meters per second! Nine of 13 makes started at Lyon with OHC or DOHC four-valve engines, three with OHC two-valve engines, and Pic-Pic with its sleeve engine. The crankshafts ran either in pressure-lubricated plain bearings or in splash-lubricated ball bearings. Springs mounted below the axles and double-drop frames reduced the frontal area to 1.2 m$^2$, good for 180 km/h along the Montagnes Russes.

A week before the great encounter the teams began taking up their positions around the set of roads on which their fate was to be decided. Untertürkheim had shipped enough spare parts to put together a couple of engines, and a reserve chassis without engine stood in readiness to go into service should an accident eliminate one of the racers. Delage had a big, old-fashioned farm, a stone's throw from the course, the barns converted into garages and workshops. At the Fiat headquarters in Givors there was the most complete collection of vehicles to be found in the whole countryside, in contrast to the beautifully finished racers "on which Italian workmen give that refining touch of which they alone seem to be capable." The Nagant men had found a charming retreat in a quiet, shady valley at Orlié-

July 1914—GP de l'ACF, Lyon. After the *pesage* at Brignais: on the left the Mercedes of Pilette, then Lautenschlager (with mechanic Hans Rieger), Wagner, Sailer (with Otto Eckerle), on the right Salzer (with Grupp). Originally the entry was different: no. 14 for Lautenschlager, 28 for Wagner, 39 for Salzer, 40 for Sailer, 41 for Pilette. Tactics made the change necessary.

July 1914—GP de l'ACF, Lyon. Cars started in pairs for the first time: here the Alda of Szisz and the Opel of Joerns. (Opel)

nas, where they occupied the whole of a farmhouse hotel and had emptied the barn of hay and straw to give room for the yellow Belgian racers. Nazzaro also secured a picturesque old-world home at Soucieu-en-Jarret, a village of obvious Roman origin. Two days before the race the Aquila-Italiana men had not put in an appearance at their headquarters and the anxiety of the landlady was increasing as the stack of unopened letters grew higher. Sunbeam selected the heights of Saint-Maurice-sur-Dargoire, in a little French inn with an obliterated sign over the door, and the Union Jack fluttering above it, and a spacious, poorly illuminated barn containing the racers. In addition to the drivers a big staff of mechanics was sent over from Wolverhampton, and Mesdames Coatalen, Resta and Claudel, of carburetion fame, were part of the party. The Vauxhall men had the advantage of the equipment of a modern garage in Lyon. An exciting field of 38 racers lined up for the start, the mysterious Caesars and Marsaglia's Aquila staying at home, while the Marquis de Moraes replaced his colleague Beria at the last moment.

| *No.* | *Make* | *Driver* | | |
|---|---|---|---|---|
| 1, 15, 29 | Alda | Szisz | Pietro | Tabuteau |
| 2, 16, 30 | Opel | Joerns | Erndtmann | Breckheimer |
| 3, 17 | Nagant | Elskamp | Esser | |
| 4, 18, 31 | Vauxhall | Hancock | DePalma | Watson |
| 5, 19, 32 | Peugeot | Boillot | Goux | Rigal |
| 6, 20, 33 | Schneider | Champoiseau | Gabriel | Juvanon |
| 7, 21 | Caesar | | | |
| 8, 22, 34 | Nazzaro | Nazzaro | Porporato | Cenisio |
| 9, 23, 35 | Delage | Bablot | Guyot | Duray |
| 10, 24, 36 | Sunbeam | Chassagne | Resta | Guinness |
| 11, 25 | Pic-Pic | Tournier | Clarke | |
| 12, 26, 37 | Aquila | de Moraes | Marsaglia | Costantini |
| 13, 27, 38 | Fiat | Cagno | Fagnano | Scales |
| 14, 28, 39 | Mercedes | Sailer | Lautenschlager | Salzer |
| 40 | Mercedes | Wagner | | |
| 41 | Mercedes | Pilette | | |

Who else but the great Boillot could be the first to come round, at top speed over the Montagnes Russes, braking hard for the Piège de la Mort, the Trap of Death? All eyes and glasses were fixed on the little piece of road at the top of the hill which seemed to come out of the heavens. Someone with powerful glasses shouted: "C'est Boillot!" The cry was quickly echoed: "Oui! C'est Boillot!" Anywhere between fifty and a hundred thousand eyes watched him swoop down as some invisible hand seemed to restrain him. "Ce sont les freins avant!" was the conclusion of the versed folk, the front-wheel brakes. Boillot had already overtaken Hancock, Elskamp, Joerns and Szisz. When he accelerated out of the hairpin at Les Sept-Chemins and passed the grandstand at full speed, victory was in the bag, and there was frantic applause. Then the time of Max Sailer was announced, to deathly silence. With 21 min 11 sec the Mercedes of the Swabian pace-setter lay 18 seconds ahead of Boillot's Peugeot, 19 seconds ahead of Duray's Delage, 41 seconds ahead of Resta's Sunbeam, then Goux, Pilette, Rigal, Lautenschlager, Guinness and Fagnano. Szisz stopped at the depot to change the radiator on his Alda. A. J. Hancock battled to bring his Vauxhall around the circuit in two and one half hours. Lap two changed nothing at the front. Sailer increased his lead over Boillot by a further 38 seconds.

July 1914—GP de l'ACF, Lyon. The Peugeot team: on the left Georges Boillot, then Jules Goux, Victor Rigal and reserve driver André Boillot, the younger brother of Georges.

July 1914—GP de l'ACF, Lyon. A pair of Mercedes about to start: no. 39 Salzer, no. 40 Wagner.

July 1914—GP de l'ACF, Lyon. The great DePalma appeared at the wheel of a Vauxhall.

July 1914—GP de l'ACF, Lyon. The Opel of Franz Breckheimer leading the Alda of Maurice Tabuteau.

Lautenschlager moved forward to position six, while Wagner lay fourteenth and Salzer nineteenth. Bartolomeo Costantini, in the twenties a successful Bugatti driver and director of the racing department at Molsheim, parked his Aquila with a damaged magneto.

Sailer was out to set the breakneck pace and continued to extend his lead, now to 31 seconds in lap three. Duray and Resta were not quite able to keep close and fell back. Lautenschlager took fifth place, Wagner eleventh, Salzer seventeenth. Rigal, in the third Peugeot with the previous year's head, could only hold position. The Delages of Bablot and Guyot were not at all up to general expectations and far slower than during their practice period. Just before the race, all three of the Delages had experienced trouble with backfiring into the carburetors, attributed to a slightly imperfect seating of the desmo valves. A new adjustment was made a few hours before the start, but the desmo engines lost their power. The unpreparedness of the Vauxhall team became manifest, Hancock and Watson retiring with engine trouble. Why DePalma finished up at the wheel of a Vauxhall remained a mystery. Didn't the American press report about an official offer from Untertürkheim? In lap four Max Sailer opened up for a lap of 20 min 6 sec. The great Georges could not believe it—the greenhorn had shown him up by 43 seconds! The Peugeot depot began to hang its head since Boillot regularly pulled out, execrating his Dunlops. The front-wheel brakes were making their impact! Whether smooth, ribbed or steel-studded, the Peugeot wore down every tire. With 1 h 22 min 36 sec

July 1914—GP de l'ACF, Lyon. The Peugeot of Boillot rounding the *fourche* of Les Sept-Chemins.

Sailer assumed his lead, two minutes ahead of Boillot, 2 min 37 sec ahead of Duray, 2 min 42 sec ahead of Resta, 3 min 25 sec ahead of Lautenschlager; Goux, Guinness, Wagner, the Fiats of Fagnano, the former mechanic of Nazzaro, and Jack Scales followed further back. Felice Nazzaro, who reached Lyon only the day before the race, withdrew because of engine trouble. Pilette drove his car into the ditch; at least there was one Mercedes fewer! Boillot tried a new set of tires but lost just a minute for the change, quick enough to hold position two in front of Duray. Lautenschlager passed Resta and was 57 seconds behind Boillot. The battle between Peugeot, Delage, Mercedes and Sunbeam was raging, with less than one minute separating positions two through five.

What should be thought of Sailer? Would the Mercedes be able to set the current pace for long? The Peugeot camp got cold feet. In lap six the grandstand breathed a sigh of relief as Sailer broke down with a defective oil-feed pipe. In the Mercedes camp nobody took it to heart, as the breakdown had been scheduled. Now the Swabians knew that only one Peugeot, the number five of Boillot, was able to keep pace when the Mercedes opened up. The Peugeot of Goux, the Delage of Duray and the Sunbeam of Resta were overstrained. Thus Lautenschlager and Wagner attacked Boillot, and Salzer backed them up. Boillot's Peugeot no. 5 lay half a minute ahead of Lautenschlager's Mercedes no. 28. With the huge advantage of a massive, constantly advancing rear cover, the Swabian began to increase his pace. Under these conditions victory was certain against every other competitor; only

July 1914—GP de l'ACF, Lyon. The Pic-Pic of Paul Tournier at the depot.

Boillot had the stuff to counter. As best non-favorite, Willy Esser held position 13 with his Nagant and Elskampf position 20, just behind Paul Tournier, who showed an excellent performance in his Pic-Pic, while his teammate Theo Clarke, an Englishman living in France, brought up the rear.

As if the breakdown of Sailer had given him a boost, Boillot turned a lap in 20 min 20 sec, "taking his turns as he had never taken them before, pushing his engine to the limit on the long switchback stretch." Goux moved up to position three ahead of Duray; Wagner was fifth ahead of Guinness; Salzer was seventh ahead of Fagnano. Resta changed the plugs and regained position six in the next lap with 20 min 31 sec. Juvanon's Schneider, DePalma's Vauxhall and Clarke's Pic-Pic withdrew. The famous pilot and Alda dealer Tabuteau left the road in the Madeleine corner near Châteauneuf, finishing up in the river Giers. In lap nine Jack Scales parked his elegant Fiat with a broken valve, de Moraes his Aquila with unknown engine trouble, Gabriel his Schneider and Guinness his Sunbeam, both with broken pistons. Duray fell back to twelfth after a tire defect. At the depot Bablot drove over the foot of the faithful Lausson and took along Laly as substitute.

Boillot completed ten laps in 3 h 31 min 4 sec, lying 1 min 9 sec ahead of Lautenschlager, 4 min 38 sec ahead of Goux, 5 min 29 sec ahead of Wagner, 6 min 33 sec ahead of Salzer. The Sunbeams of Resta and Chassagne followed further back, then the Fiat of Fagnano, the Delages of Bablot and Guyot, and the Nagant of Esser. Lautenschlager changed all tires and took on fuel as planned, losing 3 min 15 sec.

July 1914—GP de l'ACF, Lyon. The Peugeot of Boillot did not complete the last lap.

While changing a wheel on the course, Szisz was struck by the overtaking Opel of Joerns and suffered a dislocated shoulder. The Alda of Pietro broke down somewhere on the course. The team of Fernand Charron could go home. Cagno's Fiat swallowed a valve. In lap twelve Wagner passed Goux and squeezed up close to Lautenschlager. And in lap 14 the order was Boillot, Wagner, Lautenschlager. Chassagne withdrew his Sunbeam with a broken connecting-rod bolt, Franz Breckheimer, the former mechanic of Joerns, his Opel with a broken oil pump and Emil Erndtmann his Opel with a broken valve.

Lautenschlager was unflappable. Wagner had still to change tires, the Swabian knew. As the brakes of the no. 5 began to die away, Lautenschlager attacked. With three-quarters of the distance run, Boillot lay 2 min 28 sec ahead of Lautenschlager, 3 min 24 sec ahead of Wagner. In lap 16 Lautenschlager reduced the gap by 23 seconds, in lap 17 by nearly two minutes. Boillot fought back tooth-and-nail. There was nothing for it; the ball was in his court, and he had found his match in the stolid, sturdy Swabian. On this hot summer day Lautenschlager was better, not faster but simply better. He was wearing Boillot out, slowly but surely. In lap 18 two Mercedes passed two Peugeots, Lautenschlager passed Boillot and Salzer passed Goux. Fagnano held position six for Fiat, Duray position eight for Delage. Bablot and Guyot? A completely depressed Monsieur Louis had pulled them back.

The Mercedes had the great Georges in its grip. Now Boillot was forced to break down. Wagner, knowing his pride, increased the pace. Boillot got the impossible

July 1914—GP de l'ACF, Lyon. Christian Lautenschlager crossing the finish: "We'll sum-up at the end!"

July 1914—Untertürkheim. Greeting of the victors in Mercedes Street.

out of his Peugeot. But he did not come back from the last lap, as a valve broke near the *virage de la Madeleine*: "Boillot threw up his hands in despair as his engine spluttered and stopped, wrecked in the supreme battle of speed." Goux fell behind Salzer. Fagnano fell back to eleventh. Christian Lautenschlager won in 7 h 8 min 18 sec (105.55 km/h), 1 min 36 sec ahead of Wagner, 4 min 57 sec ahead of Salzer, nine minutes ahead of Goux, twenty minutes ahead of Resta, and half an hour ahead of Esser, whose fine performance was forgotten in the frenzy of the Mercedes triple victory. The front-wheel brakes had decided the finish, not in favor of the avant-garde but just as Daimler and Schnaitmann had foreseen: Lautenschlager stopped only once, fitting a new set of tires at half-distance; Boillot stopped every three laps, and changed tires four more times on the course. The clear-sightedness of the young Daimler was frightening. On examination, Boillot's Peugeot was found to be falling to pieces, the front-wheel brakes worn out and inoperative, the steering column broken away from its mounting. How did the great Boillot manage to drive as he had done for the last few laps? Lautenschlager, for his part, beat the best possible field, as he had done in 1908. But he never became a superstar who inspired the masses à la Boillot; the quiet Swabian lacked the showman's flair. Wasn't this his strong point? The closer the struggle, the more he followed his motto: "We'll sum-up at the end!"

The revenge in the Grand Prix de France to be held on 16 August was cancelled. At the end of July, in the Boulogne meeting, Boillot and the 4.5-liter Peugeot covered three kilometers with a standing start in 1 min 14 sec. Then, at half-past four on the afternoon of 2 August, a small unimportant-looking poster was posted on the walls of every public building in France announcing the general mobilization. In the great motoring district to the west of Paris, at Levallois, Suresnes and Courbevoie, machinery was stopped, workmen laid down their tools and within five minutes were on their way to the railroad station. The DMG supplied the armed forces with all possible touring cars, trucks and aero engines. The heroes of Le Mans, Dieppe, Amiens and Lyon were sent to the front. The whole Peugeot team drove for the French general staff. Once Boillot was too fast, and the officers finished up in the ditch. The engines continued to roar on the speedways until 1916.

**July 1914—GP de l'ACF, Lyon. Lautenschlager and mechanic Hans Rieger: better than Boillot?**

# 26

# *Oval Tracks*

The bare result of the Grand Prix battle at Lyon distorted the real conditions within the empire of the constructors. The stiff Swabian Paul Daimler was not alone on the throne. The chary Swiss Ernest Henry kept pace. Untertürkheim designs were austere, conservative and weight-saving, allowing for all possible finesse to go easy on the tires. The distinctive features were the steel singles, the OHC head, the over-lubricated crankshaft running in five plain bearings, and the rigid frame with its torque-tube axle. Levallois designs were more lively, taking more pleasure in difficult engineering and more risks. The Peugeot stood out with its elaborate, already mature DOHC engine, the crankshaft running in three ball bearings within a one-piece crankcase, with its flexible frame and Hotchkiss axle. Levallois did not polish like Untertürkheim, hence was forced to upgrade by a streamlined body and front wheel brakes. The Mercedes and the Peugeot provided nearly all ingredients for future cocktails. With his elegant Fiat, Giuseppe Coda gave a foretaste of the Mediterranean splendor of later Alfa Romeos and Maseratis, and with the two-piece roller bearings of his Théo Schneider, Gratien Michaux showed how to resolve lubrication problems. A last element of the puzzle was provided by the oval courses in America, the concept of the speedway special, the flawless track racer. Was it coincidence that, on the very day when the Mercedes, Peugeot and Fiat struggled on a classic road course near Lyon for the hegemony on the old continent, the Duesenberg brothers succeeded in winning their first great race on an equally classic two-miler near Sioux City?

Actually the Duesenberg brothers were born in Kirchheide near Lemgo, Germany, Friedrich in 1877, August in 1879, the younger brothers of Conrad, Wilhelmine, Caroline, and Amalie. Their father, Konrad Düsenberg, died at the beginning of the eighties. Their mother, Luise Conradine, decided to leave Germany and try her luck in America. In 1895, she crossed the Atlantic, then took the train to Iowa in the company of her six children. Friedrich, now called Fred, took a job with a farm-implement dealer where he set up windmills and repaired all possible machinery; built bicycles for a couple of years; opened a garage in Des Moines; and finally, in 1904, with the financial assistance of a young attorney called Mason, founded the Mason Motor Car Co. Hence the first 230-cubic-inch racers, which were successful in the 1912 Milwaukee races, started as Mason specials. These Masons provided the basis for all Duesenberg racers until the appearance of the OHC straight-eights at the end of the Great War. In October 1913, Fred and Augie moved to St. Paul, Minnesota, renamed their shop the Duesenberg Motor Company and painted their racers in the national colors, red, white and blue. The horizontal-valve four had a standard stroke of six inches or 152.4 mm, and was available with a multitude of

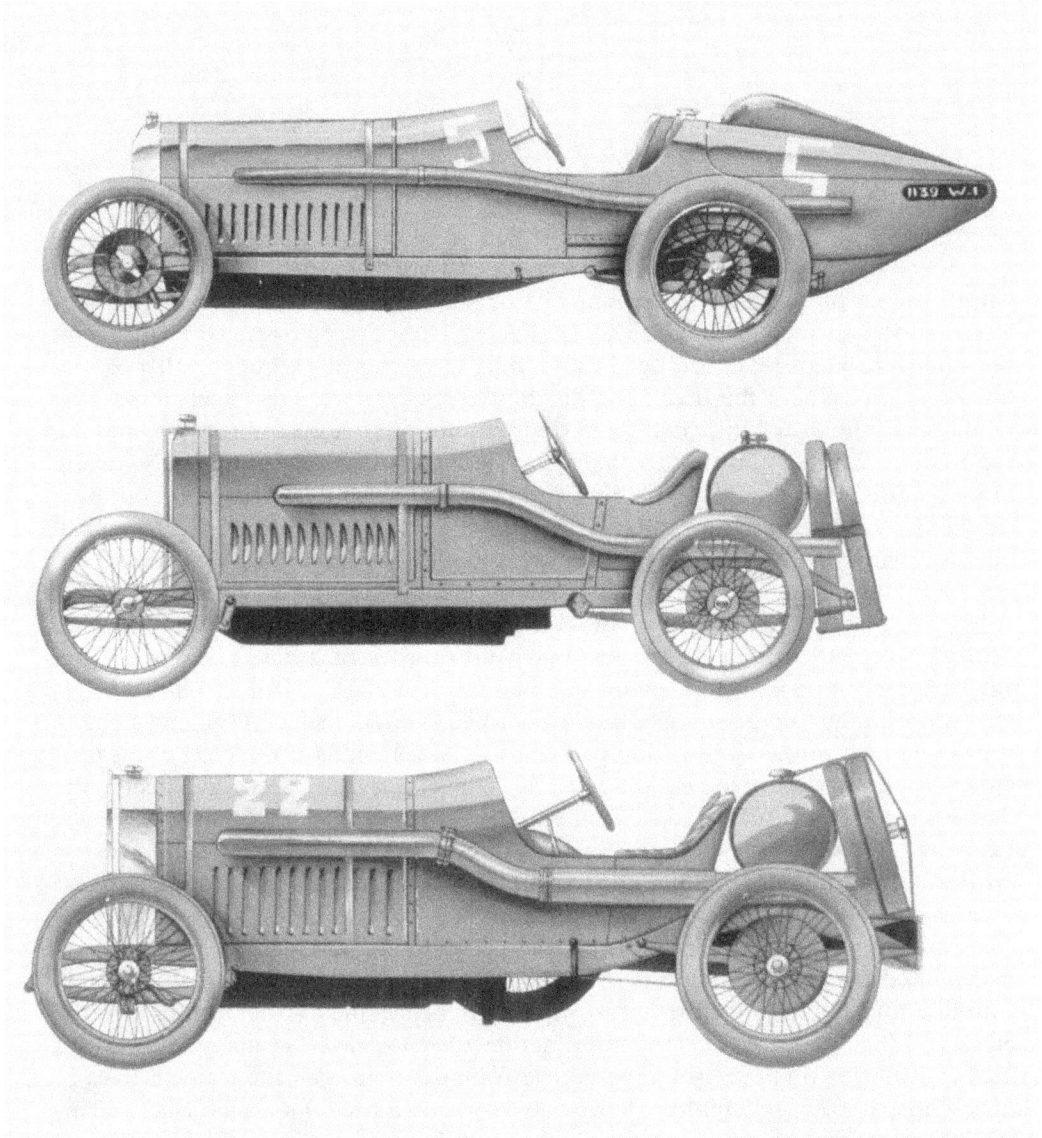

**Peugeot dynasty: at the top the 4.5-liter EX 5 of 1914, in the middle the 5.6-liter EX 3 of 1913, at the bottom the 7.6-liter EX 1 of 1912. (Peugeot)**

bores: 3.98 inches, 101 mm, for the 300-cubic-inch class, 109, 110, 111 or 112 mm to keep pace with the heavy calibers.

By the beginning of July 1914, at Sioux City, Eddie Rickenbacher (the original spelling) and the former DePalma mechanic Tom Alley started in the most powerful version, with extra-light magnalium block in the dimensions of 4.4" × 6", 112 mm × 152 mm, 6 liters. The crankshaft now ran in two big ball bearings, lubricated by means of a dry-sump system, with output of 110 hp at 3000 rpm transmitted via cone clutch to a three-speed gearbox in the rear axle. The Duesy weighed 900 kg

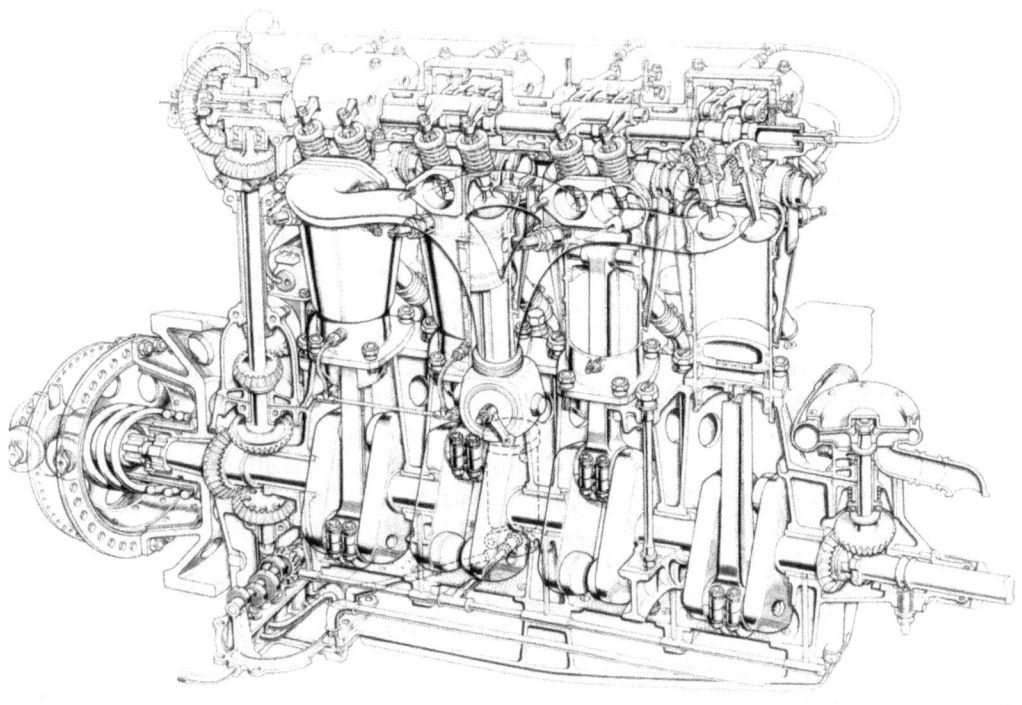

Cutaway of the 4.5-liter Mercedes. The intake opened at TDC and closed 35° after BDC; the exhaust opened 50° before BDC and closed 9° after TDC.

dry, 1100 kg with full tanks. The tires were pleased about it. Rickenbacher made the 300 miles with but one change, the right rear, and won in 3 h 49 min 2 sec, with a margin of 48 seconds in front of Wishart's Mercer, 3 min 8 sec in front of teammate Alley. The two 5.6-liter Peugeots of Burman and Mulford, which had not been thoroughly overhauled since the Indianapolis 500, the older 7.4-liter of Stringer and the two six-cylinder Sunbeams of Grant and Babcock all broke down. On the oval courses, the specials of Fred and Augie Duesenberg came closer to perfection, but on the classic road course at Elgin, the transmission of their lightweights was to reach its limits.

"DePalma dual winner at Elgin" was the headline by the end of August. E. C. Patterson had again purchased a Mercedes racer from Untertürkheim, after the former Salzer six-cylinder, now the 4.5-liter, which had finished second at Lyon in the hands of Wagner. DePalma, too, knew how to handle it. On 21 August he took the Chicago Automobile Club Trophy, winning after 36 laps of 8.36 miles (13.4 km) and a racing time of 4 h 5 min 1 sec, ahead of Anderson's Stutz and Mulford in the 5.6-liter of the Peugeot Auto Import. Indeed DePalma was fortunate. With a lead of not less than nine minutes, Wishart's Mercer fell out in lap 25 with a leaking fuel tank. The two Duesies of Rickenbacher and Alley withdrew with gearbox trouble. The next day, DePalma secured the Elgin National Trophy, covered the same distance of 36 laps in 4 h 6 min 18 sec, 1 min 10 sec ahead of Pullen's Mercer, nearly 18 minutes ahead of Oldfield's Stutz. In lap 14, on the backstretch of the course, near the Coombs' farm, Wishart, who had labored far into the night to repair his Mercer, attempted to overtake his teammate Otto Henning. Wishart's car grazed the other Mercer, swerved, shot off the road and crashed against a tree. Wishart died two hours after the accident; mechanic John Jenter escaped with a broken arm and internal injuries. The Duesy driven by Rickenbacher and Alley was able to keep the pace until lap 33 when the driveshaft broke. The old warrior Fritz Walker, Jenatzy's oil-pumper in the 1903 Bennett Cup, started at the wheel of a 1903 Mercedes entered under the name of Rae, but withdrew after a few miles with a broken intake valve. A few weeks later, by the end of October, "Mercedes Fritz" was severely hurt while serving as mechanic for Jack Gable when their Burman special turned over in a 100-mile race at Galesburg, Illinois. Walker died from his injuries.

By the end of November 1914, on Thanksgiving Day, the Corona road race was held over 109 laps of a 2.76-mile course encircling the small California city with the appropriate name, a few miles east of Los Angeles. The purse of $12,000, the largest amount ever given for a California speed event, attracted a fine field and 100,000 speed fans. Eddie Pullen and his Mercer, once yellow but painted crimson now, smashed the road-racing record, covering 301.8 miles in 3 h 26 min 2 sec, averaging 87.86 mph or 141 km/h, followed by Barney Oldfield (Maxwell), Eddie O'Donnell (Duesenberg) and Ralph DePalma (Mercedes). Bob Burman, whose sensational work in practice made him a favorite, tore the engine of his 5.6-liter Peugeot to pieces while warming up, breaking a wrist pin and connecting rod and driving a piston through the cylinder wall. Burman towed the sick racer to Los Angeles, to the workshop of Harry Miller, and tried to patch it up for the San Diego race on 9 January 1915. But the Peugeot fell out again with a blistered piston and broken connecting rod. Burman, determined to rebuild the car along his own lines, made a flying trip from Los Angeles to Chicago to purchase the steel for the axles and returned to work in the Miller shop.

Since 1909, the Master Carburetor Co. of Harry Armenius Miller, located at 922 Los Angeles Street, manufactured the well-known "Master" rotary throttle instruments, more or less a copy of the French Claudel. The 1.5" Master for handling gasoline was sold for $35 and was used on 12 of the cars competing in the 1914 Vanderbilt at Santa Monica, including DePalma's winning Mercedes. Recently Miller had offered a revolutionary alloy, named alloyanum, density 3.532, nothing less than a new form of magnalium. In addition there was a trump card by the name of Fred Offenhauser, a 25-year-old top-class artisan and former toolmaker at the Pacific Electric Railway. Burman took advantage of the offer and transformed his Peugeot into a Burman special. The new block had two removable water-jacket plates, made of alloyanum and bearing "Bob Burman" in large letters. The bore was reduced to 93 mm (93 mm × 180 mm) to comply with the 300-cubic-inch formula which became effective in 1915. New connecting rods, made of tubular chrome-vanadium steel, replaced the old I-beam rods. The cylinder sides, which had never received an adequate supply of oil with the old splash system, were lubricated through holes. Furthermore the cure included a new crankshaft, alloyanum pistons with rings of Burman's own design, tungsten steel valves, new gears and axles, and of course a Master carburetor. The finishing touch was the emblem of the Chicago Automobile Club which Burman always carried as a mascot. The Peugeot had been pushed into Miller's shop weighing 1040 kg; after three months the Burman left it at 950 kg. Costs for mechanical work and material were $2000. Burman looked back with pride on his racer, "the peer of any racing machine in America."

The Burman-Peugeot did not feel lonely in Miller's shop. Certainly not. Its twin brother stood by its side, the 5.6-liter of the Peugeot Auto Import Co., the former Indy racer of Jules Goux, in order to be overhauled after the San Diego race. Dario Resta, who had replaced Ralph Mulford at the beginning of the season and was the new star driver of Alphonse G. Kaufman, demanded more power. Fred Offenhauser applied the standard solution and mounted alloyanum pistons. Resta was content. Or was it due to his recent marriage to a sister of Spencer Wishart? In any case, by the end of February 1915, they were in top form, the Peugeot and Resta, winning the Grand Prize and the Vanderbilt Cup which were held within one week at San Francisco, within the grounds of the Panama-Pacific Exposition. Neither DePalma in an exhausted Mercedes nor Wilcox nor Anderson in brand-new Stutzes could counter.

Anyway Harry Clayton Stutz was not seeking prize money, but regarded San Francisco as a test for the new 300-cubic-inch racer. It was only by the end of May, on the brickyard at Indianapolis, that Stutz turned up with a team of three fully developed cars for Gil Anderson, Howdy Wilcox and Earl "Lucky" Cooper. In the qualifying trials, Wilcox promptly achieved fastest time, sending his racer around in 1 min 31 sec, 98.9 mph, 158 km/h. A new racer? It was a fine OHC four-valve four (3.808" × 6.484", 97 mm × 165 mm), strictly speaking a white OHC Peugeot! At Indianapolis, Stutz, too, was able to copy, not as unscrupulously as in the Sunbeam factory of Wolverhampton, but from the same sample: In June 1914, just after Duray's sensational second-place finish in the Indianapolis 500, a pragmatic Harry Stutz purchased the 3-liter Peugeot from the Menier family for $10,000. No bad deal, either for Menier or for Stutz who immediately tore the mechanism to pieces and incorporated the three-ball-bearing crankshaft and the spur pinion camshaft drive. Originally he may have used the DOHC head too, but only until the triple victory of the Mercedes at Lyon. One overhead camshaft was fully sufficient. The Stutz delivered 130 hp, at 3000 rpm.

DePalma achieved the second-best qualifying time, 1 min 31.3 sec, at the wheel of an overhauled Mercedes. The inspection took place at Detroit, in the Packard factory, where chief engineer Jesse G. Vincent looked after the 4.5-liter, not least in view of new insights for Packard's own aero engines. The Mercedes turned up with Packard carburetor and pointed tail. Mechanic Louis Fountaine fitted Goodrich "Silvertown" cord tires, 33 × 4.5 front and rear. The absolute steadiness of the front wheels immediately attracted the specialist's attention, "this being due to a caster wheel system worked out by Mercedes for the French road racing classic." For possible relief no less than Caleb Bragg was sitting in the pits.

The Peugeot Auto Import of Alphonse Kaufman and Arthur Hill had imported the Lyon reserve racer for Resta, good for 1 min 31.4 sec: "Resta drove the track well, but shut off on all four turns, whereas DePalma did not throttle down on any of them. Resta's car was designed to carry two extra tires on the rear for road racing and without these on the speedway, the tail is a little light and skids on the turns." Did wild Bob Burman open up his special? He was six seconds slower. Nine seconds back came the small ex–Duray, ex–Stutz 3-liter of George Babcock. New in America were two 4.5-liter Sunbeams for the former Grégoire star Jean Porporato and Guinness friend Noël van Raalte, while Harry Grant handled the well-known Ziegler six-cylinder, repainted in deep maroon. It was Barney Oldfield who qualified the van Raalte Sunbeam, and shortly after also the Garros Bugatti (98 mm × 160 mm) which was owned by Charles Fuller and driven by George Hill. Barney played the humble role of spectator! W. E. Wilson entered a Delage Y with a new block (93 mm × 180 mm) for John DePalma, Ralph's younger brother. The Maxwells (3.75" × 6.75", 95 mm × 172 mm) started with a revamped head, with four vertical 70-mm valves. The two-piece crankshaft ran in three ball bearings à la Peugeot. Otherwise Ray Harroun left everything unchanged. Fred and Augie Duesenberg relied on their traditional 300-cubic-inch dimensions: 3.98" × 6", 101 mm × 152 mm. There were Duesy engines, too, in the Kleinart of Art Klein and in the Sebring, built at Sebring, Ohio, of Joe Cooper. The 115-cubic-inch Cornelian (2.932" × 4.25", 74.5 mm × 108 mm) of Louis Chevrolet was the grasshopper among the elephants. The Blood brothers of Allegan, Michigan, had built a monocoque, a "sheet-steel body acting as a frame as well," with independent wheel suspension by transverse springs, weighing 450 kg. The Mais, the Cino-Purcell and the Emden played only minor roles. The new 4.9-liter Mercers never found their feet. Guy Ruckstell turned a few laps, the best in 1 min 47.4 sec. Too slow! Trenton withdrew. Maybe star engineer Finley R. Porter was missing there; he was responsible for his own sleeve-valve FRP Porter-

Summer of 1914—Untertürkheim. After the Vauxhall interlude at Lyon, DePalma immediately traveled to Untertürkheim to pick up the 4.5-liter for E. C. Patterson.

Knights which failed to qualify because of broken piston rings. Because of inclement weather, the 500-mile race was postponed from Saturday, 29 May, to Monday, 31 May:

| No. | | | Make | Driver | | | |
|---|---|---|---|---|---|---|---|
| 1, | 4, | 5 | Stutz | Wilcox | Earl Cooper | Anderson |
| 2 | | | Mercedes | Ralph DePalma | | |
| 3, | 8, | 16 | Peugeot | Resta | Burman | Babcock |
| 6, | 7, | 14 | Sunbeam | Porporato | van Raalte | Grant |
| 9 | | | Kleinart | Klein | | |
| 10, | 15, | 22 | Duesenberg | Alley | O'Donnell | Mulford |
| 17 | | | Delage | John DePalma | | |
| 18 | | | Sebring | Joe Cooper | | |
| 19, | 21, | 23 | Maxwell | Carlson | Orr | Rickenbacher |
| 24 | | | Mais | Mais | | |
| 25 | | | Purcell | Cox | | |
| 26 | | | Bugatti | Hill | | |
| 27 | | | Cornelian | Chevrolet | | |
| 28 | | | Emden | Haupt | | |

As usual the pack had a flying start, after the initial lap behind the Packard six of Carl Fisher. Howdy Wilcox took the lead in his white Stutz, in front of the blue Peugeot of Dario Resta and the beige Mercedes of DePalma. In lap two the order was Resta, Wilcox, DePalma, Earl Cooper, Anderson and Rickenbacher. In lap three it was Wilcox, Resta, Cooper, after 25 miles Resta, DePalma, Porporato, Wilcox and Cooper. The first to go to the pits was the Mais of Johnny Mais. After 20 laps Anderson had a small margin over DePalma, Resta, Cooper, Wilcox and Rickenbacher, this batch at least one lap ahead of the others. The Purcell of Cox fell out with a broken pump gear. Smiling Ralph Mulford changed the right rear tire of his Duesy. When Wilcox and Anderson pulled out to change tires, Resta took over the lead in front of DePalma, Cooper, Porporato, Rickenbacher and van Raalte. Resta achieved the first 100 miles in 1 h 7 min 30 sec, averaging 88.88 mph or 142 km/h. He lay just one second ahead of DePalma, four seconds ahead of Cooper, six ahead of Porporato and Rickenbacher, seven ahead of van Raalte, followed two laps back by the Duesy of Eddie O'Donnell, the Maxwell of Billy Carlson, the Duesy of Tom Alley and the black Maxwell that Tom Orr was driving in green buckskin shoes.

The race was a wheel-to-wheel battle between two swarthy-skinned Italians who had the same hobby: They liked to drive fast. After 125 miles they were well up ahead of Wilcox, Rickenbacher, van Raalte, Cooper and Anderson. John DePalma parked his Delage with a broken flywheel. Porporato was repairing at the pits. Rickenbacher dropped back a little. Orr, still in green shoes, doctored his Maxwell. After 63 laps DePalma came in for a right rear tire, losing one minute. After 75 laps the Mercedes was again in the lead. DePalma took the 200-mile record in 2 h 14 min 23 sec, equaling 89.22 mph or 142.5 km/h, 38 seconds ahead of Resta, 40 ahead of Anderson, 1 min 16 sec ahead of Cooper, four minutes ahead of Porporato. The little Cornelian fell out with a broken piston, the Maxwell of Rickenbacher with a broken crankshaft, the Peugeot of Babcock with a cracked cylinder. Van Raalte skidded off the track, lost the hood. The Englishman did not stop to pick it up. Referee Pardington did not agree, called him in. Van Raalte started out again, looking for the hood. Anderson came in with the right rear tire gone, no wonder given the number of left hand turns! After 300 miles DePalma led with 3 h 19 min 33 sec, nearly one minute in front of Resta, five minutes in front of Cooper and Anderson, then Porporato, Wilcox and Burman who was out in his Sunday suit, trousers and shirt of blue serge with his initials, B. B., embroidered in yellow silk on the right sleeve. For a few laps Carlson was relieved by Hughie Hughes, Anderson by Johnny Aitken.

In lap 121 DePalma stopped for four tires, losing 2 min 21 sec. When he started out, his Mercedes and Resta's Peugeot were a hood's-length apart, with Resta a lap to the good over DePalma. The Mercedes made up the ground lost on the straightaways by a burst of speed in the turns. DePalma stuck to the outside of the track and forced Resta to slow down before taking the turns. Due to a great deal of slack in the steering, Resta lost control of his Peugeot, touched the concrete wall and was forced to stop for a rear tire. The duel was resumed. DePalma gradually drew away from his weakening rival and at the completion of 400 miles he had an advantage of one lap. The Sebring of Joe Cooper skidded into the safety wall, breaking a wheel. The Maxwell of Orr was taken out with a broken rear axle, the Sunbeam of Porporato with a broken piston, the six-cylinder Sunbeam of Harry Grant with a loose mud apron.

Had DePalma overcome his jinx? Again it happened five miles before the finish when a connecting rod saw the light of the day. But DePalma continued to run wide open. The crankcase withstood the pounding. DePalma, Fountaine and the Mercedes won in 5 h 39 min 56 sec. Resta followed 3 min 29 sec back, then Anderson, Cooper, O'Donnell, Burman, Wilcox, Alley, Carlson and van Raalte. The record average of 89.84 mph or 144 km/h stood until 1922. While the crowd was congratulating him, DePalma thought only of his grease-splattered helper: "Louis, you're an awful little runt, but believe me, you're some mechanic!" Examination of the steering of Resta's Peugeot showed a damaged worm gear and 10 cm free movement on the rim of the wheel.

Already in December 1913 starter Fred Wagner had written:

> Were you to ask me to pick the most sympathetic driver, I would name DePalma. I never have known a more altruistic, a more considerate man. He has traits that are lovable, a heart as big and as fine as a mother's. Other drivers say that I favor Ralph. If their allegation is true, it is because I respect him, not only for his sportsmanship and tenacity but for his manliness. Ralph has done some fine things, but nothing finer than what he did at Elgin this year. Just before the second day's race and as DePalma was leaving the Mercer camp, a boy volunteered to crank Ralph's car. The motor kicked back and the cranking handle broke the boy's arm. He was taken to the hospital, placed in a public ward and given only ordinary attention. Two nights after, members of the Chicago Automobile Club tendered a dinner to the drivers and officials at which trophies were presented to the winners of the two races. DePalma, who captured the C.A.C. cup, sent word that he could not attend. Few knew the reason why Ralph stayed away. He sacrificed an evening of pleasure that he might sit for an hour at the bedside of the injured boy and make arrangements with the hospital authorities for a private room and special nurse before he left for California to drive in the Corona meeting. I consider that act of DePalma's his greatest achievement, greater by far than his victory in the Vanderbilt Cup race of 1912.

By the end of June 1915, the Maywood speedway was inaugurated at Burnside on the western edge of Chicago, a two-mile board track with banked turns, a "modern circus maximus." In 36 working days, 1500 workmen laid down and spiked 3000 km of lumber using 150 tons of nails. The track width was 25 meters, the maximum angle of banking in the turns 19.5°, costs of the track alone $300,000, costs of the speedway plant $1,250,000. Speed king Oldfield established a new lap record at the wheel of his front-drive Christie, covering the two miles in 1 min 4.4 sec, equaling 111.4 mph or 178 km/h. In the absence of DePalma, Resta qualified his Peugeot in 1 min 5.4 sec and drove it to a comfortable victory in front of Porporato's Sunbeam and Rickenbacher's Maxwell. New York was replacing the historic turf track of the Coney Island Jockey Club with a wooden two-miler, the Sheepshead Bay speedway. Among the prominent stockholders were Carl Fisher, A. C. Newby, Ralph DePalma, Fred Wagner and Alphonse Kaufman. Harry Harkness looked for management and promotion. His friend Vincent Astor donated a $2000 trophy and on 9 October 1915 the Astor Cup was run over 350 miles. Harkness quickly imported a whole set of 4.5-liter Delages from Courbevoie. Alphonse Kaufman entered all four 4.5-liter Peugeots for the first time, for his star Dario Resta, for Johnny Aitken, Howdy Wilcox and smiling Ralph Mulford. But the Peugeots had an off day. The Stutzes of Gil Anderson and Tom Rooney finished first and second. During the 1915 season, Resta won three great races, the Grand Prize and the Vanderbilt Cup at San Francisco and the 500-miler at Chicago. DePalma and his Mercedes took first place at Indianapolis. Eddie Rickenbacher won the 300-milers of Sioux City and Omaha for Maxwell, Anderson won for Stutz at Sheepshead Bay and on the road course at Elgin, his teammate Earl Cooper in a 500-miler at Minneapolis. Mulford drove his Duesy to victory in a 300-miler at Des Moines.

The 1916 season opened tragically: At the beginning of April, Bob Burman and his mechanic Eric Schroeder were killed in an accident at Corona when the Peugeot special blew a tire. America lost one of its most dazzling drivers. Also, the war began to make its impact. In 1916 Indianapolis was run over only 300 miles. DePalma and the whole Stutz team were absent. Fiat wanted to enter the 4.9-liter type S 57 A (104 mm × 143 mm), a rebored S 57 matching the 300-cubic-inch formula, with revised OHC head, valves inclined at 30°, and dual ignition. But the planned Atlantic crossing had to be cancelled, and the S 57 A had to wait until the twenties to achieve its great success, a Targa victory with the Florentine Count Giulio Masetti. Somehow Wolverhampton succeeded in shipping a new 4.9-liter Sunbeam. At the suggestion of Josef Christiaens a lengthened Tourist Trophy engine was mounted into the Grand Prix frame. The six-cylinder (81.5 mm × 157 mm) matched the 300-cubic-inch formula and delivered 152 hp at 3200 rpm. The Duesenberg brothers had engaged a young engineer named Cornelius van Ranst who gave the Duesy a second set of walking beams. And the Chevrolet brothers, Louis, Arthur and Gaston, turned up with a trio of brand-new Frontenacs (98 mm × 162 mm), with aluminum block, OHC four-valve head driven via vertical shaft.

Resta and his Peugeot won easily, ahead of Wilbur d'Alene's Duesenberg, Ralph Mulford's Peugeot, Christiaens' six-cylinder Sunbeam and Oldfield's desmo Delage. The Frontenacs fell out. Resta also took the 300-miler on the Maywood speedway, since DePalma's Mercedes began to splutter two laps from the finish because of overheated plugs, and the Vanderbilt Cup at Santa Monica. America entered into the war. Rickenbacher changed the spelling of his name to Rickenbacker and became America's top-scoring fighter pilot, the Ace of Aces. Fred and Augie Duesenberg focused on aero engines. The racing scene was forced to hibernate.

# 27

# *Wartime*

Until the autumn of 1914 the matériel battle of the Marne was deadlocked and guzzled such amounts of ammunition that the pure armament factories were overstrained. The Défense Nationale was forced to draw on the resources of the empty automobile factories. Thus, by the end of the year, at Billancourt, Argenteuil and Puteaux, Renault, De Dietrich and De Dion received orders for over one million shells and one thousand aircraft engines. Just the beginning of the war boom! Delaunay-Belleville, Chenard & Walcker, Brasier, Clément-Bayard and Georges Richard filled in as well. By the end of 1914, the now predominantly female personnel of the reactivated factories produced ten thousand shells per day, by the middle of 1915 not less than two million! And it paid off. The Défense Nationale remitted promptly, for a 75-millimeter shell 22.50 francs. Twenty units covered one monthly wage. Of course Hotchkiss continued to produce machine guns at Saint-Denis. Peugeot supplied 1.7 million bombs and large-calibre shells during the war years, 4.3 million 75-millimeter shells, 1400 tank engines, 10,000 aircraft engines, 6000 trucks, 3000 passenger cars, 1000 motorcycles and more than 60,000 bicycles. The truck specialists Panhard and Latil relied on four-wheel-drive tractors for the heavy cannon. Who came off best? André Citroën. As manager of the Mors factory he was not very active. However with the help of state money he established a model factory at the Quai de Javel employing 13,000 workers and instantly yielding 35,000 shells per day. In November 1918, to secure eight million francs' turnover per day, he took steps to begin building automobiles on a moving assembly line, Ford fashion. From the middle of 1919 the line produced one hundred units of the 7500-francs type A per day. It was the only way to use a factory which had long been paid off.

The situation on the German side was similar. In 1914 the DMG employed six thousand workers, in 1918 nearly 25,000, a large number of whom were involved with aero engines. The Kaiserpreis engine and the Lyon 4.5-liter charted the course. By the beginning of the war, the dimensions of the aero six were stretched to 140 mm × 160 mm, the crankshaft being carried in seven bearings instead of four. Displacement was 14.8 liters, weight 300 kg, output 175 hp at 1400 rpm. The German airforces demanded more. Paul Daimler added two cylinders. Nearly 20 liters and 405 kg delivered 240 hp at 1350 rpm and a compression of 4.75:1. After a short development time the engine was making 285 hp at 1750 rpm. The elongated straight-eight set new standards. The French manufacturers were forced to counter since the shaky aeroplane was maturing into an all-around machine, indispensable for reconnaissance and directing the fire of the heavy cannon. In September 1914 the French air forces used 150 airplanes; in 1918 they had no fewer than 3600, much more reliable and powerful machines. The improvements were mainly due to the raw materials, better valves and valve springs, lighter pistons and housings. Components like magnetos and plugs that were reliable at 2000 rpm in the air were good for 4000 rpm on the ground where a failure resulted only in a breakdown and not in a crash. The aero-engine specialists from Anzani, Clerget, Canton-Unné or Le Rhône were unable to match the German pace. Hispano director Marc Birkigt developed his own interpretation of an eight-cylinder made of steel, a compact eight-cylinder, a V-8. In the Hispano, the Swabian steel-sheet periphery gave way to a water jacket made of low-priced, rather low-grade and porous aluminum casting; the enamelling, applied for the purpose of sealing, made for a finish in elegant black! With this "8 A," Hispano supplied the standard engine for the Allied airplanes. When, on 11 November 1918, bugler corporal Pierre Sellier sounded at last the ceasefire and the end of the war, Citroën, Hispano, Salmson, Farman and Voisin were not the only profit-takers of the recent financial and technical background; Ballot was part of the same group.

In 1906 the former navy engineer Ernest Ballot had begun to manufacture conventional, reliable L-head engines in a small factory located at no. 105, Boulevard Brune, in the south of Paris, for stationary purposes, for boats and voiturettes. Delage and Barré purchased engines from Ballot & Cie. Due to the defense activities, the Ballot factory, which in 1912 had been relocated to no. 39, Boulevard Brune, was better equipped than ever. Ballot decided to invest in complete automobiles. In order to stimulate sales he was thinking of winning the 1919 Indianapolis 500. This high-flying idea was in accordance with Ballot's tailor-made wardrobe, his high polish footwear, his persnickety fob chain and his filigree moustache. And how was he going to do this? With a straight-eight Peugeot! Ballot was not only vain, he was clever and lured Ernest Henry to the Boulevard Brune. He contacted Indy victor René Thomas who acted as manager of the Ballot engined Barré team in the 1914 Tour de France and had known Henry for a long time. Henry and Thomas were good friends. Hadn't they reached the same dead end? Neither Henry nor Thomas was accepted as a master of their craft. Thomas was graciously appointed Delage reserve driver for the Grand Prix at Lyon. No surprise that Henry, despite the great successes at Dieppe, Amiens, Indianapolis and Boulogne, was on the black list after Boillot's dramatic breakdown. From the outset, the director of the Peugeot drawing office at Levallois passed for an opportunistic dabbler and *arriviste*. The old-established high priests of the Peugeot engineering department, above all the trio Vasselot, Chamuseau and Grémillon, mercilessly checked all drawings of the intruder and informed the company management of the slightest mistakes. In August 1914 Thomas placed his friend Henry with Barré. When, by the end of 1918, Monsieur Ballot decided to create a racer, both were standing by: the chance of a lifetime! During the first discussions at the Boulevard Brune, an updated remake of the 4.5-liter Peugeot was the point, in the dimensions of 95 mm × 172 mm, matching the American 300-cubic-inch formula. But there were countless Peugeot copies, in England from Sunbeam and Humber, in Belgium from Nagant, and recently at Indianapolis from Premier, as speedway representative Bradley aptly remarked. However a dual 2.5-liter Coupe de l'Auto would certainly be a big hit, in the eyes of the public, of the press, and also of the potential customers for the future production type. Thus Ernest Henry was more or less forced to devise an eight-cylinder, an advertisement eight...

The 4.9-liter Ballot (74 mm × 140 mm) included the peculiarities of the Peugeot, a cast-iron block with two overhead camshafts and four valves per cylinder, and a flexible frame in combination with a Hotchkiss axle. The valve tappets were of the cup type, and of course the crankshaft of the straight-eight had to run in five ball bearings now, with plain big ends, as usual, still receiving their few drops of oil by centrifugal force. The output was disappointing: 125 hp at 3000 rpm, for short periods 140 at 3500. A peak of 4000 rpm would only be possible with an adequate lubrication system. Henry missed the point and the great Laurence Pomeroy later commented: "Henry sowed but did not reap so far as the eight-cylinder in-line engine is concerned." The Ballot's distaste for high revolutions was well known; in view of the 1919 Indianapolis race it was countered by long axle ratios. Certainly too long! Bablot and Wagner preferred to fit smaller wheels and promptly left the track as they broke. Thomas and Guyot struggled with the plugs. The popular Howdy Wilcox won in an old 4.5-liter Peugeot, beating Eddie Hearne in a Stutz, Jules Goux in a Premier-engined Peugeot, and Guyot in the best Ballot. By the end of November 1919, René Thomas drove his 4.9-liter Ballot to Sicily, in view of the Targa, which was to be run over four long laps of 107 km. He met a lot of old friends, the 2.5-liter Coupe de l'Auto Peugeots of André Boillot and Samy Réville, the 4.5- and 4.9-liter Fiats of Antonio Ascari and Giulio Masetti, the 1913 Grand Prix Italas of Moriondo and Landri, and the 4.5-liter Nazzaros of Baldoni and Negro. Enzo

October 1920—Gaillon hillclimb. Maurice Rouvier at the wheel of his 4.5-liter Alda: During the twenties many amateurs thoroughly enjoyed the performance of the former Amiens and Lyon racers.

Ferrari started on a CMN (Costruzioni Meccaniche Nazionali). Boillot, Thomas and Ascari struggled for the lead. Thomas was forced to withdraw because of a broken differential. Ascari left the road. The young Boillot was too fast in the last corner before the finish, hit a wall, and rolled backwards over the line. Didn't this mean disqualification? Ernest Ballot lifted him back in the seat. Boillot crossed the line again, so exhausted that he passed out murmuring "c'est pour la France." Henry continued to work for Ballot until 1921, devising a 3-liter straight-eight (65 mm × 112 mm) at the wheel of which DePalma won the 1920 Elgin race and Goux the 1921 Italian Grand Prix at Brescia. He also designed a 2-liter four (69.9 mm × 130 mm) which appeared in the autumn of 1920 at Gaillon, finished third in the 1921 Grand Prix de l'ACF and started in 1922 with a streamlined cigar-like body. When a wealthy clientèle was able to purchase the 2-liter as 2 LS, as *deux liters sport*, for nearly the same price as the grandiose Hispano H 6, Henry was long out of it. By the end of 1921 Ballot dismissed him. Henry switched to the west of Paris, to Suresnes, settled down in an office of the former Darracq factory, the French domicile of the Sunbeam-Talbot-Darracq group, and designed a Sunbeam. Jean Chassagne was responsible for the data flow between Suresnes and Wolverhampton where the 2-liter racer (68 mm × 136 mm) was assembled under the direction of Louis Coatalen. The Sunbeam was not up to the mark and Henry disappeared from the scene. After some subordinate employments, unworthy for a man who was one of the heads of the great Peugeot racing team, he died in poverty, in 1950.

July 1921—GP de l'ACF, Le Mans. The three-liter Ballot of Ralph DePalma and his nephew and mechanic Pete DePaolo, designed by Ernest Henry.

By the beginning of the war, the Italian counterpart of Henry, Giuseppe Coda, left Fiat to manage a workshop building Hispano engined Spad airplanes under license. He was a good friend of the Italian aces, of Baracca, Ancilotti, Ranza and Piccio. After the hostilities he founded the Veltro Fabbrica di Automobili, having in mind the production of a little brother of his S 57 Fiat displacing 2 liters, but was unable to secure the financing. He sold the project to Diatto, an old Turin factory making carriages, railway material and, since 1905, cars under Clément license. Coda's 2-liter became the Diatto tipo 20, and Coda himself technical director. The Diatto (79.7 mm × 100 mm) was available as touring and sports car with wheelbases of 265, 300 and 310 cm, and at Ponte Vecchio, a suburb of Bologna, the Maserati family prepared a few short chassis for competition work. No surprise that in 1922, in the new *autodromo* at Monza, the numberless *tifosi* thought they saw two scaled-down S 57 Fiats as Alfieri Maserati and Guido Meregalli pushed their 2-liter Diattos to the start of the Italian Grand Prix. Later, between 1925 and 1936, Coda worked for Citroën in Paris but remained in contact with Alfieri Maserati in view of the development of a straight-eight which became the first Maserati. Coda died in Biella in October 1977.

The jolly Michela fell out with Delage and left Courbevoie. He finished up at Marseille, in the small factory of Léon Paulet where he designed a fine 3.5-liter six (75 mm × 130 mm), in principle a small Hispano, which was displayed at the 1921 Paris salon but unfortunately was produced only in small quantities and

September 1922—Gran Premio d'Italia, Monza. The two-liter Diatto of Guido Meregalli, a scaled down 1914 GP Fiat, devised by Giuseppe Coda.

remained virtually unknown even in his homeland. By the beginning of the thirties, after Delage had been taken over by Delahaye, he returned to Courbevoie and designed the D 6-65, the last real Delage. At the beginning of the war, Jellinek was taking a cure at Bad Kissingen. His French assets were seized, the villa Mercédès, the hotels in Paris and Nice, his Rolls-Royce and the yacht *Mercedes II* which was lying at anchor in the port of Monaco. He moved to Vienna, then to Meran, and, just before the outbreak of the hostilities with Italy, to Geneva where he stayed in the Grand Hôtel National and succumbed to a cerebral apoplexy in January 1918. His wife Madeleine died in Neuilly in 1940. Wilhelm Maybach stood by his son Karl and died in 1929. Josef Brauner worked for NAG in Berlin, until 1930. Paul Daimler adapted the supercharger to the Mercedes before switching to Horch in 1922, going on pension six years later and living in Berlin where he died in 1946. Ferdinand Porsche was his successor at Untertürkheim. Marius Barbarou left Delaunay-Belleville in April 1914 and switched to Lorraine-Dietrich where he designed the famous 3.5-liter six which was to make Le Mans history. Otto Hieronimus drove for Gaggenau, Austro-Daimler and Steyr but had a fatal accident in May 1922, during the practice for the Ries hillclimb near Graz. Franz Heim built his own sports cars in his hometown of Mannheim from 1921 until his death in 1926. Christian Lautenschlager and Otto Salzer remained faithful to their Swabian employer and drove Mercedes during the twenties. Fritz Erle looked after the Benz agency in Berlin, until 1935. René Hanriot built airplanes with his brother.

In December 1913 Camille Jenatzy "took a group of friends boar hunting in a forest near Brussels. Unfortunately, the hunting was poor and the group resorted to a long dinner and drinking session instead. Jenatzy was convinced their luck was about to improve and offered bets they would be shooting within the next two hours. After everyone had gone to bed, he sneaked outside and began making sounds like a wild boar to arouse the sleepy interests of his buddies. But his own cunning plan backfired as the windows were suddenly flung open and shots were fired." It was his friend Alfred Madoux, editor of the Brussels newspaper *L'Ètoile Belge*, who hit him. Jenatzy was dead within a few minutes. Willy Poege died of heart disease in May 1914, Théo Pilette in a car accident near Luxembourg in 1921. Louis Wagner took the wheel of every racer falling into his hands, from Fiat, to Rolland-Pilain, Alfa Romeo, Delage and Talbot, was later in charge of the Montlhéry racetrack to the south of Paris. Léon Théry died of tuberculosis in 1909. During the twenties Ferenc Szisz managed a repair shop at Neuilly, rue du Château, before retiring at Auffargis near Paris where he died in 1944. Felice Nazzaro concluded his driving career with Fiat, Ralph DePalma with Packard, Ballot and Duesenberg, Victor Hémery with Rolland-Pilain, Jules Goux with Ballot, Schmid and Bugatti. Paul Bablot initiated the track of Miramas near his hometown Marseille. Albert Guyot drove for Duesenberg and Rolland-Pilain before designing his own Guyots with sleeve-valve engines. René Thomas was promoted to star driver at Delage, sold at the same time his own steering wheels. Georges Boillot took on aviation by the end of 1914, as a sport rather than in the business of war, and was killed in May 1916 in a fight with five German pilots, bringing down one of them before the bullets hit him. Teddy Tetzlaff drove his last race on the Corona circle in 1916 and died in December 1929. Eddie Hearne became 1923 National Champion and died in February 1955. Dario Resta was killed in an accident at Brooklands in September

1924. And speed king Oldfield? Barney made money with tires and died at Beverly Hills in October 1946.

The monumental dinosaurs were mercilessly hunted to death, in numberless hillclimbs and kilometer sprints, on pebbly dirt tracks and the wavy concrete of Brooklands. The handicaps there irresistibly attracted them, especially the chain-drive racers whose sprockets could be changed in the turn of a hand. Douglas Hawkes turned up in the 1912 Lorraine "Vieux Charles III," John Duff either in the freshly prepared Fiat Mephisto or in a 10-liter S 61, Pilette in the indestructible 1906 Mercedes, Barlow in the big Benz, the former Blitzen of Cupid Hornsted. Then there was the Zborowski gang, the 25-year-old Louis Zborowski, the son of Paris–Vienna hero William Elliott, and his friends, Jack and Dick "Shuggar" Cooper. Louis let off steam at the wheel of a 1914 Lyon Mercedes, allegedly the winning Lautenschlager car, Jack in a 10-liter, Shuggar in a 1908 Grand Prix racer or a Blitzen with a new tapered tail. Eventually the gang was bored, despite the jazzy clothing and the spectacularly colored Florida golfing caps. During the spring of 1921, Zborowski had a Maybach aero engine mounted in a Mercedes chain drive

Spring of 1921—Brooklands. Louis Zborowski, son of Paris–Vienna hero William Elliott, at the wheel of "Chitty-Bang-Bang," a cocktail of Mercedes chain-drive frame, Maybach aero engine and body from the Bligh brothers, Canterbury. By his side mechanic Wigglesworth, behind the hood the Cooper brothers with their unmistakable golfing caps.

frame, a 23-liter six-cylinder (165 mm × 180 mm) with OHV four-valve head, with 300 hp and a stovepipe as exhaust. The fearsome combination was called "Chitty-Bang-Bang" and disconcerted every handicapper. Chitty number two was not long in coming, again a chain-drive chassis from Untertürkheim, but now with an aero engine from Benz, a 19-liter (145 mm × 190 mm). Zborowski used number two for a trip through the Sahara, in company of his wife. Chitty number three? Originally a 28/95 in which a 14.8-liter (140 mm × 160 mm) was mounted, the perfect service car for the desert tour. Shuggar Cooper kept pace, replacing the four-cylinder of his Grand Prix Mercedes with a 20-liter V-8 from Clerget (140 mm × 160 mm). His brother Jack had a fatal accident during a test drive. And the Zborowski gang dropped the aero engine monsters.

It was surprising how quickly the overhead camshaft became accepted in touring-car circles. DOHC four-valve sports cars were manufactured in many countries, in France not by Peugeot but by Ballot, in Germany as a copy by Simson, in Italy as a six-cylinder by SPA, in America as eight-cylinders by Duesenberg and Stutz. In the luxury sports car, the OHC head was standard, in the Mercedes, Austro-Daimler, Hispano and Farman, and in the Bentley: After its victory at Lyon and its lap of honor through Untertürkheim, the Lautenschlager Mercedes was displayed in Berlin, then shipped to London, confiscated a few days after the beginning of the war, the engine finally finishing up at Derby where it was inspected by Rolls-Royce engineers and by W. O. Bentley who was "tremendously impressed." In the Mercedes era, in the great races of the Belle Époque, the gasoline engine found its definitive form. Afterwards came the adjustment to mass production. It seems strange that, with the exception of Opel, just the winning makes survived: Renault, Fiat, Peugeot, Mercedes and Benz. The rest—as they had so often been on the track—were left behind in the dust of history.

# Appendix A: Forgotten Cars— and Forgotten Heroes

The first pure Mercedes racer was the Eighty. In the spring of 1903, Cannstatt delivered a batch of six cars (170 mm × 140 mm), followed by two engines to be used in power boats:

Commission 19/24—delivered in April 1903—driven by Otto Hieronimus in the Paris–Madrid race, with Gustave Girard as riding mechanic—sold via Richard von Stern to Andrew Fletcher who started in the 1904 Circuit des Ardennes.

Commission 19/25—delivered in April 1903—driven by Henri Degrais in the Paris–Madrid race—sold via Henri de Rothschild to Léopolde of Belgium.

Commission 19/26—delivered in April 1903—driven by Köhler in the Paris–Madrid race—exhibited at the 1903 Paris Salon—sold via Charley Lehmann to Willie Vanderbilt who used it on the beach of Daytona in February 1904.

Commission 20/22—delivered in April 1903—driven by Pierre de Caters in the Paris–Madrid race—owned by de Caters, remuneration for his starts in the Paris–Madrid race and the Bennett Cup—not rebuilt after the factory fire.

Commission 20/23—delivered in April 1903—driven by Camille Jenatzy in the Paris–Madrid race, with Fritz Walker as riding mechanic—rebuilt after the factory fire—sold in July 1903 via Jenatzy to Eugène Lefebvre, Avenue du Midi, Brussels, with tonneau body.

Commission 19/27—delivered in May 1903—driven by Wilhelm Werner in the Paris–Madrid race—rebuilt after the factory fire—sold via Dinsmore to William Gould Brokaw, New York.

Commission 22/42—delivered in December 1903—engine for power boat.

Commission 22/3—delivered in April 1904—engine for power boat—sold to Albert Bostwick, New York.

Due to the 1903 Bennett victory, the next batch comprised 15 racers (165 mm × 140 mm):

Commission 21/20—delivered in March 1904—assembled in Wiener-Neustadt—driven by Hermann Braun in the 1904 Bennett Cup—sold to Henri de Rothschild.

Commission 21/87—delivered in March 1904—assembled in Wiener-Neustadt—driven by John B. Warden in the 1904 Bennett Cup—owned by Warden.

Commission 29/71—ordered by Jellinek in September 1903—delivered in March 1904—driven by Camille Jenatzy in the 1904 Bennett Cup—sold to Dinsmore.

Commission 29/72—delivered in June 1904—driven by Pierre de Caters in the 1904 Bennett Cup—owned by de Caters.

Commission 29/76—delivered in June 1904—assembled in Wiener-Neustadt—driven by Wilhelm Werner in the 1904 Bennett Cup—sold to Jellinek's secretary Ferdinand Spiegel, Vienna, with red tonneau body.

Commission 29/73—delivered in July 1904—sold to Luigi Storero, Corso Valentino no. 37, Turin.

Commission 29/75—delivered in July 1904—sold to Willie Vanderbilt.

Commission 29/86—delivered in September 1904—assembled in Wiener-Neustadt—sold to Alfred Harmsworth, London.

Commission 29/74—delivered in October 1904—sold to Vincenzo Florio, Palermo.

Commission 29/77—delivered in November 1904—exhibited at the 1904 Paris Salon.

## Appendix A: Forgotten Cars—and Forgotten Heroes

September 1905—Coppa Florio, Brescia. Cortese at the wheel of his friend Florio's twelve-liter Mercedes. The racer had been delivered to Palermo in October 1904.

Commission 29/87—delivered in November 1904—sold to Sultan of Jahore, Wellington Court, Knightsbridge, London—driven by Georges Teste in the 1905 Gaillon hillclimb.

Commission 29/101—delivered in November 1904—red racing body.

Commission 29/88—delivered in December 1904—sold to Rittergutsbesitzer Kees (Knight Kees), with Truffault shock absorbers.

Commission 22/42—delivered in December 1904—sold to Prince Alexis Orloff, Rue Saint Dominique no. 47, Paris.

Commission 29/10—delivered in January 1905—exhibited at the Berlin show—sold to Hutton, London.

In 1905, the batch comprised twelve cars (175 mm × 146 mm and 175 mm × 150 mm):

Commission 29/11—delivered in April 1905—driven by Camille Jenatzy in the 1905 Bennett Cup—sold to Vincenzo Florio, Palermo—driven by Florio in the 1905 Coppa Florio and the 1906 GP de l'ACF—driven by Otto Salzer in the 1906 Circuit des Ardennes.

Commission 29/113—delivered in April 1905—assembled in Wiener-Neustadt—driven by Hermann Braun in the 1905 Bennett Cup—sold via Dinsmore to Marieaux—driven by Marieaux in the 1906 GP de l'ACF.

Commission 29/114—delivered in April 1905—driven by Wilhelm Werner in the 1905 Bennett Cup—sold to Henri de Rothschild.

Commission 29/115—delivered in April 1905—driven by Pierre de Caters in the 1905 Bennett Cup—sold to Harvey du Cros.

Commission 29/116—delivered in April 1905—assembled in Wiener-Neustadt—driven by Otto Hieronimus in the 1905 Bennett Cup—sold to Robert W. Graves—driven by Campbell in the 1905 Vanderbilt Cup.

Commission 22/51—delivered in June 1905, directly to Clermont-Ferrand—driven by Burton in the 1905 Bennett Cup—owned by Burton—driven by Jenatzy and Burton in the 1906 GP de l'ACF—driven by

## Appendix A: Forgotten Cars—and Forgotten Heroes

September 1905—Coppa Florio, Brescia. Vincenzo Florio at the wheel of his latest Mercedes racer, the 14-liter which had been driven by Jenatzy in the Bennett Cup through the Auvergne.

Salzer in practice for the 1906 Circuit des Ardennes and 1906 Semmering hillclimb—in 1907 sold to Camaracescu, Bucharest.

Commission 29/46—delivered in July 1905—sold to Pierre de Caters—driven by de Caters in the 1905 Gaillon hillclimb.

Commission 29/47—delivered in August 1905—sold to John B. Warden—driven by Warden in the 1905 Vanderbilt Cup.

Commission 29/56—delivered in August 1905—sold to Foxhall Keene, New York—quoted as "90 hp" with cylinder dimensions 175 mm × 150 mm—driven by Keene in the 1905 Vanderbilt Cup.

Commission 29/57—delivered in September 1905—sold to Alberto Santos-Dumont, Paris—driven by E. T. Stead in the 1905 Salon (southern-France) meeting.

Commission 29/12—delivered in October 1905—sold to Charley Lehmann, Paris—exhibited at the 1905 Salon.

Commission 29/43—delivered in November 1905—sold to Demartini, Rome.

For the 1908 Grand Prix, Unter-türkheim built five cars:

Commission 38/83—delivered in April 1908—cylinder dimensions 155 mm × 170 mm, tires 875 mm × 105 mm front and 895 mm × 135 mm rear—driven by Christian Lautenschlager in the 1908 GP de l'ACF.

Commission 38/84—delivered in April 1908—cylinder dimensions 155 mm × 180 mm—driven by Willy Poege in the 1908 GP de l'ACF.

Commission 38/85—delivered in April 1908—cylinder dimensions 155 mm × 180 mm—driven by Otto Salzer in the 1908 GP de l'ACF.

Commission 38/86—delivered in April 1908—cylinder dimensions 155 mm × 180 mm—sold to Willy Poege—155-mm engine replaced in the last week of August by new 175 mm × 180 mm engine. Commission 38/87—delivered in April 1908—cylinder dimensions 155 mm × 170 mm—spare car for 1908 GP de l'ACF.

In August 1914, the magazine *Motor Age*, "published weekly by The Class Journal Company, 910 South Michigan Avenue, Chicago," printed a poem describing the fortunes of those forgotten men of the great sport, the riding mechanics:

"The Mechanician," by J.-C. Burton

When the throng is goin' mad
Over some dust-eatin' lad
That's raced with Death to win its fickle praise,
There's another hero there
Who ain't gettin' half his share
Of the plaudits under which the gray stand sways

He don't figure in the lead
Of the stories that you read
Of the boys who rode to fortune and to fame,
'Less his car should leave the track
And the surgeons bring him back—
Then the papers turn a rule around his name.

He is smeared with grime and oil
And his hands are cut from toil,
He hasn't copped a purse that's made him rich;
But because he's on the job
He has kept a morbid mob
From gath'rin' round a smashup in the ditch.

When a tire jumps a rim
Then they yell and curse at him;
The driver stops a minute—then is off,
Still the leader in the race
With another wheel in place
And the engine spittin' grease at ev'ry cough.

There is chaos in the pit
For the motor's took a fit
and is missin' about three times out of four.
There's rattle at the hood—
Then she's actin' smart and good
And eatin' up the road with strident roar.

So I smite my bloomin' lyre
In a sort of mad desire
To give the mechanician what's his due;
For I cannot help but feel
'Side the man who's at the wheel
That another hero helped to put it through.

Usually the mechanics remained anonymous in the background, but from time to time some names were mentioned:

## French Bennett elimination—Circuit de l'Auvergne—June 1905

| car | driver | mechanic |
|---|---|---|
| no. 1 Brasier | Léon Théry | Muller |
| no. 2 Renault | Ferenc Szisz | Dimitriévitch |
| no. 3 C.G.V. | Léonce Girardot | Loupi |
| no. 4 Clément-Bayard | Albert Clément | Vénus ainé (the elder Vénus) |
| no. 5 Hotchkiss | Hubert Le Blon | Duchesne |
| no. 6 Automoto | Lapertot | R. Foureau |
| no. 7 De Dietrich | Fernand Gabriel | Vauthier |
| no. 8 Darracq | Victor Hémery | Victor Demongeot |
| no. 9 Panhard & Levassor | Georges Heath | Louis |
| no. 10 Gobron-Brillié | Louis Rigolly | Campagne |
| no. 11 Brasier | Gustave Caillois | Pouxe |
| no. 12 Renault | Edmond | Rassat |
| no. 14 Clément-Bayard | René Hanriot | Vénus junior |
| no. 15 Hotchkiss | Achille Fournier | Reigenbach |
| no. 17 De Dietrich | Henri Rougier | D. Miellon |
| no. 18 Darracq | Louis Wagner | Guillot |
| no. 19 Panhard & Levassor | Georges Teste | Artault |
| no. 21 Brasier | E. T. Stead | Janot |
| no. 22 Renault | Maurice Bernin | Hennin |
| no. 24 Clément-Bayard | Villemain | Paris |
| no. 25 Hotchkiss | Lavergne | Klein |
| no. 27 De Dietrich | Arthur Duray | Franville |
| no. 28 Darracq | de La Touloubre | Yvon |
| no. 29 Panhard & Levassor | Henry Farman | Monge |

## Appendix A: Forgotten Cars—and Forgotten Heroes

Spring 1906—Outskirts of Paris. Edmond and mechanic Rassat testing the Renault GP prototype, still using non-detachable wire wheels. Their first names have passed into oblivion. (Renault)

### Bennett Cup—Circuit de l'Auvergne—July 1905

| car | driver | mechanic |
|---|---|---|
| no. 1 Brasier | Léon Théry | Muller |
| no. 7 Brasier | Gustave Caillois | Pouxe |
| no. 13 De Dietrich | Arthur Duray | Franville |
| no. 2 Napier | Clifford Earp | A. Earp |
| no. 8 Wolseley | Charles S. Rolls | Hands |
| no. 14 Wolseley | Cecil Bianchi | M. Wilde |
| no. 3 Mercedes | Camille Jenatzy | Menzel |
| no. 9 Mercedes | Pierre de Caters | R. Cozic |
| no. 15 Mercedes | Wilhelm Werner | ? |
| no. 4 F.I.A.T. | Vincenzo Lancia | Pietro Bordino |
| no. 10 F.I.A.T. | Alessandro Cagno | ? |
| no. 16 F.I A.T. | Felice Nazzaro | Antonio Fagnano |
| no. 5 Austro-Mercedes | Hermann Braun | ? |
| no. 11 Austro-Mercedes | Otto Hieronimus | Schloz |
| no. 17 Austro-Mercedes | J. T. Alexander Burton | ? |
| no. 6 Pope-Toledo | Herbert H. Lytle | Billy Knipper |
| no. 12 Pope-Toledo | Albert Dingley | Tattersall |
| no. 18 Locomobile | Joe Tracy | W. Poole |

### Grand Prix de l'ACF—Dieppe—July 1908

| car | driver | mechanic |
|---|---|---|
| no. 1 Austin | Dario Resta | Lambetti |
| no. 2 Mercedes | Willy Poege | Bott |
| no. 3 Motobloc | Pierron | Sonan |
| no. 4 Renault | Ferenc Szisz | Marteau |
| no. 5 Lorraine-Dietrich | Arthur Duray | Henry Matthys |
| no. 6 Benz | Victor Hémery | Gilli |

## Grand Prix de l'ACF (cont.)

| car | driver | mechanic |
|---|---|---|
| no. 7 Fiat | Vincenzo Lancia | Pietro Bordino |
| no. 8 Brasier | Léon Théry | Mignot |
| no. 9 Porthos | Émile Stricker | Bergez |
| no. 10 Opel | Fritz Opel | Weyl |
| no. 11 Clément-Bayard | Victor Rigal | Gilbert |
| no. 12 Itala | Alessandro Cagno | Moriondo |
| no. 13 Weigel | Pryce Harrison | Colman |
| no. 14 Mors | Camille Jenatzy | Dayssiolles |
| no. 15 Thomas | Lewis Strang | Guichard |
| no. 16 Panhard & Levassor | Georges Heath | ? |
| no. 17 Germain | Degrais | Salvator |
| no. 18 Austin | Moore Brabazon | Lane |
| no. 19 Mercedes | Otto Salzer | Stegmaier |
| no. 20 Motobloc | Pierre Garcet | Gauderman |
| no. 21 Renault | Gustave Caillois | Vivet |
| no. 22 Lorraine-Dietrich | Henri Rougier | Bohn |
| no. 23 Benz | René Hanriot | Franz Heim |
| no. 24 Fiat | Felice Nazzaro | Antonio Fagnano |
| no. 25 Brasier | Paul Baras | Godin |
| no. 26 Porthos | Gaubert | Chartier |
| no. 27 Opel | Carl Joerns | Franz Breckheimer |
| no. 28 Clément-Bayard | Fernand Gabriel | Alézy |
| no. 29 Itala | Henry Fournier | Ayana |
| no. 30 Weigel | Laxen | Robinson |
| no. 31 Mors | Landon | Bache |
| no. 32 Panhard & Levassor | Maurice Farman | Kohler |
| no. 33 Germain | Roch-Brault | Jargot |
| no. 34 Austin | Warwick Wright | Hadley |
| no. 35 Mercedes | Chr. Lautenschlager | Mäckle |
| no. 36 Motobloc | Courtade | Malafaye |
| no. 37 Renault | Dimitriévitch | Saglini |
| no. 38 Lorraine-Dietrich | Ferdinando Minoia | Cenotti |
| no. 39 Benz | Fritz Erle | Gass |
| no. 40 Fiat | Louis Wagner | Antonio Ferro |
| no. 41 Brasier | Paul Bablot | Lausson |
| no. 42 Porthos | Simon | Kinsch |
| no. 43 Opel | Michel | Sitaritz |
| no. 44 Clément-Bayard | Lucien Hautvast | Jean Chassagne |
| no. 45 Itala | Giovanni Piacenza | Craviolo |
| no. 46 Weigel | Shannon | Deavis |
| no. 47 Mors | Landon | ? |
| no. 48 Panhard & Levassor | Henri Cissac | Schaube |
| no. 49 Germain | Perpère | Ghide |

## Grand Prix des Voiturettes—Dieppe—July 1908

| car | driver | mechanic |
|---|---|---|
| no. 1 Delage | Albert Guyot | Reyrol |
| no. 2 Martini | Beck | Segesmann |
| no. 4 Grégoire | Pinaud | Jusant |
| no. 5 Alcyon | Barriaux | Long |
| no. 6 Le Métais | Birnbaum | Besson |
| no. 7 Demeester | Martin | Kupperschmidt |
| no. 9 Thieulin | Zetwood | Guth |
| no. 10 Lion-Peugeot | Giuppone | Paul Péan |
| no. 12 Bailleau | Bailleau | Gant |
| no. 13 La Roullière | Jean de La Roullière | Routichon |
| no. 14 Ariès | Meaux de Saint-Marc | Guérin |
| no. 17 Werner | Léon Molan | Triguili |
| no. 18 Isotta-Fraschini | Vincenzo Trucco | Rossi |
| no. 21 Guillemin-Le Gui | Hamilton | Faviot |
| no. 22 Taine-La Joyeuse | Ménard | Soulès |

Appendix A: Forgotten Cars—and Forgotten Heroes

## Grand Prix des Voiturettes (cont.)

| car | driver | mechanic |
|---|---|---|
| no. 23 Truffault | Charlas | Constantin |
| no. 25 Sizaire et Naudin | Georges Sizaire | Rochette |
| no. 28 Monier | Pizzagalli | Poitoux |
| no. 29 Delage | René Thomas | Plot |
| no. 30 Martini | Boris | Kaeser |
| no. 31 Grégoire | Philippe de Marne | van den Hewelt |
| no. 32 Alcyon | Dominique | Dumas |
| no. 33 Le Métais | Haubourdin | Rousor |
| no. 34 Demeester | Dacier | Gérard |
| no. 35 Thieulin | Thieulin | Sarner |
| no. 36 Lion-Peugeot | Jules Goux | Duvernois |
| no. 38 Bailleau | Farcy | Lemaître |
| no. 39 Ariès | Perrot | Margoutte |
| no. 40 Werner | Lucien Molon | Dubreuil |
| no. 41 Isotta-Fraschini | Alfieri Maserati | Pontiroli |
| no. 45 Werner | d'Avaray | Le Guen |
| no. 46 Sizaire et Naudin | Louis Naudin | Winter |
| no. 49 Delage | Lucas | Chenard |
| no. 50 Martini | Sonvico | Perret |
| no. 51 Grégoire | Gasté | Max |
| no. 52 Alcyon | Roisant | Aublet |
| no. 53 Le Métais | Pernette | Perlat |
| no. 54 Demeester | Léon Demeester | Liny |
| no. 55 Lion-Peugeot | Georges Boillot | Lenoble |
| no. 57 Ariès | Richez | Danart |
| no. 58 Werner | Vallée | Georges |
| no. 59 Isotta-Fraschini | Buzzio | Butti |
| no. 60 Rolland-Pilain | Louison | Métais |
| no. 62 Guillemin-Le Gui | Rivière | Rodet |
| no. 63 Sizaire et Naudin | Jules Leboucq | Dettelin |

## Coppa Florio—Bologna—September 1908

| car | driver | mechanic |
|---|---|---|
| no. 1 Lorraine-Dietrich | Arthur Duray | Henry Matthys |
| no. 2 Motobloc | Gauderman | Chalus |
| no. 3 Mors | Victor Demongeot | Bauer |
| no. 4 Fiat | Vincenzo Lancia | Pietro Bordino |
| no. 5 Clément-Bayard | Fernand Gabriel | Alézy |
| no. 6 Itala | Alessandro Cagno | Moriondo |
| no. 7 Lorraine-Dietrich | Ferdinando Minoia | Cinotti |
| no. 8 Motobloc | Charles Faroux | Tolin |
| no. 9 Mors | Pierre Garcet | Mellinger |
| no. 10 Fiat | Felice Nazzaro | Antonio Fagnano |
| no. 11 Clément-Bayard | Lucien Hautvast | Jean Chassagne |
| no. 12 Itala | Henry Fournier | Riva |
| no. 13 Lorraine-Dietrich | Vincenzo Trucco | Alfieri Maserati |
| no. 14 Mors | Landon | Bèche |
| no. 15 Fiat | Louis Wagner | Antonio Ferro |
| no. 16 Clément-Bayard | Fitch Shepard | Lehman |
| no. 17 Itala | Giovanni Piacenza | Cosso |

## Grand Prix of America—Savannah—November 1910

| car | driver | mechanic |
|---|---|---|
| no. 3 Marquette-Buick | Arthur Chevrolet | Albert Seraye |
| no. 4 Lozier | Ralph Mulford | Ed Chandler |
| no. 6 Pope-Toledo | Charlie Basle | his brother |
| no. 7 Alco | Harry Grant | Frank H. Lee |
| no. 8 Marmon | Joe Dawson | Bruce Keene |
| no. 9 Benz | Victor Hémery | Franz Heim |
| no. 10 Fiat | Felice Nazzaro | Antonio Fagnano |

## Grand Prix of America (cont.)

| car | driver | mechanic |
|---|---|---|
| no. 12 Lozier | Joe Horan | George Ainsley |
| no. 13 Pope-Hartford | Louis Disbrow | R. Church |
| no. 14 Marmon | Ray Harroun | Harry Goetz |
| no. 15 Benz | David Bruce-Brown | Fritz Craemer |
| no. 16 Fiat | Louis Wagner | Antonio Ferro |
| no. 17 Marquette-Buick | Bob Burman | Howard Hall |
| no. 18 Benz | Willie Haupt | Harris Feyhle |
| no. 19 Fiat | Ralph DePalma | Joe Pozzo |

# Appendix B: Technical Data

## Panhard

Daimler V-2 and Phénix-engined
Original engine design by Wilhelm Maybach
Production at Ivry under Mayade

| year of construction | 1894 | 1895 | 1896 | 1896 |
|---|---|---|---|---|
| cylinder | 16° V-2 | 2 | 2 | 4 |
| bore (mm) | 75 | 81 | 91 | 81 |
| stroke (mm) | 140 | 120 | 130 | 120 |
| displacement (liter) | 1.29 | 1.25 | 1.7 | 2.5 |
| output (hp) | 4 | 4 | 5.5 | 8 |
| at rpm | 600 | 700 | 700 | 800 |
| wheelbase (cm) | 138 | 150 | 165 | 200 |
| track front (cm) | 112 | 112 | 112 | 112 |
| track rear (cm) | 126 | 126 | 126 | 126 |
| tires front | 810 | 810 | 810 | 810 |
| tires rear (outer diameter mm) | 1110 | 1110 | 1110 | 1110 |
| dry weight (kg) | 650 | 605 | 650 | 800 |

The V-2 was also available in the dimensions of 60 mm × 100 mm, 62 mm × 106 mm, 67 mm × 108 mm, 72 mm × 126 mm, 72 mm × 140 mm and 75 mm × 146 mm; the two-cylinder Phénix in the dimensions of 66 mm × 104 mm, 67 mm × 108 mm and 75 mm × 120 mm.

The Cannstatt Phoenix car was available from 1897 as two-cylinder in the dimensions of 75 mm × 120 mm, 90 mm × 120 mm and 100 mm × 140 mm; from 1899 as four-cylinder in the dimensions of 70, 75, 84 and 100 mm × 120 mm, 90 mm × 140 mm and 102 mm × 150 mm.

## Peugeot

Design by Louis Rigoulot and Auguste Doriot

| year of construction | 1896 | 1897 | 1897 | 1898 | 1899 |
|---|---|---|---|---|---|
| cylinder | 2 | 2 | 2 | 2 | 2 |
| bore (mm) | 84 | 98 | 105 | 115 | 140 |
| stroke (mm) | 126 | 144 | 144 | 160 | 190 |
| displacement (liter) | 1.4 | 2.2 | 2.5 | 3.3 | 5.85 |
| output (hp) | 4.5 | 7 | 8 | 11 | 20 |
| at rpm | 700 | 700 | 700 | 800 | 800 |

## Mors

Design by Henri Brasier

| year of construction | 1897 | 1898 | 1899 | 1899 | 1900 | 1901 |
|---|---|---|---|---|---|---|
| cylinder | 2 | 90° V-4 | 4 | 4 | 4 | 4 |
| bore (mm) | 70 | 80 | 95 | 98 | 119 | 130 |
| stroke (mm) | 110 | 110 | 135 | 140 | 165 | 190 |
| displacement (liter) | 0.78 | 2.2 | 3.8 | 4.2 | 7.35 | 10 |
| ouput (hp) | 2.5 | 8 | 16 | 18 | 30 | 55 |
| at rpm | 700 | 700 | 900 | 900 | 1000 | 1000 |

## Panhard

Design by Émile Mayade and Arthur Krebs
two cast iron pairs, three main bearings

| year of construction | 1898 | 1899 | 1900 | 1901 |
|---|---|---|---|---|
| cylinder | 4 | 4 | 4 | 4 |
| bore (mm) | 94 | 96 | 110 | 130 |
| stroke (mm) | 132 | 138 | 138 | 140 |
| displacement (liter) | 3.65 | 4 | 5.25 | 7.4 |
| output (hp) | 14 | 16 | 24 | 40 |
| at rpm | 1000 | 1000 | 1000 | 1000 |
| wheelbase (cm) | 230 | 240 | 240 | 260 |
| track front (cm) | 120 | 135 | 135 | 135 |
| track rear (cm) | 135 | 135 | 135 | 135 |
| tires front(mm) | 900 × 65 | 900 × 65 | 870 × 90 | 870 × 90 |
| tires rear (mm) | 1100 × 90 | 1100 × 90 | 900 × 120 | 900 × 120 |
| dry weight (kg) | 900 | 950 | 1200 | 1250 |

## Panhard

Design by Arthur Krebs, steel cylinders, five main bearings, from 1903 with T-head

| year of construction | 1902 | 1903 | 1904 | 1905 | 1906 | 1907 | 1908 |
|---|---|---|---|---|---|---|---|
| cylinder | 4 | 4 | 4 | 4 | 4 | 4 | 4 |
| bore (mm) | 160 | 160 | 170 | 170 | 185 | 170 | 155 |
| stroke (mm) | 170 | 170 | 170 | 170 | 170 | 170 | 170 |
| displacement (liter) | 13.6 | 13.6 | 15.5 | 15.5 | 18.2 | 15.5 | 12.8 |
| output (hp) | 70 | 80 | 100 | 120 | 130 | 120 | 125 |
| wheelbase (cm) | 275 | 275 | 250 | 280 | 285 | 265 | 265 |

## Phoenix, Mercedes and Simplex

Design by Wilhelm Maybach and Josef Brauner
two cast-iron pairs, three main bearings, low-tension ignition from 1901 T-head

| year of construction | 1900—Phoenix | 1901—Mercedes | 1902—Simplex |
|---|---|---|---|
| cylinder | 4 | 4 | 4 |
| bore (mm) | 106 | 116 | 118 |
| stroke (mm) | 156 | 140 | 150 |
| displacement (liter) | 5.5 | 5.9 | 6.55 |
| output (hp) | 26 | 35 | 50 |
| at rpm | 950 | 1000 | 1200 |
| engine weight (kg) | 320 | 238 | 247 |
| wheelbase (cm) | 190 and 217 | 233 | 245 |

*Appendix B: Technical Data*

### Phoenix, Mercedes and Simplex (cont.)

| year of construction | 1900—Phoenix | 1901—Mercedes | 1902—Simplex |
|---|---|---|---|
| track (cm) | 128 | 140 | 145 |
| tires front (mm) | 910 × 90 | 910 × 90 | 870 or 910 × 90 |
| tires rear (mm) | 920 or 1020 × 120 | 920 or 1020 × 120 | 880 or 920 × 120 |
| dry weight (kg) | 1400 | 1050 (Nice) 1150 (Paris–Berlin) | 1000 |

## Mercedes

Sixty and Eighty (80, 80/90 hp or 90 hp)
Design by Wilhelm Maybach and Josef Brauner, F-head, one camshaft

| year of construction | 1903—Sixty | 1903—Eighty |
|---|---|---|
| cylinder | 4 | 4 |
| bore (mm) | 140 | 170 |
| stroke (mm) | 150 | 140 |
| displacement (liter) | 9.25 | 12.7 |
| output (hp) | 65 at 1100 | 85 at 1100 |
| at rpm | 70 at 1200 | 95 at 1200 |
| wheelbase (cm) | 260 or 275 | 260 |
| track (cm) | 140 | 145 |
| tires front (mm) | 910 × 90 | 910 × 90 |
| tires rear (mm) | 920 × 120 | 920 × 120 |
| dry weight (kg) | 1000 | 1000 |

Tires for the Eighty driven by de Caters: 870 mm × 90 mm front, 880 mm × 120 mm rear.

## Mercedes

95 hp and 125 hp Bennett cars
Design in 1904 by Wilhelm Maybach and Josef Brauner, in 1905 by Brauner alone
F-head, two camshafts, by the end of 1906 with detachable rims

| year of construction | 1904—95 hp | 1905/06—125 hp |
|---|---|---|
| cylinder | 4 | 4 |
| bore (mm) | 165 | originally: 175 × 146 |
| stroke (mm) | 140 | end of 1905: 175 × 150 |
|  |  | 1906: 185 × 150 |
| displacement (liter) | 12 | 14—14.4—16.1 |
| output (hp) | 98 at 1150 | 1905: 125 at 1300 |
| at rpm | 105 at 1380 | 1906: 130 at 1300 |
| wheelbase (cm) | 260 | 290 |
| track (cm) | 145 | 140 |
| tires front (mm) | 870 × 90 | 870 × 90 or 875 × 105 |
| tires rear (mm) | 880 × 120 | 880 × 120 |
| dry weight (kg) | 1000 | 1000 |

Tires for the Sultan of Jahore 95-hp: 910 mm × 90 mm front, 920 mm × 120 mm rear; for the Prince Alexis Orloff 95-hp: 920 mm × 120 mm front, 1000 mm × 150 mm rear.

## Mercedes

Design by Paul Daimler, Josef Brauner, Eugen Link and Karl Schnaitmann
F-head, two camshafts

| year of construction | 1907—130 hp | 1908—135 hp | 1909—sprint racer |
|---|---|---|---|
| cylinder | 4 | 4 | 4 |
| bore (mm) | 180 | 155 × 170 and | 175 |
| stroke (mm) | 150 | 155 × 180 | 180 |
| displacement (liter) | 15.3 | 12.8 and 13.6 | 17.3 |
| output (hp) | 120 | 135 | 170 |
| at rpm | 1200 | 1400 | 1400 |
| wheelbase (cm) | 285 | 270 | 270 |
| track (cm) | 140 | 140 | 140 |
| tires front (mm) | 875 × 105 | 875 × 105 | 875 × 105 |
| tires rear (mm) | 880 × 120 | 895 × 135 | 895 × 135 |
| dry weight (kg) | 1040 | 1150 | 1200 |

## Brasier

Design by Henri Brasier, L-head, three-speed gearbox, chain drive

| year of construction | 1904 | 1905 | 1906 | 1907 | 1908 |
|---|---|---|---|---|---|
| cylinder | 4 | 4 | 4 | 4 | 4 |
| bore (mm) | 150 | 160 | 165 | 165 | 155 |
| stroke (mm) | 140 | 140 | 150 | 140 | 160 |
| displacement (liter) | 9.8 | 11.25 | 12.8 | 12 | 12.1 |
| output (hp) | 80 | 96 | 105 | 105 | 119 |
| at rpm | 1200 | 1300 | 1380 | 1350 | 1350 |
| wheelbase (cm) | 260 | 265 | 275 | 265 | 265 |
| track (cm) | 125 | 125 | 135 | 125 | 130 |
| tires front (mm) | 815 × 105 | 875 × 105 | 870 × 90 | 875 × 105 | 875 × 105 |
| tires rear (mm) | 820 × 120 | 880 × 120 | 880 × 120 | 895 × 135 | 895 × 135 |
| dry weight (kg) | 950 | 1000 | 1000 | 1020 | 1184 |

## Renault

Design by Paul Viet, L-head, three-speed gearbox, shaft drive, no differential

| year of construction | 1905 | 1906 | 1907 | 1908 |
|---|---|---|---|---|
| cylinder | 4 | 4 | 4 | 4 |
| bore (mm) | 150 | 165 | 165 | 155 |
| stroke (mm) | 150 | 150 | 150 | 160 |
| displacement (liter) | 10.6 | 12.8 | 12.8 | 12.1 |
| output (hp) | 85 | 105 | 113 | 120 |
| at rpm | 1200 | 1200 | 1300 | 1400 |
| wheelbase (cm) | 280 | 280 | 285 | 270 |
| track (cm) | 135 | 135 | 135 | 130 |
| tires front (mm) | 870 × 90 | 870 × 90 | 870 × 90 | 875 × 105 |
| tires rear (mm) | 880 × 120 | 880 × 120 | 880 × 120 | 895 × 135 |
| dry weight (kg) | 1000 | 1000 | 1010 | 1151 |

# Darracq

Design by Paul Ribeyrolles, OHV head, one camshaft, vertical valves

| year of construction | 1904 | 1905 | 1906 | 1907 |
|---|---|---|---|---|
| cylinder | 4 | 4 | 4 | 4 |
| bore (mm) | 160 | 150 | 180 | 180 |
| stroke (mm) | 140 | 140 | 150 | 140 |
| displacement (liter) | 11.25 | 9.8 | 15.3 | 14.3 |
| output (hp) | 85 | 85 | 125 | 120 |
| at rpm | 1100 | 1200 | 1200 | 1300 |
| wheelbase (cm) | 250 | 240 | 285 | 250 |
| track (cm) | 130 | 135 | 135 | 135 |
| tires front (mm) | 810 × 90 | 870 × 90 | 870 × 90 | 870 × 90 |
| tires rear (mm) | 820 × 120 | 880 × 120 | 880 × 120 | 880 × 120 |
| dry weight (kg) | 950 | 1000 | 1000 | 1000 |

# Benz

Design by Hans Nibel, Georg Diehl and Louis de Groulart
OHV head, high-tension ignition,
GP engine with three main bearings, 21-liter with five main bearings

| year of construction | 1908–1911 GP Benz | 1909 Blitzen Benz |
|---|---|---|
| cylinder | 4 | 4 |
| bore (mm) | 155 × 160 or | 185 |
| stroke (mm) | 155 × 200 | 200 |
| displacement (liter) | 12.1 or 15.1 | 21.5 |
| output (hp) | short-stroke: 130 at 1600 | 184 at 1500 |
| at rpm | long-stroke: 158 at 1500 | 200 at 1600 |
| | in 1911: 175 at 1650 | in 1912: 225 at 1575 |
| wheelbase (cm) | 275 | 275 |
| track (cm) | 135 | 135 |
| tires front (mm) | 870 × 90 or 875 × 105 | 875 × 105 or 32" × 4" |
| tires rear (mm) | 895 × 135 or 935 × 135 | 895 × 135 or 34" × 5" |
| dry weight (kg) | 1245 | 1300 |

In 1908, two short-stroke (155 mm × 160 mm) and one long-stroke car (155 mm × 200 mm) were built for the Grand Prix.

In 1910 two new long-stroke cars were shipped to America, in 1911 one new car.

The Jumbo Benz dimensions of 200 mm × 250 mm are not confirmed by the factory. Between 1909 and 1913, one 21-liter was built per year.

At the end of 1913 an additional 21-liter in a 345-cm frame was delivered to Ghent.

# Mercedes

Design by Paul Daimler, Eugen Link and Karl Schnaitmann
three-valve OHV head, high-tension ignition, four main bearings

| year of construction | 1911<br>130-mm formula | 1913<br>450-cubic-inch formula |
|---|---|---|
| cylinder | 4 | 4 |
| bore (mm) | 130 | 114 |
| stroke (mm) | 180 | 180 |
| displacement (liter) | 9.5 | 7.35 |
| output (hp) | 90 at 1300 | 100 at 2000 |
| at rpm | 110 at 1600 | 120 at 2500 |

## Mercedes

| year of construction | 1911<br>130-mm formula | 1913<br>450-cubic-inch formula |
|---|---|---|
| wheelbase (cm) | 270 | 270 |
| track (cm) | 140 | 140 |
| tires front (mm) | 880 × 120 | 880 × 120 |
| tires rear (mm) | 895 × 135 | 895 × 135 |
| dry weight (kg) | 990 | 960 |

## Outstanding Engines 1908 to 1911

| make<br>year of construction | Sizaire et Naudin<br>1908 | Lion-Peugeot<br>1909 | Fiat S 61<br>1910 | Hispano-Suiza<br>1910 |
|---|---|---|---|---|
| cylinder | 1 | 1 | 4 | 4 |
| bore (mm) | 100 | 100 | 130 | 65 |
| stroke (mm) | 250 | 250 | 190 | 200 |
| output (hp) | 30 | 33 | 130 | 45 |
| at rpm | 2400 | 2400 | 1900 | 2500 |
| displacement (liter) | 1.96 | 1.96 | 10.08 | 2.65 |
| cylinder head | F-head | 6 horizontal valves | OHC 4 Valves | T-head |

| make<br>year of construction | Benz<br>Prince Henry<br>1910 | Austro-Daimler<br>Prince Henry<br>1910 | Lion-Peugeot<br>VX 5<br>1910 | Delage X<br>1911 |
|---|---|---|---|---|
| cylinder | 4 | 4 | 20° V-2 | 4 |
| bore (mm) | 115 | 105 | 80 | 80 |
| stroke (mm) | 175 | 165 | 280 | 149 |
| output (hp) | 104 | 95 | 40 | 60 |
| at rpm | 2050 | 2100 | 2200 | 2600 |
| displacement (liter) | 7.26 | 5.71 | 2.81 | 2.99 |
| cylinder head | OHV 4 valves | OHC | 3 valves | 2 hortizontal valves |

## Mercedes

entered in August 1913 in the GP de France at Le Mans
Design by Paul Daimler, Eugen Link and Karl Schnaitmann
steel cylinders, OHC two-valve head
last Mercedes chain-drive racers

| year of construction | 1913 | 1913 |
|---|---|---|
| cylinder | 4 | 6 |
| bore/stroke (mm) | 140 × 150 | 105 × 140 |
| displacement (liter) | 9.2 | 7.2 |
| cylinder head | OHC | OHC |
| output (hp) at rpm | 90 at 1150<br>120 at 1800 | 90 at 1350<br>120 at 2000 |
| wheelbase (cm) | 270 | 270 |
| track (cm) | 140 | 140 |
| tires front | 875 × 105 | 875 × 105 |
| tires rear (cm) | 895 × 135 | 895 × 135 |
| dry weight (kg) | 850 | 850 |

## 1914—1915 American Cars

| make | Mercer<br>1913 & 1914 | Duesenberg<br>1914 | Maxwell<br>1914 | Stutz<br>1915 | Maxwell<br>1915 |
|---|---|---|---|---|---|
| *engine* | | | | | |
| bore/stroke (inch) | 4.8 × 6.189 | 4.38 × 6 | 4.21 × 8 | 3.816 × 6.484 | 3.75 × 6.75 |
| bore/stroke (mm) | 122 × 157 | 112 × 152 | 107 × 204 | 97 × 165 | 95 × 172 |
| output (hp) at rpm | 130 at 2400 | 110 at 3000 | 140 at 2400 | 130 at 3000 | 125 at 3000 |
| displacement (liter) | 7.34 | 5.99 | 7.34 | 4.86 | 4.86 |
| cylinder head | T | 2 horizontal valves | OHC | OHC 4 valves | OHC 4 valves |
| *transmission* | | | | | |
| clutch | discs | cone | discs | discs | discs |
| speeds | 4 | 3 (at rear axle) | 4 | 4 | 4 |
| drive | shaft | shaft | shaft | shaft | shaft |
| *frame* | | | | | |
| wheelbase (cm) | 285 | 270 | 270 | 265 | 280 |
| track (cm) | 135 | 135 | 140 | 135 | 140 |
| tires front (inch) | 33" × 4.5" | 33" × 4.5" | 33"× 4.5" | 33" × 4.5" | 33" × 4.5" |
| tires rear (inch) | 35" × 5" | 35" × 5" | 34" × 4.5" | 33" × 5" | 33" × 5" |
| dry weight (kg) | 1225 | 890 | 1060 | 1070 | 1110 |

The Mercer started in the 300-cubic-inch class with the dimensions of 4.37" × 5" = 111 mm × 127 mm.

## 1906—I

The cars are arranged according to the best laps times in the Grand Prix:

| make | Brasier | Lorraine-Dietrich | Renault | F.I.A.T. | Mercedes |
|---|---|---|---|---|---|
| *best lap—driver* | | | | | |
| Le Mans (103 km) | 52:19—Baras | 52:32—Duray | 53:03—Szisz | 53:08—Weill-Schott | 55:23—Jenatzy |
| Ardennes (85 km) | 48:57—Barillier | 45:59—Duray | | | 46:39—Salzer |
| Long Island (44 km) | | 26:50—Duray | | 27:57—Nazzaro | 28:05—Jenatzy |
| *loss of time (sec/km)* | | | | | |
| Le Mans | 0 | 0.13 | 0.43 | 0.47 | 1.77 |
| Ardennes | 2.44 | 0.35 | | | 0.82 |
| Long Island | | 0 | | 1.52 | 1.7 |
| *engine* | | | | | |
| bore/stroke (mm) | 165 × 150 | 185 × 160 | 165 × 150 | 180 × 160 | 185 × 150 |
| output (hp) at rpm | 105 at 1380 | 130 at 1100 | 105 at 1200 | 135 at 1300 | 130 at 1300 |
| displacement (liter) | 12.82 | 17.19 | 12.82 | 16.27 | 16.1 |
| cylinder head | L | T | L | OHV | F |
| *transmission* | | | | | |
| clutch | cone | cone | cone | discs | scroll |
| speeds | 3 | 4 | 3 | 4 | 4 |
| drive | chain | chain | shaft | chain | chain |
| *frame* | | | | | |
| wheelbase (cm) | 275 | 295 | 280 | 290 | 290 |
| track (cm) | 135 | 140 | 135 | 135 | 140 |
| tires front (mm) | 870 × 90 | 870 × 90 | 870 × 90 | 875 × 105 | 875 × 105 |
| tires rear (mm) | 880 × 120 | 880 × 120 | 880 × 120 | 880 × 120 | 880 × 120 |
| dry weight (kg) | 1000 | 1000 | 1000 | 1000 | 1000 |

## 1906—II

| make | Panhard & Levassor | Darracq | Hotchkiss | Clément-Bayard |
|---|---|---|---|---|
| *best lap—driver* | | | | |
| Le Mans (103 km) | 55:28—Tart | 55:39—Hémery | 56:31—Shepard | 56:31—Clément |
| Ardennes (85 km) | | 45:29—Hémery | | 48:05—Clément |
| Long Island (44 km) | | 27:22—Wagner | | 27:02—Clément |
| *loss of time (sec/km)* | | | | |
| Le Mans | 1.83 | 2 | 2.5 | 2.5 |
| Ardennes | | 0 | | 1.84 |
| Long Island | | 0.73 | | 0.27 |
| *engine* | | | | |
| bore/stroke (mm) | 185 × 170 | 180 × 150 | 180 × 160 | 160 × 160 |
| output (hp) at rpm | 130 at 1100 | 125 at 1200 | 120 at 1100 | 105 at 1200 |
| displacement (liter) | 18.26 | 15.26 | 16.21 | 12.86 |
| cylinder head | T | OHV | F | T |
| *transmission* | | | | |
| clutch | Hele-Shaw (discs) | cone | cone | discs |
| speeds | 4 | 3 | 4 | 3 |
| drive | shaft | shaft | shaft | shaft |
| *frame* | | | | |
| wheelbase (cm) | 280 | 285 | 265 | 290 |
| track (cm) | 135 | 135 | 145 | 135 |
| tires front (mm) | 870 × 90 | 870 × 90 | 870 × 90 | 870 × 90 |
| tires rear (mm) | 880 × 120 | 880 × 120 wire wheels | 880 × 120 wire wheels | 875 × 105 |
| dry weight (kg) | 1000 | 1000 | 1000 | 1000 |

## 1906—III

| make | Gobron-Brillié | Itala | Grégoire | Vulpès |
|---|---|---|---|---|
| *best lap—driver* | | | | |
| Le Mans (103 km) | 59:15—Rigolly | 1:23:32—Cagno | retirement first lap | did not start |
| Ardennes (85 km) | | | | |
| Long Island (44 km) | | | | |
| *loss of time (sec/km)* | | | | |
| Le Mans | 4.04 | | | |
| Ardennes | | | | |
| Long Island | | | | |
| *engine* | | | | |
| bore/stroke (mm) | 140 × 220 | 180 × 145 | 140 × 130 | 180 × 150 |
| output (hp) at rpm | 110 at 1200 | 110 at 1250 | 70 at 1200 | 120 at 1200 |
| displacement (liter) | 13.53 | 14.75 | 8 | 15.26 |
| cylinder head | L | F | OHV | F |
| *transmission* | | | | |
| clutch | Hérisson (band) | discs | cone | discs |
| speeds | 4 | 3 | 3 | 3 |
| drive | chain | shaft | shaft | chain |
| *frame* | | | | |
| wheelbase (cm) | 300 | 295 | 225 | 290 |
| track (cm) | 140 | 140 | 120 | 135 |
| tires front (mm) | 870 × 90 | 870 × 90 | 870 × 90 | 870 × 90 |
| tires rear (mm) | 880 × 120 | 880 × 120 | 880 × 120 | 880 × 120 |
| dry weight (kg) | 1000 | 1000 | 850 | 1000 |

In the case of Lorraine-Dietrich, F.I.A.T., Darracq, Hotchkiss, Itala and Vulpès the outputs have been measured by the Commission Sportive.

## 1907—I

| make | Fiat | Brasier | Lorraine-Dietrich | Renault |
|---|---|---|---|---|
| *best lap—driver* | | | | |
| Dieppe (77 km) | 38:16—Nazzaro | 38:22—Barillier | 39:00—Duray | 39:05—Szisz |
| loss of time (sec/km) | 0 | 0.08 | 0.57 | 0.63 |
| *engine* | | | | |
| bore/stroke (mm) | 180 × 160 | 165 × 140 | 180 × 170 | 165 × 150 |
| output (hp) at rpm | 135 at 1300 | 105 at 1350 | 127 at 1100 | 113 at 1300 |
| displacement (liter) | 16.27 | 11.96 | 17.29 | 12.82 |
| cylinder head | OHV | L | T | L |
| *transmission* | | | | |
| clutch | discs | cone | band | cone |
| speeds | 4 | 3 | 4 | 3 |
| drive | chain | chain | chain | shaft |
| *frame* | | | | |
| wheelbase (cm) | 290 | 265 | 270 | 285 |
| track (cm) | 135 | 125 | 137 | 125 |
| tires front | 875 × 105 | 875 × 105 | 875 × 105 | 870 × 90 |
| tires rear (mm) | 880 × 120 | 895 × 135 | 935 × 135 | 880 × 120 |
| dry weight (kg) | 1060 | 1020 | 1080 | 1010 |

## 1907—II

| make | Clément-Bayard | Mercedes | Darracq | Panhard & Levassor |
|---|---|---|---|---|
| *best lap—driver* | | | | |
| Dieppe (77 km) | 39:07—Garcet | 39:08—Jenatzy | 40:28—Hanriot | 42:01—Le Blon |
| loss of time (sec/km) | 0.64 | 0.70 | 1.72 | 2.9 |
| *engine* | | | | |
| bore/stroke (mm) | 160 × 160 | 180 × 150 | 180 × 140 | 170 × 170 |
| output (hp) at rpm | 105 at 1200 | 120 at 1200 | 120 at 1300 | 120 at 1100 |
| displacement (liter) | 12.86 | 15.26 | 14.24 | 15.42 |
| cylinder head | T | F | OHV | T |
| *transmission* | | | | |
| clutch | discs | scroll | cone | discs (Hele-Shaw) |
| speeds | 3 | 4 | 3 | 4 |
| drive | shaft | chain | shaft | shaft |
| *frame* | | | | |
| wheelbase (cm) | 283 | 285 | 250 | 265 |
| track (cm) | 135 | 140 | 135 | 135 |
| tires front | 870 × 90 | 875 × 105 | 870 × 90 | 870 × 90 |
| tires rear (mm) | 880 × 120 | 880 × 120 | 880 × 120 | 880 × 120 |
| dry weight (kg) | 1000 | 1040 | 1000 | 1080 |

## 1907—III

| make | Gobron-Brillié | Motobloc | Weigel | Germain |
|---|---|---|---|---|
| *best lap—driver* | | | | |
| Dieppe (77 km) | 43:16—Rigolly | 45:36—Pierron | 46:37—Harrison | 47:47—Degrais |
| loss of time (sec/km) | 3.9 | 5.7 | 6.5 | 7.4 |
| *engine* | | | | |
| bore/stroke (mm) | 140 × 220—double piston | 165 × 140 | 8 × 120 × 140 | 102 × 110 |
| output (hp) at rpm | 110 at 1200 | 90 at 1200 | 85 at 900 | 45 at 1800 |
| displacement (liter) | 13.53 | 11.96 | 12.66 | 4.33 |
| cylinder head | L | F | L | T |
| *transmission* | | | | |
| clutch | Hérisson (band) | band | cone | cone |
| speeds | 4 | 4 | 3 | 3 |
| drive | chain | chain | shaft | shaft |
| *frame* | | | | |
| wheelbase (cm) | 300 | 278 | 290 | 266 |
| track (cm) | 140 | 130 | 130 | 124 |

Appendix B: Technical Data

## 1907—III (cont.)

| make | Gobron-Brillié | Motobloc | Weigel | Germain |
|---|---|---|---|---|
| tires front (mm) | 870 × 90 | 870 × 90 | 870 × 90 | 810 × 90 |
| tires rear (mm) | 880 × 120 | 880 × 120 | 880 × 120 | 815 × 105 |
| dry weight (kg) | 1000 | 1100 | 1200 | 900 |

## 1907—IV

| make | Christie | Porthos | Corre-La Licorne | Dufaux |
|---|---|---|---|---|
| best lap—driver | | | | |
| Dieppe (77 km) | 48:19—Christie | 51:41—Stricker | 52:14—Collomb | 53:32—Dufaux |
| loss of time (sec/km) | 7.8 | 10.5 | 10.9 | 11.9 |
| engine | | | | |
| bore/stroke (mm) | V-4 × 184 × 184 | 8 × 120 × 120 | 150 × 150 | 8 × 125 × 150 |
| output (hp) at rpm | 130 at 1000 | 80 at 1000 | 80 at 1200 | 90 at 900 |
| displacement (liter) | 19.56 | 10.85 | 10.59 | 14.71 |
| cylinder head | automatic intake | T | L | L |
| transmission | | | | |
| clutch | cone | cone | cone | discs |
| speeds | 2 | 4 | 3 | 3 |
| drive | front wheel drive | shaft | shaft | chain |
| frame | | | | |
| wheelbase (cm) | 255 | 295 | 280 | 290 |
| track (cm) | 135 | 135 | 140 | 135 |
| tires front (mm) | 880 × 120 | 870 × 90 | 875 × 105 | 870 × 90 |
| tires rear (mm) | 875 × 105 | 870 × 90 | 880 × 120 | 880 × 120 |
| dry weight (kg) | 1200 | 1200 | 1000 | 1100 |

Aquila entered a production type (130/140 mm), but did not start.

## 1908—I

| make | Mercedes | Brasier | Renault | Fiat SB 4 | Clément-Bayard |
|---|---|---|---|---|---|
| best lap—driver | | | | | |
| Dieppe (77 km) | 36:31—Salzer | 36:40—Bablot | 37:06—Szisz | 37:13—Wagner | 37:28—Rigal |
| Bologna (52.88 km) | | | | 23:24—Lancia | 24:40—Gabriel |
| Savannah (43 km) | | | 22:12—Szisz | 21:36—DePalma | 22:59—Hautvast |
| loss of time (sec/km) | | | | | |
| Dieppe | 0 | 0.11 | 0.45 | 0.55 | 0.74 |
| Bologna | | | | 0 | 1.43 |
| Savannah | | | 0.84 | 0 | 1.93 |
| engine | | | | | |
| bore/stroke (mm) | 155 × 170 and 155 × 180 | 155 × 160 | 155 × 160 | 155 × 160 and 155 × 175 | 155 × 185 |
| output (hp) at rpm | 135 at 1400 | 119 at 1350 | 120 at 1400 | 135 at 1400 | 138 at 1450 |
| displacement (liter) | 12.83–13.59 | 12.08 | 12.08 | 12.08–13.21 | 13.96 |
| cylinder head | F | L | L | OHV | OHC |
| transmission | | | | | |
| clutch | scroll | cone | cone | discs | discs |
| speeds | 4 | 3 | 3 | 4 | 4 |
| drive | chain | chain | shaft | chain | shaft |
| frame | | | | | |
| wheelbase (cm) | 270 | 265 | 270 | 275 | 275 |
| track (cm) | 140 | 130 | 130 | 135 | 130 |
| tires front (mm) | 875 × 105 | 875 × 105 | 875 × 105 | 875 × 105 | 875 × 105 |
| tires rear (mm) | 895 × 135 | 895 × 135 | 895 × 135 | 895 × 135 | 895 × 135 |
| dry weight (kg) | 1151 | 1184 | 1151 | 1205 | 1204 |

Additional weight at the start: 250 kg fuel and water, 50 kg tools and spare parts, 80 kg tires, altogether 380 kg.

## 1908—II

| make | Lorraine-Dietrich | Benz | Itala | Panhard & Levassor |
|---|---|---|---|---|
| *best lap—driver* | | | | |
| Dieppe (77 km) | 37:55—Duray | 37:55—Hémery | 38:55—Fournier | 39:37—Cissac |
| Bologna (52.88 km) | 24:15—Minoia | | 24:58—Fournier | |
| Savannah (43 km) | 23:07—Duray | 21:52—Hanriot | 22:47—Cagno | |
| *loss of time (sec/km)* | | | | |
| Dieppe | 1.09 | 1.09 | 1.87 | 2.41 |
| Bologna | 0.96 | | 1.77 | |
| Savannah | 2.1 | 0.37 | 1.65 | |
| *engine* | | | | |
| bore/stroke (mm) | 155 × 180 | 155 × 160 and 155 × 200 | 155 × 160 | 155 × 170 |
| output (hp) at rpm | 135 at 1400 | 130 at 1600 resp. 158 at 1500 | 120 at 1400 | 125 at 1300 |
| displacement (liter) | 13.59 | 12.08—15.10 | 12.08 | 12.83 |
| *transmission* | | | | |
| clutch | discs | cone | discs | discs (Hele-Shaw) |
| speeds | 4 | 4 | 3 | 4 |
| drive | chain | chain | shaft | chain |
| *frame* | | | | |
| wheelbase (cm) | 271 | 275 | 295 | 265 |
| track (cm) | 130 | 135 | 140 | 130 |
| tires front (mm) | 870 × 90 | 870 × 90 | 875 × 105 | 870 × 90 |
| tires rear (mm) | 880 × 120 | 835 × 135 | 895 × 135 | 880 × 120 |
| dry weight (kg) | 1285 | 1243 | 1414 | 1224 |

## 1908—III

| make | Mors | Weigel | Opel | Motobloc |
|---|---|---|---|---|
| *best lap—driver* | | | | |
| Dieppe (77 km) | 40:13—Landon | 40:29—Laxen | 41:14—Joerns | 41:28—Garcet |
| Bologna (52.88 km) | 25:39—Garcet | | | 28:15—Gauderman |
| Savannah (43 km) | | | | |
| *loss of time (sec/km)* | | | | |
| Dieppe | 2.88 | 3.1 | 3.75 | 3.85 |
| Bologna | 2.55 | | | 5.5 |
| Savannah | | | | |
| *engine* | | | | |
| bore/stroke (mm) | 155 × 170 | 155 × 170 | 155 × 160 | 155 × 170 |
| output (hp) at rpm | 120 at 1300 | 115 at 1300 | 115 at 1300 | 120 at 1300 |
| displacement (liter) | 12.83 | 12.83 | 12.08 | 12.83 |
| cylinder head | OHV | OHC | F | F |
| *transmission* | | | | |
| clutch | band | cone | cone | band |
| speeds | 3 | 4 | 4 | 4 |
| drive | chain | shaft | shaft | shaft |
| *frame* | | | | |
| wheelbase (cm) | 263 | 290 | 265 | 264 |
| track (cm) | 126 | 130 | 135 | 130 |
| tires front (mm) | 875 × 105 | 870 × 90 | 875 × 105 | 870 × 90 |
| tires rear (mm) | 895 × 135 | 880 × 120 | 880 × 120 | 880 × 120 |
| dry weight (kg) | 1250 | 1395 | 1169 | 1264 |

## 1908—IV

| make | Porthos | Austin | Germain | Thomas |
|---|---|---|---|---|
| *best lap—driver* | | | | |
| Dieppe (77 km) | 43:21—Stricker | 43:45—Wright | 44:40—Roch-Brault | 54:34—Strang |
| Bologna (52.88 km) | | | | |
| Savannah (43 km) | | | | |

## 1908—IV (cont.)

| make | Porthos | Austin | Germain | Thomas |
|---|---|---|---|---|
| loss of time (sec/km) | | | | |
| Dieppe | 5.25 | 5.63 | 6.35 | 14 |
| Bologna | | | | |
| Savannah | | | | |
| *engine* | | | | |
| bore/stroke (mm) | 6 × 120 × 127 | 6 × 127 × 127 | 155 × 170 | 155 × 150 |
| output (hp) at rpm | 90 at 1500 | 90 at 1500 | 110 at 1200 | 80 at 1200 |
| displacement (liter) | 8.61 | 9.58 | 12.83 | 11.32 |
| cylinder head | T | T | T | |
| *transmission* | | | | |
| clutch | cone | cone | band | discs |
| speeds | 3 | 4 | 3 | 4 |
| drive | shaft | shaft | chain | chain |
| *frame* | | | | |
| wheelbase (cm) | 270 | 275 | 305 | 275 |
| track (cm) | 120 | 135 | 135 | 135 |
| tires front (mm) | 875 × 105 | 875 × 105 | 870 × 90 | 875 × 105 |
| tires rear (mm) | 880 × 120 | 880 × 120 | 880 × 120 | 880 × 120 |
| dry weight (kg) | 1102 | 1340 | 1164 | 1228 |

## 1912—I

| make | Fiat S 74 | Peugeot EX 1/L 76 | Lorraine-Dietrich |
|---|---|---|---|
| *best lap—driver* | | | |
| Dieppe (77 km) | 37:18—Bruce-Brown | 37:35—Boillot | 39—Hémery |
| loss of time (sec/km) | 0 | 0.22 | 1.32 |
| *engine* | | | |
| bore/stroke (mm) | 150 × 200 | 110 × 200 | 155 × 200 |
| output (hp) at rpm | 160 at 1600 | 135 at 2200 | 160 at 1500 |
| displacement (liter) | 14.14 | 7.60 | 15.10 |
| cylinder head | OHC 4 valves | DOHC 4 valves | OHV |
| *transmission* | | | |
| clutch | discs | discs | cone |
| speeds | 4 | 4 | 4 |
| drive | chain | shaft | chain |
| *frame* | | | |
| wheelbase (cm) | 272 | 275 | 275 |
| track (cm) | 135 | 135 | 135 |
| tires front (mm) | 875 × 105 | 875 × 105 | 875 × 105 |
| tires rear (mm) | 895 × 135 | 895 × 135 | 935 × 135 |
| dry weight (kg) | 1150 | 1000 | 1250 |

## 1912—II

| make | Excelsior | Rolland-Pilain | Mathis |
|---|---|---|---|
| *best lap—driver* | | | |
| Dieppe (77 km) | 40:34—Christiaens | 42:43—Fauquet | 56—Esser |
| loss of time (sec/km) | 2.54 | 4.22 | 14.3 |
| *engine* | | | |
| bore/stroke (mm) | 6 × 110 × 160 | 110 × 165 | 70 × 120 |
| output (hp) at rpm | 125 at 2000 | 75 at 2000 | 30 at 3000 |
| displacement (liter) | 9.10 | 6.27 | 1.85 |
| cylinder head | L | OHC 4 valves | L |
| *transmission* | | | |
| clutch | cone | cone | discs |
| speeds | 4 | 4 | 4 |
| drive | shaft | chain | shaft |

## 1912—II (cont.)

| make | Excelsior | Rolland-Pilain | Mathis |
|---|---|---|---|
| *frame* | | | |
| wheelbase (cm) | 280 | 265 | 240 |
| track (cm) | 137 | 135 | 117 |
| tires front (mm) | 815 × 105 | 875 × 105 | 760 × 100 |
| tires rear (mm) | 815 × 105 | 880 × 120 | 760 × 100 |
| dry weight (kg) | 1220 | 1050 | 660 |

## 1912—III

Engine data three-liter class – all cars with shaft drive

| make | bore/stroke (mm) | output (hp) at rpm | cylinder head |
|---|---|---|---|
| Sunbeam | 80 × 149 | 70 at 3000 | L |
| Vauxhall | 90 × 118 | 70 at 3100 | L |
| Alcyon | 85 × 132 | 65 at 2700 | OHV 4 valves |
| Grégoire | 80 × 149 | 70 at 3000 | T |
| Lion-Peugeot | 78 × 156 | 65 at 2500 | DOHC 4 valves |
| Singer | 85 × 132 | 65 at 2800 | F 3 valves |
| Théophile Schneider | 80 × 149 | 65 at 2800 | sleeve |
| Sizaire et Naudin | 78 × 156 | 70 at 3000 | 4 horizontal valves |
| Vinot-Deguingand | 89 × 120 | 60 at 2400 | F |
| Calthorpe | 80 × 149 | 60 at 2300 | L |
| Arrol-Johnston | 80 × 149 | 55 at 2100 | L |
| Côte | 85 × 132 | 50 at 2100 | two-cycle |
| *did not start:* | | | |
| Hispano-Suiza | 85 × 132 | 95 at 3000 | OHC—with piston compressor |
| Koechlin | 85 × 132 | 55 at 2200 | sleeve—two-cycle |

## 1913—I

| make | Delage Y | Peugeot EX 3/L 56 | Sunbeam | Théophile Schneider |
|---|---|---|---|---|
| *best lap—driver* | | | | |
| Amiens (31.4 km) | 15:17—Bablot | 15:24—Boillot | 16:07—Chassagne | |
| *loss of time (sec/km)* | 0 | 0.22 | 1.59 | |
| *engine* | | | | |
| bore/stroke (mm) | 105 × 180 | 100 × 180 | 6 × 80 × 150 | 96 × 190 |
| output (hp) at rpm | 115 at 2500 | 110 at 2500 | 100 at 3000 | 90 at 2500 |
| displacement (liter) | 6.23 | 5.66 | 4.53 | 5.39 |
| cylinder head | 4 horizontal valves | DOHC 4 valves | L | L |
| *transmission* | | | | |
| clutch | discs | cone | cone | cone |
| speeds | 5 | 4 | 4 | 4 |
| drive | shaft | shaft | shaft | shaft |
| wheelbase (cm) | 275 | 270 | 300 | 280 |
| track (cm) | 130 | 135 | 137 | 140 |
| tires front (mm) | 875 × 105 | 875 × 105 | 875 × 105 | 875 × 105 |
| tires rear (mm) | 880 × 120 | 895 × 135 | 880 × 120 | 880 × 120 |
| dry weight (kg) | 1030 | 1040 | 1070 | 1090 |

## 1913—II

| make | Excelsior | Opel | Itala | Mathis |
|---|---|---|---|---|
| *engine* | | | | |
| bore/stroke (mm) | 6 × 90 × 160 | 90 × 156 | 125 × 170 | 70 × 140 |
| output (hp) at rpm | 85 at 2000 | 80 at 2800 | 90 at 2000 | 40 at 3000 |
| displacement (liter) | 6.10 | 3.96 | 8.36 | 2.16 |
| cylinder head | L | OHC | rotary valves | L |
| *transmission* | | | | |
| clutch | cone | cone | discs | discs |
| speeds | 4 | 4 | 4 | 4 |
| drive | shaft | shaft | shaft | shaft |
| *frame* | | | | |
| wheelbase (cm) | 265 | 270 | 300 | 245 |
| track (cm) | 130 | 135 | 135 | 130 |
| tires front (mm) | 875 × 105 | 875 × 105 | 875 × 105 | 760 × 100 |
| tires rear (mm) | 880 × 120 | 880 × 120 | 880 × 120 | 760 × 100 |
| dry weight (kg) | 1005 | 842 | 1099 | 820 |

## 1914—I

| make | Mercedes M 93654 | Peugeot EX 5/L 45 | Sunbeam | Delage S | Fiat S 57-14 B |
|---|---|---|---|---|---|
| *best lap—driver* | | | | | |
| Lyon (37.6 km) | 20:06—Sailer | 20:20—Boillot | 20:31—Resta | 20:57—Duray | 21:30—Fagnano |
| *loss of time (sec/km)* | 0 | 0.37 | 0.66 | 1.35 | 2.23 |
| *engine* | | | | | |
| bore/stroke (mm) | 93 × 165 | 92 × 169 | 94 × 160 | 94 × 160 | 100 × 143 |
| output (hp) at rpm | 115 at 2800 | 115 at 3000 | 110 at 3000 | 115 at 3000 | 110 at 3100 |
| displacement (liter) | 4.49 | 4.49 | 4.45 | 4.45 desmo | 4.49 |
| cylinder head | OHC 4V | DOHC 4V | DOHC 4V | DOHC 4V | OHC |
| intake/exhaust (mm) | 43/40.5 | 52/46 | 46/46 | 48/46 | 60/60 |
| valve angle | 30° | 30° | 30° | 45° | 30° |
| *transmission* | | | | | |
| clutch | double cone | cone | cone | discs | discs |
| speeds | 4 | 4 | 4 | 5—direct third | 4 |
| drive | shaft | shaft | shaft | shaft | shaft |
| *frame* | | | | | |
| wheelbase (cm) | 285 | 270 | 280 | 270 | 275 |
| track (cm) | 132 | 135 | 140 | 135 | 135 |
| tires front (mm) | 820 × 120 | 875 × 105 | 875 × 105 | 875 × 105 | 875 × 105 |
| tires rear (mm) | 835 × 135 | 880 × 120 | 880 × 120 | 895 × 135 | 880 × 120 |
| dry weight (kg) | 930 | 1000 | 1020 | 1070 | 1110 |

## 1914—II

| make | Nagant | Alda | Opel | Théophile Schneider |
|---|---|---|---|---|
| *best lap—driver* | | | | |
| Lyon (37.6 km) | 21:58—Esser | 22:03—Szisz | 22:13—Breckheimer | 23:04—Champoiseau |
| *loss of time (sec/km)* | 2.98 | 3.11 | 3.38 | 4.8 |
| *engine* | | | | |
| bore/stroke (mm) | 94.5 × 158 | 94 × 160 | 94 × 160 | 94 × 160 |
| output (hp) at rpm | 105 at 2800 | 100 at 2800 | 100 at 2800 | 100 at 2800 |
| displacement (liter) | 4.44 | 4.45 | 4.45 | 4.45 |
| cylinder head | DOHC 4V | OHC 4V | OHC 4V | desmo OHC |
| intake/exhaust (mm) | 45/44 | 44/42.5 | 42/42 | 60/60 |
| valve angle | 30° | 15° | 30° | 10° |

## 1914—II (cont.)

| make | Nagant | Alda | Opel | Théophile Schneider |
|---|---|---|---|---|
| *transmission* | | | | |
| clutch | discs | cone | cone | cone |
| speeds | 5 | 4 | 4 | 4 |
| drive | shaft | shaft | shaft | shaft |
| *frame* | | | | |
| wheelbase (cm) | 280 | 270 | 280 | 280 |
| track (cm) | 135 | 135 | 135 | 140 |
| tires front (mm) | 875 × 105 | 870 × 90 | 875 × 105 | 870 × 90 |
| tires rear (mm) | 880 × 120 | 880 × 120 | 880 × 120 | 880 × 120 |
| dry weight (kg) | 1110 | 1110 | 1110 | 1110 |

## 1914—III

| make | Nazzaro | Piccard-Pictet | Vauxhall | Aquila |
|---|---|---|---|---|
| *best lap—driver* | | | | |
| Lyon (37.6 km) | 23:39—Nazzaro | 24:04—Tournier | 25:31—DePalma | 30:49—Costantini |
| *loss of time (sec/km)* | 5.75 | 6.38 | 8.6 | 17.3 |
| *engine* | | | | |
| bore/stroke (mm) | 94 × 160 | 97 × 150 | 101 × 140 | 6 × 85 × 132 |
| output (hp) at rpm | 95 at 2800 | 100 at 3000 | 95 at 2900 | 90 at 3000 |
| displacement (liter) | 4.45 | 4.44 | 4.49 | 4.498 |
| cylinder head | OHC 4V | sleeve Argyl-Burt/McCollum system | DOHC 4V | OHC |
| intake/exhaust (mm) | | | 46/44 | 60/55 |
| valve angle | | | 9° | |
| *transmission* | | | | |
| clutch | discs | discs | cone | discs |
| speeds | 4 | 4 | 4 | 4 |
| drive | shaft | shaft | shaft | shaft |
| *frame* | | | | |
| wheelbase (cm) | 275 | 265 | 270 | 286 |
| track (cm) | 135 | 132 | 135 | 148 |
| tires front (mm) | 875 × 105 | 875 × 105 | 875 × 105 | 820 × 120 |
| tires rear (mm) | 880 × 120 | 880 × 120 | 880 × 120 | 820 × 120 |
| dry weight (kg) | 1120 | 1110 | 1120 | 1160 |

# Appendix C: Race Results

### Nice–Aix–Senas–Salon–Nice— 25 March 1901—462.6 km

| driver | make | time | |
|---|---|---|---|
| 1. Werner | Mercedes | 6:45:48 | |
| 2. Demeester | Gladiator | 6:54:56 | tricycle |
| 3. Gleizes | De Dion | 7:11:41 | tricycle |
| 4. Degrais | Rochet-Schneider | 7:11:58 | |
| 5. de Caters | Mors | 7:14:5 | |
| 6. Schneider | Rochet-Schneider | 7:21:54 | |
| 7. Osmont | De Dion | 7:24:14 | tricycle |
| 8. Loraine Barrow | Mercedes | 7:24:40 | |

### Paris–Vienna— 26 to 29 June 1902—1120 km

| | | | |
|---|---|---|---|
| 1. Marcel Renault | Renault | 26:22:43 | 650 kg |
| 2. Henry Farman | Panhard | 26:36:30 | |
| 3. Edmond | Darracq | 26:45:10 | 650 kg |
| 4. Zborowski | Mercedes | 26:48:9 | |
| 5. Maurice Farman | Panhard | 26:54:29 | |
| 6. Baras | Darracq | 27:39:50 | 650 kg |
| 7. Teste | Panhard | 27:48:38 | |
| 8. Hémery | Darracq | 27:58:38 | 650 kg |
| 9. Marcellin | Darracq | 28:13:30 | 650 kg |
| 10. de Crawhez | Panhard | 28:40:20 | |

### Circuit des Ardennes— 30 July 1902—Bastogne— 6 x 85.4 km (512.4 km)

| | | |
|---|---|---|
| 1. Jarrott | Panhard | 5:33:39 |
| 2. Gabriel | Mors | 6:2:45 |
| 3. Vanderbilt | Mors | 6:22 |
| 4. Zborowski | Mercedes | 6:46:40 |
| 5. Girardot | CGV | 6:55:55 |
| 6. Heath | Panhard | 6:57:3 |

### Paris–Madrid—stopped at Bordeaux—24 May 1903—552 km

| | | | |
|---|---|---|---|
| 1. Gabriel | Mors | 5:13:31 | |
| 2. Louis Renault | Renault | 5:33:59 | 650 kg |
| 3. Salleron | Mors | 5:46:1 | |
| 4. Jarrott | De Dietrich | 5:51:55 | |
| 5. Warden | Mercedes | 5:56:30 | |
| 6. de Crawhez | Panhard | 6:1:8 | |
| 7. Voigt | CGV | 6:1:9 | |
| 8. Gastaud | Mercedes | 6:8 | |
| 9. Achille Fournier | Mors | 6:11:39 | |
| 10. Baras | Darracq | 6:12:49 | 650 kg |
| 11. Rougier | Turcat-Méry | 6:16:7 | |
| 12. Mouter | De Dietrich | 6:17:54 | |
| 13. Jenatzy | Mercedes | 6:24:8 | |
| 14. Max | Mercedes | 6:39:35 | |

### Gordon Bennett Cup— 2 July 1903—Ballyshannon— 4 x 83 km + 3 x 64 km (524 km)

| | | | |
|---|---|---|---|
| 1. Jenatzy | Mercedes | 6:39 | (79.162 km/h) |
| 2. de Knyff | Panhard | 6:50:40 | |
| 3. Henry Farman | Panhard | 6:51:44 | |
| 4. Gabriel | Mors | 7:11:33 | |
| 5. Edge | Napier | 9:18:48 | |

### Gordon Bennett Cup— 17 June 1904—Bad Homburg— 4 x 127.2 km (508.8 km)

| | | | |
|---|---|---|---|
| 1. Théry | Richard-Brasier | 5:50:1 | (87.24 km/h) |
| 2. Jenatzy | Mercedes | 6:1:29 | |
| 3. Rougier | Turcat-Méry | 6:47:9 | |
| 4. de Caters | Mercedes | 6:47:30 | |
| 5. Braun | Austro-Mercedes | 6:59:47 | |
| 6. Hautvast | Pipe | 7:2:35 | |
| 7. Salleron | Mors | 7:15:14 | |
| 8. Lancia | F.I.A.T. | 7:17:51 | |
| 9. Girling | Wolseley | 7:22:53 | |
| 10. Cagno | F.I.A.T. | 7:23:34 | |
| 11. Werner | Austro-Mercedes | 7:32:13 | |
| 12. Jarrott | Wolseley | 7:36:50 | |

### Gordon Bennett Cup— 5 July 1905—Clermont-Ferrand— 4 x 137.5 km (550 km)

| | | | |
|---|---|---|---|
| 1. Théry | Brasier | 7:2:42 | (78.42 km/h) |
| 2. Nazzaro | F.I.A.T. | 7:19:9 | |
| 3. Cagno | F.I.A.T. | 7:21:22 | |
| 4. Caillois | Brasier | 7:27:6 | |
| 5. Werner | Mercedes | 8:3:30 | |
| 6. Duray | De Dietrich | 8:5 | |
| 7. de Caters | Mercedes | 8:7:11 | |
| 8. Rolls | Wolseley | 8:26:42 | |

## Gordon Bennett Cup (cont.)

| | | | |
|---|---|---|---|
| 9. | Earp | Napier | 8:27:29 |
| 10. | Braun | Austro-Mercedes | 8:33:5 |
| 11. | Bianchi | Wolseley | 8:38:32 |
| 12. | Lytle | Pope-Toledo | 9:30:32 |

## GP de l'ACF—26 and 27 June 1906—Le Mans—12 x 103.18 km (1238.16 km)

| | | | |
|---|---|---|---|
| 1. | Szisz | Renault | 12:14:7 |
| 2. | Nazzaro | F.I.A.T. | 12:46:26 |
| 3. | Clément | Clément-Bayard | 12:49:46 |
| 4. | Barillier | Brasier | 13:53 |
| 5. | Lancia | F.I.A.T. | 14:22:11 |
| 6. | Heath | Panhard | 14:47:45 |
| 7. | Baras | Brasier | 15:15:50 |
| 8. | Duray | Lorraine-Dietrich | 15:26:1 |
| 9. | Pierry | Brasier | 16:15:7 |
| 10. | Jenatzy/Burton | Mercedes | 16:18:42 |
| 11. | Marieaux | Mercedes | 16:38:41 |

## Circuit des Ardennes—13 August 1906—Bastogne—7 x 85.7 km (599.9 km)

| | | | |
|---|---|---|---|
| 1. | Duray | Lorraine-Dietrich | 5:38:39 |
| 2. | Hanriot | Darracq | 5:40:21 |
| 3. | Rougier | Lorraine-Dietrich | 5:50:11 |
| 4. | Barillier | Brasier | 5:50:27 |
| 5. | Gabriel | Lorraine-Dietrich | 5:52:14 |
| 6. | Clément | Clément-Bayard | 6:2:55 |
| 7. | Sorel | Lorraine-Dietrich | 6:4:38 |
| 8. | Wagner | Darracq | 6:14:46 |
| 9. | Salzer | Mercedes | 6:14:50 |
| 10. | Jenatzy | Mercedes | 6:15:9 |

## Vanderbilt-Cup—6 October 1906—Long Island—10 x 47.8 km (478 km)

| | | | |
|---|---|---|---|
| 1. | Wagner | Darracq | 4:50:10 |
| 2. | Lancia | F.I.A.T. | 4:53:29 |
| 3. | Duray | Lorraine-Dietrich | 4:53:44 |
| 4. | Clément | Clément-Bayard | 5:1:10 |
| 5. | Jenatzy | Mercedes | 5:4:38 |

## GP de l'ACF—2 July 1907—Dieppe—10 x 77 km (770 km)

| | | | |
|---|---|---|---|
| 1. | Nazzaro | Fiat | 6:46:33 |
| 2. | Szisz | Renault | 6:53:10 |
| 3. | Baras | Brasier | 7:5:5 |
| 4. | Gabriel | Lorraine-Dietrich | 7:11:39 |
| 5. | Rigal | Darracq | 7:12:36 |
| 6. | Caillois | Darracq | 7:15:58 |
| 7. | Barillier | Brasier | 7:24:54 |
| 8. | Garcet | Clément-Bayard | 7:31:17 |
| 9. | Shepard | Clément-Bayard | 7:39:56 |
| 10. | Hémery | Mercedes | 8:25:25 |

## Circuit des Ardennes—27 July 1907—Bastogne—7 x 85.7 km (598.5 km)

| | | | |
|---|---|---|---|
| 1. | de Caters | Mercedes | 6:29:10 |
| 2. | Lee Guinness | Darracq | 6:30:34 |
| 3. | Jenatzy | Mercedes | 6:49:40 |

## GP de l'ACF—7 July 1908—Dieppe—10 x 77 km (770 km)

| | | | |
|---|---|---|---|
| 1. | Lautenschlager | Mercedes | 6:55:43 |
| 2. | Hémery | Benz | 7:4:24 |
| 3. | Hanriot | Benz | 7:5:13 |
| 4. | Rigal | Clément-Bayard | 7:30:6 |
| 5. | Poege | Mercedes | 7:32:31 |
| 6. | Joerns | Opel | 7:39:40 |
| 7. | Erle | Benz | 7:43:21 |
| 8. | Dimitriévitch | Renault | 7:54:12 |
| 9. | Heath | Panhard | 7:55:36 |
| 10. | Perpère | Germanin | 7:59:7 |
| 11. | Cagno | Itala | 8:7:56 |
| 12. | Gabriel | Clément-Bayard | 8:11:44 |

## Coppa Florio—6 September 1908—Bologna—10 x 52.88 km (528.8 km)

| | | | |
|---|---|---|---|
| 1. | Nazzaro | Fiat | 4:25:21 |
| 2. | Trucco | Lorraine-Dietrich | 4:34:7 |
| 3. | Cagno | Itala | 4:56:12 |
| 4. | Demogeot | Mors | 4:57:11 |
| 5. | Lancia | Fiat | 5:8:51 |
| 6. | Garcet | Mors | 5:22:7 |

## GP of America—26 November 1908—Savannah, Georgia—15 x 43.025 km (645.375 km)

| | | | |
|---|---|---|---|
| 1. | Wagner | Fiat | 6:10:31 |
| 2. | Hémery | Benz | 6:10:47 |
| 3. | Nazzaro | Fiat | 6:18:47 |
| 4. | Hanriot | Benz | 6:26:16 |
| 5. | Hautvast | Clément-Bayard | 6:34:5 |
| 6. | Strang | Renault | 6:43:37 |
| 7. | Rigal | Clément-Bayard | 6:45:47 |
| 8. | Fournier | Itala | 6:46:42 |
| 9. | DePalma | Fiat | 6:51:31 |
| 10. | Duray | Lorraine-Dietrich | 7:19:40 |

## GP of America—12 November 1910—Savannah, Georgia—24 x 27.71 km (665.04 km)

| | | | |
|---|---|---|---|
| 1. | Bruce Brown | Benz | 5:53:5 |
| 2. | Hémery | Benz | 5:53:6 |
| 3. | Burman | Marquette-Buick | 6:11:23 |
| 4. | Mulford | Lozier | 6:26:12 |
| 5. | Horan | Lozier | 6:30:2 |

## GP of America—30 November 1911—Savannah, Georgia—24 x 27.42 km (658.08 km)

| | | | |
|---|---|---|---|
| 1. | Bruce Brown | Fiat | 5:31:29 |
| 2. | Hearne | Benz | 5:33:34 |

### GP of America (cont.)

| | | | |
|---|---|---|---|
| 3. DePalma | Mercedes | 5:34:41 | |
| 4. Bragg | Fiat | 5:51:55 | |
| 5. Disbrow | Pope Hartford | 6:26:46 | |
| 6. Harroun/Dawson | Marmon | 6:30:22 | |

### Vanderbilt-Cup—27 November 1911—Savannah, Georgia— 17 x 27.42 km (466.14 km)

| | | |
|---|---|---|
| 1. Mulford | Lozier | 3:56 |
| 2. DePalma | Mercedes | 3:58:11 |
| 3. Wishart | Mercedes | 4:6:20 |
| 4. Grant | Lozier | 4:10:23 |
| 5. Parker | Fiat | 4:14:25 |
| 6. Disbrow | Pope-Hartford | 4:29:2 |

### Santa Monica, California—5 May 1912—36 x 13.45 km (484.2 km)

| | | |
|---|---|---|
| 1. Tetzlaff | Fiat | 3:50:57 |
| 2. Bragg | Fiat | 3:53:5 |
| 3. Bruce Brown | Benz | 3:55:32 |

### GP de l'ACF— 26 and 27 June 1912—Dieppe— 20 x 77 km (1540 km)

| | | | |
|---|---|---|---|
| 1. Boillot | Peugeot | 13:58:2 | |
| 2. Wagner | Fiat | 14:11:8 | |
| 3. Rigal | Sunbeam | 14:38:36 | three-liter |
| 4. Resta | Sunbeam | 14:39:51 | three-liter |
| 5. Medinger | Sunbeam | 14:59:41 | three-liter |
| 6. Christiaens | Excelsior | 16:23:38 | |

### Elgin Trophy + Free-for-All— 30 August 1912—Elgin, Illinois— 30 + 36 x 13.4 km

| | | | |
|---|---|---|---|
| 1. DePalma | Mercedes | 3:43:20 | 4:25:36 |
| 2. Bergdoll | Benz | | 4:30:28 |
| 2. Mulford/ Chandler | Knox | 3:46:9 | 4:34:8 |
| 3. Merz | Stutz | 3:56:43 | |
| 4. Roberts | Mason | 3:58:17 | |

### Vanderbilt-Cup—2 October 1912— Milwaukee, Wisconsin— 38 x 12.6 km (478.8 km)

| | | |
|---|---|---|
| 1. DePalma | Mercedes | 4:20:31 |
| 2. Hughes | Mercer | 4:21:14 |
| 3. Wishart | Mercedes | 4:36:35 |
| 4. Anderson | Stutz | 4:39:40 |
| 5. Clark | Mercedes | 4:51:39 |

### GP of America—6 October 1912— Milwaukee, Wisconsin— 52 x 12.6 km (655.2 km)

| | | |
|---|---|---|
| 1. Bragg | Fiat | 5:59:27 |
| 2. Bergdoll | Benz | 6:14:58 |
| 3. Anderson | Stutz | 6:15:22 |
| 4. Oldfield | Fiat | 6:37:55 |

### GP de l'ACF—12 July 1913— Amiens—29 x 31.4 km (910.6 km)

| | | |
|---|---|---|
| 1. Boillot | Peugeot | 7:53:57 |
| 2. Goux | Peugeot | 7:56:22 |
| 3. Chassagne | Sunbeam | 8:6:20 |
| 4. Bablot | Delage | 8:16:14 |
| 5. Guyot | Delage | 8:17:58 |

### GP de France—7 August 1913— Le Mans—10 x 54 km (540 km)

| | | |
|---|---|---|
| 1. Bablot | Delage | 4:21:50 |
| 2. Guyot | Delage | 4:26:50 |
| 3. Pilette | Mercedes | 4:27:53 |
| 4. Salzer | Mercedes | 4:34:52 |
| 5. Duray | Delage | 4:35:3 |
| 6. Lautenschlager | Mercedes | 4:36:51 |

### Vanderbilt-Cup—26 February 1914—Santa Monica, California— 35 x 13.44 km (470.4 km)

| | | |
|---|---|---|
| 1. DePalma | Mercedes | 3:53:41 |
| 2. Oldfield | Mercer | 3:55:1 |
| 3. Carlson | Mason | 4:2:39 |
| 4. Cooper | Stutz | 4:4:3 |

### GP of America—28 February 1914—Santa Monica, California— 48 x 13.44 km (645.12 km)

| | | |
|---|---|---|
| 1. Pullen | Mercer | 5:13:30 |
| 2. Ball | Marmon | 5:53:23 |
| 3. Taylor | Alco | 6:8:29 |
| 4. DePalma | Mercedes | 6:9:8 |

### Indianapolis 500—30 May 1914— 200 x 2.5 miles (500 miles)

| | | |
|---|---|---|
| 1. Thomas | Delage | 6:3:45 |
| 2. Duray | Peugeot | 6:10:24 |
| 3. Guyot | Delage | 6:14:1 |
| 4. Goux | Peugeot | 6:17:24 |
| 5. Oldfield | Stutz | 6:23:51 |
| 6. Christiaens | Excelsior | 6:27:24 |
| 7. Grant | Sunbeam | 6:36:22 |
| 8. Keene | Beaver Bullett | 6:40:57 |
| 9. Carlson | Maxwell | 7:2:42 |
| 10. Rickenbacher | Duesenberg | 7:3:34 |

### GP de l'ACF— 4 July 1914—Lyon/Givors— 20 x 37.6 km (752 km)

| | | |
|---|---|---|
| 1. Lautenschlager | Mercedes | 7:8:18 |
| 2. Wagner | Mercedes | 7:9:54 |
| 3. Salzer | Mercedes | 7:13:15 |
| 4. Goux | Peugeot | 7:17:17 |
| 5. Resta | Sunbeam | 7:29:17 |
| 6. Esser | Nagant | 7:40:28 |
| 7. Rigal | Peugeot | 7:44:28 |
| 8. Duray | Delage | 7:51:32 |
| 9. Champoiseau | Schneider | 8:6:51 |
| 10. Joerns | Opel | 8:17:9 |
| 11. Fagnano | Fiat | 8:26:11 |

## C. A. C. Trophy—
### 21 August 1914—Elgin, Illinois—
### 36 x 13.6 km (489.6 km)

1. DePalma      Mercedes          4:5:1
2. Anderson     Stutz             4:5:45
3. Mulford      Peugeot           4:8:16
4. Oldfield     Stutz             4:15:23
5. Chandler     Braender-Bulldog  4:27:58

## Elgin National Trophy—
### 22 August 1914—Elgin, Illinois—
### 36 x 13.6 km (489.6 km)

1. DePalma   Mercedes  4:6:18
2. Pullen    Mercer    4:7:28
3. Oldfield  Stutz     4:24:2
4. Morris    Sunbeam   4:31:9
5. Hearne    Burman    4:35:47

## Indianapolis 500—31 May 1915—
### 200 x 2.5 miles (500 miles)

1. DePalma         Mercedes    5:33:55
2. Resta           Peugeot     5:37:25
3. Anderson        Stutz       5:42:27
4. Cooper          Stutz       5:46:19
5. O'Donnell       Duesenberg  6:8:13
6. Burman          Peugeot     6:13:19
7. Wilcox          Stutz       6:14:19
8. Alley           Duesenberg  6:15:8
9. Carlson/Hughes  Maxwell     6:19:56
10. van Raalte     Sunbeam     6:35:23

# Bibliography

## Contemporary magazines

*The Automobile* (New York and Chicago)
*L'Automobile—Revue des Locomotions nouvelles* (Paris)
*The Automobile Engineer* (London)
*La France Automobile* (Paris)
*The Motor* (London)
*Motor Age* (Chicago)
*Der Motorwagen* (Berlin)
*Omnia—La Locomotion* (Paris)
*La Vie Automobile* (Paris)

## Secondary Works

Barthel, Manfred, and Gerold Lingnau. *100 Jahre Daimler-Benz—Die Technik—Das Unternehmen.* Mainz: v. Hase & Koehler Verlag, 1986.
Besqueut, Patrice. *La Coupe Gordon Bennett 1905.* France: Editions La Montagne, 1985.
Boddy, William. *The History of Brooklands Motor Course.* London: Greenville Publishing Company Limited, 1979.
Borgeson, Griffith. *The Golden Age of the American Racing Car.* New York: W. W. Norton, 1966.
Court, William. *Power and Glory: A History of Grand Prix Motor Racing, 1906-1951.* London: Macdonald 1966.
Demand, Carlo, and Paul Simsa. *Kühne Männer, tolle Wagen—Die Gordon Bennett-Rennen 1900-1905.* Stuttgart: Motorbuch-Verlag, 1987.
Ickx, Jacques. *Ainsi naquit l'Automobile.* Lausanne: Edita S.A., 1971.
Karslake, Kent. *Racing Voiturettes.* London: Motor Racing Publications Limited, 1950.
Ludvigsen, Karl. *The Mercedes-Benz Racing Cars.* Newport Beach, Ca.: Bond Parkhurst Books Publishing, 1971.
Pomeroy, Laurence. *The Grand Prix Car.* 2 vols. London: Motor Racing Publications Limited, 1956.
_____, and Kent Karslake. *From Veteran to Vintage.* London: Temple Press Ltd., 1956.
Riedler, Alois. *Wissenschaftliche Automobil-Wertung.* Berlin: R. Oldenbourg Verlag, 1913.
Souvestre, Pierre. *Histoire de l'Automobile.* Paris, Quai des Grands-Augustins: H. Dunod et E. Pinat, 1907.

# Index

ACF 21, 58, 147, 195, 251
Albert, Paul (?–1903) 83, 90
Alco 235
Amiens, circuit map 271
Antoinette engine 166
Ardennes, circuit map 143
Auger, Georges, "Augières" 84, 121
Austro-Daimler 1910 199
Austro-Mercedes 115, 119, 130
Auvergne, circuit map 132

Bablot, Paul 183, 233, 276, 287
Ballot, Ernest (1870–1937) 321
Balz, Hermann 35, 43, 103, 113
Baras, Paul 53, 152
Barbarou, Marius (1876–?) 69, 100, 173, 325
Bauer, Wilhelm (?–1900) 36
Bayard 121
Beau de Rochas, Alphonse Eugène (1815–1893) 7
Bellamy 66, 72
Bennett Cup 1900 52
Bennett Cup 1901 52
Bennett Cup 1902 66
Bennett Cup 1903 102
Bennett Cup 1904 118
Bennett Cup 1905 131
Bennett formula, 1000-kg formula 58
Benz, Carl or Karl (1844–1929) 10, 173
Benz Auto Import Co. 204, 235
Benz Blitzen 1910 208, 210
Benz Grand Prix 1908 181, 235, 246
Benz Jumbo 1912 209
Benz Lightning 1910 205
Benz Patent-Motor-Car 1886 10
Benz Prince Henry 1910 200
Benz Record Car 1909 202
Bergdoll, Erwin 246, 248, 250
Bigio, Guido (?–1913) 143, 275

Birkigt, Marc (1878–1953) 227, 321
BND steel 229
Boillot, André (1891–1932) 295, 322
Boillot, Georges (1884–1916) 222, 227, 231, 252, 259, 263, 276, 281, 302
Bollée, Amédée *fils* (1867–1926) 6, 23
Bollée, Amédée *père* (1844–1917) 6
Bollée, Léon (1870–1913) 23, 215
Bollée, steamer 6
Bosch low tension ignition 34
Boudreaux-Verdet 224
Bouton, Georges (1847–1938) 7
Bradley, William (1876–1971) 291, 293
Bragg, Caleb Smith (1888–1943) 242, 246, 250
Brasier, Henri Charles (1864–1941) 26, 54, 67, 120
Brasier 1904 120
Braun, Hermann (1878–?) 30, 33, 36, 44, 47, 50, 53, 88, 97, 103, 113, 119, 137
Brauner, Josef (1863–?) 34, 41, 42, 59, 78, 89, 115, 129, 130, 149, 164, 180
Brooklands 202
Bruce-Brown, David (1887–1912) 237, 239, 242, 246, 248, 249, 259, 263
Bugatti, Ettore (1881–1947) 75, 199, 251, 291
Bugatti Garros 1914 291, 316
Burman, Bob (1884–1916) 209, 250, 268, 314, 319
Burman special 1915 314
Burton, J. T. Alexander 131, 134, 158, 176
Busson, Guillaume (1885–?) 229
Buzio, Felice 222, 223

Cagno, Alessandro (1883–1971) 122, 162, 299
Calais Dover 1904 127

Caters, Baron Pierre de (1875–1944) 50, 84, 87, 97, 104, 119, 124, 137
Cattaneo, Giustino 143
Causan, Némorin (1883–?) 221
CGV 29, 47
chain drive 151
Charlatans 254, 270
Charley *see* Lehmann
Charron, Fernand (1866–1928) 26, 28, 47, 152, 299
Chassagne, Jean (1881–1947) 257, 277, 323
Chasseloup-Laubat, Comte Gaston de (1867–1903) 28, 87
Chauchard, Paul 50
Chevrolet, Arthur (1884–1946) 237
Chevrolet, Louis (1878–1932) 234, 319
Chitty Bang Bang 327
Christiaens, Josef (?–1919) 251, 256, 259
Christie 1907 166
Circuit de l'Argonne 1904 119
Circuit de l'Auvergne 1905 131
Circuit des Ardennes 1902 72
Circuit des Ardennes 1903 100
Circuit des Ardennes 1904 127
Circuit des Ardennes 1905 142
Circuit des Ardennes 1906 158
Circuit des Ardennes 1907 176
Circuit du Nord 1902 66
Circuit du Sud-Ouest 1901 48
Cissac, Henri (1877–1908) 189
Clark, George 249
Clément, Adolphe (1855–1928) 77, 121, 152, 287
Clément, Albert (1883–1907) 158, 172

Clément-Bayard 1908 182
Coda, Giuseppe (1883–1977) 221, 236, 246, 299, 324
Coppa Florio 1904 128
Coppa Florio 1905 143
Coppa Florio 1907 177
Coppa Florio 1908 190
Cortese 143, 330
Coupe de l'Auto 215
Coupe de l'Auto 1905 215
Coupe de l'Auto 1906 215
Coupe de l'Auto 1907 217
Coupe de l'Auto 1908 223
Coupe de l'Auto 1909 225
Coupe de l'Auto 1910 229
Coupe de l'Auto 1911 231
Coupe de l'Auto 1912 251, 257
Coupe de l'Auto 1913 281
Crawhez, Baron Pierre de 72, 100, 103

Daimler (Seelberg factory) 11, 37, 38
Daimler (Untertürkheim factory) 114
Daimler, Adolf 42, 88
Daimler, Gottlieb (1834–1900) 7, 9, 16, 17, 22, 36, 40
Daimler, Paul (1869–1945) 9, 19, 41, 63, 130, 149, 158, 164, 180, 196, 283, 296, 320, 325
Daimler Américain 1886 10
Daimler Belt Car 1896 22
Daimler-Motoren-Gesellschaft 17
Daimler Phoenix 1897 25
Daimler Phoenix engine 1895 20, 25
Daimler Phoenix 4.9-liter 1899 33
Daimler Phoenix 5.5-liter 1900 35
Daimler Riding Car 1885 10
Daimler Single-cylinder engine 1885 9
Daimler Steel-wheel-car 1889 16
Daimler V-2 engine 1889 13
Dannat, William Turner (1853–1929) 45, 53, 88
Darracq, Alexandre (1855–1931) 69, 105, 163, 195, 197
Darracq 1905 142
Darracq V-8 1905 205
Dawson, Joe 248
Daytona 1910 205
Daytona 1911 209
Deauville 1902 74
De Boiano, Clemente 175
De Dion-Bouton single-cylinder 23, 219, 224, 227
De Dion-Bouton steamer 1887 8

Degrais, Henri 50, 53, 64, 77, 87, 90, 97, 103
Delage, Louis (1874–1947) 221, 231, 273, 289, 293
Delage 1908 219
Delage S 1914 297
Delage X 1911 231
Delage Y 1913 273
Delahaye 1905 253
Denner, Paul 42
DePalma, Ralph (1883–1956) 194, 205, 237, 242, 243, 248, 249, 259, 289, 304, 313, 315, 318
désaxé 182
Desjoyeaux, Léon 29, 39, 41, 47, 52, 64, 75, 149
Desmo-head 221, 297
Deutsch, Henri, de la Meurthe (1846–1919) 54, 66, 166
Diehl, Georg (1866–1941) 175, 181, 200
Dieppe, circuit map 165
Dinsmore see Gray Dinsmore
Dion, Comte/Marquis Albert de (1856–1946) 7, 21, 28, 215, 225
Dr. Pascal see Rothschild, Henri de
Duesenberg, Augie and Fred 249, 311
Duesenberg 1912 249
Duesenberg 1914 311
Duray, Arthur (1881–1954) 131, 161, 168, 172, 213, 292
Duttenhofer, Max (1843–1903) 17, 22, 29, 35, 41, 78, 81, 105, 115, 117, 148

Edge, Selwyn Francis (1868–1940) 69, 106
Eiffel, Gustave 271
Elgin road race 1910 234
Elgin road race 1912 248
Elgin road race 1914 313
Elskamp, Leon 283, 300
Enrico, Giovanni (1851–1909) 121
Erle, Fritz (1875–1957) 175, 181, 194, 198, 202, 210
Erwin special 200
Esser, Willy 251, 299
Essling, Victor Masséna 5th Prince d' (1836–1910) 45
Eugénie, Empress (1826–1920) 5

F-head 79
Fanelli, Ernesto 228, 252, 267
Farman, Henry (1874–1958) 49, 70, 106
Farman, Maurice (1877–1964) 49, 52, 66, 131
Faroux, Charles (1872–1957) 192, 267

F.I.A.T. 121, 133
Fiat Mephisto 1908 203
Fiat 1904 121
Fiat S61 1910 236, 242
Fiat S74 1911 246
Fiat S76 1911 210
Fiat S57 1914 299
Fisher, Carl Graham (1874–1939) 133, 241, 319
Fletcher, Andrew 127
Florio, Vincenzo (1883–1959) 116, 143, 148, 152, 331
Forest, Maurice Arnold de (1879–1968) 66, 72, 74, 88, 103
Fornaca, Guido (1870–1928) 176
Fournier, Henry (1871–1919) 53, 67, 76, 87, 95, 103, 187
Friderich, Ernest 251, 291, 293
Froehlich, Jesse 205, 234, 235

Gabriel, Fernand (1880–1943) 74, 88, 96, 106, 152, 277, 297
Gaillon 210
Gasmotorenfabrik Deutz 7
Gast, Camille Crespin du 54, 93, 99, 130
Gastaud 83, 96, 119, 143, 176
Girardot, Léonce (1864–1922) 29, 47, 54, 100
Giuppone, Cesare (?–1910) 217, 225
Gobron-Brillié 118
Gordon Bennett, James (1841–1918) 22, 81, 101, 196
Gordon Bennett Cup see Bennett Cup
Goux, Jules (1885–1965) 217, 225, 231, 252, 259, 267, 276
GP de France 1911 251
GP de France 1912 265
GP de France 1913 283
GP de l'ACF 1906 152
GP de l'ACF 1907 168
GP de l'ACF 1908 182
GP de l'ACF 1909 195, 202
GP de l'ACF 1912 251, 256
GP de l'ACF 1913 270
GP de l'ACF 1914 294
GP des Voiturettes 1908 217
GP of America 1908 193
GP of America 1910 237
GP of America 1911 246
GP of America 1912 250
GP of America 1914 290
Grand Prix 147
Grant, Harry (1877–1915) 234
Gray Dinsmore, Clarence (1847–1905) 52, 59, 74, 75, 80, 88, 89, 102, 105, 107–

108, 111, 113, 116, 124, 128, 130, 133, 134, 146
Grey Ghost 243
Groulart, Louis de (1880–?) 181, 252
Guyot, Albert (1882–?) 221, 278

Hanriot, René (1876–?) 152, 176, 181, 183, 194, 252
Harkness Flagler, Harry (1870–1952) 59, 88
Harroun, Ray (1879–1968) 242, 292
Haupt, Willie (?–1966) 237
Hearne, Eddie (1887–1955) 234, 242, 246
Heath, Georges 127
Heim, Franz (1882–1926) 210, 234, 252
Hémery, Victor (1876–1950) 142, 146, 164, 168, 173, 175, 181, 183, 194, 202, 237, 246, 251
Henry, Ernest (1885–1950) 227, 252, 294, 321, 323
Hieronimus, Otto (1879–1922) 76, 83, 91, 97, 103, 119, 131, 137, 325
Hispano-Suiza 1910 227
Hollander & Joseph 235
Horan, Joe 250
Hörner, Franz 210
Hornsted, L. G. "Cupid" 213, 259
Hotchkiss axle 151, 254
Hotel Hermann 19
Hôtel Pastoret 58
Huttenlocher 44

Indianapolis 500 1911 242
Indianapolis 500 1912 248
Indianapolis 500 1913 268
Indianapolis 500 1914 291
Indianapolis 500 1915 315
Indianapolis 500 1916 319
Indianapolis Speedway 241
Itala 1905 143

Jahore, Sultan Ibrahim of 116
Jarrott, Charles (1877–1944) 66, 74, 95, 106
Jellinek, Emil (1853–1918) 29, 40, 47, 52, 63, 75, 87, 96, 103, 113, 117, 130, 148, 196, 325
Jellinek, Madeleine née Dittholer (1873–1940) 52, 63, 325
Jellinek, Mercedes (1889–1929) 31
Jellinek, Rachel née Goggman (1854–1893) 31
Jenatzy, Camille (1868–1913) 87, 97, 105, 113, 119, 137, 142, 148, 152, 158, 164, 168, 176, 202, 325
Joerns, Carl or Karl (1875–1969) 176, 187, 202, 274
Johnston, Howard 60

Kaiserpreis, aero-engines 1912 283
Kaiserpreis 1907 176
Katzenstein, Robert 52, 54, 75, 89, 100, 105
Kaufman, Alphonse 315
Kaulla, Alfred von (1852–1924) 89, 117, 149, 163
Keene, Foxhall Parker (1870–1941) 45, 53, 54, 88, 92, 105, 108, 146, 161, 194
Knyff, Chevalier René de (1865–1955) 26, 36, 54, 58, 69, 106
Köhler 91
Kraft, Wilhelm 42
Krebs, Arthur Constantin (1850–1935) 26, 43, 53, 67, 92

L-head 93
Labor-Picker 227, 252
Laly, Robert 292
Lancia, Vincenzo (1881–1937) 128, 133, 168, 192
Laumaillé, Madame 28
Lautenschlager, Christian (1877–1954) 181, 183, 283, 296, 302, 310
Lehmann, C. L. "Charley" 45, 59, 75, 77, 81, 88, 103, 113, 130, 197
Lemaître, Albert 33, 45, 47, 50, 53, 54, 64
Le Mans, circuit map 148
Léopolde II, King of Belgium (1835–1909) 59
Levassor, Émile (1843–1897) 12, 17, 20, 24, 25, 40
Linck, Karl 19, 40
Link, Eugen 42, 78, 180, 296
Lion-Peugeot 215
Lohner-Porsche 46
Loraine Barrow, Claude (?–1903) 45, 48, 60, 78, 81, 97, 103
Lorenz, Wilhelm (1842–1926) 17, 117, 149, 163
Lorraine-Dietrich 149
Lorraine-Dietrich 1912 252
Ludwig Loewe AG 44
Lüttgen, Willy 113, 128, 161
Lyon, circuit map 295
Lytle, Herb 141

Magnalium 43
Marieaux 143, 148, 152, 158
Marseille Monte-Carlo 1897 28
Maserati, Alfieri (1887–1932) 192, 222, 324
Mathieu, Victor 46
Mathis, Emil (1880–1956) 236, 251
Max, Eugen 69, 83, 88
Maxwell 1914 292
Mayade, Émile Louis (1853–1898) 13, 24, 25, 26
Maybach, Wilhelm (1846–1929) 7, 9, 19, 22, 34, 41, 56, 78, 115, 117, 130, 149, 163, 325
Mégevet, C. Jules 227
Menier family 291
Mercédès 33, 36, 38
Mercedes Eighty/Ninety 1903 81
Mercedes Forty 1902 59
Mercedes *mixte* 1901 46
Mercedes *mixte* 1902 56
Mercedes 1901 41, 53
Mercedes 1904 115
Mercedes 1905 129, 130, 146
Mercedes 1906 148, 149
Mercedes 1907 164
Mercedes 1908 180
Mercedes 1909 202
Mercedes 1911 242, 243, 268, 289
Mercedes 1913 268, 283
Mercedes 1914 296, 315
Mercedes Excelsior 1903 28, 60, 78
Mercédès-Palace 114
Mercedes-Peugeot 1914 291
Mercedes Simplex 1902 56
Mercedes Sixty 1903 78
Mérode, Cléo de (1875–1966) 59
Meyan, Paul 21, 35, 38, 50, 64, 69, 99
Michaux, Gratien 219, 227, 254, 297
Michaux, Pierre (1813–1883) 5
Michelat, Arthur "Léon" 231, 273, 297, 324
Michelin rim 155, 180, 189, 261
Miller, Harry Armenius (1875–1943) 314
Minoia, Ferdinando or Nando 177, 192
Molon, Léon 257, 287
Momo, Cesare (1876–1966) 121, 176
Moross, Ernie 205
Mors 1898 26
Mors 1901 54
Mors 1903 92, 115
Motschmann, Gustavo 45
Mulford, Ralph (1884–1974) 242, 246, 268

Nallinger, Friedrich (1863–1937) 149

Naudin, Louis 217, 254
Nazzaro, Felice (1880–1940) 133, 168, 173, 176, 193, 202, 237, 278, 306, 325
Nibel, Hans (1880–1934) 181, 200, 202
Nice 1899 33
Nice 1900 36
Nice 1901 49
Nice 1902 64
Nice 1903 83
Nice 1904 118
Nice 1905 130

Offenhauser, Fred (1888–1973) 314
Oldfield, Barney (1878–1946) 205, 208, 241, 248, 250, 289, 293, 314, 316, 326
Opel, Fritz (1875–1938) 119
Orloff, Prince Alexis 52, 55, 116
Ostend formula 179
Otto, Nikolaus August (1832–1891) 5, 7
Outhenin-Chalandre 117

Panhard, René (1841–1908) 11
Panhard & Levassor 12
Panhard 1895 21
Panhard 1896 24
Panhard 1898 25
Panhard 1901 43, 53
Panhard 1902 67
Panhard 1903 92
Panhard Phénix engine 21
Paris Amsterdam 1898 25
Paris Berlin 1901 53
Paris Bordeaux 1895 20
Paris Bordeaux 1901 52
Paris Brest 1891 18
Paris Madrid 1903 87
Paris Marseille 1896 23
Paris Rouen 1894 19
Paris Vienna 1902 66
Pascal 78
Patterson, E. C. 268, 291, 313
Pau 1901 *see* Circuit du Sud-Ouest 1901
Périgord, Boson de, Prince de Sagan (1867–1952) 22, 54
Périn, Jules 11
Peugeot, Armand (1849–1915) 15, 215
Peugeot, Robert (1873–1945) 215, 252
Peugeot Auto Import Co. 315
Peugeot 1891 17
Peugeot 4.5-liter 1914 294
Peugeot 5.6-liter 1913 270, 291
Peugeot 7.6-liter 1912 252, 266
Peugeot Lion 1909 224
Peugeot Lion 1910 227
Peugeot Lion 1911 231

Pfänder, Otto 42, 121, 176
Pickens, William Hickman 205, 234, 235
Picker, Charles and Lucien 227, 252
Pilette, Théo (?–1921) 176, 199, 202, 268, 283, 285, 306, 325
Pipe 1904 121
pneumatic tire 21, 25, 137, 154
Poege, Willy (1879–1914) 81, 128, 130, 176, 181, 183, 198, 202, 325
Pont de Neuilly Versailles 1891 8
Porsche, Ferdinand (1875–1952) 75, 199
Porter, Finley Robertson (1872–1964) 291, 316
Prince Henry Tour 198
Pullen, Eddie 291, 314

Raggio, Carletto 81
Raggio, Giovan(ni) Battista (1878–?) 143
Raustein, Ernst 42
Red Devil 122
Renault, Louis (1877–1944) 54, 96, 189
Renault, Marcel (1872–1903) 70, 97
Resta, Dario (1884–1924) 183, 259, 315, 319
Ribeyrolles, Paul 69, 93, 142, 162
Richard-Brasier 67, 129, 197
Rickenbacher, Eddie (1890–1973) 312, 319
Rigal, Victor 171, 185, 189, 257, 265, 299
Rigoulot, Louis 16, 17, 23
Robertson, George 234
Roger, Émile 14
Rothschild, Arthur de (1851–1903) 33, 38, 47
Rothschild, Henri de, "Dr. Pascal" (1872–1947) 34, 36, 45, 50, 52, 66, 77
Rothschild & Fils, Jacques Rothschild & Fils 44, 56
Rougier, Henri 120

Sailer, Max (1882–1964) 42, 296, 302
St. Petersburg Moscow 1908 182
Salon Paris 1901 46
Salon Paris 1903 103
Salon Paris 1904 129
Salzer, Otto (1874–1944) 158, 164, 168, 176, 181, 183, 202, 283, 296, 305
Santos-Dumont, Alberto (1873–1932) 38, 60, 130
Sarazin, Édouard Auguste (?–1887) 11

Sarazin, Louise née Cayrol (1847–1916) 12, 16, 36, 40
Savannah, circuit map 235
Schnaitmann, Karl 42, 180, 297
Schroeder, Edward J. 244
Semmering 1909 202
Serpollet, Léon (1858–1907) 14, 50, 64
Shepard, Elliott Fitch 152, 155, 156, 161
Sioux City 1914 312
Sizaire, Georges and Maurice 217, 254
Sizaire et Naudin 1908 219
Sizaire et Naudin 1912 254
Sloan, Tod 76, 95
Société Mercédès 148, 164, 195
Spamann, Paul 175
Spiegel, Ferdinand 39, 45, 89, 116, 129
Stead, E. T. 36, 50, 59, 64, 76, 80, 99
Stern, Richard von 45, 50, 55, 59, 75, 89
Stutz, Harry Clayton (1876–1930) 315
Système Panhard 17
Szisz, Ferenc (1873–1944) 152, 155, 168, 185, 308, 325

T-head, hammer-head 43, 77
Tarasque 120
Targa Florio 1907 175
Terry 83, 92, 97, 127, 143
Tervueren 1909 202
Teste, Georges 127
Tetzlaff, Teddy 210, 248, 249, 325
Théo Schneider 1914 297
Théry, Léon (1879–1909) 97, 119, 131, 137, 183
Thomas, René (1886–1975) 219, 226, 232, 254, 292, 321
Thorn, W. K. 45, 48, 50, 53
Tischbein, Willy 45, 53, 87, 103
Tour de France 1899 26
Turckheim, Adrien de 252

Vanderbilt, William Kissam II (1878–1944) 22, 45, 55, 59, 64, 114, 115
Vanderbilt Cup 1904 128
Vanderbilt Cup 1905 143
Vanderbilt Cup 1906 162
Vanderbilt Cup 1910 234
Vanderbilt Cup 1911 246
Vanderbilt Cup 1912 249
Vanderbilt Cup 1914 289
Varlet, Amédée 253
Velghe, Alfred "Levegh" (?–1904) 36, 54
Verdet, Louis (1869–1918) 224, 254

Viet, Paul 24, 93
Villa Daimler (Cannstatt) 9
Villa Didier (Baden) 63
Villa Mercedes (Baden) 31, 63
Villa Mercedes (Nice) 63, 85
Vischer, Alfred 199, 285
Vischer, Gustav (1846–1920) 29, 35, 41, 99, 103, 149
Voigt, Émile 29
Voiture légère 49, 231
Voiturette 23, 49, 215

Wagner, Fred 239, 318
Wagner, Louis (1882–1960) 162, 168, 194, 237, 246, 259, 296, 305
Walker, Fritz (?–1914) 113, 162, 194, 314

Warden, John B. 81, 88, 96, 119
Weill-Schott, Aldo 157
Weisweiler, Edmond de 148
Werner, Wilhelm (1874–1947) 29, 33, 36, 47, 50, 53, 64, 74, 83, 91, 96, 103, 119, 128, 137, 146
Winton, Alexander (1860–1932) 106
Winton 1903 106
Wishart, Spencer (1889–1914) 234, 242, 247, 248, 249, 314
World Exhibition Paris 1867 5
World Exhibition Paris 1889 14

Xantho 45

Zborowska, Margaret Laura, née Carey (1856–1911) 60
Zborowski, Louis Vorow (1895–1924) 326
Zborowski, William Elliott (1855–1903) 39, 61, 66, 72, 76, 84
Zuccarelli, Paolo (1884–1913) 230, 252, 259, 267, 275
Zuylen, Étienne de (1860–1934) 21, 34, 87

www.ingramcontent.com/pod-product-compliance
Lightning Source LLC
Chambersburg PA
CBHW081536300426
44116CB00015B/2645